THE SUBCONTINENT IN
WORLD POLITCS

THE SUBCONTINENT IN WORLD POLITICS

India, Its Neighbors, and the Great Powers

Edited by

Lawrence Ziring

Revised Edition

PRAEGER SPECIAL STUDIES • PRAEGER SCIENTIFIC

Library of Congress Cataloging in Publication Data
Main entry under title:

The Subcontinent in world politics.

   Includes index.
   1. South Asia—Politics and government.
2. South Asia—Foreign relations. I. Ziring,
Lawrence, 1928–
DS341.S9 1982   327′.0954   82-7634
ISBN 0-03-060287-4   AACR2
ISBN 0-03-060288-2 (pbk.)

Published in 1982 by Praeger Publishers
CBS Educational and Professional Publishing
a Division of CBS Inc.
521 Fifth Avenue, New York, New York 10175 U.S.A.

© 1982 by Praeger Publishers

23456789 052 987654321

Printed in the United States of America

for
Raye M. Ziring

Through understanding, peace
is still possible.

PREFACE TO THE REVISED EDITION

This second edition of *The Subcontinent in World Politics* is testimony to the intense interest generated by recent events in South and Southwest Asia. The first edition, published in 1978, anticipated important changes in the region but even those expectations could not envisage the high drama that eliminated the shah of Iran, that caused the Soviet Union to invade Afghanistan, and that brought Moscow and Washington into direct confrontation. Both crisis and opportunity are apparent in the arc stretching from India through Pakistan to Afghanistan, Iran, the Middle East, and East Africa. Crisis suggests retreat and the coming to grips with complex conditions; opportunity indicates the capacity to reap advantages from changes in the preexisting power structure. The first edition of this volume identified numerous problems for American policymakers in the region, but generally the theme was positive and the United States was viewed in an advantageous position vis-à-vis its principal adversary. This edition is not nearly so optimistic for the United States. The Soviet Union has moved quickly and forcefully to exploit unrest among its neighbors. It has also sought to ingratiate itself with governments that have reasons to reject the Americans. The United States has been forced to reappraise its previous policies and to evolve new strategies capable of defending its interests in an area of critical concern. This volume seeks to describe the rearrangement of power relationships in the "arc of crisis." It also addresses itself to the condition of the nations in the "arc," and how their domestic problems influence the course of global politics.

This revised edition, therefore, is essentially a new volume. All the chapters have been rewritten. Several are virtually new offerings. Two entirely new chapters have been drafted expressly for this edition, while two chapters appearing in the first edition have been dropped. The sudden passing of our colleague Baljit Singh, who contributed Chapter 5 in the first edition, necessitated one of these changes. The inclusion of a new chapter on Soviet foreign policy and another on Afghanistan were judged absolutely essential and together they offer deeper insight into the complicated factors challenging the policymaker and informed observer.

The pace of contemporary events has quickened in the past decade, making it extremely difficult to keep abreast of issues of vital concern. This is particularly true in the realm of international affairs, where personalities and political systems have always been subject to the vagaries and vicissitudes of time and inexorable change. The instability of the modern world, the inchoate nature of the nation-state system, the persistence of ideological rivalries, the enervating quest for identity and status, and the fear, suspicion, and unconcealed envy of rich and poor alike all represent conditions and forces that dominate consciousness and shape behavior. Comprehending this chaotic world in the last quarter of the twentieth century is a great challenge, and those who show indifference are not to be criticized. But those few who are committed, by background, predicament, or profession, have little choice but to strive to understand, inform, and be informed about the issues and consequences flowing from a world in flux. This volume does not pretend to be a profound commentary on the state of the world. Nor is it an exhaustive exploration of global questions. The purpose of the study is to examine one segment of this turbulent planet, to place it in larger perspective, and to suggest patterns of change and direction.

Our focus is South and Southwest Asia. Connecting links between India, Bangladesh, Pakistan, Afghanistan, and the other countries comprising the region are studied. Iran and Saudi Arabia have also become near neighbors of the subcontinent. Territorial questions on the rim of Asia cannot be analyzed without examining their roles and predicaments. The central thread in any study in world politics, however, is the posture of the great powers. The probable aims and movements of the Soviet Union and the United States in the region are given careful attention, and efforts are made to trace their historic involvement as well as project future attitudes and performance.

Domestic conditions have a way of influencing international postures, and it is one assertion of this volume that foreign policy is a response to national events. Thus changes in the local environment indubitably alter or, at least, tend to modify external behavior. In other words, international politics can neither be detached from its more limited nation-state setting nor be observed in a vacuum. Changes in government are seen as affecting changes in policy and interstate activity. The fall of the shah of Iran and the rise to prominence of Ayatollah Khomeini, the assassination of Bangladesh's Mujibur Rahman, and later Ziaur Rahman, the deaths of Mao Zedong and Zhou En-Lai, Jimmy Carter's entrance onto the world stage as president of the United States and his replacement by Ronald Reagan in 1981, the fall and political resurrection of Indira Gandhi, the overthrow and execution of Zulfikar Ali Bhutto and the reimposition of military rule in Pakistan, the death of Mohammad Daud as well as his immediate successors Noor Mohammad Taraki and Hafizullah Amin and the installation of Babrak Karmal as the new president of Afghanistan, are all events of particular significance. In combination they are developments of great moment. New governments are usually tested by the older ones, and it could be hypothesized that the continuity of leadership in Moscow between 1964 and 1981 explains an extended period of probing and testing by the Soviet Union. Despite anticipated changes in the aged Kremlin leadership, it is doubtful the course established by the current Soviet leaders will be redirected. It is more likely that the strategic objectives will remain constant, although tactics may become more aggressive.

Soviet foreign policy has moved into an activist phase. Diplomatic maneuvering has been augmented by military posturing, and future aggressive demonstrations of Soviet might cannot be ruled out. It is one hypothesis of this chapter that opportunities in the international arena have brought the Soviet armed forces into intimate relationship with the Kremlin's decision-making apparatus and that national security planning and operations dominate all other issues. Although civilian control over the Soviet military has been sustained, the Politburo is currently more heavily influenced by its defense organization than at any time since the end of World War II. If this judgment is valid, it gives rise to a number of questions concerning short- and long-term Soviet objectives, the nature and course of change in the aging Soviet leadership, and the implications for the communist and noncommunist worlds.

As with any collective effort, the contributors to this volume reveal a variety of experience and opinion. Each author has had a long, intimate, and often personal involvement with the area. All are experts in their respective fields. Together they present as comprehensive and learned a view of world politics in South and Southwest Asia as can be drawn in a limited presentation. It is hoped their individual contributions and the book's overall presentation will add to our general knowledge of the subject.

It is important for me to acknowledge my indebtedness to Kathy Grodus and Margaret McCluskey, who patiently and expertly prepared several drafts of the manuscript. I also wish to show my gratitude to my wife, Raye M. Ziring, to whom this book is dedicated, for encouraging me to stay with the project despite other distractions.

Finally, it should be noted that the ideas and comments expressed in each chapter are those of the authors. Errors of fact or interpretation are inadvertent, and if any appear, the reader has our sincerest apologies.

April 2, 1982

CONTENTS

THE SUBCONTINENT IN
WORLD POLITCS

1

SOUTH ASIAN TANGLES AND TRIANGLES

Lawrence Ziring

For almost two decades the United States endeavored to maintain a politico-military capability in and near South Asia without directly taking sides in the running controversy between the region's two most significant states. India consistently refused to help the United States assemble an anticommunist defense system and was particularly enraged when Pakistan, its primary enemy, became the recipient of large-scale U.S. military assistance. Nevertheless, India welcomed the substantial economic and technical aid that Washington provided, and its relations with the United States were proper and cordial, if not especially warm. U.S. interest in Pakistan was, in part at least, generated by U.S. failure to convince India that its cold war "nonalignment" posture was counterproductive. It was also conditioned by the Dullesian quest for a vital link in the alliance chain that the United States engineered on the rimland of the communist world.[1] Moreover, the Pakistani Muslims were judged a warrior people, and not only were they eager to build a modern military establishment, but also their strategic position as the gatekeepers of South Asia made them useful allies. Thus it could be said the United States was heavily involved in the affairs of the subcontinent. On the one side, it encouraged Pakistan to become a formidable military power, while on the other, it struggled to maintain India's friendship by showering significant quantities of foodstuffs and material necessities on the country. As a result the patterns of U.S. policy in South Asia were both multidimensional and highly compartmentalized.[2]

American policy toward Pakistan was supposedly independent of its policy toward India, or so the American decision makers wished to believe. The fact that no one in India or Pakistan viewed the situation this way did not prevent the Americans from pressing their program to its embarrassing conclusion. In 1971, given the Bangladesh crisis, the United States felt compelled to side with Pakistan against India. But its chagrin over the outcome finally caused it to reappraise its longtime performance. The futility expressed in the desire to befriend both countries while they remained unreconciled enemies, to transform the Pakistani army into the most effective military force in South Asia when the New Delhi government voluntarily entered into mutual assistance agreements with the Soviet Union, made it essential that the United States reconsider its position and interests in South Asia.

The Carter administration moreso than those preceding it sensed the need to reverse the "tilt" toward Pakistan. Relations between President Carter and Indian Prime Minister Morarji Desai were cordial, and Washington was eager to satisfy India's desires. In the meantime, relations between the United States and Pakistan soured, especially given American reaction to Pakistan's atomic energy program. The Soviet Union's invasion of Afghanistan in December 1979, however, confounded White House policymakers. The obvious threat posed toward Pakistan by the appearance of the Red Army on its borders pressed Washington to reconsider its tough position with Islamabad. This reappraisal was just getting underway when Ronald Reagan replaced Jimmy Carter. The new Republican administration left little doubt that it was giving serious thought to improving relations with Pakistan even if it meant embittering contacts with India. Indeed, the Desai government had fallen earlier, and in the 1979–80 general elections Indira Gandhi was returned to power. Prime Minister Gandhi's posture toward the United States was generally judged abrasive in Washington, and the Reagan administration was even more drawn to promoting friendship with the Zia-ul-Haq government in Pakistan. Despite efforts on several fronts to alter U.S. policy toward the subcontinent, established patterns of relationships proved virtually impossible to change.

SOUTH ASIA IN THE 1970s

Diplomatic realignments between and among major and lesser powers in the 1970s were dramatic, and South Asia was no exception. When the decade began, U.S. attention was still riveted on Southeast Asia and, in particular, Indochina. The war was winding down for the Americans, but it continued to consume the attention of policymakers and the general public. The People's Republic of China (PRC) was still considered a primary dilemma and its containment required considerable intellectual and material resources.[3] The mission of Henry Kissinger to Peking altered almost over night a course that the United States had established for itself as far back as the Korean war. It signaled the serious intention of the United States to extricate itself from the war in Indochina and to moderate its relations with the PRC. If the Chinese had been suspicious of earlier American announcements about removing their troops from the region, the Kissinger visit helped to change the atmosphere. Moreover, the arrangements that permitted President Nixon to visit the PRC, early in 1972, more than convinced the Chinese that the Americans were tiring of their role on the mainland of Asia. It is important to note, however, that the Chinese continued to see the Americans as a counterweight to the Soviet threat on their far-flung border. Thus the first step in a new detente policy was taken between the United States and the PRC, but both the Soviet Union and India were hardly idle. The Indians saw the improvement in U.S.-Chinese relations as a special problem, and it was no doubt more than coincidence that just a few weeks after Kissinger's secret mission to Peking, the Soviet Union and India signed a treaty of peace and friendship.[4]

In the midst of this major-power maneuvering was the civil war in East Pakistan, which began in March 1971 and had by that summer settled into a war of attrition. The most immediate consequence of the war was the flood of refugees that moved from East Pakistan to India. India made diplomatic capital out of the plight of the tragic millions that sought refuge and succor within its borders. The conscience of the Western world was pricked by the reports, photographs, and films that revealed the gruesome realities of the struggle in East Pakistan and the great outpouring of sympathy for India in the Western world was vividly contrasted with the bitterness directed against Pakistan and the military junta that ruled over it. The U.S. government could not ignore this comparison, but its principal concern lay in its own efforts aimed at withdrawing from Southeast Asia, and toward this end the Chinese played an important role. Kissinger's initial visit to Peking was arranged in major part by the Pakistani government, and it was from Pakistan that the American secretary of state made his secret journey. He also returned to Pakistan after completing his mission. In point of fact, the U.S. government owed a debt to the Pakistani government's action in East Pakistan.[5] Moreover, the U.S. government held the view that the civil war was an internal matter and should be resolved by the Pakistanis alone. Washington also acted as if the worst of the fighting was over, that the Pakistani army controlled the province, and that it was only a question of restoring creditable government in East Pakistan and facilitating the return of the refugees. India, of course, did not see the conflict in East Pakistan in the same manner, and it stepped up its own military preparations while providing support for the Mukti Bahini (Bangladesh Liberation Army). It also sanctioned the establishment of the Bangladesh government in exile in Calcutta.

The United States and China were equally interested in protecting the territorial integrity of the Pakistani state. Neither country could ignore the Bengali demand for self-determination, but, for their own reason, they found it impossible to support the separatists. Moreover, after the Indo-Soviet treaty of August 1971, both the United States and China were convinced that the conflict in East Pakistan was being perpetuated by outside forces. The civil war in Bangladesh therefore had ramifications far beyond the frontiers of the Pakistani state. Indian authorities perceived collusion between Pakistan, the United States, and the PRC; China and the United States were no less certain that India and the Soviet Union were determined to dismember Pakistan.

When the Indian army crossed into East Pakistan in December 1971, all these perceptions were confirmed. The United States felt the Indians would not have violated Pakistan's sovereignty had it not been for the support guaranteed it by the Soviet Union.[6] In the United Nations, India was pressured to desist and withdraw its forces behind its own frontier, but the Soviet Union sided with India and blocked any action in the Security Council. While Pakistan waited in vain for the Chinese to open a front along the Himalayan chain, the U.S. government decided to show its flag in the Bay of Bengal, and a small naval task force led by the nuclear carrier *Enterprise* steamed into Indian waters. Undeterred by the American maneuver, the Indian armed forces made short work of the isolated Pakistani garrison in East Pakistan, and, with no real sign of tangible external support, the Pakistanis surrendered. Bangladesh was recognized as an independent sovereign state by both India and the Soviet Union, and in the days that followed many more countries followed their example. Little attention was given to the fact that Bangladesh was the first country to achieve its independence since World War II through the instrument of civil war. Even those countries that usually displayed sympathy for Pakistan held the view that the Pakistanis got what they deserved and that justice had finally been done the Bengalis, even if international law had been mangled in the process.

The collapse of the Pakistani army, the criticism in the U.S. Congress and intellectual circles of the U.S. government's "tilt" toward the Pakistani junta, and the fait accompli in Bangladesh caused the White House to reappraise its position throughout South Asia. Gone were the dreams that Pakistan was the first line of defense in the subcontinent, or that India could be insulated from the influence of the Soviet Union. The new politico-military realities taking shape in the subcontinent focused on a truncated and relatively unstable Pakistan, an independent but impoverished Bangladesh, and a confident, strident, and preeminent India. The United States assured the new civilian government in Islamabad that it would continue providing Pakistan with economic assistance but that it had no intention of lifting the arms embargo (imposed on both Pakistan and India in 1965). The United States made more or less the same gesture to India and Bangladesh. Both governments were informed that the United States was prepared to assist them in their development programs, and diplomatic efforts were initiated to undo the discontent caused by the Bangladesh episode. The U.S. government had in fact concluded that an evenhanded policy was required in South Asia and that its links with Pakistan had been more extensive than the situation warranted.[7]

PAKISTAN: THE BHUTTO YEARS

Shortly after assuming control of the Pakistani government, Zulfikar Ali Bhutto removed Pakistan from both the Commonwealth of Nations and the Southeast Asia Treaty Organization (SEATO). Bhutto argued the former had done nothing to prevent the breakup of Pakistan and was heavily influenced by India, while the latter was no longer functional given the loss of East Pakistan. Bhutto emphasized, however, that he would not cut his ties with the Central Treaty Organization (CENTO) or the West. Despite a stress on socialist goals and his anti-American reputation, Bhutto could not afford to disassociate his country from a part of the world that provided Pakistan with its economic and technological essentials. Moreover, the Soviet Union's embrace of India coupled with Sino-Soviet antagonism seemed to rule out any significant turn toward Moscow, especially as such a move would be interpreted as a breach of faith in Peking. In its principal parameters, Pakistan's foreign policy was relatively unchanged. Bhutto, however, was determined to give that policy a slightly different orientation. The new realities of the Pakistani position suggested a greater interest in Southwest Asia and the Middle East, and Bhutto's major foreign policy initiatives were directed at this region. Iran came in for special attention, as did the Arab Persian Gulf states. With the exception of Iraq, these countries appeared quite receptive to Pakistani overtures of close cooperation, and programs of mutual interest were developed. In return for trained technical and professional personnel, the countries of the Persian Gulf offered Pakistan substantial sums of capital.[8] (By 1981, approximately 1.4 million Pakistanis resided in the Persian Gulf states. In FY 1980–81, these migrants remitted to Pakistan $2.1 billion, which was almost the equivalent of Pakistan's earnings from exports during the same period. Moreover, an estimated 130,000 Pakistanis sought opportunities in the Middle East countries each year, and Pakistani military missions had already been established with 22 countries, especially in Saudi Arabia, Oman, and the United Arab Emirates.)

Iran had more to offer than financial assistance. The political system that sustained the shah, replete with its special security foundation, was very attractive to Bhutto. Structures and agencies that bore the Iranian imprint were virtually transplanted in Pakistan, and the most important of these were the highly efficient and very powerful secret police and intelligence-gathering organizations. Bhutto's perception of the Pakistani scene was influenced by a long experience in politics and the personal conviction that no administration could satisfy Pakistan's political opposition. Only a firm hand, he concluded, could govern Pakistan, even if this meant neutralizing his political opponents. Bhutto, like the shah of Iran, insisted on absolute power. In order to be successful, his writ had to be considered sacred law and his judgment infallible. But the fact that some of Pakistan's politicans could not be won over or intimidated and that they refused to grant Bhutto his wishes, or blindly follow his lead, gave the country little respite from societal strife.[9] At the same time, there seemed to be little effective opposition, and it was assumed Bhutto would govern Pakistan for some time to come.

In December 1976, Bhutto completed five years as the primary ruler of Pakistan. His Pakistan People's Party (PPP) was without genuine competition, and virtually every political leader of stature had been imprisoned or otherwise silenced. Although Bhutto had received credit for leading the Pakistani nation out of the dark despite of defeat and dismemberment, Pakistan remained an inchoate entity. In some important respects the lesson of Bangladesh had had a completely reverse effect. Instead of its drawing the people of Pakistan into a tighter, more coherent nation, fissiparous tendencies intensified. The lingering Pakhtunistan dispute had been given new vitality with the 1973 seizure of power in Afghanistan by Sardar Daud. A Baluchi Liberation Organization was active in Baluchistan, and sizable contingents of the Pakistan army and air force engaged in sporadic fighting in the desolate mountain terrain that borders on Iran and Afghanistan. If these frontier troubles were not enough, the country was faced with a Sindhu Desh movement (Sind for the Sindhis), which was directed against both the Muhajirs (the refuge community that moved from India to Pakistan in the period following independence) and the Punjabis who since independence had obtained large landholdings in the irrigated northern sector of the province. As the largest demographic component and traditionally the more influential ethnic group in the country, the Punjabis have always been perceived by Pakistan's minorities as monopolizing the power and wealth of the country.[10] On the one side, the nationalities problem opened Pakistan to further meddling by India and Afghanistan. On the other, however, it provided Bhutto with the opportunity to keep his domestic foes divided and weak.

Bhutto's effectiveness as a leader was linked with his driving, demanding personality and his formidable political party. But this would not have been enough had he not also received the support of the armed forces and the permanent services, the traditional steel frame that long guided the destiny of the subcontinent's inhabitants. Bhutto's declaration seemed to promote the politicization of the country, but there was no mistaking the continuing prominence of the civil-military bureaucracy.[11] All previous Pakistani leaders had found it necessary to lean upon the civil and armed bureaucrats, and despite Bhutto's rhetoric about restoring parliamentary government, he was no less dependent on them than his predecessors. In major part, this reliance on the traditional administrative power structure called attention to the ethnic, cultural, and political divisions mentioned above. It also underlined the scarcity of national political leaders and coherent political organizations after almost two decades of arbitrary government. The civil-military bureaucracy, with its peculiar stake in the survival of Pakistan and with a national political consciousness unmatched by other important groups in the country, managed to perpetuate its guardian role.[12] Thus, the army was again ready to assert itself in July 1977, when it ousted Bhutto from office, declared martial law, and suspended all political activity.

The military coup was led by General Mohammad Zia-ul-Haq, Bhutto's handpicked chief of the Pakistani army. Assisted by key members of the armed forces, Zia at first promised and then repeatedly postponed new elections and a return to civilian government. Although declaring he had no interest in political office, the general soon declared himself to be the country's new president and proceeded to neutralize opposition to his rule. Bhutto was accused of ordering the murder of a political rival and after a lengthy trial was declared guilty and sentenced to die by hanging. An agonizing appeal process and pleas for mercy from governments all over the world could not prevent his execution in April 1979.[13] And although Bhutto predicted a massive uprising against the military government in the event he was put to death, the demonstrations that did erupt were limited and easily contained by the army and law enforcement.

The Pakistani public, like the country's politicians, were of several views and many showed mixed feelings over the demise of Zulfikar Ali Bhutto. Their fragmented organizations meant there would be no unified front to contest the power of the military government. Zia also moved quickly to reinforce his authority by claiming to transform Pakistan into an Islamic state, a much publicized but little realized goal in the first three decades since the country's birth. Zia also concluded that only by giving primary attention to Islamic principles, values, and traditions could Pakistan's nationality problems be successfully addressed.

BANGLADESH

Independence did not usher in an era of progress and prosperity for the Bangladeshis. Although free from the overbearing attitude of the West Pakistanis, they had to contend with the aftermath of a civil war that had taken hundreds of lives, and among this number some of the country's more outstanding and promising younger leaders.[14] Moreover, the bloodletting did not cease when the last Pakistani soldier lay down his arms. While the Awami League emerged as the dominant political organization and had full control of the government, numerous dissident factions protracted the conflict, especially in the hinterland, where government security was relatively weak and ineffective. But political instability was only part of the story. The war had disrupted the growing season and harvests were small compared with the enormous needs. Millions of people had lost their land and all their possessions, and they were totally dependent on the government for their survival. Prices for essential commodities soared to astronomical levels, and inflation was further aggravated by economic dilemmas in the world at large. Shortages of all goods produced hoarding and smuggling on an unprecedented scale. Corruption became a necessary and functional component of the politico-administrative process. With industry virtually paralyzed, there was little employment for the many needing work, and the nation's productivity was almost nonexistent. This was the Bangladesh to which Mujibur Rahman triumphantly returned from his prison in Pakistan. Released by Bhutto in a gesture of goodwill, Mujib hoped to rally the Bengalis behind his leadership. United, he declared, the Bangladeshis could realize their "Sonar Bengal" (Golden Bengal).[15]

Not even Mujib, however, expected that Bangladesh could be reconstructed without outside assistance. India was instrumental in the creation of Bangladesh, and that country was now called upon to lend whatever material assistance it could offer. But the real burden of aid for Bangladesh could not be placed upon India, given its own economic problems. Western Europe, the Soviet Union, and the United States had to bear this responsibility, and it is striking the amount of basic assistance they rendered. The United States was perhaps most prominent, providing several hundred million dollars worth of foodstuffs and other essentials. Still, it was India that wielded a heavy hand in Bangladesh, and Mujib's Awami League government had to content itself with an Indian presence that disturbed many Bangladeshis. It was perhaps Mujib's dependence on India that prevented him from capitalizing on his extensive popularity; his mystique as a "Great Leader" certainly suffered by his subordination to India's Prime Minister Indira Gandhi.[16]

Mujib's program for developing Bangladesh had to wait on the building of a firm governmental foundation. But the Bengali leader was suspicious of those in the conventional bureaucracy, and his army and party were disorganized and faction-ridden. Given this unstable situation, Mujib's unreconciled opposition resorted to violent methods in order to discredit him. Although the Awami League was successful in the elections that followed independence, the key problem remained the establishment of a governmental structure capable of managing the country's affairs. And this was compounded by terrorists who assassinated scores of Awami League government officials. As a defensive gesture, Mujib drew around him only his family members and loyal friends upon whom he could absolutely trust. He also built a personal militia, the Rakkhi Bahini, which, rather than the divided army, was ordered to contain, and if possible liquidate, all so-called terrorist and antistate elements. The Rakkhi Bahini membership was estimated at approximately 20,000, and like the dissidents it too soon earned the reputation for terrorizing the countryside.[17] Search-and-destroy tactics did not work for the United States in Vietnam, and it was destined to be counterproductive in Bangladesh. The Rakkhi Bahini had as its mission the destruction of all anti-Mujib and anti-Awami League guerrillas. The identification of these guerrillas was no simple task, however, and when the Bangladesh countryside could not be pacified, the Rakkhi Bahini engaged in wanton destruction, taking a heavy toll of the innocent. None of these activities added to Mujib's esteem or charisma. Moreover, the Bangladesh army was particularly disturbed. Not only had the prime minister not given it his patronage, but, by organizing and unleashing the Rakkhi Bahini, he had minimized and possibly undermined their professional role. The army was also incensed by the tactics employed by the Rakkhi Bahini and the manner in which members of the force sought to aggrandize themselves. If "Mujibism" had any chance of developing in Bangladesh, it apparently died amid the burned villages and broken hopes of the Bengali peasantry.

In December 1974 Mujib took the drastic step of suspending the constitutional system and declaring a state of emergency that gave the prime minister virtual dictatorial powers. On January 3, 1975, press censorship was imposed, mail was intercepted, political parties were banned, and many foreigners were ordered out of the country on short notice.[18] Fundamental guarantees were suspended, and hundreds of persons were rounded up and detained without charges being brought against them, and with little promise that they would ever come to trial. Any criticism of the government was cause for police action, and the jails throughout Bangladesh were filled to overflowing. Curiously, Mujib had not declared martial law. The army had not been called upon to enforce the prime minister's action. Rather, it was Mujib's police agencies and the Rakkhi Bahini that were ordered to carry out the prime minister's directives. On January 25, Mujib took the next fatal move by abrogating the Bangladesh constitution. The parliamentary system, he argued, was not suited to Bangladesh's needs, and he insisted on the adoption of a presidential system that would better allow him to consolidate power. The decree dissolving the parliament had wide-ranging effects on the political process. The Awami League, which had spawned a number of factions, now split apart and ceased to be an effective political organization. It had been alleged that Mujib no longer relied on the Awami League and wanted it dismantled so that he could build a new party that would be more responsive to his ideas and ambitions. From hindsight it can be said that Mujib created a situation in which he alienated most of the personalities and undermined the very institutions upon which the success of his regime depended.

Mujib was blinded by a perception of himself as the "Father of Bangladesh." Like Bhutto in Pakistan, his behavior reflected that of a venerable paternal leader who could do no wrong and who the people of Bangladesh would follow with unquestioning conviction. Mujib no doubt also gained a false sense of power from his relations with India. India had proved to be the difference in the war against Pakistan, and his relations with Indira Gandhi were cordial and encouraging. In point of fact, however, Mujibur Rahman failed to understand the realities of the Bangladesh condition or the increasing opposition to his rule from many sectors of society. After imposing one-man rule, Mujib drew himself into his tight family circle and all but ignored his cabinet as a reign of terror was launched by the Rakkhi Bahini.

On August 15, 1975, suddenly and without prior warning, elements of the Bangladesh army attacked the home of Mujibur Rahman and killed him as well as all the members of his family, with the exception of two daughters who were traveling in Germany. Other detachments struck the homes of Mujib's powerful relatives, and they and other close supporters were put to death on the spot. The headquarters of the Rakkhi Bahini was attacked simultaneously, and although there was some resistance, the installation was quickly put out of action, and the corps' leaders were killed. Within hours of the coup, word spread that the Father of Bangladesh was dead and a new civilian government was being organized under army supervision. Martial law was declared, but the new government led by a civilian, Khondakar Mushtaque Ahmed, moved to restore some of the freedoms that had been suspended by Mujib's emergency orders. Newspapers closed by Mujib were reopened, and more than 1,000 political prisoners were turned out of the Bangladesh jails. New elections were forecast but in the meantime the government announced its decision to rule by decree.[19]

As the new rulers of Bangladesh moved to consolidate their power, the factions that had been vying for control ever since the Pakistani surrender again asserted themselves. And on November 6, 1975, Mushtaque Ahmed was overthrown by another military junta, this time led by Major General Ziaur Rahman, whom Mustaque Ahmed had dismissed from his post as army chief. Mustaque Ahmed was accused of being the instrument behind the young officers who had overthrown and killed Mujib. These same officers had arrested Bangladesh's other celebrated politicians, particularly those who had been in the vanguard of the Bangladesh movement. When it was revealed that they (namely, Tajuddin Ahmed and Mansoor Ali, former prime ministers of Bangladesh; Syed Nasrul Islam, an ex-vice-president; and A. H. M. Kamaruzzaman, onetime minister of commerce) had been executed while in prison, the older, more established members of the military could not ignore the deepening crisis overtaking Bangladesh. Thus when Major General Ziaur Rahman was dismissed from his post, the only conclusion to be drawn was that the young revolutionaries were about to unleash another bloody purge.

In an effort to gain control of the government, Ziaur Rahman moved to arrest the officers responsible for the political killings and fighting broke out between various factions of the army. The leader of the young officers, Khalid Musharaf, was killed in the ensuing battles, and ultimately Ziaur Rahman, with the cooperation of the other heads of the military services and bureaucracy, established his authority, Bangladesh's parliament was abolished, and no political parties were permitted to operate in the immediate aftermath of the countercoup. Bangladesh's orgy of blood and violence did not completely end, but for the first time in two years the country seemed ready to opt for a more tranquil condition.

The Ziaur Rahman government shunned the flamboyant style of Mujib and was primarily concerned with laying a foundation for coherent policy planning and execution in critical economic and demographic areas. The weather, a perennial enemy of the people of Bangladesh, was unusually good in 1976 and agricultural yields were the highest since the country gained its independence from Pakistan. In addition, the government's stern policies aimed at checking official corruption and smuggling, a problem of historic dimensions, were somewhat reduced. Smuggling had always sapped the vitality of the state, and India was always seen as the culprit and ultimate beneficiary. In general, relations with India took a turn for the worse with Mujib's death, but genuine tensions did not emerge until the Ziaur Rahman regime began to consolidate its power.

Shortly after Zia's successful maneuver there were reports of skirmishes between Indian and Bangladeshi forces on their mutual frontier. The Indian high commissioner in Dacca was also the target of an assassin, and although he escaped unharmed, the Gandhi government issued a harsh warning to Bangladesh that serious consequences might follow if terrorist activities were not stopped. The deterioration in India-Bangladesh relations was also advanced by the alacrity with which Pakistan moved to recognize the Ziaur Rahman government. Despite the earlier recognition of Bangladesh by Pakistan, relations were cool and circumspect. Mujib had insisted on Pakistan paying indemnities and settling economic and financial matters resulting from the division of the country. Pakistan had balked at all such settlements, and as a consequence there were few transactions between the two countries. Growing discontent between Bangladesh and India, however, seemed to draw the Bengalis into a closer relationship with Pakistan. The death of Mujib and subsequent developments made it possible for the two countries to develop an intimacy that they had not enjoyed since long before their civil war. Islam was again raised as a force drawing them together. While no one seriously entertained the idea that the countries would once more merge into a single union, speculation was rife about their establishing something akin to a confederal economic system. Emphasis was placed on maximizing economic cooperation without minimizing political sovereignty.

India was clearly unhappy with developments in Bangladesh, despite Ziaur Rahman's apparent success in establishing a modicum of law and order.[20] The new opening to Pakistan also brought the Chinese into Bangladesh. Bangladesh and China agreed to exchange ambassadors early in 1976, well in advance of the restoration of Sino-Indian diplomatic relations. It may not be inaccurate to suggest that India was prompted to accelerate its normalization of relations with China because the Bangladeshis had already done so. India was disquieted by the thought of a hostile Bangladesh, which in league with the PRC and Pakistan might exploit conditions in India's turbulent northeast quadrant.

In April 1976 there were renewed hostilities on the Indo-Bangladesh border, and this time the Indians let it be known that they believed it was officially inspired from Dacca. At the same time the Bangladeshis reopened the 20-year-old Farakka Barrage problem. The Farakka Barrage controlled the flow of Ganges water into Bangladesh. It was built by India as a means to saving the port of Calcutta, but it has had adverse effects on Bangladesh's agriculture during the dry months. Mujib and Indira Gandhi arrived at a tentative agreement over the question of how to manage the distribution of the Ganges waters in 1974, but the Indians promptly violated it, thus further antagonizing the volatile Bangladeshis. With Mujib gone and anti-Indian sentiment rising, the issue was not only revived, it became a cause célèbre.[21] In March 1976 the Indians announced they would increase the flow of water to Bangladesh, but the authorities in Dacca were neither impressed nor satisfied. They now called for a general settlement that would require the Indians to dismantle much of the construction, a position the Indian government refused to entertain. Bangladesh raised the issue in third world forums and in November 1976 called upon the United Nations to add the Farakka Barrage dispute to its agenda. Although India blocked a full-scale debate in the United Nations, it found the pressure disconcerting.

Indira Gandhi's government apparently was determined to erode General Ziaur Rahman's position by assisting clandestine elements opposed to his regime. The Bangladeshi leader spoke publicly of just such a plot, hence reinforcing anti-Indian sentiment in the country.[22] The Indian threat also enabled Ziaur Rahman to improve his personal status. As a Bengali he believed his people required a "great leader." But he also knew from bitter experience that Bengalis derive particular satisfaction from destroying those they proclaim as "great leaders." Numerous public and secret trials by martial law courts tried politicians and members of the armed forces who were suspected of or implicated in guerrilla and other conspiratorial activities. The political parties and the army were hotbeds of intrigue and plots to overthrow the government. Thus General Ziaur Rahman broke with the Jatiya Samajtantrik Dal (JSD), the National Socialist Party, which had helped him achieve power, and arrested hundreds of its members. Members of Mujib's defunct Awami League were forced to flee India while others set up a resistance movement in the Mymensingh area north of Dacca. The Islamic parties, which had been instrumental in the overthrow of Mujib, were also becoming more troublesome for Zia and stern action was directed at their forces. Each of the parties could expect to attract some military support, and the divided nature of the armed forces perpetuated a condition of general uncertainty.

Zia's government gave the appearance of hesitating to take the kind of action deemed necessary to root out the discontent. Essentially the problem resolved around the fragmented politico-military scene and the inability to consolidate power long enough to root out the more fanatical elements. A mutiny of armed units in Chittagong in February 1976 followed by another near Dacca and Bramanbaria were treated gingerly. General Zia also permitted some army officers to return from exile while others were still being arrested or expelled from the country. For example, a number of ranking military officers who had been involved in the overthrow of Mujib and subsequently fled the country were permitted to return and some were offered diplomatic assignments. On the other hand, Lieutenant Colonel Abu Taher, one of the more notable guerrilla leaders during the civil war and an officer who played a crucial role in bringing Zia to power in November 1975, was tried for crimes against the state, found guilty, sentenced to death, and hanged on July 21, 1976. Numerous other military and political personalities were also executed or given long prison terms. Even a Dutch relief worker and journalist, Peter Custers, was accused of plotting to establish "scientific socialism" in Bangladesh with the help of Taher. He too was sentenced to death, but after international intervention on his behalf he was later pardoned and expelled from the country.[23]

In order to stabilize the political scene the Bangladesh government ordered the country divided into 11 zones, each coming under the control of a martial law administrator drawn from the armed forces. Martial law regulations were developed with the purpose of maintaining law and order, and severe punishment was threatened for any violations. Another ordinance made it a high crime to criticize any of the martial law actions. At the same time the government declared its intention to permit political party activities, and approximately 45 parties applied for government approval. Newspapers that had been suppressed under previous ordinances were also permitted to resume publication but under the watchful eye of government security agents. On November 29, 1976, President A. M. Sayem transferred his office of chief martial law administrator to Zia, who heretofore had the title of deputy martial law administrator. Although for all practical purposes little was changed, the move tended to concentrate legal power in Zia's hands, thus enhancing his legitimacy. Shortly before the transfer, President Sayem announced the indefinite postponement of national elections. Elections to village and district councils, however, were permitted to go ahead as originally scheduled. Following this announcement Zia ordered a new round of arrests, and approximately 2,000 political figures were imprisoned on charges ranging from criticism of the government to high treason. It was estimated that Bangladesh jails held as many as 25,000 political prisoners by the end of 1976. While these arrests were underway Ziaur Rahman paid an official visit to Peking, and the Bangladesh government entered into its first direct contact with PRC leaders since the country gained its independence in 1971.

The methodical building of Ziaur Rahman's authority took another step forward in April 1977, when Sayem resigned his position for what was reported to be health reasons. Before leaving office, however, he nominated Ziaur Rahman to succeed him. The legality for the maneuver was found in a presidential proclamation of August 20, 1975, that empowered a resigning president to identify his successor before the expiration of his term. Thus Major General Ziaur Rahman became president as well as chief martial law administrator, and on April 22 he announced he would call a referendum to ascertain if the Bangladesh public had confidence in his leadership. In order to further bolster his authority, Zia announced an amendment to the Bangladesh constitution that shifted the country from its status as a secular nation to that describing it as an Islamic state.[24] The change was not meant to please India, however, which looked on the events in Bangladesh with considerable trepidation.

India-Bangladesh relations continued to deteriorate up to the Indian elections in March 1977. Guerrilla raids against the Bangladesh government in the Mymensingh and Chittagong areas were said to have been mounted from bases in India. Bomb and grenade attacks in Dacca also were alleged to have been inspired by the Indian government. Deliberations on the Farakka Barrage dispute also were at an impasse. Prime Minister Gandhi's defeat in the elections and the crushing of the Congress Party, however, created new opportunities for a rapprochement, and the new Janata government of Morarji Desai moved quickly to calm the fears of Ziaur Rahman.[25]

Desai and Zia met for the first time at the Commonwealth meeting of heads of government in London, and on June 10, 1977, both leaders announced that progress had been made on all their outstanding differences. While India promised to police its border and prevent Indian territory from being used as a sanctuary for guerrillas operating against the Bangladesh government, Bangladesh agreed to control the movement of Bangladesh refugees into India, where they were alleged to be engaging in political acts prejudicial to the Indian Union. Desai also told Rahman that his government would work arduously to resolve the Farakka problem. General Zia halted his verbal attacks on India, and for the first time since the death of Mujibur Rahman, tension between India and Bangladesh was reduced.

In May 1977 the Bangladesh voting public gave Ziaur Rahman an overwhelming vote of confidence. He received 98.87 percent of the votes cast from the approximately 34 million people who went to the polls.[26] The government was quick to point out that more persons had voted in the referendum than had cast ballots during the 1973 elections that Mujibur Rahman's party had monopolized. It was less publicized that the voters had only the one choice before them. While Zia had clearly not won the hearts of all his countrymen, he was increasing his power, and, generally speaking, most Bangladeshis were ready for a respite from the constant strife. Thus when dissident military units again attempted to overthrow the government in October 1977, there was little popular support for the revolutionaries.

This coup had been planned to coincide with the highjacking of a Japan Air Lines passenger plane that had been allowed to land at Dacca. It was during the negotiations with the Japanese Red Army highjackers that the rebellion broke out and much of the fighting centered near the airport. Within a few days the rebellion had been crushed, and numerous military and political figures were again arrested. Martial law tribunals were quickly assembled, and this time it was obvious that the government of Ziaur Rahman would be neither cautious nor lenient. By the end of October 37 persons implicated in the coup attempt were executed, and 20 more were given life imprisonment.[27] The government also announced it was banning Bangladesh's three leading political parties, accusing them of attempting to infiltrate the armed forces and generally inciting them and the public to violence. At the top of the ban order was the Bangladesh Communist Party (BCP), a pro-Moscow organization. Its leaders Moni Singh and Muhammad Farhad were also detained under emergency provisions for what was termed "prejudicial activities." The centrist Democratic League of former President Khondakar Mushtaque Ahmed and the National Socialist Party were the other parties that were ordered to cease functioning.[28]

Zia's strengthened domestic position was further improved when after crash negotiations, India agreed to yield to many of Bangladesh's demands over

Farakka, and an agreement was officially signed on November 5, 1977. The five-year agreement could be extended by mutual understanding until a new arrangement was developed, but for the time being, Bangladesh was guaranteed an even flow of Ganges water during the dry months. In Bangladesh there was quiet jubilation that contrasted with the heavy criticism directed at Desai's government by sections of the Indian press and especially public opinion in West Bengal.[29] The Indian government, however, made it clear that it was more interested in promoting and strengthening good relations with its neighbors than in sustaining economic advantage. General Zia, who was hopeful of turning his country toward normalcy after long years of bitter internecine conflict, praised the Indian government for its statesmanship and opined that relations between Bangladesh and India would markedly improve in the new atmosphere of equality and shared responsibility. In order to dramatize the termination of his conflict with India, President Ziaur Rahman visited India on December 19, 1977, and was received warmly by Indian President Sanjiva Reddy and Desai. In his response to Reddy's words of welcome and friendship, Zia said he attached great importance to the development of mutual cooperation between their two countries.[30] At the conclusion of his two-day visit, Zia flew on to Pakistan, where he met with General Zia-ul-Haq, Pakistan's chief martial law administrator. It was the first state visit by a ranking Bangladeshi to Pakistan since the East Pakistan session in 1971. Pakistan's President Fazal Elahi Choudhury noted that the visit "seals the process of normalization and reconciliation" between Bangladesh and Pakistan.[31] The leaders of Pakistan and Bangladesh also went out of their way to emphasize that they had no intention of distressing India, that accommodation and cooperation were preferred to competition and antagonism.

In a display of his political strength Zia Rahman permitted the holding of a presidential election in June 1978. His major competition came from another general, M. A. G. Osmani, who headed a coalition of disparate political parties that was essentially interested in returning to the ideas and policies of the late Mujibur Rahman. Despite heightened emotions caused by the campaign it was generally free of incident. And when the ballots were counted Zia Rahman had won a resounding victory and a vote of confidence. The official tally gave him slightly less than 80 percent of the total vote and although the opposition cried foul, Zia basked in his success. He commented that the people of Bangladesh had given him a five-year "mandate" to rehabilitate the country and that he would tolerate no interference from any quarter, including his still feuding army.

No one expected societal tensions to completely dissipate but Ziaur Rahman showed himself to be an adept political leader. In 1979 he permitted the reinstatement of civilian government and the convening of a full-fledged parliament with an extremely vocal opposition. Zia also promoted economic development and family planning that aimed at producing the country's first food-grain surplus. He also took his government into the remote rural areas and personally interacted with the simple folk of the Bangladesh countryside. This popular base of power was deemed essential given Zia's vigorous opposition from among the more sophisticated segments of the population. Indeed, perennial flooding, uncontrollable inflation, continuing acts of political terror, economic crime, and persistent divisions within the army alienated the urban elites and brought heavy criticism on his person and regime. Moreover, relations between India and Bangladesh became strained again with the return of Indira Gandhi to high office in New Delhi. The Ganges water problem and related territorial questions jeopardized the understanding that Zia and Morarji Desai had developed several years before. Difficulties with India also provided the opposition with more ammunition to fire at their beleaguered president.

Zia attempted to master the situation by playing at the politicians' own game. He formed the Bangladesh National Party (BNP) in 1980 and declared it would represent the ethnic, philosophical, and social diversity comprising the nation. But observers quickly concluded that the organization was a temporary phenomenon, was solely dependent on Zia for its raison d'être, and would wither and disappear as soon as he departed the political stage. Despite this judgment, it was also noted that the opposition parties were themselves weak, amorphous congeries of factional groups, solely dependent on personal leaders and unable to achieve national status.[32] Bangladesh, despite some material progress, passed into the decade of the 1980s in largely the same anarchical state that heralded its beginning in 1971.

Bangladesh was also exposed to similar tribal and ethnic problems that plagued northeastern India. Rebellious elements in the Chittagong Hill Tracts, particularly those identified with the Buddhist Chakma tribesmen, organized the Shanti Bahini or Peace Army and carried on guerrilla attacks against government installations and forces. Major arms supplies for the insurgents were smuggled into the region from India. Other tribal groups such as the Mukti Parishad and a radical faction from the Sarbohara (Marxist-Leninist) Party added to the general unrest. These guerrilla bands, however, were not part of a united front in singular opposition to the government. Often they clashed with one another, thus making for even greater confusion and unpredictability in the region. Government plans to swamp the tribal people by opening the area to unlimited Bengali settlement provoked more bitterness and hence greater resistance from the indigenous population and Dacca was slow to take advantage of tribal rivalries and differences. Toward the close of 1980 and in the early months of 1981 Ziaur Rahman seemed to indicate a new policy for the region and promised to meet some of the demands of the tribal population and to increase the level of development. At the same time he expressed the view that his patience was not unlimited and that his government would use force to crush the rebellious elements.

But the tribal area was only one sector receiving President Zia's attention. Overall, the Bangladesh leader was concerned with the creation of a support base to ward off the many groups and personalities challenging his authority. Therefore, in 1976 he began to experiment with a system of grassroots government that in many respects resembled the Basic Democracies System of Ayub Khan (1958-69). In 1980 Zia ordered the establishment of 68,000 Gram Sarkars, or village governments. The villagers were linked with district development coordinators, much like the old district councils of the Pakistan era. Not only was power and privilege concentrated in the district headquarters, but the Union Parishad that already existed at the village level was brought into direct conflict with the new Gram Sarkars. Zia's motives were suspect and opinion held that the new Gram Sarkar was not a decentralization of power and responsibility but a means toward increasing and spreading the power of the Bangladesh National Party at the expense of the many opposition organizations. Efforts by the opposition to coalesce had not been so much frustrated by the government, but by the sheer inability of the personalized political factions to agree on a common program and leadership. The politicians, such as those in the Awami League (Malek), the Bangladesh Samajtantric Dal, the Democratic League, the Islamic Democratic League, the GONOFRONT (comprising seven small organizations), the Jatiya Ganomukti Union, the Jatiya Samajtantric Dal, the Krishak Sramik Party, the Muslim League, the National Awami Party, and the United People's Party, represented such a variety of causes, interests, and regions that a genuine alliance appeared impossible to create. So long as Ziaur Rahman held his army together, sustained the loyalty of the bureaucracy, provided positive payoffs for private sector groups, and maintained the fascination of the peasantry, it was doubtful the divisive argumentive political organizations could effectively challenge his authority. In the 1980s, Zia's principal competition would be found within, not outside his administration.

Then the inevitable happened. A disgruntled and demoted general in the Bangladesh army organized a conspiracy to destroy the Ziaur Rahman government. In the spring of 1981 Zia was engaged in another of his many tours of the country, meeting with his local administrators and the general population. His entourage paused for a night's lodging at the government rest house in Chittagong and it was in the middle of the night, while Zia and his aides lay asleep, that the conspirators struck. On May 30, 1981, President Ziaur Rahman and a number of his associates were murdered in their beds. The conspirators, led by Major-General Mohammad Abdul Manzur, anticipated widespread support from the armed forces and political opposition but it was soon obvious this would not happen. The government refrained from announcing the death of the president while loyal forces maneuvered into position and an assault was made on the rebellious group. By the time news of the tragedy was circulated, General Manzur and his forces had been surrounded and the majority taken prisoner. General Manzur was apprehended, but in a subsequent announcement, Dacca revealed he had been killed by irate members of the armed forces. This conspiracy was over, but it had taken its heavy toll.

General Ziaur Rahman's body was borne to Dacca for an emotional state funeral. Tens of thousands turned out for the ceremony, and unlike Mujibur Rahman, Ziaur Rahman was laid to rest amid public grieving and significant emotional expression. Crisis leadership was assumed by Vice-President Abdus Sattar, a gentle septuagenarian who had held a cabinet post in the 1950s before assuming duties as a judge of the East Pakistan High Court and then a justice in the Pakistan Supreme Court. After his repatriation to Bangladesh in 1972, General Zia made him his advisor, and then vice-president in 1977. Sattar had had a long, distinguished career, but it was doubtful he could fill the power vacuum left by Ziaur Rahman's death. Bangladesh has known little peace since its independence in December 1971. And the period ahead did not promise a respite from chaos.

Internationally, Bangladesh was a bit-player, living in the shadow of its Indian neighbor. Ziaur Rahman had tried to balance New Delhi's influence by recultivating relations with Pakistan and by seeming to remain aloof from Sino-Soviet quarrels. The death of Zia, however, again brought out the rivalry between Chinese and Soviet leaders. Moscow was quick to assert in its Asian broadcast that the Chinese had assisted the conspirators. The implication of this charge was that China was not a disinterested bystander, and Moscow was determined to prevent Bangladesh from allying itself with forces judged detrimental to its own as well as New Delhi's interests. Although the death of Ziaur Rahman could not pass unnoticed by Pakistan's martial law administrators, and notably by Zia-ul-Haq, Islamabad was less concerned with the international repercussions of the Bengali leader's passing and more on how it might influence their rule. The fragile nature of leadership in the region was again underlined. Nevertheless, the Bangladesh authorities were able to restore sufficient equilibrium in the country to conduct a formal election for the presidency. Despite riots in September following the execution of a number of army figures implicated in Zia's death, acting President Abdus Sattar ran on a platform of peace and stability, and won a five-year presidential term in November 1981.

President Abdus Sattar faced a test of strength in January 1982 with the appointment of a new ten-member National Security Council, which replaced the National Defense Council. The armed forces, through army Chief of Staff Lieutenant General H. M. Ershad, called for a dominant role in Bangladesh's political system, and that the military should be written into the constitution. The new council comprised the president, the vice-president, four civilian ministers (finance, home affairs, foreign affairs, and industries) as well as the chiefs of the three services. General Ershad publicly declared his opposition to such a body. He argued for a smaller council to be made up of the president and the three service leaders. This council, he said, would operate as a supercabinet and the highest policymaking body in the nation. Under pressure from his Bangladesh National Party to reject the army's proposition, the president declared there would be no supercabinet in his government. The National Security Council would also be confined to advisory functions and the president and parliament would remain accountable to the nation. The military, Sattar asserted, was responsible to him and should not tamper with Bangladesh's fragile democratic structure. The president, however, could not conceal the increasing restlessness in the armed forces or the divisive disputes that had split his party. Given the president's advanced age and his inability to prevent open controversy, General Ershad's demands had to be taken seriously.

How seriously was revealed on March 24, 1982, when General Ershad and the other armed forces chiefs deposed Sattar and took control.of the government. The military establishment banned political parties, abrogated the constitution and desolved the legislature. There was little indication that civilian government would be restored in the foreseeable future.

PAKISTAN AFTER BHUTTO

Pakistan seemed to fare better than Bangladesh in the first five years following their separation. Compared with Bangladesh, Pakistan was viable, and had it not been for two calamitous floods between 1972 and 1976 the country might have shown a remarkable economic recovery from the 1971 civil war. Nevertheless there were important strides toward self-sufficiency in agriculture. Export forecasts for rice and cotton were pegged at high levels, suggesting ample supplies for domestic consumption. The government also engaged in developing necessary infrastructure, such as electrification schemes, microwave radio relay systems, drainage and irrigation networks, and improved roads. The frontier regions and heretofore underdeveloped lands in Sind were target areas for many of these projects. A major focus was on reclaiming uncultivated lands that supposedly would be distributed to the landless rural poor.

Aiding Pakistan's economic development was the assistance it received from Iran and some of the petroleum-rich Arab states. The government was also on the receiving end of sizable sums of money in the form of remittances from thousands of Pakistanis working abroad, and especially in the Persian Gulf region. On October 7, 1976, Prime Minister Bhutto addressed a tripartite labor conference of labor leaders, employers, and government officials in which he recounted the economic achievements of his administration. He stressed the reforms that made the government the primary employer in all sectors: Bhutto insisted that "the labor reforms instituted during the past four years of People's rule should convince the workers that the government belonged to them. The industrial peace now prevailing is a revolutionary peace and not a calm imposed by oppression."[33]

Convinced that his administration's performance could be translated into broad-gauge popular support, Bhutto announced the first national election since his coming to power in December 1971. With the balloting slated for March 7-10, 1977, a campaign was launched in mid-January of that year. It was apparent from the outset, however, that the PPP government would not have the field to itself. The first surprise was the ability of nine relatively small political parties to coalesce under the banner of the Pakistan National Alliance (PNA). The second was the personal attack launched against Bhutto by those in the opposition and the large audiences they attracted. Bhutto was therefore compelled to drop the demeanor of the confident statesman and wade into the campaign with a counterattack aimed at discrediting his detractors. Given the government's control of the media and the special protection provided by the expanded police establishment, the opposition could not hope to compete with the PPP. Moreover, the government could promise and deliver special favors as well as improve the salary scales of workers and government servants alike. Finally, Pakistan was still operating under a state of emergency, the most prominent political leaders were in prison, and the only nationally influential party outside the ruling PPP had been banned in February 1975. The ability of the PNA to challenge Bhutto's authority was clearly limited, but its combined leadership provoked a debate that put virtually every member of the PPP on the defensive.[34]

When the election results were tabulated it was apparent the PPP had won a smashing victory. But the magnitude of the PPP success led many to question the fairness of the polling, and the PNA charged Bhutto with rigging the elections, hence making them null and void. The opposition contrasted the elections in Pakistan with those in India during the same period. It was pointed out that India's elections were fair, and thus Indira Gandhi had been compelled, despite her great power, to step down when the vote ran against her and her party. Pakistanis had always perceived themselves as more forthright than their Indian neighbors, and the thought that India had a higher standard of political morality than Pakistan only added fuel to the fire. The PNA and their followers took to the streets, the only forum where an impact could be registered. They called upon Bhutto to resign and demanded that an interim government be formed and that new elections be conducted under military scrutiny. The PNA demands precipitated countrywide demonstrations that quickly degenerated into rioting, necessitating the use of the special police and finally the army to quell them. Several hundred people died in the weeks that followed. Pakistan's economy ground to a halt, and the government was in a state of near paralysis. Even after the arrest of almost every PNA leader, at all levels, and the declaration of martial law and shoot-to-kill orders, the street disorder continued.

Bhutto was forced to delegate authority to the civil-military bureaucracy, which in turn pressured the prime minister to yield on some of the principal demands made by his opponents. Reluctantly Bhutto agreed to negotiate with the PNA leaders, and their exchange extended over several weeks, with the latter displaying a single-mindedness that exasperated the PPP chairman. Bhutto offered to hold a referendum on his rule, but this was rejected by the opposition. On June 14, 1977, the new Pakistani government announced that the opposition demand for new elections would be accepted if the prime minister were permitted to retain his post. Bhutto's opponents refused to accept this offer, too.

The military, sensing a protracted struggle, and fearful about widening cleavages in Pakistani society, moved to end the chaos. On July 5, 1977, it arrested Bhutto and his ministers and declared martial law throughout the country. Army chief Zia-ul-Haq announced he had taken over the government as chief martial law administrator and would continue to govern Pakistan until such time as the politicians were able to conduct another election. Initially it was stated new elections would be held in October and that a brief campaign would be permitted prior to that date. General Zia released Bhutto and the PNA leaders after several weeks of incarceration, but their appearance among their supporters sparked new demonstrations that only the army could contain. The fragility of the political situation convinced the military junta that the holding of elections in October was premature and Zia rescinded his earlier order.

In the view of informed observers Zia had been pressured by his corps commanders in Rawalpindi, Lahore, and Karachi to postpone the elections. Under no circumstances would these and other military officers sanction Bhutto's return to power. Prior to the declaration of martial law, serious divisions had opened within units of the armed forces, and the ranking officers were concerned that if a vindicated Bhutto were to be returned to office, nothing could prevent the disintegration of the military establishment. In other words, if Zia could not guarantee Bhutto's isolation, other generals would have to step in.[35] Bhutto was the consummate politician, and the generals knew from personal experience that he still commanded a large following in the Punjab and Sind. In such circumstances it was deemed best to postpone the election and to expose Bhutto's abuse of public trust. In August 1977, Pakistan's Law Association accused Bhutto of ordering political murders and engineering official corruption during his tenure as prime minister. In September he was arrested on a charge of conspiring to murder a political opponent. The politician, Ahmed Raza Kasuri, had not been injured, but his father, who was accompanying him, had died in the attack. Members of the Federal Security Force (FSF) that had taken part in the episode, including the FSF leader Masood Mahmood, were reported to have given testimony about Bhutto's direct involvement. A few days after Bhutto's arrest, Zia revealed that he had documentary evidence implicating the former prime minister in political murders. Zia described Bhutto as "an evil genius" and "Machiavelli of 1977, the Prince of Pakistan." He also remarked that the country had been administered along "Gestapo lines" and that Bhutto was "misusing funds and blackmailing people" on a regular basis.[36] Zia said that he wished he "had known one-hundredth" of the crimes that Bhutto was now alleged to have perpetrated.[37]

Bhutto was placed on trial, found guilty, sentenced to death, and after a protracted and tense appeal proved ineffective, he was hanged in a Rawalpindi prison in April 1979. His wife and daughter assumed leadership of the PPP but they were impeded in reorganizing the party by the government, which placed both women under repeated house arrest.

The FSF was disbanded, and accused officers were ordered to face prosecution. Directives were issued establishing special courts for the purpose of trying other former holders of public office. The Holders of Representative Offices (Punishment for Misconduct) Order of 1977 was amended in January 1978 to widen the scope of the proceedings. The ordinance was aimed at reaching all levels of political organization, and it especially targeted former PPP office holders. The military junta's decision to broaden the attack on the PPP was precipitated by increasing tension in the major urban centers where Bhutto's party had called for the observance of Democracy Day to coincide with their fallen leader's birthday. The PPP also sought to exploit labor unrest in the Punjab, where thousands of persons were reported to have rioted. Continuing disturbances reinforced the resolve of the military to avoid an early return to political activity. But while the Zia government was focusing its attention on neutralizing the PPP, it could not ignore those political prisoners languishing in Pakistani jails because of their opposition to Bhutto.

Abdul Wali Khan, the leader of the banned National Awami Party (NAP) who had been imprisoned since February 1975, was released from custody and his trial terminated. Forty of his close associates were freed with him. Mairaj Muhammad Khan, an early supporter of Bhutto, had been released earlier and immediately set himself the task of organizing a new political party. In a grand gesture on January 1, 1978, Zia announced the release of more than 11,000 political detainees and they too were expected to return to the political wars as soon as conditions permitted. Although the military regime was determined to control political performance, it was doubtful it could sustain public support if it insisted on its right to monopolize power indefinitely. Moreover, the collapse of Bhutto's regime only whetted the appetite of his many adversaries who now saw their opportunity to help refashion Pakistan's political life. There was no mistaking the conviction of these politicians that they were in a better position to promote political development in the country.

The dilemma facing the military leaders was how to manage Pakistan's divided political condition, adapt to the preference for provincial rather than national parties, and at the same time promote national solidarity. Zia's belief that Islam remained the only unifying force in the country, his decision to judge Pakistani behavior according to tenets of Islamic law, and his broad call to piety are suggestive of a continuing ideological quest. In addition, Zia's many references to Jinnah and Iqbal, the creators of and spirit behind the Pakistan dream, had symbolic importance in the again reborn Pakistan nation. But all of these approaches had been used before. It was obvious that for Pakistan to surmount its present difficulties, greater political innovation and certainly more provincial autonomy would have to be countenanced. And this clearly meant permitting the regional political leaders substantial latitude in reforming Pakistan's political system. (This theme is examined in detail in Chapter 4.)

The political situation demanded giving attention to social questions, and resources had to be allocated to projects that were more concerned with political payoffs than economic progress. The announcement that the Integrated Rural Development Program (IRDP) would be activated placed stress on the rural hinterland and the need to make the villages self-sufficient in foodstuffs. Another scheme to develop rural development councils held out the promise of administrative and technical expertise. Both national and local governments were also given the task of developing market facilities and agro-based industries, essentially through peasant cooperatives and local IRDP units. Recognizing that peasant skills and resources were limited, Zia's government also announced the creation of a national commission charged with examining the administrative system so that recommendations could be made concerning its developmental responsibilities. Attempts to transform the bureaucracy into a service institution had been made before, and all had failed. The Zia government had the benefit of hindsight, however, and it could examine the causes for the collapse of the Village-AID Program, the Basic Democracies System, and the rural works projects of the 1950s and 1960s. And despite political tensions from domestic and foreign sources, the government could cite some impressive economic achievements between 1979 and the first half of 1981. Outgoing World Bank President Robert McNamara visited Pakistan in March 1981 and personally noted the country's socioeconomic improvements. He was especially impressed with the integrated population welfare program, which he described as "realistic and innovative."[38] The program sought to combine the talents of a variety of government agencies ranging from health to agricultural assistance to education and social services, and necessitated the utilization of vast stores of Pakistan's human resources.

The Pakistani economy also showed remarkable resiliency during the period. The 1979–80 wheat crop was the largest in the nation's history. The surplus in food grains seemed to promise a future export potential, but for the time being the government continued to import wheat in order to build up the country's reserve supplies. Cotton production also exceeded expectations and the higher world price for the commodity gave Pakistan higher earnings for its exports. Rice exports also rose to new levels. Agricultural successes were not the only positive signs. Industrial output and sales also increased. Although not as dramatic as the increases in agricultural yields, the overall economic picture encouraged greater confidence in Pakistan's future and investors were more eager to plow their profits back into expansion programs. Generally speaking, government cooperated with the private sector and statistically Pakistan's economic performance began to look like the early years of the Ayub Khan administration.

In November 1980, the International Monetary Fund extended a credit of $1.7 billion to Pakistan. It was the largest credit arrangement ever entered into by the IMF with a third world country. In December a consortium of 36 international commercial banks offered Islamabad an additional $200 million to help finance the nation's commodity imports. As in the 1950s and early 1960s the government hoped to enlist the support of foreign investors, and Zia himself spoke to a group of key financial and corporate leaders during a visit to New York City, where he also addressed the United Nations.[39] Pakistan's debt rescheduling problems are still and will remain weighty. Although the improved economy has elevated foreign exchange reserves, the country has great difficulty in meeting its outstanding obligations. The Aid-to-Pakistan Consortium, while not about to write off Pakistan's debt, has been reasonably patient and international money circles seem to understand that they are more likely to satisfy their own interests by giving Islamabad as much breathing space as the economic situation permits.

PAKISTAN UNDER PRESSURE

Pakistan's tenuous equilibrium is not lost on investors and would-be investors in the nation's economy. Attention must be given to Zia-ul-Haq's lack of overall popularity, and the prevailing public perception that he is a power-seeker and opportunist. The skyjacking of a domestic Pakistan International Airlines (PIA) flight in March 1981 and its diversion to Kabul and finally Damascus dramatized the political difficulties with which the administration must deal. Zia was quick to describe the skyjacking as "a conspiracy" aimed at turning Pakistan from the Islamic path that he had charted. He left no doubt that he judged the terrorists to be anti-Pakistan as well as antigovernment. Nevertheless, Zia was compelled by the nature of the problem and the skyjackers' proved determination to kill their hostages (a Pakistani diplomat was murdered and dumped from the aircraft at Kabul airport) to yield to their demands. The terrorists, calling themselves members of *Al Zulfikar*, possibly an extremist splinter of the Pakistan People's Party and reported to be dedicated to the memory of Zulfikar Ali Bhutto, insisted on the release of more than 50 political prisoners. Reluctantly, the government flew the identified prisoners to Damascus where the skyjackers released their hostages and were in turn given refuge in Syria. Zia, however, was not about to permit this act of mercy to undermine his rule. The government spread a wide net, arresting numerous members of the political opposition. They again seized Nusrat and Benazir, Bhutto's wife and daughter respectively, and the reputed leaders of the Pakistan People's Party as well as other opposition figures.

To display his toughness and defiance of the opposition Zia also issued a Provisional Constitution Order in March 1981 that reaffirmed the superior power of the martial law authority. The principal features of the order allowed for the suspension of many of the salient aspects of the 1973 constitution. The Zia government was still unwilling to abrogate the document but the new directive virtually eliminated its significance. One or more vice-presidents, beholden to the president and chief martial law administrator, were to be appointed, hence avoiding the need for a prime minister. A Federal Council, or Majlis-i-

Shura, also selected by the president was to serve in the place of a formal legislature. Political activity was also severely restricted for the foreseeable future. When the martial law administration considered it appropriate to permit political party interaction, only those parties recognized as legitimate by the chief election commissioner as of September 1979 could perform their customary roles. All other parties were ordered dissolved and their assets seized by the federal government. No new party could be formed without the consent of the chief election commissioner. Moreover, it was the president's prerogative to determine if a particular political party was acting in a manner "prejudicial to the sovereignty, integrity, or security of Pakistan." If any party were so judged, the president had the power to advise the chief election commissioner to dissolve it.

No less important, the Provisional Constitution Order legitimated all actions and decisions of the chief martial law administrator from that date in July 1977 when the Bhutto government was overthrown. The 1973 constitution was declared to be in abeyance so long as martial law remained in force, with certain specific exceptions that further reinforced the power of the military government. In this connection, the high courts of Pakistan were prevented from interfering with the actions of the martial law authority in detaining individuals (thus neutralizing references to fundamental rights as described in the 1973 constitution that might otherwise be cited to gain their release). The courts also surrendered any claim to the right of judicial review and were prevented from challenging the validity of a martial law regulation, judgment, or sentence passed by a military court. Finally, the Provisional Constitution Order empowered the president and the chief martial law administrator to amend the constitution and provided a new oath for judges who pledged themselves to uphold the decisions of the martial law government.[40]

Zia justified these actions with the expressed view that it was demanded by the people of Pakistan. The 1973 constitution, he remarked, is a "sacred document" but the ideology and solidarity of Pakistan came first—and they were threatened by nefarious elements supported by external powers. The president noted that his regime was strict but he argued that the country's integrity would be endangered if it lessened its resolve. He also emphasized his intention to hold elections and eventually to return the government to civilian control. But unlike previous announcements, he did not suggest that elections were on the horizon. The Islamic state was still in the process of formation and when elections were held they would be in a mode sanctioned by Islamic principle. "We are now at a crossroads where we have to decide whether we like Islam or not. Those who do not want Islam are at liberty to go anywhere they like," he reiterated.[41]

President Zia's action in virtually eliminating political party activity was prompted by a deterioration of his authority. Representatives of seven opposition parties had met secretly in Lahore and later publicized a joint demand that Zia resign and that martial law be lifted within three months or they would unleash the pent-up fury of their members and the larger public. They also announced the formation of the Movement for the Restoration of Democracy (MRD), which was supposed to mobilize mass elements for strikes, demonstrations, and widespread civil disobedience. The leaders of the MRD were in fact prompted to act given the general disorder that rocked some of the country's major cities in January and February 1981. The government had been forced to close the universities and to prevent the assembling of groups exceeding five persons. But the students were not the only problem for the regime. Teachers, doctors, and lawyers also paraded through the urban areas, portraying the martial law government as tyrannical and in violation of basic freedoms. President Zia's reference to Islam, his critics insisted, was mere cover for his seizure of absolute power. Zia's answer to his detractors was both carrot and stick. He finally agreed to expand the size of his cabinet, and admitted a significant number of civilians to his government. He also cracked down on all those threatening his status, and given the embarrassment caused by the skyjacking of the PIA aircraft, he issued an order to tighten martial law controls and to deal more swiftly with proved and would-be antagonists.

Zia-ul-Haq's capacity to strengthen his regime must be observed against a background of Soviet aggression in neighboring Afghanistan. The Pakistani military and bureaucracy are especially mindful of the divisions within the country and how they could be exploited to weaken not only the government, but the nation as well. They were no less aware of how rivalries and differences within their own ranks thwarted effort to deal with centrifugal forces and exposed the country to significant jeopardy from unfriendly neighbors. Clearly the decision to shift Pakistan away from the parliamentary model as described by the 1973 constitution was not what the politicians desired, but it was widely accepted in military and bureaucratic circles. Moreover, the new cabinet that was installed in March 1981, after almost a year of promises and expectations, proved to be a mixture of military officials, high-placed bureaucrats, old-time luminaries, and political personalities who were essentially removed from the political competition. The Provisional Constitution Order of 1981 also underlined Zia's and his administration's exasperation with the parliamentary process.

All during 1980 Zia had permitted the politicians to voice their desires on the type of political system they deemed best for the country. They all opted for the parliamentary system. Zia's attempt to experiment on a limited basis with that process, however, was impeded by the political parties that continued to call for the lifting of martial law. The political parties also prevented some key personalities from assuming positions in the administration, i.e., as prime minister or chief minister in the provinces. Frustrated, Zia focused his attention on the Local Bodies or grassroots councils that resembled Ayub Khan's Basic Democracies System. Another curiosity was the almost similar approach that both Zia-ul-Haq and Ziaur Rahman took in "restoring" the political life of their respective nations. In both countries the military and bureaucratic establishments found it more convenient to isolate the urbanites and cater to the needs of the rural masses. In each instance the strength of the regime depended upon the weaving together of the permanent services with the peasant population. The more sophisticated elements it was judged needed to be held in check.

Zia's Islamic state was better received in the countryside but the government had to tread lightly on the sensitivities of the rural folk. The enforcement of *zakat*, or the tax on wealth, was relatively successful because it fell hardest on the well-to-do and was supposed to assist the deprived.[42] The *ushr*, or agricultural tax, was another story. In this instance the peasant population was directly affected and given resistance, the government was advised to move with great caution. On the other hand, as of January 1981, the nationalized commercial banks in Pakistan were called upon to commence a 15-month program in which all interest-bearing accounts would be phased out. Again the masses were little affected by this latter measure. Nor were the rural folk concerned about the government's order for women to clothe themselves in a floor-length veil or *burka* while in public. Feminine members of the urban communities, however, were unhappy with the order and demonstrations were taken out in Karachi to protest the government action. Zia was unconcerned with these manifestations of popular discontent and concluded that the protests were inspired by the political opposition, not by genuine dissatisfaction with his directives.

Zia moved steadily forward in an effort to collect support for his position. In August 1980 he convened a conference of the country's *ulema*, the leaders of the religious community. He formed an Ulema Board to act as presidential advisors, and he announced his intention to place the ulema on the Shariat Courts (Religious Courts) as well as on federal and provincial councils. He also emphasized the right of the ulema to fill the political vacuum created by the suspended parliament. The political opposition had sufficient grounds to suggest Zia was using Islam for his own purposes. It was also true that the Nizam-i-Mustafa (Rule of the Prophet) that Zia envisaged establishing in Pakistan had yet to materialize. In fact, the sophisticated population were convinced the goal could not be achieved under military rule.

President Zia-ul-Haq formally announced the creation of the Federal Council or Majlis-i-Shura on December 24, 1981. The well-publicized assembly was an appointed body, and Zia declared that 287 of its 350 seats had been filled. In response to criticism that the Federal Council lacked the stamp of legitimacy, that only a popularly elected body would have the support of the population, Zia reiterated his determination to reshape Pakistan's political structure. His principal intention, he declared, was not the acquisition of greater power for the ruling junta, but the sincere conviction that Pakistanis wanted the political process to reflect their Islamic heritage. Zia also insisted that the Majlis-i-Shura was an advisory body and not a formal legislature and that it was a transitional institution pending the construction of a more permanent Islamic constitutional system. Zia's political opposition, however, was unconvinced. From their vantage point, the establishment of the Majlis-i-Shura was one more indication of the military junta's decision to destroy the political parties and ultimately to discard Pakistan's conventional political and legal apparatus. Moreover, there was reason to accept the politicians' complaint. On the one side, the government had banned all political party operations. On the other, it prepared the ground for the replacement of the European-influenced court system by Shariat and Qazi courts. Indeed, training of Qazis or Islamic judges had been accelerated, cases were reserved for the Qazi courts, and the traditional courts already had lost their authority to question an act of the martial law government. Furthermore, military tribunals had become supreme instruments of government dictat.

On January 11, 1982, Zia inaugurated the first session of the Majlis-i-Shura in the national assembly building in Islamabad. Although the Majlis was supposed to be nonpolitical, scores of politicians had been named to seats. These same councillors had heretofore represented a variety of political parties. Surprisingly the largest contingent was drawn from the Pakistan People's Party, approximately 100 having identified with that organization. Approximately 40 others were former Muslim Leaguers. Lesser officials of the National Democratic Party, the Tehrik-i-Istiqlal, the Jamaat-i-Islami, the Jamiatul-Ulema-i-Pakistan, and the Jamiat-Ulema-i-Islam also obtained some of the coveted places. Only the splinter parties on the extreme left were without any representation. The appearance of these politicians in the Majlis was judged a victory for the administration, especially given earlier declarations by party leaders to ignore the assembly.

The Majlis-i-Shura initially comprised 147 members from the Punjab, 70 from Sind, 52 from the North West Frontier Province, and 18 from Baluchistan. Forty-eight of the Punjabi politicians in the Federal Council were former central or provincial ministers in previous governments. The other provinces also had their representation of former officials and ministers. In addition to these luminaries, the Council was made up of ulema, jurists, engineers, journalists, medical doctors, trade unionists, and feminists. President Zia also appointed a chairman or speaker for the Council. Khwaja Mohammad Safdar was an old-line politician and once a leading member of the opposition. He was responsible for managing the affairs of the assembly, and was assisted by four vice-chairmen, one representing each of Pakistan's four provinces. Safdar was cognizant of the burden he had assumed and in order to avoid being accused of opportunism, he declared his intention to use the Council as a legislature until such time as a new national assembly was formed. During a press conference in late January, Safdar opined that elections for a national assembly could be held within months and possibly no later than one year. Safdar also noted that he favored the early reinstatement of the political parties and that he was prepared to seek amendments in the existing laws, which forbade their operations.

General Zia was forced to respond to the statements of the Majlis chairman. He again emphasized that the Federal Council was not a legislature, that it could not criticize actions or policies of the government, and although he still wanted to hold elections, he would continue to argue against hasty decisions. The political climate in the country was too unsettled, he noted. Terrorist organizations had perpetrated assassination and arson and were planning clandestine actions against government persons and installations. Moreover, the government had information that seemed to tie some of the political parties to the terrorists.

Despite Zia's insistence that the time was neither right to permit political party activity or elections, his creation of a Majlis-i-Shura, and his subsequent decision to lift some of press restrictions, breathed new life into the political opposition. The military junta, therefore, faced new tests in governing the troubled nation.

NATIONAL SECURITY QUESTIONS IN SOUTH ASIA

South Asia is a continuation of the Middle East and the two regions have long seen their destinies intertwined. The Soviet Union's forceful entry into Afghanistan only tends to give this observation renewed creditability. Pakistan is in fact the link tying the two areas together. The future of Pakistan therefore suggests what may be the course for both the Middle East and South Asia in the decades to come. Pakistan is located in a brittle zone of international political activity. Forces course through the region that seek to take advantage of domestic unrest and ideological uncertainty. Afghanistan, heretofore the least involved state of the area has become the most troubled, and the first to feel the direct presence of a superpower. Iran remains enigmatically divided and burdened by both internal conflict and alien invaders. The revolutions that convulsed Iran and Afghanistan in 1978-79 were initially aimed at reorganizing national polities; each, however, precipitated the intervention of an ambitious power that sought to exploit the weaknesses inherent in their respective situations. The shift from essential stability to gross disorder in Iran and Afghanistan has had repercussions in numerous places across the globe, but no country has had to contend with such significant questions as Pakistan.

Since achieving independence in 1947 Pakistan has judged India its primary enemy. Afghanistan was seldom friendly but problems between the two Muslim countries were considered more irritant than threat. Indian-Pakistani relations have improved since their 1971 clash over Bangladesh, but the two countries have by no means settled their outstanding differences or agreed to enter into genuine regional cooperation. India is still perceived a major threat to Pakistan's continuation as an independent state; whereas India remains sensitive to any sign of improvement in Pakistan's military position. Indira Gandhi's return to power in New Delhi in 1980 signaled a hard road for Indian-Pakistani affairs. Prime Minister Gandhi does not enjoy negotiating with Pakistan's military leaders, moreso given General Zia's Islamic state program and how it impacts on Indian Muslims. Zia's lack of popularity at home also necessitates his maintaining the posture of a defiant Pakistan, insistent on achieving "justice" for the Kashmiri Muslims. Moreover, Pakistan's determination to construct a nuclear deterrent is linked to Islamabad's perception of New Delhi's undiminished hostility, and India's already demonstrated atomic capability.

This animus between the subcontinent's two principal neighbors early on established the pattern of relationships that they were to pursue down to the present period. Those patterns provided an important place for the superpowers and they have been significant intermediaries in the clash of opposing forces. Although India has long prided itself on following a nonaligned foreign policy, its association with the Soviet Union had been intimate and useful. The Kremlin has made available large quantities of modern weaponry and has assisted in the modernization of the Indian armed forces (see Chapter 2). Diplomatically, the Soviet Union has supported India in virtually every foreign policy pursuit launched by New Delhi. Moreover, the Soviet Union must find the turn of events in South Asia more compatible with their own philosophy and behavior than does the United States. Ideologically the Soviet Union is inclined to interpret the turbulence in the subcontinent as a phase of history in which older elitist systems are inevitably giving way to more popular ones. Conflict, violence, and chaos are therefore natural occurrences. Instead of seeking to prevent or delay them, they are to be encouraged as the necessary avenues to revolutionary change. In the zero-sum world of power politics, the United States is destined to lose its influence in the countries of South Asia as a bourgeois class is replaced by "progressive" forces. A major component of Marxist-Leninist ideology underlines the inability of the capitalist world to adjust to the inexorable pressure of change while the socialist forces find the same unsettled conditions conducive to their growth and general advantage.[43] Indeed, the Soviet Union has mentioned over and again in recent years its belief that the West is in a period of precipitous decline and that the correlation of forces now and in the future favors the Marxist-Leninist world.[44]

The problem facing the Soviet Union in South Asia is not the United States but China. China would like to displace the Soviets in South Asia, or at least carve out a region or regions of the subcontinent from where it can influence the course of events. For China, South Asia is linked with its interests in Southeast Asia and its general security posture vis-à-vis Japan and Taiwan, but especially the Soviet Union. For the Soviet Union, South Asia is connected with its deeper concern for the Middle East and Africa. Not only does the subcontinent dominate the Indian Ocean from Indonesia to the eastern coast of Africa, it also could provide the Soviet Union with the needed leverage to offset the West's power in the Persian Gulf region. These conventional geopolitical interests would appear to be more determinative in the making of policy than any reference to ideological unity. Moreover, Soviet determination to deny the Chinese an exclusive sphere of influence in Vietnam and Laos and the complicating aspects of a continuing Kampuchean-Vietnamese war make it all the more necessary that the Chinese sustain their involvement in Pakistan as well as attempt to maintain pressure on India while befriending Bangladesh.

The U.S. threat to the Soviet Union therefore stems not from its presence on the mainland of South Asia but rather from the American decision to establish itself as an Indian Ocean power.[45] The Soviet Union will not be disturbed no matter how much economic and technical assistance the United States pours into the countries of South Asia. Certainly the Soviet Union does not have the volume of resources required to satisfy the economic demands of the people of the subcontinent. In other words, the Americans are welcome to spend as much as they wish in the region. The Soviet Union long ago concluded that such aid is not going to reverse the process of change and in fact may well accelerate it. But the U.S. military policy that focuses on the Indian Ocean is another matter. New developments in weapons technology and the Western world's dependence on Persian Gulf petroleum are the principal components of this policy. With improved submarine-launched ballistic missile (SLBM) capability, the Soviet Union fears that American submarines operating in the Indian Ocean or near the Persian Gulf can cover a deeper arc of targets in Soviet Central Asia, the Caucasus, the Ukraine, and as far as Moscow. An American low-frequency communication base is already operational in Australia, and despite Britain's declared end to its East of Suez policy, there is a joint Anglo-American base on the Indian Ocean island of Diego Garcia.

The intensification of Soviet-Cuban involvement in the Ethiopian-Somali war greatly disturbed Washington, and apart from the questions raised about the Kremlin's decision "to go for broke" on the Horn of Africa, it is interesting to note how American attention dramatically shifted from the Southeast Asian extremity of the Indian Ocean to the Southwest Asian-East African sector. In these circumstances it appears the United States is determined both to improve its nuclear deterrent and to protect the vital sea lanes that carry the industrial world's major supply of petroleum. But beyond this the United States cannot be oblivious to Soviet machinations aimed at radicalizing the regimes all along the Indian Ocean periphery. While the United States may not require base bases in India, Pakistan, or Bangladesh, it has a very real stake in preserving the noncommunist character of those countries.

The United States may be searching for a foreign policy in South Asia that will enable it to deal with Soviet imperialism in Afghanistan and the threat posed to both Iran and Pakistan by both subversion and an aggressive Red Army. Pakistan's dependence on military assistance from the United States remains unchanged, despite earlier U.S. government reluctance to make significant transfers to Islamabad, and the public statements by Pakistani officials that Pakistan wants no part of American alliances, bases, or close support. Nevertheless, Pakistani authorities anticipated the United States would make a greater contribution to Pakistan's national security once the Reagan administration was firmly entrenched in Washington. The Soviet invasion of Afghanistan did not move

President Carter to assist Islamabad with military supplies commensurate with the threat posed by the Soviet forces on its frontier. Zbigniew Brzezinski's visit to Islamabad and the Pakistan-Afghanistan border brought declarations and gestures of American intention to support Pakistan. General Zia's rejection of the proffered aid package, however, and his characterization of the proposed arms transfer as "peanuts," spelled the doom of meaningful relations between the two governments. President Reagan and his supporters, however, moved rapidly to repair this damage, and in May 1981 Washington revealed it would develop a long-range military assistance program with Pakistan.[46]

The Reagan announcement came on the heels of an American government decision to back off on another promise made to India. President Carter had agreed to press for the delivery of nuclear fuel for India's Tarapur Reactor. The original agreement with New Delhi had been entered into in 1963 and had been carefully honored ever since. When congressional action threatened to terminate the sale, President Carter pressured the legislators to satisfy India's request. The Carter administration consistently supported New Delhi vis-à-vis Islamabad and hoped by its performance to reduce India's dependence on Moscow as well as develop the necessary leverage to protect its vital interests in the larger Indian Ocean area. But Indira Gandhi's continued hard-line attack on U.S. maneuvers in the region and India's reluctance to permit the United States to satisfactorily monitor its use of nuclear products led the Reagan administration to suspend the long-standing sale policy.

Coupled with the American administration's intention to step up its shipment of weapons to the Pakistanis, and the Reagan government's attempt to reduce pressure placed on the Islamabad government because of Pakistan's secret nuclear program, New Delhi had reason to be apprehensive. The United States pledged to provide Pakistan approximately $500 million in arms and economic assistance on an annual basis for the next five years, the total package amounting to $3.2 billion. Included in the deal were advanced F-16 fighter-bombers, which India immediately described as a threat to its security. Although these transfers were small compared to Soviet arms agreements with India, they represented the largest commitment of U.S. military support to Pakistan since the late 1950s and early 1960s. Moreover, the Reagan administration convinced the U.S. Congress to sidestep the Symington amendment, which had blocked U.S. economic and military sales because Islamabad had embarked on a nuclear weapons program. The Congress generally favors India over Pakistan, and since the Bangladesh crisis there had been little movement in the American legislature to promote Pakistan interests over those of India.[47] The Soviet occupation of Afghanistan (see Chapter 5) proved to be a turning point, and it appeared to return relationships to where they were in 1958 when General Ayub Khan seized control of the Pakistan government. The difference now, however, was that the specter of nuclear confrontation also hovered over the subcontinent.

NOTES

1. John Foster Dulles's commitment to the American containment policy was in considerable measure influenced by Nicholas John Spykman. See Spykman's *The Geography of the Peace*, ed. Helen R. Nicholl (New York: Harcourt, Brace, 1944) and *America's Strategy in World Politics* (New York: Harcourt, Brace, 1942).

2. William J. Barnds, *India, Pakistan and the Great Powers* (New York: Praeger, 1972), pp. 83–106.

3. Perhaps the most significant work on this subject is David Halberstam, *The Best and the Brightest* (New York: Random House, 1972).

4. Anwar H. Syed, *China and Pakistan: Diplomacy of an Entente Cordiale* (Amherst: University of Massachusetts Press, 1974), p. 49.

5. James Reston's column entitled "Politics and Strategy" published in New York *Times*, January 12, 1972, would seem to support this view. See also the article by William Safire "Opening to China," New York *Times*, February 16, 1978.

6. Concern over the Soviet role in the Indo-Pakistan war of 1971 can be seen in the publication of the papers of the Washington Special Actions Group, chaired by Henry Kissinger. The documents appeared in the Washington *Post*, January 5, 1972.

7. See the foreign policy articles by Howard Wriggins, William Barnds, and Norman Palmer in *Pakistan: The Long View*, ed. Lawrence Ziring, Ralph Braibanti, and Howard Wriggins (Durham, N.C.: Duke University Press, 1977).

8. Don Peretz, "Foreign Policies of the Persian Gulf States," paper delivered at Western Michigan University, October 8, 1976, pp. 15–16.

9. Lawrence Ziring, "Pakistan: A Political Perspective," *Asian Survey* 25, no. 7 (July 1975): 629–44.

10. Keith Callard, *Pakistan: A Political Study* (London: George Allen and Unwin, 1975), p. 184.

11. Lawrence Ziring and Robert LaPorte, Jr., "The Pakistan Bureaucracy: Two Views," *Asian Survey* 24, no. 12 (December 1974): 1086–1103.

12. Ralph Braibanti, *Research on the Bureaucracy of Pakistan* (Durham, N.C.: Duke University Press, 1966) and Henry Goodnow, The Civil Service of Pakistan: Bureaucracy in a New Nation (New Haven, Conn.: Yale University Press, 1964) examine the guardian role performed by the bureaucrats.

13. See Victoria Schofield, *Bhutto: Trial and Execution* London: Cassell, 1979.

14. Anthony Mascarenhas, *The Rape of Bangladesh* (Delhi: Vikas Publications, 1971), pp. 111–20; and Mohammed Ayoob and K. Subrahmanyam, *The Liberation War* (New Delhi: S. Chand, 1972), pp. 165–81. See also David Loshak, *Pakistan Crisis* (London: Heinemann, 1971), pp. 95–107.

15. See A. T. R. Rahman "Administration and Its Political Environment in Bangladesh," *Pacific Affairs*, Summer 1974.

16. M. Rashiduzzaman, "Changing Political Patterns in Bangladesh: Internal Constraints and External Fears" *Asian Survey* 17, no. 9 (September 1977): 797.

17. *Statesman Weekly* (Calcutta), December 21, 1974.

18. *Dawn* (Karachi), January 23, 1975.

19. An interesting summary of these events in Bangladesh can be found in the Washington *Post*, August 23, 1975.

20. New York *Times*, October 4, 1976.

21. The origins of the Farakka Barrage Dispute will be found in S. M. Burke, *Pakistan's Foreign Policy: A Historical Analysis* (London: Oxford University Press, 1973), pp. 381–83.

22. General Ziaur Rahman was quoted as saying: "We have apprehended several hundred of them [guerrillas], and they tell of being trained by Indian troops along the

border, or even as far away as Calcutta. . . . We know they [India] have also set up a few camps on the western border, and on the eastern border as well." An Indian official is reported to have replied: "It's not our fault that there are people in that country who roam about shooting things up because they don't like the government that is being imposed upon them from Dacca." New York *Times*, September 27, 1976.

23. For an account of unrest and defection in the Bangladesh military see Rashiduzzaman, "Changing Political Patterns in Bangladesh," pp. 801-2.

24. For a good discussion on Bangladesh's quest for an ideology, see Zillur R. Khan, "Leadership, Parties and Politics in Bangladesh," *Western Political Quarterly*, March 1976.

25. "India Will Not Interfere in the Internal Affairs of Any Country," *Indian and Foreign Review* 15, no. 4 (December 1, 1977): 6.

26. New York *Times*, June 2, 1977.

27. *Dawn* (overseas ed.), October 30, 1977.

28. Ibid.

29. "Ganga Waters Agreement Comes into Force," *Indian and Foreign Review* 15, no. 3 (November 15, 1977): 6.

30. *India News*, December 26, 1977.

31. New York *Times*, December 23, 1977.

32. Azizul Haque, "Bangladesh in 1980: Strains and Stresses-Opposition in the Doldrums," *Asian Survey* 21, no. 2 (February 1981): 193-97.

33. *Pakistan Affairs*, November 1, 1976, p. 4.

34. M. G. Weinbaum, "The March 1977 Elections in Pakistan: Where Everyone Lost," *Asian Survey* 17, no. 7 (July 1977): 599-618, and Lawrence Ziring's article in the same issue, "Pakistan: The Campaign Before the Storm," pp. 581-98.

35. *Financial Times* (London), September 1, 1977. Reprinted in *Scanner*, September 5-18, 1977, pp. 1563-64.

36. New York *Times*, September 7, 1977.

37. New York *Times*, September 18, 1977.

38. *Pakistan Affairs* (Washington, D.C.), 34, no. 8 (April 16, 1981): 1.

39. *Dawn* (overseas weekly), October 25-31, 1980, p. 1.

40. *Pakistan Affairs* (Washington, D.C.), 34, no. 8 (April 16, 1981): 1-3.

41. Ibid., p. 3.

42. The Shia population rebelled against the Zakat order in July 1980, claiming it was counter to their religious law. The government agreed to yield on the matter so as to avoid further disturbing the Shia minority.

43. See the comments by Henry Kissinger in "Secretary Kissinger's Statement on U.S. Soviet Relations," *Special Report*, Department of State, September 19, 1974, p. 3.

44. Wynfred Joshua, "Detente in Soviet Strategy," Defense Intelligence Agency Department of Defense, September 2, 1975. See also *Wall Street Journal*, March 1, 1978.

45. S. Weiss, "U.S. Interests and Activities in the Indian Ocean Area," *Department of State Bulletin* 70 (April 8, 1974): 371-75; A. J. Cottrell and R. M. Burrell, "Soviet-U.S. Naval Competition in the Indian Ocean," *Orbis* 18 (Winter 1975): 1109-28; A. O. Ghebhardt, "Soviet and U.S. Interests in the Indian Ocean," *Asian Survey* 15 (August 1975): 672-83.

46. New York *Times* May 12, 1981.

47. *Pakistan Affairs* (Washington, D.C.), 34, no. 20 (October 16, 1981): 3.

2

INDIA AND ITS NEIGHBORS: REGIONAL FOREIGN AND SECURITY POLITICS

Leo E. Rose

The South Asian subcontinent has a long history of invasion and conquest by outsiders, the latest only a couple of centuries ago. While the most recent onslaught of conquerers were Europeans who came by sea, all the others had poured into South Asia via one of the land routes to the northwest of the subcontinent. National security consciousness in India, thus, has long been particularly sensitive about the subcontinent's land frontiers with western and central Asia, and New Delhi's foreign and security policies since 1947 have been strongly influenced by this factor. Western imperialism by sea in the sixteenth to the nineteenth centuries was an aberration that is unlikely to be repeated under contemporary geopolitical conditions. While the Indian government and press frequently expound on the threat posed by external (i.e., American) naval forces in the Indian Ocean, few Indians really apprehend the advent of new imperial masters from this direction. The land frontiers, in contrast, still seem vulnerable, raising a range of difficult political and security problems for New Delhi.

The northwestern frontier of the subcontinent—most of which is controlled by Pakistan—has been the most difficult for India in policy terms. Until recently, however, the principal security problem in this area was seen as coming from an "adversary" South Asian state, Pakistan, rather than from outside the subcontinent. This does not mean that the Indian foreign policy elite was unaware of a potential Soviet threat to both Afghanistan and Pakistan (i.e., South Asia) in what has sometimes been portrayed as a historical Russian drive to gain an outlet on the Indian Ocean. But as long as Iran, Afghanistan, and Pakistan maintained their national integrity reasonably intact and various international deterrents were operative, the opportunities for intervention by the Soviets were seen as limited and manageable. From 1947 to the 1970s, therefore, New Delhi could devise strategic and security policies for the northwest that were primarily designed to advance India's immediate objectives vis-à-vis Pakistan rather than the more distant but far more serious problem of Soviet power in Central Asia.[1] Developments in 1978–80, in particular the direct Soviet military intervention in Afghanistan and the collapse of the shah's regime in Iran, made a reconsideration of India's order of priorities unavoidable but extremely painful because of the "special relationship" with Moscow exemplified in the 1971 Indo-Soviet Treaty of Peace, Friendship and Cooperation as well as the increasingly important economic relationship that was just emerging with the royal government in Iran.

At the same time of independence in 1947, the central Himalayas were considered virtually impenetrable by external forces but posed some difficulties because of the existence of three kingdoms in the region that preferred to remain outside the Indian federation. The frontier region to the northeast was seen more as an internal political than an external security problem. The Indian elite was vaguely aware that Assam had undergone periodic invasions from Burma (most recently by the Japanese in World War II) over several centuries, but it was the complex "ethnic" population structure that made the northeast into a potential problem area.

The Indian perception of security issues on its northern and northeastern frontiers, however, changed drastically with the absorption of Tibet into the Chinese political system and the development of Tibet as an area of substantial Chinese military concentration in the aftermath of the 1956–59 Tibetan rebellion. The situation was further complicated by the outbreak of a Sino-Indian border dispute in 1959, which, in one way or another, involved the entire Himalayan frontier and eventually culminated in a brief but embarrassing border war with China in 1962. Thereafter, the prospect of Sino-Pakistani collusion in their separate but related border disputes with India dominated New Delhi's decision making on security issues for the next decade. It was only after India's victory in the third war with Pakistan in 1971 during which China was unable (or unwilling?) to provide any real assistance to its Pakistani "allies" that New Delhi's concern over this particular security scenario gradually diminished.

Looking back in an historical perspective, one can see that British India's imperial policy (which was not always the same as London's) is still an intrinsic element in Indian approaches to security questions. This is not surprising, as British Indian policy on the frontiers was primarily directed toward assuring security for the subcontinent rather than imperial expansion into adjacent areas. Most of the geopolitical and strategic factors that motivated British thinking on defense issues have not changed since 1947 and are still persuasive to Indian decision makers despite their use of a different rhetoric to justify similar policies. Unfortunately for New Delhi, the world outside the subcontinent is now far more complex and threatening than it was prior to World War II, making it necessary to adjust and, in some respects, stiffen the security policies that worked so well for British India.

FUNDAMENTAL PRINCIPLES OF INDIAN POLICY

Before commencing an analysis of Indian policies toward specific frontier areas, it would be useful to summarize some of the basic objectives of New Delhi's broader regional policies—the context within which decisions on the border areas are usually made. The first point to note is that the universalist "moral" principles that are generally proclaimed as providing the basis for India's foreign policy—such as anticolonialism and neocolonialism, the sovereign equality of all nation-states, peaceful coexistence rather than balance-of-power politics, and a more equitable distribution of economic rewards—are rarely very evident in the policies adopted toward its neighbors in the subcontinent. New Delhi is no more hypocritical than other major powers in this respect; but neither is it less so. When it gets down to immediate and vital interests, India has generally been hard-line and uncompromising in projecting its influence and power in the subcontinent. The only substantive exception to this general rule was the 1977-79 period when the Janata Party government was in office and New Delhi adopted a more "liberal" approach in its policies toward the subcontinent that had some positive results for both the advancement of India's regional objectives and the improvement of relations with neighboring states. Unfortunately, this encouraging trend has been at least partially reversed under the successor Lok Dal (1979) and Congress (1980 on) governments.

Since 1947, India's primary objective in the subcontinent has been to gain acceptance of its paramount (hegemonic or dominant are other terms that are frequently used) position in South Asia's economic, political, and security systems from both the major external powers and the other states in the region.[2] New Delhi's attitude toward *formal* regional institutions on the model of the European Economic Community (EEC) in Western Europe or even the more loosely structured Association of South East Asian Nations (ASEAN) in Southeast Asia, however, has been rather negative. Generally, the Indian preference has been for bilateral relations with each of its neighbors in the subcontinent that tie them into the Indian economic and security systems in a cooperative but inevitably subordinate relationship.[3]

This was first evident in New Delhi's intensive efforts to organize South Asia as a regional economic and security system in the 1947–54 period.[4] The eventual failure of this endeavor is usually interpreted as a consequence of the cold war, and in particular Pakistan's decision to join the military alliance systems of the U.S.-sponsored Middle Eastern Central Treaty Organization (CENTO) and the Southeast Asia Treaty Organization (SEATO). One could argue with equal validity, however, that it was the increasing intransigence of both India and Pakistan in their dispute over Kashmir that made a viable regional system implausible at that point in time. In 1954 India offered to settle the Kashmir dispute essentially on Pakistan's terms (a plebiscite) if Pakistan did not accept U.S. military assistance. The Pakistanis rejected this offer, as they felt it would leave them weak and vulnerable to both India and other neighbors—such as the USSR and China—that then appeared threatening. Later, in 1959, Pakistan offered a "joint defense system" to India on the same terms (a satisfactory settlement of the Kashmir issue) in the context of the Sino-Indian border dispute. In this instance, New Delhi rejected the offer as detrimental to India's regional interests and in conflict with its objective of transforming the Soviet Union into a guarantor of Indian security.

The inability of India and Pakistan to achieve an amicable relationship eventually induced New Delhi to quietly abandon its effort to organize the subcontinent into an informal regional system centered around India for bilateral relations with each of the South Asian states that served more limited and immediate Indian interests. Its victory in the 1971 Bangladesh war with Pakistan, however, revived India's interest in an informal regional system, as its bargaining power with its neighbors, including Pakistan, and the major external powers was now far greater than at any time since 1947. Substantial progress was made in this endeavor until developments in 1978 and thereafter once again raised very complex problems for New Delhi in its relations with its neighbors and the major external powers. India's status as the paramount regional power in the subcontinent is again interpreted in New Delhi as being challenged from several sides—the United States, Pakistan, and even the Soviet Union. (After all, if the Soviets should maintain and solidify their direct involvement in the subcontinent through their military intervention in Afghanistan, how can anyone pay serious attention to India's claim to paramountcy in the region.)

A second objective of India's broader policy toward the subcontinent has been the maintenance of a generally stable regional political system—by implication, at least, the preservation of the status quo. India's neighbors—particularly but not only the Pakistanis—would certainly disagree that this has been a basic aspect of Indian foreign policy, and one would have to admit there is ample evidence that New Delhi has not always been consistent in the pursuance of this goal. Covert Indian intervention in Nepal in 1950–51 and again in 1961–62 and overt Indian intervention in the 1971 Bangladesh crisis are only three of the most obvious instances in which New Delhi's actions were disruptive of the status quo, and intentionally so. Nevertheless, a broader analysis of India's responses to innumerable situations that virtually invited intervention by the largest power in the region makes it apparent that in most instances New Delhi has exercised considerable restraint. There are, of course, a number of factors external to the power balance within the subcontinent that help explain India's behavior. But some importance should also be attached to a sense of reluctance on the part of Indian decision makers to upset the status quo except under what seems to them extreme provocation and/or a perceived threat to vital Indian interests.

Several foreign powers, and in particular the United States, Soviet Union, and China, have played important roles in South Asian developments since the mid-1950s. The Indian perception of the roles of these external intrusions into the region has varied over time, depending largely upon how New Delhi interpreted their impact on Indian policy objectives in the region. The policies adopted by both the United States and the Soviet Union in the pre-1960 period were major obstacles to a South Asian regional system. The inclusion of Pakistan in CENTO and SEATO and the provision of massive U.S. military aid to that country certainly helped dissuade the Pakistanis from coming to terms with India. Similarly, the Russian "opening to India" in the mid-1950s, which involved a position of total support to India in its disputes with other noncommunist countries, made it unnecessary for New Delhi to accommodate Pakistani demands. During this period, China was a negligible factor in South Asia but, on balance, moderately supportive of Indian policy objectives.[5] As one would expect, New Delhi was appreciative of Soviet support and China's more noncommittal position, but strongly critical of the "negative" role of the United States in the subcontinent.

During the 1960s the attitudes of the three major external powers toward South Asia shifted significantly. Both Washington and Moscow were attracted by the concept of a South Asian regional system with India as the focal point, and their policies in the subcontinent reflected such a bias. The Indus River Project—the only major regional cooperative economic venture to date—was to a considerable extent the product of U.S. initiatives, while in the late 1960s the Soviets became strong advocates of a regional economic system that extended beyond South Asia to include Iran and Afghanistan. This was rejected by the Pakistanis and Iranians at the time because of their suspicion that Moscow was using its close relationship with India in an effort to expand its own presence and influence on a regional basis. It is interesting to note, however, that in 1978 both the shah of Iran and the Indian foreign minister made virtually the same proposal for a regional economic system, though without the inclusion of the Soviet Union.

It was also in the early 1960s that the Soviets extended their support of India to disputes involving not only Pakistan but also their former ally in the socialist camp—China. The United States substantially reduced military assistance to Pakistan and introduced a military aid program to India, thus assuming a more nonpartisan position in the subcontinent. After the 1965 Indo-Pakistani war the United States terminated its military aid programs to both countries, but the impact of this decision was favorable to New Delhi, which had better alternative sources for the development of its military capacity.

Throughout the 1960s and 1970s, China has done everything it could (that did not involve any major price) to encourage the other South Asian states to resist India's plans for the region. Peking's substantial military and economic assistance to Pakistan, its economic aid to Nepal and Sri Lanka, and its hard-line position against the Bangladesh "national liberation" movement were all a consequence of China's interest in providing South Asian states with at least the illusion of alternative options to coming to terms with India.

In retrospect, we can conclude that none of the major external powers were particularly successful in their respective endeavors in South Asia. American and Soviet efforts to discourage internal regional strife and direct attention to the external Chinese threat were unproductive, as the 1965 and 1971 Indo-Pakistani wars testify. But the Chinese have been no more successful in projecting themselves as an effective counterbalance to the Indians, much as some Pakistanis and Nepalis relish them in this role. China's failure to offer effective assistance to Pakistan in 1965 and 1971 or to neutralize Indian economic and political pressure on Nepal on various occasions reduced its credibility in this regard.

In the latter half of the 1970s, China began to redefine its South Asian policies in terms that were, by and large, quite satisfactory to the government of India. This has involved both the elimination of the more blatantly anti-Indian aspect of Chinese policy in its relations with the other South Asian states as well as the "normalization" of Beijing's political and economic relations with New Delhi.[6] While a settlement of their border dispute through a formal treaty would still seem unlikely in the near future, a de facto agreement based upon the existing "lines of control" in the Himalayas is now honored by both the Chinese and Indians. In the past few years the two governments have also exercised restraint in supporting dissident elements in the territory of the other as they had in the past. Moreover, in the rapidly deteriorating situation on the northwest frontier of the subcontinent, the care and caution with which China has supported Pakistan on Afghanistan developments has been appreciated in New Delhi. The highly vocal pro-Soviet press and intellectuals in India continue to emphasize the Chinese "threat" to India in grossly exaggerated terms, reflecting of course Moscow's distress with the improvements in Sino-Indian relations. But while this may set some political limits on what the Indian government may be prepared to do, it has not yet been allowed to interfere with the normalization process itself.

China's increasingly cautious attitude toward overinvolvement in South Asia in the late 1970s, however, was more than countered by the substantial expansion of Soviet and American involvement in the region. While the Indian authorities (but not always the Indian press) prefer to downplay Soviet military intervention in Afghanistan and the potential threat this poses to both Indian and Pakistani interests, it cannot easily disguise the fact that this constitutes a quantitative and qualitative transformation of Moscow's role in the subcontinent on terms that are not necessarily advantageous to India. As is usually the case, the Indians exercise much less restraint in commenting on the recent expansion of American involvement in Pakistan, West Asia, and the Indian Ocean; but so far New Delhi has had nothing to suggest toward the resolution of the crisis in this area that is at all persuasive to Washington—or to any other government in the region. Indeed, if anything, the openly biased and often highly emotional public response in India to a growing crisis in a region in which it has major and legitimate interests has probably, on balance, hindered rather than helped the few tentative efforts made by various sources to negotiate a mutually acceptable settlement.

It is particularly disturbing to some Indians that New Delhi is now out-of-step with the other South Asian states, the Islamic bloc states of West Asia, ASEAN in Southeast Asia, and a large majority of the Nonalignment Movement (NAM) on recent developments. While most of these states have a rather ambivalent attitude toward American security policies in Southern Asia, they are all strongly critical of the Soviet intervention in Afghanistan and suspicious of Soviet policy objectives. The propensity in New Delhi to criticize Washington and excuse Moscow, thus, has seriously undermined India's credibility among those third world states with which purportedly it seeks a close identification. The Indian government's distress with this situation is clear, but its capacity to adjust policies accordingly is still to be demonstrated. New Delhi's almost total preoccupation with the superpowers-plus-China syndrome in its own decision making limits its capacity for effective interaction with its neighbors in South Asia and adjacent regions. This was probably most clearly demonstrated in the NAM conference hosted by India in February 1981. New Delhi's detailed policy proposals were totally rejected on all the critical issues by the moderate majority in the NAM. Eventually India found itself having to accept the latter's formulas, calling for the withdrawal of "foreign troops" from Afghanistan and Kampuchea as well as to withdraw its own resolution criticizing the American naval facility on Diego Garcia in order to maintain the pretense that India was still a leading force in the movement founded by Jawaharlal Nehru!

THE NORTHWESTERN FRONTIER

The basic political and strategic factors that permeate international relations in the northwestern frontier of the subcontinent's land frontiers are mostly unpalatable to India but extremely difficult for New Delhi to rearrange. The most important is the fact that all of the highly strategic frontier regions in the northwest, with the exception of Kashmir Valley and Ladakh, are part of Pakistan and thus, in India's view, in uncertain and unreliable hands. As noted earlier, there was no great concern in New Delhi that Pakistan might become—perhaps voluntarily—a channel for an external invasion of the subcontinent via the historical routes, such as the Khyber Pass. Up to 1971, however, New Delhi did project the possibility of Pakistani-Chinese collusion (for limited gains presumably) on their respective frontiers with India, and the Indian government's security policy in that period was formulated with such a contingency in mind.

A two-front war with Pakistan and China would have involved the entire frontier but would have been most critical on the northwest sector, in Kashmir. This factor added new emphasis to the strategic importance of those sections of Kashmir state under Indian control and made any political settlement with Pakistan that much more unattainable. No Indian government would accept a settlement that obligated it to withdraw from Kashmir Valley and Ladakh because such a change would leave India virtually impotent in the highly volatile northwest frontier region. The continuance of the dispute with Pakistan and China, therefore, probably was a more acceptable option.

New Delhi's Soviet policy since the mid-1950s has also been conditioned by India's strategic weaknesses in the northwest. A close Soviet-Pakistani relationship, for instance, would constitute a far greater problem for India than a Pakistan allied with the United States or China. This was one factor in India's decision to forge a strong working relationship with the USSR that—it was hoped—would remove any ambiguity in Moscow's policy toward South Asia. It was greatly disturbing to New Delhi, therefore, when the Soviets assumed an increasingly nonpartisan position on Indo-Pakistani relations during and after the 1966 Tashkent Conference, and even more so in 1968 when Moscow introduced an arms aid program to Pakistan that was projected to make the USSR the principal source of more advanced weapon systems for the Pakistan military. Eventually in mid-1970, India had to concede acceptance of a Soviet-proposed Treaty of Peace and Friendship, signed in August 1971, in order to obtain an agreement from Moscow to terminate its arms aid program with Pakistan. And since December 1979, when the USSR intervened directly in Afghanistan, New Delhi has probably been more concerned with the possibility that Pakistan would decide to use the "Soviet option" that Moscow has clearly indicated is available to Islamabad, rather than renew a military relationship with the Americans. India's own "special relationship" with the USSR has been seen as having the added advantage of complicating any expansionist ambitions the Soviets might entertain in the subcontinent by tieing Moscow to Indian policy in the region. There is perhaps less confidence in New Delhi on this matter since December 1979, but it is still considered a better way to handle the Soviets than any transregional security system of the type such as the one Washington has proposed.

The basic principles underlying Indian claims to hegemonic status in South Asia are fully evident in New Delhi's policy toward the northwest, since this has been the arena for some of the most serious conflicts in the subcontinent since independence. Pakistan has been the only viable challenge to India's dominant position in the region and, moreover, had the temerity to seek a power balance system in South Asia rather than to accept gracefully a position of inherent inferiority. The United States was accused of encouraging Pakistani ambitions in this respect in the 1950s, and Indian suspicions lingered on long after Washington had reversed its South Asia policy in the 1960s. The current Indian attitude toward arms aid programs reflects this perception. Massive Soviet and Western arm sales to India is right and proper because India, as the dominant power, is responsible for the region's security. On the other hand, any arms aid to Pakistan, no matter how insignificant in the total military-balance context, is wrong as it constitutes a destablizing factor that encourages Pakistan to avoid coming to terms with India.

The policy usually pursued by India of supporting the domestic and international status quo in South Asia (for example, its advocacy of acceptance of the "line of control" in Kashmir as the international boundary between India and Pakistan) has not always been evident in Indian policy toward Pakistan. At times, New Delhi had actively encouraged and supported dissident and divisive forces in Pakistan, particularly in the frontier tribal areas bordering on Afghanistan and Iran, in an effort to redirect Pakistani attention and resources away from the disputed border in Kashmir. But this became unnecessary and even counterproductive after India's victory in the 1971 war with Pakistan.[7] Since at least the mid-1970s New Delhi has not usually viewed the disintegration of Pakistan into three or four separate states with any enthusiasm since it is apprehended that India lacks the capacity to absorb these "states" into a new and greater "Indian empire." In this event, the northwest would almost certainly become an arena of competitive involvement by the other powers with important interests at stake—the USSR, China, the United States, Iran, and Afghanistan. This would be an explosive situation with potentially dangerous consequences for India. It would also remove the very useful Afghan and Pakistani buffers between India and the Soviet Union, and a common boundary with the USSR is something New Delhi would prefer to avoid. A viable, stable Pakistan that lacks the capacity to challenge India militarily is much less trouble than three or four nonviable states that could well become clients of states other than India.

During the 1970s, therefore, India and Pakistan initiated a series of prolonged negotiations that had a fundamental transformation of their relationship as the objective. This commenced with the Simla Agreement in 1972 in which Prime Minister Gandhi of India and Bhutto of Pakistan modified certain conflictual aspects of Indo-Pakistani relations in the past. India gradually reduced its support of disintegrative political forces on Pakistan's northwest frontier; Pakistan carefully refrained from pushing the Kashmir issue in international forums (although it occasionally continued to refer to Kashmir as an issue in dispute—to India's irritation).

When the Janata Party took over control of the government of India in March 1977, the efforts to expand and improve relations with Pakistan moved into high gear. The first serious attempt to negotiate an economic relationship that would be far more comprehensive than the occasional short-term ad hoc agreements made in the past got underway. Cultural and intellectual exchange programs were initiated, and the terms under which the residents of one country could visit the other were greatly liberalized. There were even more tentative moves toward collaboration on security issues, particularly after the emergence of a revolutionary regime in Kabul in April 1978 that reactivated Afghanistan's old territorial dispute with Pakistan that had seemed on the verge of a settlement, with Indian encouragement, just a short time before.

The Soviet military intervention in Afghanistan in late December 1979 and Indira Gandhi's resumption of the premiership of India about three weeks later added new complications to the Indo-Pakistani negotiation process, but did not bring it to a halt. The new government in New Delhi was unhappy with what was termed President Zia's "obsession" with the threat to Pakistan's security because of Soviet military intervention in Afghanistan and his search for external sources of support. Islamabad found India's initial justification of Soviet intervention in the debate on this issue in the UN in early 1980 as well as its slight retreat later to a leave-them-alone-and-they-may-withdraw-on-their-own-initiative position unpersuasive. In the view of Pakistan and the other South Asian states, India has performed dismally in its self-proclaimed role as the dominant power in the subcontinent by its abject failure to do anything to counter intervention in "its region" by an outside power. New Delhi is now depicted as always eager to assume the rewards and privileges of a dominant power status in the subcontinent but to shy away from the responsibilities that go along with this position when this could be expensive. The Indian government's attempt to portray the American response to Soviet intervention with the reintroduction of a rather modest arms aid program to Pakistan as the primary threat to Indian security and to peace and stability in South Asia is considered particularly irresponsible and unbecoming of a major regional power.

In any case, by late 1981 some observers in South Asia and elsewhere were predicting yet another Indo-Pakistani war in which India would take the initiative. This scenario is usually based upon two developments that have been described as "intolerable" to India: the renewal of U.S. military aid to Pakistan in the fall of 1981 that included the provision (by 1985) of 40 highly sophisticated F-16 fighter-bombers, and the prediction that Pakistan would have a nuclear weapons capacity—and possibly even nuclear weapons—by 1982 or 1983. This has induced some Indian political sources, including several leaders in the ruling party, to contemplate a preemptive military strike at Pakistan before the latter, in their perceptions, had attained the capacity to launch a war against India with the "liberation" of Kashmir as its objective.

But while a "war psychology" was evident in India, at least in some government circles, in early 1982 the deterrents to overt military action against Pakistan were also understood in New Delhi. The United States, Western Europe, Japan, and the international financial institutions such as the International Monetary Fund (IMF) and the International Development Association (IDA)—the sources of most external financial and technological assistance to India—would be likely to respond very negatively at a time that the Indian economy appears to be very vulnerable to economic sanctions. The Islamic states of West Asia, which supply approximately half of India's vital oil resources, would also be certain to react very strongly to an attack on Pakistan. On the domestic side, the politically important Muslim minority community in India would be unlikely to accept an Indian-instigated war with Pakistan in the 1980s as meekly as they did the 1971 Indian military action in support of another Muslim society, Bangladesh. Some sections of the Indian public suspect that Indira Gandhi's government might be tempted to launch a military campaign not for external security reasons but in an effort to regain support among the majority and some minority (e.g., the Sikhs) communities in India. But this would be a strategy of desperation that hardly seemed warranted by the political situation in India in early 1982.

There is, moreover, still the possibility of an accommodation with Pakistan on mutually acceptable terms, and some interesting recent developments in this direction. President Zia's September 1981 endorsement of a "no-war pact" with India—first proposed by Nehru in 1949 and subsequently by other Indian governments but always before with a negative response from Pakistan—raised the Indo-Pakistani dialogue on security issues to a new level. Pakistan has clearly indicated its interest in continuing the dialogue with India; after some initial hesitation, New Delhi had no reasonable option but to respond in kind. While it is difficult to be very optimistic about the prospects for an accommodation, at least the process of negotiation goes on. The northwest remains the most difficult frontier problem area for the government of India and one in which policy miscalculations could be disastrous rather than just embarrassing. But there is still a variety of policy options in the northwest available to New Delhi and it could well once again "muddle through" in reasonably satisfactory fashion.

THE NORTHERN BORDER'S CENTRAL FRONTIER

The central frontier of the subcontinent's northern border is usually defined as consisting of the three (now two) Himalayan kingdoms of Nepal, Sikkim, and Bhutan as well as the mountainous areas of India lying between Nepal and Kashmir. The central frontier region was once defined by Curzon, the viceroy of India at the turn of the century, as the "inner belt" of the buffer zone upon which British India's security depended. Tibet, which was then virtually independent (and after 1913 actually independent), and Afghanistan were the principal buffer areas between British India and the Chinese and Russian empires. While both Tibet and Afghanistan were responsive to British influence, they were never areas in which the writ of British "paramountcy" applied.

The three Himalayan states had a somewhat different status in their relations with the British Indian empire, one of whose basic principles was that the Himalayan kingdoms must accept "advice" on security and foreign relation issues in exchange for varying degrees of internal autonomy—nearly total for Nepal and Bhutan but more restricted for Sikkim. British India had achieved this objective by the first decade of the twentieth century, either through formal treaties or informal but effective tacit agreements.

The format of the relationship with the Himalayan states was retained in its essence after India had gained independence in 1947, first through "standstill agreements" and later through new treaties. The operating principle of India's security policy was stated explicitly by Prime Minister Jawaharlal Nehru at the time of the Chinese invasion of Tibet in the fall of 1950 when he declared: "The fact remains that we cannot tolerate any foreign invasion from any foreign country in any part of the Indian sub-continent. Any possible invasion of Nepal would inevitably involve the safety of India."[8] The statement referred specifically to Nepal, where an internal political crisis had just exploded, but it was fully understood that the principle applied to the entire frontier area. The policy was further reinforced by formal treaties with Bhutan, Sikkim, and Nepal that defined, in somewhat different ways, their respective roles in the Indian-managed regional security system.

The British policy under which internal autonomy had been conceded to Nepal and Bhutan was also retained by New Delhi after 1947, if in an attenuated form in Nepal in the 1951–56 period. Nehru's advocacy of a "middle way" approach that sought to preserve traditional institutions and processes while gradually "modernizing" them was, in effect, generally supportive of the existing monarchical structures. New Delhi encouraged the liberalization of the political systems in the Himalayan states, but only to the extent that this either served India's national interests or did not disrupt stability in this strategic but difficult area.[9]

That India considered it necessary to adopt a more activist role in the Himalayan states than the British was directly the consequence of the loss of Tibet as a buffer in 1951. Some Indians who were close to Nehru in that period have insisted that he expected trouble with the Chinese over the northern border and devised policies that would prevent or at least delay such a confrontation. Military intervention in support of the Tibetan government was rejected as beyond India's capabilities[10] and against New Delhi's broader Asian foreign policy objectives, which projected a close working relationship with China. Rather, Nehru sought an accommodation with Beijing under which Chinese sovereignty in Tibet would be recognized in exchange for China's acceptance of India's primacy south of the Himalayas. A short-lived working relationship based upon this formula was eventually negotiated and then formalized in the 1954 Sino-Indian treaty, which included the five principles of peaceful coexistence.

The responses of the Himalayan states to India's frontier policy since 1950 have varied over time. Nepal initially accepted the concept of a "special relationship" (including membership in the Indian security system) with India, but in the late 1950s began a long-term effort to modify its dependent status. The history of Bhutan's relationship with India is almost the exact reverse of that of Nepal. Bhutan initially sought to avoid any direct involvement in the Indian security system by maintaining its traditional isolationist foreign policy, but since 1960 it has closely integrated both its economic development and defense policies with those of India. Sikkim had no choice, as its administrative structure has been dominated by Indian officials since 1949 and, under the 1950 treaty, defense was the responsibility of the Indian army.

Nepal and India

The protagonist role in India in the 1950-51 revolution in Nepal and in the negotiations that led to a compromise agreement formulated by New Delhi earned for the Indians a dominant influence in Nepal's internal politics and external relations. The meek compliance of the Nepal government with this situation, however, began to change with the ascension of King Mahendra to the throne in 1955. The new ruler sought to modify Nepal's identification with India's regional security and economic systems through a number of policy innovations. The most important of these was the adoption in 1956 of the principle of "equal friendship" (with India and China) as the basic feature of Nepal's foreign policy. This was intended to provide the framework for the eventual neutralization of Nepal, as it implied the rejection of the concept of a "special relationship" with India and expressed Katmandu's interest in the revision of the 1950 Indo-Nepali treaty.

After King Mahendra had dismissed an elected government and assumed dictatorial powers in 1961, he intensified these efforts to define a more independent role for Nepal in the frontier region. The increasingly serious Sino-Indian dispute on the 2,500-mile frontier between China and the subcontinent aroused concern in Nepal over its involvement in the Indian security system; but at the same time it provided King Mahendra with some policy options that had previously seemed unrealistic.[11] In 1963, Nepal sought and obtained from the British and Americans limited quantities of military assistance—provision of which was previously an Indian monopoly. In the late 1960s India reluctantly acceded to Nepal's request that the Indian military mission in Katmandu and the Indian-manned security posts on Nepal's border with China be withdrawn. One prime minister of Nepal also suggested the abrogation of the 1950 treaty, but this was more than the Indians were prepared to accept or Katmandu could extract.

The new ruler, King Birendra, who came to the throne in early 1972, has intensified Katmandu's efforts to gain New Delhi's acceptance of Nepal's neutral status. The innovative feature of Birendra's policy is his proposal that Nepal be recognized as a "zone of peace," which, under Katmandu's interpretation, would remove Nepal as an area of contention between India and China. In making this proposal, Nepal specifically disavowed any intention of using China as a counterbalance to India, the most prominent feature of King Mahendra's foregin policy in the 1960s. But, in fact, the responsible authorities around the palace continued to speak in familiar terms on this subject, and for obvious reasons, for even as a zone of peace, Nepal would be far more vulnerable to political and economic pressure from India than China. Thus a counterbalance would still be required if Nepal's neutralized status was to have any meaning.

It is now evident that a quarter century of earnest endeavor has brought Nepal only limited success in achieving the basic goals of its foreign policy. The

1950 treaty with India, which made Nepal a participant in an Indian-defined security system in the Himalayas, is still in force and presumably binding on both governments. Prime Minister Morarji Desai, during a state visit to Nepal in 1977, made it perfectly clear that India considers the treaty fully operative and not in need of revision. Similar views were reportedly expressed by Indira Gandhi's Foreign Minister, Narasimha Rao, when he visited Katmandu in late 1981. The security relationship implicit in the 1950 treaty has never been put to the test and thus one cannot state categorically how New Delhi or Katmandu would respond if it were. But it is apparent that the government of India intends to keep its options open if intervention in Nepal should be considered necessary for the protection of the Indian security system along the entire Himalayan range.

Nepal also has had no success in extracting from the Chinese the firm commitments Katmandu requires to play its balance-the-powers foreign policy politics successfully. Starting in about 1958, Beijing began encouraging Nepal to assume an independent posture directed at the modification of its dependency relationship with India, and even provided some economic and rhetorical support to make this appear feasible. But China was never prepared to make a security commitment, formal or implicit, to Katmandu in the event of Indian intervention. More recently, China has largely abandoned its verbal encouragement of Nepal's efforts to assume a more independent role in the Himalayas. In 1981, a high Chinese official on a state visit to Katmandu reportedly even encouraged the Nepal government to come to terms with India. Thus, the regional environment in which Nepal must now operate is probably less conducive to the attainment of its proclaimed foreign policy goals than at any time since 1960.

This is even more evident when we consider Katmandu's efforts to reduce its economic dependence on India through a diversification of Nepal's external economic relations. There has been a small diversion of trade in percentile terms; now as much as 20 percent of Nepal's foreign trade is with countries other than India (if the large-scale smuggling between India and Nepal is not included). But in any real sense, Nepal is still as much an adjunct of the Indian economy in the 1980s as it was three decades earlier. Perhaps even more so, as Nepali dependence upon India both as a market and as a source for essential imports is greater today than in 1950 when Nepal still followed an isolationist policy and had a largely subsistence economy. Third-country aid donors and UN agencies have been generous in providing Katmandu with economic aid, but this has had only a minimal impact upon the Indo-Nepali economic relationship.

The Indian response to the Nepali foreign policy innovations discussed above have been remarkably consistent since the late 1950s—that is, to be accommodating on small points but to resist any fundamental changes in their economic and security relationships. India's response to Nepal's proposal that it be declared a zone of peace is typical. New Delhi has never specifically rejected the proposal but has merely suggested instead that *all* of Asia be declared a zone of peace. Obviously this is not what Katmandu has in mind. Another example was the Indian response to Katmandu's repeated requests for separate treaties on trade with India and on transit trade through India with third countries. New Delhi finally conceded this point in 1977, but the specific terms the Indians insisted upon were no more liberal than the provisions of the 1970 treaty that had encompassed both trade and transit in a single agreement.

There are several ways in which the Indians can exert pressure upon Katmandu. The one employed most frequently by New Delhi is the imposition of subtle, unofficial, but persistent economic pressure. A wide variety of tactics can be employed—delaying Indian exports to Nepal through contrived procedural complications, restricting access to Indian markets for Nepali products, or failing to provide transport and storage facilities for Nepali imports and exports in transit through India. All are quite effective and usually sufficient. When necessary, economic pressure can be supplemented by political pressure, usually involving quiet warnings from New Delhi that India might be disposed to extend support to one or the other opposition forces in Nepal. Katmandu has concluded, regretfully, that the likely response of the rest of the world to Indian intervention in Nepal would be the same as in other such cases (e.g., Kashmir, Hyderabad, Goa, Bangladesh, Sikkim)—vocal criticism of India but no assistance for the "victim."

In the 1960s, when India faced a formidable challenge from China on the Himalayan frontier, New Delhi usually considered it less expensive to make minor concessions to Nepal on some issues rather than to insist upon its own terms. Since the 1971 Bangladesh war, however, India has generally tended to be more hard-line on issues in dispute. The problems in their relationship are as formidable and perplexing as ever, reflecting the quite different perspectives on their national interests in India and Nepal. In recent years, this has been most apparent in their respective positions on the utilization and control of river systems that have their sources in Nepal but eventually feed into the Gangetic system in India and Bangladesh. The potential for hydroelectric power and for the development of irrigation facilities is enormous—but is seen in quite different terms in New Delhi, Katmandu, and Dacca. An agreement on this vital issue has yet to be achieved despite intensive negotiations on the subject over the past decade. The tone of Indo-Nepal relations in the 1980s will probably be determined more by this issue than any other factor. And in this case there are some grounds for optimism.

Sikkim and India

Sikkim was a far simpler problem for New Delhi than Nepal, and conversely the policy options available to the Sikkim government (prior to the state's accession to the Indian Union in 1975) were much more limited. Since

1949, when Indian troops were called in by the ruler of Sikkim to suppress a dissident political movement, India has been the de facto ruling power in this Himalayan state. New Delhi allowed Sikkim limited autonomy on a range of internal questions, but always within a context in which India's "paramountcy" (to use the old British Indian term) was recognized. Moreover, foreign relations, defense, and communications were India's responsibility under the 1950 Indo-Sikkimese treaty, and Sikkim became an arena of major Indian military concentration.

According to some authoritative Indian sources, the ruler of Sikkim, his American wife, and some of his palace coterie had begun to express interest in a broader degree of internal autonomy in the late 1960s, even suggesting that this Indian "protectorate" (under the 1950 treaty) should be allowed to apply for membership in the United Nations. Initially, New Delhi's response to these overtures was rather moderate, merely suggesting to the Sikkim ruler that he would be well advised to be satisfied with what he had. In the 1970s, and particularly in the aura of euphoria prevalent in India following the victory in the 1971 Bangladesh war, the Indians began to react more forcefully. In 1973, the Indians allowed the Sikkim opposition parties to organize a political movement, which came close to being an uprising directed against the palace. In contrast to its policy in similar situations earlier, New Delhi only intervened to restore "law and order" once the ruler had been compelled to request Indian assistance.

Having created a new political environment in Sikkim through their intervention, the Indians then approved the opposition parties' demands for general elections to the state assembly. The opposition won an overwhelming victory and proceeded to form a government that passed legislation severely limiting the power of the ruler. Even more important, the new government announced its support for accession to India and, with New Delhi's consent, held a national referendum on this question. The vote was nearly unanimous in favor of accession. The Indian Parliament, in response to this "expression of the will" of the Sikkimese people, passed an enabling act that allowed Sikkim's admission as a state in the Republic of India.

Most of the commentaries on this series of events have stressed New Delhi's concern over the Sikkim ruler's expressed interest in greater autonomy for his state, and the possible weakening effect this could have on India's security system in a highly strategic area. This must have been one factor in Indian decision making, but perhaps not the most important. It would have been relatively easy for the Indians to keep the palace in line without insisting upon the abolition of the monarchy and Sikkim's accession to India. But this would not have satisfied the highly vocal and increasingly better-organized political forces in Sikkim that were critical of the earlier Indian policy of accepting the predominant role of the palace in the Sikkimese governmental and political systems. Whether New Delhi will be any happier dealing with these troublesome political forces within the Republic of India than they were when Sikkim had the convenient status of a protectorate outside the Indian political system seems unlikely but is now unavoidable. Sikkim continues to have the highest priority in the Indian northern border security system because of its role as the shortest and easiest route between Tibet and the plains of India (and Bangladesh) as well as the line of defense for the narrow but vitally important access channel to northeast India. The events of 1973-75 did not in any way reduce the responsibilities of the Indian military in Sikkim, but it is possible that the army will eventually find it less convenient to work with an elected state government under the Indian federal system than with the old autonomous royal regime.

Bhutan and India

In the early postindependence period, Bhutan's role in the Indian security system was never clearly defined. From 1947 to 1960 Bhutan retained its traditional isolationist foreign policy, carefully avoiding contacts with all external powers except India and the Dalai Lama—but not the Chinese—in Tibet. In the 1949 Indo-Bhutanese treaty, Bhutan had conceded to India the right to "advise" the Bhutan government on its external relations, but this right was of limited significance as long as Bhutan was not interested in contacts with foreign powers.[12]

Initially, in 1949, the isolationist policy had been retained to limit India's involvement in Bhutan, at that time the only serious external threat. The Chinese invasion of Tibet in 1950 and, even more persuasively, the impressive assertion of Chinese military power in Tibet in 1959-60 radically changed the Bhutanese perception of their regional environment. The construction of a road complex tying Lhasa with the northeast sector of the border with India, paralleling the Tibetan-Bhutanese border for most of its length, raised the specter of Chinese military intervention, and moreover one the Indian army at that time had no capacity to counter. This was the context in which Bhutan finally decided (under Indian prodding, to be sure, but on its own appraisal of the situation) to reverse its foreign policy totally by accepting a broad alignment with India on security questions as well as wholesale Indian involvement in Bhutan's economy. Under the new policy, an impressive road network has been constructed by the Indian army connecting all of the major areas of Bhutan to India, a number of Indian advisers and technicians are associated with Bhutanese government offices, the Indian army is present in the country in various training and security capacities, and most of the Bhutanese economic development programs are financed through Indian aid.[13]

By the mid-1960s, there was a general feeling in the Bhutan government that it may have overreacted to the Chinese "threat," in the process becoming too closely aligned with and dependent upon India. A modest step backward was decided upon, primarily through seeking admission to the United Nations and at least limited diversification in sources of foreign economic assistance. But the semiconfrontation strategy adopted by Nepal a few years earlier in its efforts to modify relations with India was carefully avoided by Bhutan. Rather, Thimphu has done everything it can to reassure India about the new directions in Bhutan's foreign policy and even to solicit New Delhi's cooperation in its implementation.

The Indian response, while not satisfactory on every issue to the Bhutanese, has generally been considered good. The Indian officials on deputation to Bhutan have been instructed to leave decision making to the Bhutanese. Compliance with these instructions has not been total, and under the circumstances could not be total. But at least Indian intervention in internal Bhutanese affairs has been kept to an acceptable minimum and may even be less in the 1980s than it was ten years earlier. India also, after protracted negotiations, sponsored Bhutan's admission to the UN.

There are, of course, continuing tensions in the relations between the two countries, but these appear to be of manageable proportions to both sides. Any basic changes in either Indian or Bhutanese policy, thus, seem unlikely. This is all very satisfactory to New Delhi, which sees its security and related regional policy objectives well served by the maintenance of the status quo in its relationship with Bhutan.

THE NORTHEASTERN FRONTIER

The northeastern frontier, consisting of the mountain areas to the east of Bhutan that separate Assam (the Brahmaputra valley) from Tibet and Burma, is all part of India, with the exception of the narrow Bangladesh-Burma border on the extreme South. Thus the northeast is distinct from the northwest and central sections of the frontier, where India has to work through, with, and/or against other South Asian states. While this situation simplifies matters for New Delhi in most respects—that is, not having to deal with foreign governments with very different ideas from those of India on some aspects of regional interests and needs—it has drawbacks as well. It is important, for instance, that the northeast is largely inhabited by ethnic communities ("tribes") quite distinct from the "plains Indians" that constitute the vast majority of the population of India and dominate the Indian political, economic, and social systems. While some of these tribal communities have adjusted to membership in the Indian federation, others are still in the process of negotiating terms of association. There are, thus, several dissident tribal elements in the northeast that are partially in and partially out of the Indian political system.

Virtually all of the major tribal groups insist on the preservation of tribal lands through the exclusion (except on their own terms) of Indians who are not members of their community as well as on broad autonomy for their federal political unit. To accommodate these tribal demands, New Delhi has had to concede separate states within the Indian federation to the larger tribes, in the process abandoning its earlier plan to include the entire northeast in a unified Assam state. This hodgepodge of small, ethnically defined states is a continuing political problem for New Delhi, complicated even further by the historically strained relationship between the Assamese, Bengalis, and most of the tribal communities in the frontier region.

Three neighboring powers—China, Burma, and Bangladesh (East Pakistan until 1971)—are also important ingredients in India's policy planning in the northeast. Since 1959, the Chinese have usually been perceived by New Delhi as antagonistic to Indian interests and objectives. East Pakistan's status prior to 1971 was somewhat more ambivalent, even during crisis periods in Indo-Pakistani relations. Dominating all the land routes that connect India with the northeast except for a narrow strip of Indian territory at the foot of the Sikkim and Bhutan hills, East Pakistan was a major problem for Indian defense planning in the region. But, virtually indefensible, it also served as a hostage that limited Pakistan's freedom of action on the northeast—that is, Kashmir. From 1972 until 1975, Bangladesh integrated its foreign and defense policies with those of India; since then, however, it is behaving more like another Pakistan or Nepal than a pliant client state. Burma has generally been quietly cooperative with India in devising policies for their rugged and difficult border, as Rangoon usually identifies its interests in much the same way as New Delhi.

The mountains to the north of Assam—now the state of Arunachal but formerly NEFA, or the North East Frontier Agency—was one of the two areas (Ladakh was the other) that the Chinese invaded during the 1962 border war with India. This strategy reflected careful planning by Beijing as NEFA was the section of the Himalayan frontier in which Indian military and logistic capabilities were most limited. Pakistani and some Western commentators on the 1962 war have argued it was India that provoked and started the hostilities on the NEFA-Tibet border.[14] To anyone familiar with the incredibly difficult logistic problems the Indians faced in battling overwhelmingly superior Chinese forces in this sector of the frontier, this is implausible. More convincing, however, are some Indian critics—including high military officers—who have expressed their distress with the Nehru government for allowing India to become involved in hostilities in a section of the frontier where the consequences could only be disastrous.[15] This area of the border is still very vulnerable militarily despite the intensive efforts made by India since 1962 to improve the road network and administrative infrastructure in Arunachal.[16] Fortunately for New Delhi, Chinese efforts to encourage dissidence among the numerous tribal groups in this state have met with little success, and Arunachal is still probably the most stable area politically in the northeast.

The internal situation in Indian territory on or near the Indo-Burmese borders, on the other hand, has been marked by open rebellions against Indian authority by sections of the two major communities in this area—the Nagas and the Mizos—for more than two decades. While the Chinese had not instigated these movements, following the 1962 Sino-Indian war Beijing eagerly provided both ideological and guerrilla warfare training as well as a small amount of arms aid to the rebels. This program was seriously affected by the 1971 Bangladesh war as the Chinese-operated guerrilla training camps that the Pakistan government had permitted in East Pakistan were overrun by the Indian army and many of the Nagas and Mizos undergoing training there were captured. Some half-hearted attempts were made to revive these programs through the difficult and danger-ous communication route through western Burma into the Naga and Mizo tribal areas.[17] But even these were abandoned in the late 1970s when Beijing terminated its support of dissident forces in India in favor of the normalization of relations with New Delhi. The rebel movement lost a valuable source of assistance; this induced some of the leadership to seek and, in some cases, achieve a precarious accommodation with the Indian government. The northeast is still an extremely difficult problem for New Delhi and tribal dissidence has by no means disap-peared. But at least now the Indian administration and security forces do not have to contend with rebel movements enjoying external support.

The northeast frontier has not been the arena for even small-scale skir-mishes between the Indian and Chinese military forces since 1968, and there would seem to be a de facto boundary settlement on the ground that only re-quires legitimation through a treaty. As far back as 1960, Zhou En-Lai had offered India a compromise formula under which Peking would accept the MacMahon line (the basis for India's territorial claims) as the boundary on the eastern sector in exchange for New Delhi's recognition of Chinese claims to the Aksai Chin area on the Tibet-Kadakh border. It is probable that any agree-ment on the border that may eventually emerge from the efforts being made by both sides to "normalize" their relationship would be based on some such terms, as these reflect the existing situation with respect to administrative control.

Burma and India

The border with Burma also poses some serious problems for India, but for totally different reasons than that with China. There have been no boundary dis-putes between India and Burma since the British settled that question in 1937 when they separated Burma from their Indian empire. But what New Delhi and Rangoon do share are problems with certain dissident tribal communities, in particular the Nagas and Kachins whose traditional homelands lie on both sides of the border. The Burmese Nagas have been relatively quiescent but have on occasion rendered various kinds of assistance to the Indian Naga rebels. Similarly, the small Kachin and Kachin-related communities in the extreme northeast of India reportedly are sympathetic to the demands for independence of the Kachin national movement in Burma.

Both the Burmese and Indian governments have been "correct" in their policies toward tribal separatist movements in the other country. Rangoon, for instance, is fully prepared to cooperate with India in the Naga area by inter-cepting and returning Naga and Mizo rebels trying to make their way to China through Burma. Unfortunately for India, the efficacy of Burmese control on the frontier, and even more in the Kachin area through which the route to China passes, was very limited. India, thus, had to depend on its own border posts to intercept the rebels. While the Indians have been much more successful in carrying out this task in the post-Bangladesh war period on the Burma border, the India-Bangladesh border is still comparatively porous.

One other aspect of Indo-Burmese relations that impinges on New Delhi's regional security system concerns Burma's occasionally difficult and threatening relations with China. One of the several active insurrectionary movements in Burma is led by the pro-Chinese wing of the Burmese Communist Party (BCP), which exercises a tenuous control over a fringe area on the China-Burma border. Peking's support of the BCP has varied between periods when it did the minimum necessary to keep the party alive to times when the Chinese extended substantial material support, including small-scale incursions by Chinese troops across the border to counteract Burmese military operations directed against the BCP.

Rangoon has usually considered the BCP more of a nuisance than a real threat, but the prospect of massive Chinese intervention in support of the BCP with the overthrow of the present regime as its goal would present quite a different problem. The only occasion to date when this seemed a possibility was in 1967, when the Cultural Revolution distorted China's relations with most of its neighbors. It was in this context that President Ne Win of Burma made a hurried trip to New Delhi to solicit assurances of Indian support in the event the Chinese actually invaded Burma under one guise or another. If reports are correct, the Indians gave a positive response, in the process implicitly extending their South Asian security system to a Southeast Asian neighbor. Fortunately for New Delhi, the credibility of its support guarantee to Burma has never been put to the test. Ne Win visited China twice in 1977, and Deng Xiaoping came to Rangoon in early 1978. According to reports, these discussions led to a substantial improvement in Sino-Burmese relations, including presumably some guarantees to Rangoon on China's support of the BCP. But extreme variations in Chinese policy toward Burma have been the norm in the past, and yet another reversal is not beyond the range of possibilities. If this should occur on a serious scale, Rangoon might attempt to reactivate the tacit agreements of the late 1960s between Burma and India on security issues as one of its responses to a perceived threat from China.

Bangladesh and India

The former province of East Pakistan achieved independence in 1971 with the assistance of the Indian army. The Bangladesh government established shortly thereafter was, as one would expect under the circumstances, closely allied with India in what some Bangladeshis now call a client state relationship.

For nearly three years Dacca coordinated its foreign and defense policies with those of New Delhi. Then, in the latter half of 1975, a series of coups led to the installation of a military-dominated regime with evident, if only rarely expressed publicly, anti-Indian proclivities. Dacca has cautiously been redefining its foreign policy, primarily through programs directed at the diversification of its economic and political relations with such former "adversary" countries as the United States, China, Pakistan, and the Islamic states of West Asia. India is still far too powerful and important a neighbor to be denied a major presence in the country, but the authorities in Dacca are now resistant to involvement in any Indian-devised regional security system and even have strong reservations about the Indian proposals for economic cooperation on the Ganges-Brahmaputra project, which could be a major boon to the Bangladesh economy.

Bangladesh is, moreover, a different kind of problem for New Delhi from that of any other South Asian state as it contributes to potentially separatist tendencies within India. Most Bangladeshis are Bengali Muslims sharing the same language and many of the same cultural values and traditions of the Hindu Bengalis in India (Bangladesh means "country of the Bengalis"). In 1971, several prominent members of the Indian foreign policy decision-making elite reportedly doubted the wisdom of Indian intervention in support of an independent Bangladesh, arguing that this could prove to be a dangerous precedent for the Indian Bengalis. The government of India's decision eventually went against their advice. Concern on this matter has not totally disappeared but is perhaps less today because the post-1975 rulers in Dacca have virtually abandoned the pretense of being a secular Bengali state and again tend to emphasize the Islamic traditions that separate Bengali Muslims and Hindus. While there is an "Arma Bangal" (Our Bengal) movement in India that advocates the establishment of a separate united Bengali nation, it has had only a very limited appeal among Bengalis in India and virtually none in Bangladesh. Religion rather than a common language and literary culture still appears to be the decisive determinant of political identification among most Bengalis, and both Dacca and New Delhi apparently prefer to keep it that way.

The Indian government is indecisive and somewhat baffled on how best to respond to the various problems, domestic and international, raised by the existence of Bangladesh, which is too large (and not landlocked) to be handled like Nepal and Bhutan but too strategically located in India's northeast to be ignored. New Delhi has usually adopted a moderate line, despite the indignation among some Indians over Bangladeshi "ingratitude" for the assistance rendered in their 1971 struggle for independence. One exception was the policy adopted by the Gandhi government in 1975-76 in arming and assisting small antigovernment terrorist gangs operating in Bangladesh, close to the Indian border.[18] But this was limited in scope and apparently designed more to demonstrate India's capacity for intervention than the overthrow of the Bangladesh government. In any case, in 1977 the new Janata government in New Delhi reversed this policy and instead embarked upon some vigorous efforts to improve relations with Dacca.

There are a number of issues in dispute between the two states that have long defied settlement and occasionally strain their relationship.[19] The old "enclave" issue, inherited from the 1947 partition of Bengal, has never been resolved. More critical to both countries and thus not easily compromised are the disagreements over the division of the waters of the Ganges and Brahmaputra river systems and over the new islands formed at the mouth of the Brahmaputra that involve important maritime boundary questions in the Bay of Bengal. And the reportedly substantial migration of Bangladeshis into Assam and Tripura since 1975 has become a major political issue in both of these Indian states, and between India and Bangladesh. The negotiating process on all these issues goes on, but is seriously handicapped by the suspicion and even antagonism with which both sides view each other.

Obviously India is unhappy with the general trend of developments in Bangladesh's domestic and foreign policies and with the potentially disruptive role Dacca could play in the northeast of the subcontinent. But while the Bangladesh government is often seen as uncooperative, it is also very vulnerable to a wide range of Indian pressures. And in Bangladesh as in Nepal, there is no really effective external counterforce to India despite Dacca's intensive efforts to expand contacts with ASEAN, Japan, China, the United States, and the Islamic world. Bangladesh is yet another complication for India in the already difficult northeastern sector of the frontier, and this New Delhi could do without. But it is probably a mangeable problem—at least as long as everything does not start coming apart in West Bengal, Assam, and the tribal hill states in the northeast.

INDIA, SRI LANKA AND THE MALDIVES

While New Delhi's attention is generally directed toward security issues on its land frontiers to the north, the oceanic areas that surround the subcontinent on three sides can hardly be ignored. Thus, policies toward Sri Lanka and the Maldives, two insular neighbors to the south, and toward the Indian Ocean now constitute increasingly important factors in Indian foreign policy.

It is only infrequently that Indo-Sri Lankan relations receive much public notice, even in the press of the two countries. There have been occasional periods of tension in their relationship, but for the most part both sides have adopted "low-posture" rather than confrontationist strategies toward each other. A number of agreements on issues in dispute have been concluded; while these have not always solved the problem, they have defused potentially difficult situations and permitted the postponement of decisions that could be embarrassing to either or both governments. Probably the most important factor in New Delhi's perception of Colombo concerns the latter's role in the South Asian region, for it is on this question that the two governments pursue quite distinct policies. As noted earlier, for most of the period since 1947 India has sought to restrict the role of the major external powers in the subcontinent or, when this was not possible, to direct their involvement in ways that were supportive of Indian objectives. Sri Lanka, like the other South Asian states, has generally encouraged the external powers to maintain a substantial presence as a contribution to Colombo's capacity to adopt more flexible policies toward its giant neighbor to the north. In brief, China, the Soviet Union, and (usually) the United States have been viewed as essential counterbalances to the overwhelming political, economic, and military power of India.[20]

Sri Lanka's "China connection" became a matter of concern for the Indians. While Nehru not only endorsed but actually sponsored closer economic (the rubber/rice agreements) and political (the Panchshila pact) relations between China and Sri Lanka in the 1950s, these were viewed with a notable lack of enthusiasm after Sino-Indian relations reached a stage of public hostility in the 1960s. But New Delhi felt that China's limited capabilities in Sri Lanka made a direct response on India's part unnecessary, and the Indians have normally preferred to depend upon Sri Lanka's own balance-of-power politics to make sure that China did not gain an inordinate influence in Colombo.

There are several specific issues that also complicate the relationship between India and Sri Lanka. Probably the most important and insoluble is the presence of a large Tamil minority of Indian origin concentrated in northern Sri Lanka. Under agreements signed in 1964 and 1974, a part of this Tamil community is eligible for Sri Lankan citizenship and continued residence in the country while the rest is to be repatriated to India. But, despite the precise terminology used in the agreements, it has proved difficult to divide the Tamil minority into these respective categories, and repatriation to India has not moved at the stipulated annual rate by a considerable margin.

The Indian government has been reasonable in its negotiations with Sri Lanka on this question—indeed, to the point where it has overlooked injustices in the treatment of Tamil's long resident in the country. Colombo has appreciated New Delhi's restraint on this issue but nevertheless is still apprehensive that the plight of the Tamils might be used as a pretext for Indian intervention—as nearly happened in 1981. The increasing tendency for Tamil political organizations in Sri Lanka to support separatist goals rather than, as in the past, demands for greater autonomy complicates decision making on this issue for both Colombo and New Delhi, as it is evident that Tamil leaders are now less inclined to accept agreements between the two governments that determine the fate of the Tamil community in Sri Lanka.[21]

Economic relations between India and Sri Lanka are another continuing problem, primarily because of the heavy trade imbalance in India's favor and the competition between the two countries for the world's tea market. While Sri Lanka may not be as vulnerable to Indian economic dominance as Nepal or Bangladesh, it still prefers to maintain a multilateral approach on external economic relations. This has been particularly true since the 1977 elections, which brought a new government with radically different economic policies to power in Colombo. Borrowing heavily from the "Singapore model," Sri Lanka has introduced free industrial zones, in which foreign firms are granted special incentives, as a basic feature of its development strategy. Indian corporations are involved in these operations to some extent, but it is the ASEAN states and Japan that have been the big investors—to Colombo's satisfaction.

Colombo's reservations on its economic ties with India are even evident in the one field in which cooperation would obviously be mutually beneficial—tea exports. Between them, the two powers provide about 85 percent of the tea on the world market, and 60 percent of Sri Lanka's export earnings are from this commodity. But while Colombo has agreed in principle to coordinate the marketing of tea with India in order better to control world prices,[22] in practice it has continued to adopt a competitive strategy at a high cost to itself. The terms offered by New Delhi have been attractive, but the strong suspicion with which the other South Asian states approach economic cooperation with India is once again evident in this case.

The one area of Sri Lanka's foreign policy in which there would appear to be an identity of interests with India is on their respective policies toward the Indian Ocean. Indeed, one of the major achievements of India's regional policy is the success it had in persuading—if persuasion was necessary—Sri Lanka to take the lead in the movement to have the Indian Ocean declared a "zone of peace."[23] India's concern over security interests on its oceanic frontiers had first become public in the 1963–65 period, when China, Indonesia, and Pakistan were increasingly identifying their interests in the Bay of Bengal and the Southeast Asian straits in mutually supportive terms. The replacement of the Sukarno government in Indonesia by a strongly anti-Chinese military regime in 1966 relieved Indian apprehensions on this score, at least for the time being. Subsequently, however, the expansion of U.S. and Soviet naval activity in the Indian Ocean after 1968 and the emergence of Iran as a significant naval force in the 1970s has revived interest in India's sea frontiers. New Delhi's response has been to expand its own navy while at the same time calling for the total-withdrawal of the naval and air forces and bases of the nonlittoral powers from the Indian Ocean.

Sri Lanka has adopted Indian rhetoric on this issue, but there have been occasions when its behavior was inconsistent with its public policy position. In 1971, for instance, shortly after Sri Lanka had formally submitted a Declaration of the Indian Ocean as a Zone of Peace proposal to the UN calling for the non-littoral powers to withdraw or at least reduce their military forces in the Indian Ocean, war broke out between India and Pakistan over East Pakistan. During the hostilities, both the United States and the Soviet Union sent naval units into the Indian Ocean without eliciting one word of protest from Sri Lanka. While this failure to respond reflected Colombo's critical attitude toward what it described as a "secessionist" movement in East Pakistan (and, hence, a bad example for the Tamil minority in Sri Lanka) as well as its distress with India's armed inter-vention in a neighboring state (another bad precedent), one would have expected at least a pro forma protest to Moscow and Washington.

Sri Lanka's reaction to two events in 1974—the Anglo-American agree-ment on the Diego Garcia base and the CENTO naval and air exercises in the Indian Ocean in which the United States participated—was also one of restraint. Sirimavo Bandaranaike finally expressed "regrets" over the base agreement, but Colombo made no comment on the CENTO maneuvers.

Perhaps the strongest evidence that there are important differences between India and Sri Lanka on the Indian Ocean, however, was the association made in Colombo between the zone-of-peace proposal and renunciation of nuclear weapons by regional powers. In a 1974 position paper, Sri Lanka's official policy was stated as follows: "As far as the countries in the region are concerned, they will have to commit themselves to a policy of de-nuclearization which would entail the permanent renunciation by them of nuclear weapons."[24] This consti-tuted an endorsement of the Pakistani addition to the zone-of-peace proposal (made after India's explosion of a "peaceful nuclear device") that New Delhi had specifically rejected.

Sri Lanka continues to support the zone-of-peace formula in appropriate international forums, but with less enthusiasm than when it first made the pro-posal in 1971. Several leading Sri Lankan officials, journalists, and scholars pri-vately express the view that Sri Lanka adopted this policy position without proper consideration of its ultimate consequences. More specifically, they ques-tion whether Sri Lanka's foreign policy objectives would be served by an agree-ment under which India would assume an unchallenged position as the dominant naval power in the section of the Indian Ocean in which Sri Lanka is located. The preference for multilateral balances may be surfacing again even in this aspect of Sri Lankan foreign policy. Colombo's reluctance to host the Indian Ocean conference originally scheduled for late 1981 led to its "postponement" to a more "convenient" time, to New Delhi's discomfiture. But then even the government of India recognizes that the "zone of peace" in the Indian Ocean lacks feasibility under existing circumstances, though they keep pushing it on every possible occasion in order to keep the concept alive.

More disturbing to New Delhi, however, were two Colombo policy deci-sions: the application for membership in ASEAN and an agreement with an American firm for the construction of an oil refinery at Trincomolee, the former British naval base that had been closed for more than two decades. While the government of India demonstrates little enthusiasm for formal South Asian regional institutions, it does get upset when other countries in "its region" opt for membership in regional systems in adjacent areas—e.g., Pakistan in West Asia or Sri Lanka in ASEAN. The Trincomolee issue aroused suspicion in India that Sri Lanka was prepared to allow the United States to establish a naval base or facility there that would be a threat to Indian security. Colombo explained to

New Delhi that while naval units of any foreign power would be permitted to use the facilities at Trincomolee for normal resupply operations (on the same basis as Soviet naval vessels use India ports), there was no intention to allow anything resembling a base there.

The foreign policy of the present government in Colombo is directed at establishing a more balanced, "equidistance" relationship with India, China, the USSR, the United States, ASEAN, and the more moderate West Asian states in contrast to the previous regime's policy of leaning toward the Socialist bloc and stressing its membership in the Nonalignment Movement. But, in fact, this constitutes the reemergence of the long-range policy objectives adopted by Sri Lanka in the early 1950s rather than a dramatic innovation. In the process, India's important role in Sri Lankan decision making has not been diminished significantly, and the relationship between the two states continues to be marked by what one observer aptly termed "watchful cordiality."[25] Sri Lanka may well have a higher priority in India's regional security policy because of its growing concern with developments in the Indian Ocean, but as yet this has not induced New Delhi to revise its basic policy approach toward its southern neighbor.

The Republic of the Maldives, an archipelago of over a thousand small sparsely populated islands located about 500 miles southwest of the southern tip of the subcontinent, has only recently begun to assume some importance in South Asian geostrategy. Never formally colonized, the Maldives accepted a dependency relationship with the British in the nineteenth century similar to that which British India had with Nepal and Bhutan. In a treaty signed in 1887, the Maldives "entrusted" defense and foreign policy to the British in exchange for guarantees of internal autonomy. This relationship lasted until 1965, operating through the British colonial administration in Colombo until 1948 and directly from London thereafter.

The importance of the Maldives to its neighbors and other powers is directly attributable to its highly strategic location in the Indian Ocean, and in particular to the air base at Gan that was first constructed by the British during World War II and then considerably expanded and improved under agreements signed in 1953 and 1965. In 1976, however, the British withdrew completely under their policy of reducing security commitments "east of Suez," leaving the air base intact.[26] This had the effect of enhancing the attraction of the Maldives to some outside powers. In 1977, Moscow offered to "rent" the base at Gan (ostensibly as a refuelling and maintenance facility for Soviet fishing vessels in the Indian Ocean!), but the Maldives turned it down.[27]

Since 1976, India, Pakistan, Sri Lanka, the USSR, the United States, Great Britain, China, Japan, and several ASEAN and West Asian states have sought to assert roles for themselves in the Maldives on a low-profile but nonetheless competitive basis. The Maldives has adopted an "open to all" development policy in which it solicits economic assistance from a wide variety of sources. Its traditional rice, sugar, and fish barter trade relations with Sri Lanka have been maintained, while old ties with India through several Indian merchant families long resident in the Maldives have been expanded through the introduction of a substantial Indian economic aid program. The West Asian Islamic states now also provide large financial grants, while Japan and some ASEAN and Western states extend the technological assistance the Maldives requires to modernize its vital fishing industry and establish a tourist industry.[28]

So far, New Delhi has found little to object to in the Maldives' foreign and economic policies. The effective "neutralization" of the Maldives in the increasingly important geopolitics of the Indian Ocean through its accessibility to all policy serves Indian objectives quite well. The Indian government would not want to have the Gan base leased out to any other external power, including the Soviet Union, but the Maldivian authorities have made the right moves on this issue as far as India is concerned after initially entertaining some aspirations to lease it out in the period immediately after the British withdrawal.[29] The Maldives may identify a little too loudly and closely with the Islamic states in West Asia for New Delhi's tastes, but as long as this is done primarily to extract financial rewards from the oil-rich governments in West Asia rather than to establish substantive regional affiliations, India is unlikely to complain. There is also an implicit competition between India and Sri Lanka for the old British role as principal channel for the Maldives with the outside world, but in some respects this is already passé. The objective of the Indian government is to prevent any single third state or bloc from obtaining a dominant influence in the Maldives or its transformation into another Diego Garcia. In this, India would appear to have the full cooperation of the present Maldivian government and, as yet, there have been no serious, concerted attempts by an outside power to persuade the Maldives to change their policy in this respect. New Delhi will certainly watch developments in the archipelago closely, but at the same time will keep its own presence in the Maldives to nonthreatening proportions unless, in its views, circumstances make interference unavoidable.

REGIONAL INSTITUTIONS

South Asia has been perhaps unique among the regions of the world in lacking any kind of formal regional institutional structure, and it has only been in the 1980s that there have been some efforts to fill this gap. While there have been informal regional systems of various sorts consisting of combinations of India's bilateral relations with two or more of the other South Asian states, none of these functioned on a multilateral basis nor did they involve cooperative decision-making processes.[30] The reasons for this situation are readily apparent— the lack of any strong demand for regional institutions by the states in the subcontinent. Since the mid-1950s, at least, New Delhi has tended to interpret proposals for multilateral regional bodies from any source with suspicion, viewing them as either plots by outside powers to undermine India's primacy in the subcontinent and/or as attempts by the other regional states to improve their bargaining position with India by "ganging up" against it in an institution in which the principle of the equality of sovereign nations would apply. On their part, the other South Asian states usually perceived a regional system as yet another instrument through which India's dominance in the subcontinent would be reinforced.

By the latter part of the 1970s, when India's predominant position in South Asia seemed well-established, the attitude of some of the other South Asian states toward regional institutions had changed. It now seemed preferable to negotiate political and economic relations with India within a broader institutional framework rather than on a strictly bilateral basis. In 1979, therefore, Bangladesh proposed a conference of all South Asian states to discuss the formation of a regional institution. The responses from Nepal, Sri Lanka, the Maldives, and Bhutan were very positive. The Indian and Pakistani reactions, in contrast, were cautiously negative, though for quite different reasons. New Delhi still adhered to its preferences for bilateral relations with regional states; Pakistan was more interested in affiliations with West Asian rather than South Asian regional organizations, and was uncertain whether it should get involved in the proposed conference.

After some informal discussions, however, all the governments agreed upon a preparatory conference at the foreign secretary level—slightly lower than the foreign minister level proposed by Bangladesh. The first of these was held in Colombo in late 1980 and a follow-up meeting in Katmandu a year later. Six subcommittees, each responsible for different aspects of interregional relations, were established at Colombo, met in various capitals in mid-1981, and submitted preliminary reports at the Katmandu meeting.

While no startling progress was made at either meeting, on the whole they went better than expected. Indian and Pakistani reservations about the process were somewhat mitigated; the enthusiasm of the other states was retained. It was agreed that the negotiation process should continue, and there was a public acceptance "in principle" of the concept of regional institutions. But it is assumed that in this delicate introductory stage, the regional body would deal with lesser, more manageable, problems rather than those that really divide the countries of the region—such as the division of river waters on a multilateral basis, security issues, or responses to external power involvement in the subcontinent. While only a first step has been taken, even this had eluded the countries of South Asia for more than three decades since the achievement of independence.

CONCLUSIONS

India is still beset by a wide range of problems, both internal and external, but severely limit its capacity to assume the mantle of leadership in the subcontinent that most of the Indian elite consider to be the country's rightful destiny.

Since the mid-1960s, and particularly after the 1971 Bangladesh war, India had appeared to be on the verge of universal acceptance of its status as the paramount power in South Asia. Developments in and around the region in the early 1980s, however, have revived old problems that had seemed resolved only a few years earlier and also raised several new, even more intractable complications. Domestic political developments—including the curious combination of a powerful prime minister who is virtually immune to challenges to authority from any source with a weak and inept administrative structure that is a poor instrument for the implementation of policy—have further complicated decision making in the foreign policy sphere. The result has been more inconsistencies and contradictions in policies and policy declarations than at any time in the past.

While the primacy of India's position in South Asia is still generally accepted, New Delhi cannot dictate to its sensitive neighbors nor unilaterally decide the terms upon which external powers become involved in the subcontinent. This is perhaps most apparent in the emerging security relationship between the United States and Pakistan and in the Soviet military intervention in Afghanistan. Both of these have aroused strong Indian disapproval, but this has had little impact on the course of developments as yet. But it is also probable that New Delhi can make the price paid for persistent deviations from Indian-determined norms high, as Nepal and Bangladesh have discovered in the past and Pakistan may in the future. While the intrusions of external powers into the subcontinent—usually with the cooperation of a regional power—cannot be prevented by New Delhi, it probably can be contained to tolerable proportions. The Soviet military involvement in Afghanistan is not yet at a level that seriously threatens Pakistan's viability; the U.S.-Pakistan security relationship has been limited to the sale of arms (at high world market prices) and has not yet been expanded to include security commitments or the provision of base facilities. Thus, the situation on the northwest could—and eventually may—become considerably more difficult and dangerous for India, but there is some optimism in New Delhi that it has sufficient leverage on the powers involved to prevent this from happening.

One of the casualties of the reemergence of a limited confrontation environment in southern Asia has been India's comparatively liberal and generous policies toward neighboring states introduced in the mid-1970s. This policy has by no means been completely abandoned, but it is more difficult to persuade the foreign policy decision makers in New Delhi in 1982 that this serves India's vital interests than it was a few years earlier. The response of the other countries in the region has been predictable: concern with avoiding unnecessarily irritating New Delhi combined with a dogged determination to adhere to their own views on critical regional and international issues. The growing tendency in the 1970s for a regional consensus in various international forums—the UN, its specialized agencies, the Nonalignment Movement, and so forth—has been partially dissipated in the 1980s. India will have to play the critical role if this dangerous trend toward divisiveness and sullen antagonism in the subcontinent is to be reversed. Whether New Delhi is interested enough to make the effort should become clearly evident in the 1980s.

NOTES

1. For a wide variety of Indian views on regional and international developments in the 1970s, see the special combined issue of *International Studies* 17, nos. 3 & 4 (October/ December 1980). An excellent analysis of the general principles underlying Indian foreign policy is included in Shashi Tharoor, *Reasons of State: Political Development and India's Foreign Policy under Indira Gandhi, 1966-1977*, (New Delhi: Vikas, 1982), which also includes an "epilogue" on foreign policy in the Janata period.

2. See, for instance, the contributions by several Indian scholars in S. P. Varma and K. P. Misra, eds., *Foreign Policies in South Asia* (Delhi: Orient Longmans, 1975).

3. This analysis of the Indian perspective on regional cooperation is based upon discussions with Indian officials, scholars, and journalists by the author over the past two decades as well as a survey of the Indian literature on the subject.

4. See Sisir Gupta, *India and Regional Integration in Asia* (Bombay: Asia, 1964).

5. William J. Barnds, *India, Pakistan and the Great Powers* (New York: Praeger, 1972), pp. 136–41.

6. Nepali press reports and comments on China's capabilities and intentions in the Himalayan region and South Asia have generally been much more restrained since Deng Xiaoping's visit to Katmandu in 1978. The previous assumption that China constituted an effective counterbalance to India in the central Himalayas is now much less evident.

7. Dilip Mukherjee, "Afghanistan under Daud: Relations with Neighboring States," *Asian Survey* 15, no. 4 (April 1975): 309.

8. Speech to Parliament on December 6, 1950, *Jawaharlal Nehru Speeches 1949-53*, vol. 2 (New Delhi: Government of India, 1957), p. 177.

9. For a representative Indian view on India's relations with the Himalayan states see S. D. Muni, "India and the Himalayan Kingdoms: Security Interests and Diplomacy (1947–75)," prepared for the series on Indian Foreign Policy and Contemporary Diplomacy, School of International Studies, Jawaharlal Nehru University, New Delhi, 1977.

10. B. N. Mullick, *My Years with Nehru: The Chinese Betrayal* (Bombay: Allied, 1971), pp. 250–76.

11. Leo E. Rose, *Nepal: Strategy for Survival* (Berkeley: University of California Press, 1971), pp. 250–76.

12. Leo E. Rose, *The Politics of Bhutan* (Ithaca, N.Y.: Cornell University Press, 1977), pp. 72–73.

13. K. J. Holsti's chapter on Bhutan in his forthcoming volume *Why Nations Realign: Foreign Policy Restructuring in the Postwar World*, analyzes Bhutan's decision to abandon isolationism and accept an alignment with India.

14. See, for example, S. M. Burke, *Mainsprings of Indian and Pakistani Foreign Policies* (Minneapolis: University of Minnesota Press, 1974), and Neville Maxwell, *India's China War* (New York: Pantheon, 1970).

15. See, for instance, J. P. Dalvi, *Himalayan Blunder* (Bombay: Thacker, 1969); B. M. Kaul, *The Untold Story* (Bombay: Allied, 1967); and Parshotam Mehra, *The McMahon Line and After* (Madras: Macmillan, 1976).

16. Leo E. Rose and Margaret W. Fisher, *The North-East Frontier Agency of India* (Washington, D.C.: U.S. Department of State, 1967), pp. 65–66.

17. *Far Eastern Economic Review* 97, no. 36 (September 9, 1977): 5.

18. Talukder Maniruzzaman, "Bangladesh in 1976: Struggle for Survival as an Independent State," *Asian Survey* 17, no. 2 (February 1977): 191–94.

19. Ishtiaq Hossain, "Bangladesh-India Relations: Issues and Problems," *Asian Survey* 21, no. 11 (November 1981): 1115–27.

20. See S. U. Kodikara, *Indo-Ceylon Relations Since Independence* (Colombo: Ceylon Institute of World Affairs, 1965); S. U. Kodikara, "Ceylon's Foreign Policy; Global Compulsions and Regional Responsibilities," in *Foreign Policies in South Asia*, ed. S. P. Varma and K. P. Misra (Delhi: Orient Longmans, 1975); and Dhirendra Mohan Prasad, *Ceylon's Foreign Policy under the Two Bandaranaikes (1956-1965): A Political Analysis* (Delhi: S. Chand, 1973).

21. Robert N. Kearney, "Language and the Rise of Tamil Separatism in Sri Lanka," *Asian Survey* 18, no. 5 (May 1978).

22. Urmila Phadnis, "Foreign Policy of Sri Lanka in the Seventies," *Institute for Defence Studies and Analyses Journal* (New Delhi) 8, no. 1 (July-September 1975): 104, 119.

23. K. P. Misra stresses Sri Lanka's leading role in the UN resolution declaring the Indian Ocean as a "Zone of peace." See his "Indian Ocean as a Zone of Peace: The Concept and Alternatives," *India Quarterly* 33, no. 1 (January-March 1977): 19–20.

24. Justice Siriwardene, "Sri Lanka and the Indian Ocean," in *Indian Ocean Power Rivalry* ed. T. T. Poulose (Delhi: Youn Asia, 1974), p. 90.

25. Phadnis, "Foreign Policy of Sri Lanka," p. 119.

26. Urmila Phadnis and Ela Dutt Luithui, "The Maldives Enter World Politics," *Asian Affairs* 8, no. 3 (January-February 1981): 174–75.

27. The Soviets had just lost their base at Berbera in Somalia, and it was suspected that Gan was looked upon as a substitute.

28. On the Maldive's economic policies, see Republic of Maldives, National Planning Agency, "Republic of Maldives: Programmes and Projects for the 1980s," mimeographed (Paper prepared for the UN conference on Lesser Developed Countries, Paris, September 1981); and World Bank, *The Maldives: An Introductory Economic Report* (Washington, D.C.: World Bank, 1980).

29. The Maldives government advertised in various newspapers around the world that it was prepared to lease "the island and facilities for any purpose considered reasonable" (New York *Times*, October 27, 1977). However, the offer was withdrawn shortly thereafter, according to the Maldivian authorities, in order to avoid arousing "suspicion amongst our friends in the non-aligned movement" (*Daily Telegraph*, October 28, 1977).

30. For a discussion of some of these informal regional systems, see Leo E. Rose and Satish Kumar, "South Asia," in *Comparative Regional Systems*, ed. Werner J. Feld and Gavin Boyd (New York: Pergamon Press, 1980), pp. 237–73.

3

NATIONAL SECURITY AND
MILITARY POLICY IN INDIA

Onkar Marwah

The revolutionary convulsions in Iran, the Soviet invasion of Afghanistan, the Iraq-Iran war, and the intensification of major power rivalry have transformed the Indian Ocean from a quiescent backwater into an area of great strategic preoccupation. Most of the new interest in the Indian Ocean, however, centers on the northwest quadrant of the ocean. Two-thirds of the world's known oil reserves are located in and off its shores, and there are Western fears of oil supply interdiction if regimes hostile to the West's interests come to power in that area. Soviet support to radical states in the Middle East, the Horn of Africa, and perhaps in the future to sub-Saharan African states, fuels such fears.

Among Western states' responses, possibly the most significant has been in the form of an immense supply of modern weapons to a select number of the Persian Gulf-Middle Eastern states, notably Iran in the 1970s, and Egypt, Saudi Arabia, and Pakistan in the 1980s.[1] Additionally, the United States has moved toward the establishment of a permanent strategic presence in the Indian Ocean through the upgrading of its earlier communications facility on the island of Diego Garcia (800 miles due south of the southern tip of India). A matching Soviet military base, initially sited at Berbera on the Somali coast, was lost as a consequence of the Soviet switch of military support to Ethiopia in the latter's war with Somalia. The Soviets, however, have obtained an alternative base at Aden in an effort to minimize U.S. strategic capability in the Indian Ocean. The United States also seeks to establish bases or use facilities in Oman, Somalia, Kenya, and Egypt. The Soviet Union, on the other hand, is continuing to bolster its position in Syria, South Yemen, and Libya.

India has played a minimal role in the preceding developments. While wary of their effect on subcontinental politics, the country has been unwilling to criticize the Gulf-Middle Eastern states for their oil price hikes and arms purchases and has been unable to coax the superpowers into a deescalation of their strategic presences in the Indian Ocean. (It is to be noted that the United States and the Soviet Union have been engaged, through bilateral negotiations in Geneva, in efforts to find a mutually acceptable formula to limit their strategic presences in the Indian Ocean. These talks were adjourned due to U.S. objectives of the extent of Soviet involvement in the Ethiopian-Somali war, and suffered further by the increased rivalries in the region compounded by the Soviet invasion of Afghanistan.)

Despite its low profile in recent events concerning the northwestern Indian Ocean, India remains the biggest of the littoral states in size, population, skilled personnel, most minerals save oil, industrial capacity, and military power. It could be said that, irrespective of its low per capita position, the country is the only "developed" state among the developing countries surrounding the ocean. (The statement excludes South Africa and Australia as not falling in the category of developing states.) India's capacity to build upon what exists is also likely to remain higher than that of any other Indian Ocean state. That assessment would hold in spite of the vast arms supply to the Gulf states, the petrodollar-financed economic and military activity in that area, or the Gulf-oriented focus of great-power interests. It is probable that India's military capability will remain superior to that of other Indian Ocean states, notwithstanding assumptions to the contrary arising from the arms imports into the Gulf region.

INDIA'S POLITICAL OBJECTIVES VIS-À-VIS THE INDIAN OCEAN STATES

Behind a facade of high fractiousness, India's internal and external frameworks of political action have been based on a large measure of consensual agreement since independence in 1947.* The choices within the country have been for centrist policies largely sympathetic to the Left. The external effort has been to interact positively with both the socialist and nonsocialist sectors of the international system.

In more specific form, the objectives of India's external consensus have been to mediate the country's conflicted position with the two major ideological camps of the international system, open channels of communication with both of them and seek to define the level and intensity of participation with either according to Indian preferences. Since the ability of the Indian state to accomplish these tasks is limited by the ability and power of other states, the real

---

*India's former foreign minister, Atal Bihari Vajpayee, said as much in behalf of the Janata government of India: "Foreign policy was not an issue in the election campaign [which led to the Congress Party's ouster after thirty years in power in India]. There has always been a broad national consensus on external affairs in this country" (New York *Times*, March 31, 1977, p. 8).

definition of action frameworks in the external sphere could not be undertaken entirely within Indian choices. Despite that, Indian leaders view their state's nonaligned posture as having engaged the world's major competing ideologies and their adherents in separate but cumulative support of India's needs. Meanwhile, the posture itself is seen as having exhibited a comprehensive appeal through its acceptance as the external policy stance of 104 states in the world. Many of the Indian Ocean states fall in the preceding category. Those among the latter not formally "nonaligned" participate in the international system through the Group of 77 forum, with policy activity fairly similar—though not the same—to those of the nonaligned. In effect, India's differences with the developing states of the Indian Ocean littoral arise in relation to a few states, occur in limited form, and are amenable to resolution without any potential for large-scale conflict.

India has neutralized the potential for active Middle Eastern or Gulf states' support to Pakistan in the latter's disputes with India, through an unwavering Indian alignment behind Arab-Islamic causes in international forums. Minor forms of support—such as token arms and sympathetic statements provided Pakistan—have been ignored to maintain and stabilize the larger framework of good relations with the Middle East and Persian Gulf states. India's relations with the black states of East Africa have been smooth and friendly throughout, as have those with the Southeast Asian states of the ocean littoral. A temporary, active, but nominal Indonesian support under Sukarno for Pakistani causes during the mid-1960s was—as with the Middle Eastern cases—ignored for the sake of the wider consensus with Indonesian policies.

Cast in low-keyed terms, Indian policies in respect to the Indian Ocean states have, in recent years, begun to provide a substantial dividend. The Middle East, Gulf, and East African states have become large importers of Indian skilled personnel, manufactures, and engineering services. Ironically, the oil price increases by Middle East-Gulf suppliers have provided India with both an argument and an opportunity to persuade those states to import more from India. Though modest in comparison to Western states' exports, Indian sales to the area have tended to increase by an average of 20 percent per annum. The same process, at a slower rate, is occurring in relation to the East African states. Future Indian objectives call for expanding trade with the Southeast Asian countries in a similar manner. Indian economic strategy has now enlarged to include the provision of substantial aid and credit facilities to importing states beyond South Asia. Thus, in March 1978, India undertook to provide a wide range of Indian goods and consultancy services to Vietnam financed by a $100 million credit from Indian coffers. Similar deals with other states are forecast, some of the candidates being along the Indian Ocean littoral in the direction of the Persian Gulf.

The calls for greater regionwide economic cooperation, made by the more vigorous and financially secure littoral states, aid the Indian economic push among the Indian Ocean states. As the state with the largest industrial, scientific, and economic capability as well as a diverse range of natural raw materials, India is in a position to benefit substantially if such plans find acceptance. Under the shah, Iran was the prime mover in expounding the concept of a "common market" for the Indian Ocean states. It sought to begin the process by an enlargement of the Regional Cooperation for Development (RCD) so as to include India in the arrangement along with the initial membership of Turkey, Iran, and Pakistan. Pakistan objected to such Iranian schemes, but what was important was the newer and more innovative frameworks for interaction between long-standing adversaries. In the wake of the Iranian revolution, India and Pakistan have begun to display new interest in mutual cooperation. Although Pakistan continues to advance a dynamic Middle East policy, Islamabad recognizes its need to live within the subcontinent, and especially with its larger neighbor. The Pakistani government might be more agreeable to India's request for overland transit facilities to allow for the increasing two-way trade between the Persian Gulf states and India. The Pakistanis seem more inclined to honor the request and for a normalization of Indo-Pakistani contacts—a process that began in small ways with the slow renewal of trade, rail, and postal communications between the two subcontinental states.

It seems that Indian leaders now place a heavier emphasis on symbolic and practical affirmation for their state among the Indian Ocean states. More understanding is being accorded to the anxieties of the smaller South Asian states in their relations with India. Thus, India relented in 1977 from its earlier strongly held position on the division of the Ganges waters with Bangladesh and in matters of trade and transit facilities affecting Nepal. In both cases, India signed agreements that assuaged the fears and met the terms demanded by the latter two states. Prime Minister Gandhi's policies, however, appear to threaten these arrangements engineered by the Janata government.

In Southeast Asia a new grouping of states under the title of the Asian and Pacific Regional Commonwealth (APRC) has come into being. Its membership includes India, Australia, and ten other local states, and it might eventually replace the Association of South East Asian Nations (ASEAN), which has a membership of five, two of whom, Singapore and Malaysia, have also joined the APRC. In an independent development, Indian-Chinese contacts have been renewed without the rancor of the past and have led to the exchange of delegations, greater diplomatic contacts, and negotiations for trade. The Indian foreign minister visited Beijing, and his Chinese counterpart engaged in talks in New Delhi in 1981.

In quiet ways, therefore, a range of political, economic, and diplomatic activities relating to the Indian Ocean have involved India in significant measure. Neither spectacular nor dramatic, the cumulative effect of those activities is, nonetheless, supportive of India's general political and strategic objectives: to reduce the country's reliance on external powers, first, in matters that effect India's internal situation and, second, in relation to geographical areas whose conditions influence Indian security.

In a separate development, Indian security managers now tend to view nonalignment with military power as maintaining the benefits that existed earlier for their state without a basis in power. In this context, the substance of Indian nonalignment has become somewhat indistinguishable from the policies of other larger states. That is, for a relatively weaker India, nonalignment in the short term was a balancing act that sought reductions in the "laws of the political framework" and increases in the "laws of reciprocity" across the conflicts of the international system. Today, in discounting the present for future gains and with the experience of numerous wars, India's nonalignment appears to have become a search for equal status with other large states, and hence a search for equal power.

INDIA'S SECURITY PERCEPTIONS

In terms of the usual indicators, the changes in India's "power" over the past 34 years seem quite impressive. At independence in 1947, India had possessed an army of 300,000, an air force of two fighter and one transport squadrons, and a navy comprising four sloops, two frigates, and some harbor-defense craft. Lethal armament-manufacturing capacity was almost nonexistent, the military officer corps consisted mainly of noncommissioned officers (NCOs), captains, and majors, and the new leadership had had little experience with the role or use of armed forces as instruments of state policy.

By the 1980s, India had acquired the world's third largest standing army, fifth largest air force, and eighth largest navy. Its indigenous armament industry was the largest among third world noncommunist states in value, volume, diversity of manufacture, and research and development (R&D) facilities. The country's military officer corps numbered anywhere from 20,000 to 40,000, large numbers of whom were trained for staff-level duties. It has also absorbed lessons from four substantial external wars and one continuing internal war in northeast India. In all of those conflicts, negative interactions had occurred for India with one or another of the world's major military powers.

Through its nuclear and space activities India has exhibited an ability—and some would say the intent—to acquire a strategic weapon and delivery system in the coming decade. New Delhi, however, has consistently emphasized the peaceful uses of nuclear energy and the need for a total ban on all nuclear weapons. India's intentions notwithstanding, Pakistan's efforts to join the nuclear club have not been lost on Indian decision makers.* Supporting the military effort is

---

*See Prime Minister Indira Gandhi's reply to a debate on Defense Ministry Grants, *India News*, April 20, 1981, p. 7; and "Must India Have the Bomb: A Debate," *World Focus* 18 (June 1981).

the world's tenth largest industrial base and third largest stock of skilled and technical manpower. Understanding India's security experience is, therefore, a useful means for assessing national perceptions of threat, the policy measures employed to counter those threats, and the frameworks within which the nation's governing elites have moved to synthesize, over time, the varying needs of development and defense.

1947-50. Immediately upon independence, the Nehru government took steps formally and effectively to reduce the public eminence of the (British) Indian army, which, in nationalist perceptions had previously discharged the functions of "an army of occupation" in India. The military's draft on the public exchequer was drastically reduced, its senior officers' ranks in state warrants of precedence were lowered, and its subordinate role relative to civilian-political authority was abundantly clarified. The military organization was to be maintained as an arm of state in a world of nation-states, but it seemed during the early years of independence that its strength was to be worked out on no more meaningful a sense than an ability to resist Pakistan. A defense committee of the cabinet took over the direction of defense policies, but—with the experience of the 1948 Indo-Pakistani war over Kashmir—defense planning and strategic contingency provided for little more than Indian army movements across the Punjab plain in case of future wars with Pakistan. With an initial two-to-one superiority in men and arms, India took hold of two-thirds of Kashmir in 1948. It was assumed that Pakistan would remain inferior in military strength to India and be unable to force her hand in the dispute over Kashmir.

1950-54. The second event of importance during the early years with a bearing on Indian security occurred in 1950 with the Chinese takeover of Tibet. A high-level North and North-Eastern Border Defense Committee was established in 1951 and submitted its report in early 1953. The effect of its recommendations was mainly to permit a shoring up of border defenses on the Indo-Tibetan boundary. As one writer has noted: "While fully aware of the strategic implications of China's occupation of Tibet, the Indian government . . . responded to the altered Himalayan situation in a manner that must be described as politically discreet, diplomatically cautious, economical of financial and material resources, and projected over a long time."[2] At least up to 1957, the Indian government seemed to avoid a "vigorous and publicized program of Himalayan security measures" in the belief that such activities would "compromise the government's professions of friendship and goodwill toward China and provoke the very response which Indian diplomacy sought to prevent an overt challenge along the long Himalayan frontier."[3]

In a broader geopolitical context, Indian leaders harbored no deep-seated anxieties about the global intent of the United States or the Soviet Union in relation to their country. To obviate any doubts that may have existed, Nehru announced a policy of opening detente with the Soviet Union parallel to the detente that already existed with the Western states. While stating that "we intend cooperating with the United States of America and we intend cooperating fully with the Soviet Union,"[4] the Indian prime minister also explained in Parliament that "in accepting economic help, or in getting political help, it is not a wise policy to put all your eggs in one basket."[5] Indeed, the wider strategic implications of what came later to be termed as "Indian neutralism" (and now as "nonalignment") had been enunciated by Nehru in 1931:

> It may be that some will covet her, but the master desire will be to prevent any other nation from possessing India. No country will tolerate the idea of another acquiring the commanding position which England occupied for so long. If any power was covetous enough to make the attempt, all the others would combine to trounce the intruder. This mutual rivalry would itself be the surest guarantee against an attack on India.[6]

It can be said with a fair measure of certainty that, from 1947 until today, India's broad framework of security policymaking has not diverged from the preceding geostrategic assessment. Such changes as have occurred have been tactical and temporary and, once played through, have provided mainly for an increase in Indian military power and a restatement of the country's "nonalignment."

1954-62. When the third event of importance calling for Indian security countermeasures occurred in 1954 with the signing of a mutual security pact between the United States and Pakistan, the Indian response was twofold. Viewing the pact as one that "brought the cold war to its doorstep," India first tried to dissuade the cosignatories from going ahead with their plan. When that attempt failed, and large quantities of American arms-without-payment started flowing into Pakistan, India responded with purchases of her own from sundry non-American sources (but not, at that stage, from the Soviet Union). As it happened, India lost its earlier two-to-one superiority over Pakistan in armor and aircraft and retained it only in numbers of infantry. For a short period there was some alarm about the possibility of "Pakistan Patton tanks clanking down the Grand Trunk Road to Delhi." However, Pakistan equaled but never acquired a substantial edge over India in attack weapons systems either on the ground or in the air. As such, Pakistan managed to "balance" India in the early stages of its security relationship with the United States but never possessed—probably according to American design—any offensive capacity against India. With such an assessment of "curbs" upon the overall Pakistani capability, India security managers were at liberty to institute long-term measures to thwart the Pakistanis. The answer was to commence work on the indigenous production of arms so that, over time, Pakistan could be militarily neutralized without requiring heavy changes in future Indian "neutralist" policies to suit external weapons suppliers. By the end of the 1960s, it was apparent to Indian security analysts that American arms transfers to Pakistan, though eventually amounting to $2 billion worth and large in absolute terms, would come in such annual appropriations as India could match from its own financial resources.* This it proceeded to do, while at the same time slowly laying the foundations of an indigenous armament industry.

1962-65. The fourth event of security importance for India occurred in 1962 in the form of the "border war" with China. While highly alarming at the time for the Indian leadership, its long-term effect on security planning was really one of degree rather than of kind in policy purpose. In the first panic of reverses at Chinese hands, India appeared to abandon selectivity in the sources of its weapons supplies. Equipment came, in the short term, from as contradictory sources as the United States, the Soviet Union, Great Britain, West Germany, Canada, and Yugoslavia. China, in fact, charged that Western imperialists had allied with Soviet revisionists in support of Indian reactionary ruling circles. However, the long-term defense needs of the country were assessed not in the context of a large-scale supply of arms purchased from other countries but on gearing local production to meet those needs. Interim purchases would be undertaken, but the substantive change was that the earlier leisurely pace of developing an indigenous conventional weapons production base was speeded up and its requirements formalized as high-priority items within the general context of planned development. Beginning in 1964, five-year defense plans became "rolling" adjuncts on a continuous basis of the country's five-year economic development plans.

The second major effect of the border war was that the Indian government took the decision, in its aftermath, to upgrade considerably the numbers, weapons, training, firepower, and mobility of the country's armed forces. In summary, what had until then been jocularly described—even by ministers of the Indian cabinet—as "our parade ground armed forces" was to be converted into a modern and integrated military establishment. Its tasks and hence its functional complement of men and material were defined in precise terms so as to provide the country with the ability simultaneously to fight—and dominate—all of Pakistan's military forces and all Chinese forces in Tibet.

1965-71. It is probable that the large-scale increases and modernization of the Indian armed forces following the border war with China led to India's fifth significant security event. Aware of the reality that India's armed strength would soon become overwhelming, Pakistan may have sought a solution to the Kashmir problem before time ran out for her. In any case, a 22-day war broke out between the two countries in September 1965—that is, within a year of the

---

*U.S. official sources admit military assistance and sales to Pakistan from 1950 to 1973 of only $672.5 million and $89.1 million respectively. (See Department of Defense, Security Assistance Agency, *Foreign Military Sales and Military Assistance Facts*, April 1974, pp. 17, 19.) However, Indian estimates totally discount the above figures, interpreting them as a function of the frequent procedure whereby military grants and sale items are declared as "excess defense items," or items in surplus, and marked down in value for accounting purposes.

commencement of India's first five-year defense plan.[7] Pakistan, however, was unable to wrest Kashmir from India. The tactical gains by either side during the military campaign were minor, and they were traded off in the peace negotiations that followed at Tashkent.

The Russian venue and sponsorship of the peace negotiations were themselves unusual. For separate reasons, both Pakistan and India rejected Western initiatives for settling the peace. Pakistan objections were that the United States and Britain withheld military supplies to the two combatants once the war started, thereby hurting Pakistan's U.S.-created military capability more than India's diversified weapons base. India, on the other hand, had always held the Western states more partisan in behalf of Pakistan. Likewise, the Russian offer to sponsor negotiations was accepted by the subcontinental states for varying reasons. India's case on Kashmir had consistently found more favor in Moscow than Washington, and so had its rearmament plans following the border war with China. Pakistan, meanwhile, sought to diversify the sources of its military and political support and complicate those of India by inviting Russian aid for itself. In addition, the Indians had feared collusive military action between China and Pakistan ever since the 1962 border war. During the campaign in 1965, the Chinese did signal hostile intent, accusing Indian troops of having transgressed into Tibetan territory and undertaking military maneuvers of their own close to the northern Indian border. While an attack did not materialize, the obvious attempt at joint Sino-Pakistani pressure on India reinforced Indian images of a possible two-front war contingency in the future. In relation to security assessment and planning, the perceptive effect was to make India that much more determined to implement its extensive rearmament goals. Pakistan's ability to seek accommodation and receive benefits in varying amounts from such ideologically diverse states as the United States, China, and the Soviet Union impressed Indian security analysts immensely. It ensured that Indian recompense would be sought by—and in the long term only by—an indigenously based, and therefore independent, arms industry and military organization.

1971-77. By the time that India's sixth crucial security event in the form of the 1971 Indo-Pakistani war over (then) East Pakistan occurred, the Indian armed forces had been thoroughly reorganized.[8] The first five-year defense plan, 1964-69, had been implemented, and the second one had commenced. When the war came in late 1971, India embarked upon the campaign with a superiority over Pakistan in effective-equivalent combat terms of eight to one in aircraft, four to one in troops, three to one in armor, and five to one in naval vessels. More important, all the small arms and ammunition, and significant proportions of the aircraft, artillery, armor, and naval vessels on the Indian side were of local origin. Staff planning for the war on the Indian side was of subcontinental dimensions. Three hundred thousand troops were on combat alert—and if necessary, deployable—on the northern borders, and 500,000 soldiers were evenly divided on the western and eastern fronts against Pakistan. The ground movements were integrated with naval attack squadrons deployed across the Bay of Bengal and the Arabian Sea and an air campaign that implemented an average of 1,500 sorties per day. Although not so obvious to external observers, the war's results were a foregone conclusion in Indian assessments prior to the war.

Certain events before and during the hostilities could not be predicted, and it is possible that they will eventually carry wider implications than the immediate consequences of the war. The first of the unpredictable events was an initial wavering in Soviet support for India in the months preceding their Treaty of Peace and Friendship of August 1971. The second one was the dramatic U.S. opening to China, with the secret Kissinger trip to Peking via Islamabad and Pakistani help and knowledge of the arrangement. The third was the statement of Washington intent delivered to Indian leaders by Kissinger soon after his Peking visit: If India intervened in the East Pakistan situation and China responded militarily along with Pakistan, India could not count on U.S. support.[9] Indian leaders viewed the Kissinger statement as a direct threat carried on behalf of Peking and a visible sanction on behalf of Washington. Finally, during the hostilities itself, the United States ordered Task Force 74, led by the nuclear powered and armed aircraft carrier *Enterprise*, into the Bay of Bengal. By all informal accounts, the Indian decision to proceed with a nuclear test was taken in the context of the preceding series of occurrences. Likewise, India's rocket and electronics development programs were sharply upgraded in the months that followed the 1971 war.

1977–85. Current Indian security concerns relate to two events that are still in the process of unfolding. The first is the likely geostrategic impact of increasing and permanent superpower naval deployments in the Indian Ocean. Substantial bases are being constructed by the United States and the Soviet Union at various points in and near the Indian Ocean. The second arises from the immense supply of arms into the Persian Gulf region and the possibility that a significant proportion of them might be surreptitiously released—and in a hostile situation, openly provided—to Pakistan. Thus, from the Indian perspective, a totally new and geographically wider area of strategic interaction has arisen. The perception of security threats in the altered circumstances is novel inasmuch as the threats imply Indian responses whose spatial framework would have to be larger than the subcontinent. Such a situation has not existed in the past 30 years so that Indian security analysts have little experience deliberating the related issues. It seems clear, however, from a series of statements by Indian spokesmen that superpower naval ingress into the Indian Ocean and weapons supply activity in the Persian Gulf area are of prime concern to them.[10] The visit of British Prime Minister Margaret Thatcher to India in April 1981, again prompted Indira Gandhi to voice her concern over increasing military tensions in the region. The Indian prime minister left no doubt that she considered United States arms policies to be primarily responsible for the area's high volatility. India, she intimated, had no choice but to sustain its military preparedness.

Prime Minister Gandhi had earlier noted that her government spent only 3.9 percent of its GNP on armaments, a figure supposedly lower than that of Pakistan and the great powers.

POLITICAL AND MILITARY RAMIFICATIONS OF INDIA'S SCIENTIFIC, TECHNOLOGICAL, AND INDUSTRIAL GROWTH

The keys to understanding Indian application science, technology, industrial capacity, and economic means to military preparedness are the following: the primal value placed on achieving a large measure of self-sufficiency for the economy as a whole; the policy and capability of drafting support for the country's economic development within its own network of choices from both the socialist and nonsocialist sectors of the international economy; the decision to accept the transfer of manufacturing techniques and plant and to reject contracts that seek merely to assemble goods in India from components manufactured abroad; the requirement that Indian personnel be inducted for training in the construction and running of any plants set up in India by foreign contractors; the early emphasis on the creation of a heavy industrial base for the national economy; and the absolute size, growth, and structural transformation of the Indian economy rather than its performance in per capita terms.

Given the preceding conditions, India's defense production sector has grown as a normal and not a special part of the industrial economy. Its growth and its shortcomings parallel the overall experience with industrialization, the only difference being that security assessments demanded a speedier advance for defense procurement after the border war with China than before it. India's economic growth rates have averaged between 3 and 4 percent per annum since the 1950s, hiding the fact that its industrial growth rate has been about 7 to 8 percent compounded annually over the same period. In the crucial field of machine building and heavy industry—a sector of direct relevance to defense production—the compounded growth rates have been in the region of 10 to 11 percent annually. These figures are fairly similar to China's in percentage-change terms, although the absolute size of the Chinese economy was initially and remains larger than the Indian. Like China, India now produces 95 percent of all its ongoing requirements for heavy industrial machinery, plant, and equipment. The "self-reliance" of the People's Republic of China (PRC) is no greater than India's.

Complementing the structural transformation of its industrial economy, India has also developed a large reservoir of skilled and technical manpower across a wide range of scientific disciplines. Numbering close to 2 million, it is the third largest absolute stock of trained manpower in the world, smaller than those of the United States and the Soviet Union and larger than those of China, Great Britain, France, Germany, or Japan. It is doubling on base every ten years, and future plans call for tripling the current annual output of science and technology graduates by 1986. As one study assesses, India now has "an autonomous scientific community."[11]

To stabilize the process of scientific and technological change, the Indian government organized in 1971 a separate Department of Science and Technology and a policymaking National Committee on Science and Technology. A science and technology plan that was implemented and integrated with the five-year economic and defense plans has the clear objective of promoting "science and technology and their application to the development and security of the nation."[12] The areas of special endeavor are energy, mining, metallurgy, heavy and design engineering, chemicals, atomic energy, outer space, electronics, agriculture, housing, health, and education. Of an outlay of $2 billion in nominal exchange parities over the 1974-79 period—but 2.5 times higher if the rupee's internal purchasing power is taken into account—approximately one-third was allocated to atomic energy and space research and another significant proportion to electronics and computer-related research. As will be discussed later, the allocations to nuclear, space, and electronics research serve the needs of both development and defense.

Distinct from the general scientific and technological effort, which is geared to socioeconomic developmental objectives and defense sophistication in a wider sense, there exists in India a specific organization for conventional weapons research, design, and prototype production. The Defense Research and Development Organization (DRDO) manages 34 major establishments and laboratories, employs a scientific and technical staff of approximately 6,000 and is concerned with narrowly focused weapons projects, namely: duplication, modification, improvement, standardization, and import substitution of components; the development of prototype weapons to suit local terrain; the creation of facilities for the local repair and refitting of foreign weapons; the provision of spares through local entrepreneurs; and research in special materials and alloys.[13] The actual weapons development projects in hand remain classified, but the general areas in which the DRDO's own seven-year research plan (1972-79) lays emphasis have been indicated as follows: missile technology, aeronautics, radar technology, underwater naval weaponry, infrared devices, low-level night photography equipment, solid and liquid propellants, inertial navigation systems, sonobuoys, and armored vehicles. The budgetary allocations for the DRDO are probably in ranges of $50 to $100 million in nominal exchange parities (and 2.5 times higher with the rupee's internal purchasing power).[14]

During the period up to 1962,

India has made substantial progress in developing local sources of defense equipment, particularly after 1959, on a foundation that was built in less spectacular fashion between 1947 and 1958. HAL's [Hindustan Aircraft Limited] Aero-Engine Division had achieved the distinction of being the first organization in noncommunist Asia to manufacture a gas turbine aero-engine. The HJT-16 was the first jet aircraft designed by an Afro-Asian country without help from either of the two power blocs. The HF-24 project gave India the distinction of being one of only four or five countries to proceed with the development of a supersonic fighter aircraft.[15]

For the army, the country was manufacturing almost 80 percent of all the required equipment. The number of ordnance factories was increased to 22, with production lines newly created for heavy trucks, jeeps, and patrol wagons. In 1962, a contract was signed with Vickers-Armstrong for the progressive manufacture of a modified version of the British Chieftain tank. In the naval field, the Indian government acquired two private shipyards for expansion and modernization with a plan to build small defense vessels, minesweepers, frigates, and eventually destroyers and submarines.

The deficiencies that nevertheless remained can be summarized as follows: the design base was largely foreign, sophisticated equipment was still imported, the supporting chemical-industrial base was narrow, and production was mainly of a prototype rather than of an assembly line nature. Considering the subsequent confrontation with China, no attempt had been made for the provision of mountain warfare equipment. Finally, financial allocations for defense production took their (low) turn in central budget disbursements to all the ministries. Indeed, whatever additional outlays were gleaned were probably due to the personality of the then-minister for defense production, V. K. Krishna Menon.

After the border war with China, the whole attitude toward defense changed in India, and its sectoral needs became unquestionable elements of all succeeding annual budgetary and plan investments. The first defense plan (1964-69) laid down the following objectives: a well-equipped army of 825,000 men, and a constant review of this strength for further increases when required; a 45-squadron modern combat air force, replacement of old aircraft, and improvement of air defense and communication facilities; replacement of overage ships of the navy; improvement of the border roads network; strengthening of the indigenous defenses production base; and improvement of the country's defense organization.[16]

The expenditure on the implementation of the program was placed at 50 billion rupees ($10 billion approximately at the pre-1966 devaluation rate), with a foreign exchange component of approximately 7 billion rupees. The guidelines in planning defense production were as follows: the production of efficient and modern weapons; placing the country progressively in a position of general self-sufficiency; stockpiling of items with slow obsolescence rates; emphasis in research and development of equipment suited to Indian conditions; utilizing capacity in the civilian sector to the maximum extent; and achievement of high standards in managerial and technical skills in defense industries.

The organization of defense came to be shared by an inner Defense Committee of the Indian cabinet, an outer National Defense Council, and a specialized Defense Research and Development Council. By 1965, a Defense Planning Cell was created "to deal with all wider aspects of planning which have a bearing on defense in both the medium and long term aspects, and to maintain constant liaison with the Economic Planning Commission." By 1966–67, a reorganized Department of Defense Supplies was made responsible for substitution of imported components by indigenous producers through utilization of local industrial capacity and coordination of scientific and technological research in the country with the work of the Defense Research and Development Organization. Additionally, 15 military schools to act as feeders to the National Defense Academy (Khadakvasla) and the Indian Military Academy (Dehra Dun) were established on a statewide basis.

The second and third defense plans (1969–74 and 1974–79) called for approximate expenditures of 72 to 75 billion rupees each. Thus, by the end of the 1970s India's rearmament and force modernization, begun in 1964, cost some $30 billion, or $2 billion per year over a 15-year period.

By 1978, defense production had become the second largest sector of the Indian industrial economy and consisted of 34 major ordnance establishments, employing over 150,000 workers and manufacturing all light, heavy, and armored equipment for the army, and a wide range of stores and technical instruments for the navy and air force; and 8 large defense public-sector undertakings, with numerous factories located across the country, employing 75,000 workers, and producing specialized and sophisticated equipment and weapons for all the three services.

Indian defense plants now turn out an extensive range of conventional weapons for the Indian armed forces—small arms, field and antiaircraft radar/recoilless guns, howitzers, mortars, support electronics, antitank, antiaircraft, and naval missiles, armored tanks and personnel carriers; trainer, piston, transport, subsonic, supersonic, helicopter aircraft; antisubmarine warfare frigates, fast patrol and missile boats, seaward defense gunboats; and a variety of other specialized missiles and ordnances. On a comparative scale, India was producing all categories of weapons that China could, except submarines and nuclear defense systems. Approximately 11 percent of the government's R&D expenditure was being devoted to research in weapons systems.[17] Assessments placed the annual value of Indian arms production at $1 billion in nominal exchange ratios, but $2.5 billion at the internal purchasing power of the rupee.[18] It is to be expected that, with new projects in hand as mentioned below, the total value of weapons production will rise above present levels. The technological and manufacturing capacities now in varying stages of development are an indigenously designed main battle tank, conventional submarine construction, and design of nuclear-powered undersea craft for possible production in the mid-1980s; an indigenously designed STOL, mach. 2 fighter-interceptor-bomber jet aircraft, probably on the specifications of the European Multi-Role Combat Aircraft;

probable licensed production of late model MIG jet aircraft; a variety of missiles for ground, naval, and air warfare; supersonic remote pilotless vehicles; short-, medium-, and intermediate-range rockets and possible adaptation to sea-launch capability; development work on hydrofoil and hovercraft vessels; super alloy compounds and special steels for sophisticated equipment; large helicopters; aircraft accessories; and heavy marine diesel engines.[19]

Two important policy decisions are also being pressed. The first is that all such segments of arms design and production in India as still depend on foreign countries are to be phased out by 1985.[20] The second is that, for reasons partly political and partly commercial, India will enter the arms export market to the extent of 20 percent of its annual production. The sales will amount to $200 to $300 million in nominal exchange value or $500 to $700 million in real-value terms.[21]

The arms exports will be projected in other third world countries where India might have special advantages over traditional weapons suppliers. The principle of "no political strings" will govern Indian arms sales, and it is expected that the category of weapons normally needed in third world states can be produced and sold at lower cost by India. It is also felt that general Indian foreign policy objectives will be served by reducing the dependence on many third world states on traditional arms sources. Therefore, Indian arms export plans are being undertaken in consultation and perhaps on a joint basis with countries such as Yugoslavia. The calculation is that a further progressive capital investment of $1 billion would put the Indian armament industry on a stable basis for local and export purposes.[22]

DEFENSE AND DEVELOPMENT

Separate from the capital investments in defense are the expenditures incurred for the current maintenance of India's armed forces. On an average, between 25 and 30 percent of the Indian federal budgets since independence (that is, excluding state budgets) have been devoted to the annual upkeep of the three services (see Table 3.1).

The per capita expenditures on defense average out at $4 per head in recent years. On a comparative scale, Pakistan's defense expenditures as a percentage of GNP have varied between 7 and 10 percent and expenditure per capita between $9 and $11. While exact data for China are not available, Western assessments are that the Chinese spend about 10 percent of their GNP at a per capita burden of $15 on defense.[23] Thus, in relation to their supposed adversaries, the Indians have devoted appreciably fewer funds to defense purposes. Indeed, on a worldwide comparative scale, Indian defense expenditures figure in the lowest quartile of national defense allocations. In theoretical terms, therefore, India could increase its defense expenditures over a wide margin if it

TABLE 3.1

Defense Burden as a Percent of GNP

Year	Defense Budget ($ million) 1970 Price Exchange	Percent of GNP
1950	334.4	1.6
1951	370.4	1.8
1952	551.1	1.7
1953	548.2	1.7
1954	585.6	1.8
1955	610.2	1.7
1956	607.1	1.7
1957	730.4	2.1
1958	723.2	2.0
1959	674.2	1.9
1960	677.6	1.9
1961	728.0	1.9
1962	1,003.7	2.6
1963	1,642.5	3.8
1964	1,607.6	3.6
1965	1,567.6	3.6
1966	1,480.1	3.4
1967	1,373.2	3.0
1968	1,429.0	3.1
1969	1,511.9	3.0
1970	1,558.2	3.0
1971	1,743.9	3.7
1972	1,995.5	3.7
1973	1,929.0	3.0
1974	2,180.0	3.0
1975	2,660.0	2.8
1976	2,812.0	3.0
1977	3,450.0	3.8

Sources: SIPRI Yearbook, 1974 (Cambridge: M.I.T. Press, 1974), p. 215; United States Arms Control and Disarmament Agency, *World Military Expenditures and Arms Transfers, 1965-1974* (Washington, D.C.: Government Printing Office, 1976), p. 32; *The Military Balance, 1977-1978*, (London: International Institute for Strategic Studies, 1977).

wanted to match the percentage burdens "standardized" by its commonly perceived adversaries or by the major powers.

It is unlikely, however, that India would increase its defense burden over present rates. The conceptual trade-offs in capital or current investments as between the needs of "defense" and "development" appear to have stabilized at existing levels. The strategy implemented once security requirements were perceived as high was to program added expenditures over a time curve rather than to bunch them in a few short years. As a result, the annual burden of increased defense expenses could come from increasing budgets instead of being diverted from existing development projects. Of course, there was some substitution of funds earmarked for development to defense—especially in the initial years of defense modernization—but the negative effects of the change were relatively low and eventually absorbed quite smoothly in total governmental expenditure patterns.

The long-range programming pattern adopted for internal defense reorganization had an analogy in the policies that were to govern interim arms purchases from abroad. Following the war with China, the immediate need for modern weapons in relation to the future contingency of a two-front war were initially placed before Western states. The latters' response was conditional on Indian changes of policy regarding Kashmir, relations with the Soviet Union, and economic arrangements within the country. The recompense asked by Western supplier states was unacceptable to Indian leaders. In consequence and in the dynamics of interstate relations, the USSR became India's major foreign source, from 1964, of arms and, from 1968, of crucial items of licensed manufacture. However, purchases and manufacture agreements were also made elsewhere whenever possible (radar systems from the United States, armored vehicles from Great Britain, antiaircraft missiles from France). Weapons purchases from the USSR were arranged in rupee-payment terms and were reverse-purchase tied— that is, India paid for the weapons in its own currency, which the Soviet Union then spent on the purchase of an equivalent amount of goods from India. The economic burden of such an arrangement was no less than it would have been through more conventional payment terms. However, for a country short of hard currency, the options were limited, as were the sources. Western estimates place India's foreign arms purchases from all sources for the period 1965–75 at approximately $2 billion worth (see Table 3.2). A quantum leap in defense expenditures was forecast in May 1980 when it was revealed India had entered into an agreement with the Soviet Union to obtain $1.6 billion in armaments, including MIG-23 fighter-bombers, MIG-25 reconnaissance/fighters as well as a variety of naval vessels. Moreover, India concluded a long-range military purchase agreement with the Soviet Union, said to approximate $8 billion.*

---

*New York *Times*, July 6, 1981.

TABLE 3.2

India's Foreign Arms Purchases, 1965–75

Year	$ Million (Constant)
1965	189
1966	377
1967	133
1968	212
1969	171
1970	114
1971	257
1972	216
1973	180
1974	117
1975 (est.)	100
Total	2,066

Source: United States Arms Control and Disarmament Agency, *World Military Expenditures and Arms Transfers, 1965-1974* (Washington, D.C.: Government Printing Office, 1976), p. 62.

Before 1980, the average annual import bill for Indian arms purchases varied between $100 and $200 million. The allocations were not unduly burdensome for India and more or less matched the value of Pakistani weapons acquisitions. However, the major difference lay in that India paid for all its foreign arms whereas Pakistan received its $2 billion worth of American arms on a grant basis until 1966 and paid for those it acquired subsequently.

The announcement in June 1981 that the Reagan administration would accelerate arms transfers to Pakistan disturbed but did not surprise New Delhi. President Reagan was determined to expand and update the Pakistani armed forces given the Soviet pressure in Afghanistan and the threat this posed to Pakistan's security. Washington insisted its action was not intended to challenge Indian supriority in South Asia. Moreover, the U.S. government cited statistics that demonstrated India's own heavy commitment to defense. The U.S. decision nevertheless guaranteed an increase in Indian defense expenditures, despite efforts by both New Delhi and Islamabad to enter into serious conversations on their common and conflicted interests. During his visit to Pakistan, P. V. Narasimha Rao. India's foreign minister, attempted to underplay Prime Minister Gandhi's statement decrying Islamabad's new acquisition of U.S. arms by explaining that such comments were expected in Indo-Pakistani relations. Rao implied India was determined to improve its association with Pakistan and had little to fear from the Muslim state.

Rao's diplomacy, however, could not conceal the debate among Indian defense analysts. Representative statements by Ajit Bhattacharjea on July 27–28, 1981, by K. Subrahmanyam on August 12, 1981 (printed in *The Statesman*), and by former Vice Marshal M. B. Naik on August 13, 1981 and A. S. Abraham on August 14, 1981 (appearing in *The Times of India*) addressed themselves to the Pakistani arms buildup. The dominant opinion emphasized India's continuing need to constantly update and sophisticate its armed forces. Indeed by the end of 1981 it appeared India had succumbed to the influences of the arms race and was entering a new stage of military preparedness. A multibillion-dollar deal was arrived at with the French government to provide India with approximately 200 Mirage-2000 aircraft. India also anticipated building the Mirage-2000 in its plants. Even before the F-16 package had been arranged between the United States and Pakistan, India had signed an agreement for the purchase of $1.6 billion of Soviet weaponry on easy credit terms, reported to be 2.5 percent and repayable in 17 years. The agreement was considered to be worth between $8 and $10 billion dollars at Western prices. Moreover, the deal enabled India to obtain additional MIG-23s, T-72 heavy tanks, patrol boats, and a variety of missiles. The sale also provided India with the opportunity to assemble still larger numbers of MIG-23s and T-72s in Indian factories. The Soviet Union also promised to supply India with MIG-25s and MIG-27s. The latter, it is alleged, had not been inducted into the air forces of the Warsaw Pact countries.

The Indian government also agreed to purchase Anglo-French Jaguars from the British Aerospace Company, including a number that were to be assembled locally. Great Britain was also to make available aircraft for India's aircraft carrier, *Vikrant*, while another aircraft carrier was contemplated. West Germany was under contract to supply India with new submarines and the Soviet Union also publicized its intention to transfer eight of its older undersea craft to New Delhi. India purchased several hundred million dollars worth of arms from the United States. This deal involved long-range howitzers, battlefield missile launchers, and thousands of missile projectiles. These purchases, coupled with India's own expanding arms industry, said to be producing $2.5 billion worth of weapons annually and including heavy as well as light arms, major as well as minor systems, and not the least India's advanced nuclear capacity and improving missile delivery program, left little reason to believe India viewed Pakistan as more than a gross irritant.

Rajendra Sareen, editor of *Public Opinion Trends Analyses and News Services*, and Bharat Wariavwala of the Indian Institute for Defense Studies and Analysis were no doubt mindful of India's overwhelming military capability vis-à-vis Pakistan when they sought to influence high Indian officials to reconsider New Delhi's relationship with Pakistan. Sareen put forward his position in a paper entitled "Security Imperatives of South Asia," which was delivered at the India International Centre in December 1980. Wariavwala published the provocative "Timid Search For Status" in *Seminar*, also in December 1980. Both scholars were prompted to make their statements by the Soviet action in Afghanistan, and each concluded that India and Pakistan must find more successful avenues of communication and cooperation. Although penned before the F-16 controversy in the summer of 1981, both apparently retained their essential position. Nevertheless, the burden of Indian arguments appearing in newspapers and journals throughout the country seemed to suggest that India, both officially and unofficially, would continue pointing an angry finger toward the United States and a threatening one toward Pakistan.

STRATEGIC CHOICES AND MILITARY POLICIES

India's postindependence military experience may be visualized in a series of succeeding phases. In the first phase from 1947 to 1962, the country possessed a colonial style and equipped armed forces. National security perceptions and hence the premises for the use of military power were spatially limited to the subcontinent. Military policy was passively reactive to the intent and acts of others—toward Pakistan throughout and China in the later years of the period. Defense allocations were low, and the indigenous backup in weapons production was slow and modest. Strategically, the dependence on the great powers was total.

In the second phase from 1962–72, India proceeded to reorganize, reequip, and restructure its armed forces in a more modern style. Security projections now included the contingency of fighting a conventional war simultaneously on two fronts. One of these fronts still lay within the subcontinent, but the other verged beyond it to the north. Military tactical planning had to conceive of the possibility that in a future confrontation on the Himalayan borders, India had the ability to respond in kind to Chinese ingress into Indian territory. Hence the premises and policy of the Indian force posture moved from a reactive to an active-riposte stage. Allocations to defense took an upward turn, and a long-term rearmament plan based on indigenous sources was put into effect. Interim weapons needs were fulfilled from wherever they could be acquired. While the strategic dependence on the great powers continued as before, conventional defense dependence began to be reduced.

Toward the end of the period, it became possible for India through a combination of force and diplomatic maneuver to undertake a swift conventional military campaign that reduced the power and size of Pakistan and effectively thwarted a 25-year effort to maintain a power balance in the subcontinent. In the allied context of the Himalayan border, the Indian army could be described functionally as composed of two armies—a "mountain army" facing north and a "plains army" facing west. Both armies possessed greater numbers and firepower than their opposite numbers-in-place. Staff planning provided for the interchange of troops and reserves in relatively short order, and succeeding defense lines and roads along both fronts provided for stronger defense and easier access in either case. Considering that modern regional wars using conventional weapons are likely to be of a limited duration, India had probably acquired the ability to defend itself without outside help on the two fronts. Such dependencies as existed had a short half-life, were not crucial, and could not in the interim unduly damage the country's military capabilities.

The third phase may be viewed as beginning from 1972 and stretching to the middle or late 1980s. In terms of conventional defense and security, the country is likely to move to a position of virtual independence in the use of force within and on the borders of the subcontinent. This situation will exist despite the facility of any state within the subcontinent to invoke external military help in what could be described as "reasonable amounts" (e.g., Pakistan's arms deal with the Reagan administration) or despite the ability of states bordering on the subcontinent to apply such force as would be possible for them, given their total security needs (e.g., Iran and Afghanistan, neither of which are in a position to threaten Indian security). Moreover, China is likely to become more friendly toward India given its preoccupation with the Soviet Union and Vietnam. The June 1981 visit of Vice Premier and Foreign Minister Huang Hua to New Delhi and the cordial statements made by both parties were aimed at reducing the distance between their respective positions.

Current plans for augmentation of armed strength, military organization and management, and technical-industrial support for defense production indicate objectives that seek to reduce the unpredictabilities that could still face Indian security managers. Thus, the Indian air force of 2,000 planes, of which half are combat jets organized in 45 squadrons, is to be increased to a combat squadron strength of 64. The armored formations of the land forces, at approximately 3,000 tanks, is considered sufficient for the moment but could be subject to increases were it conceivable that Pakistan had short-order access to armor from beyond the subcontinent. India's troop strength at 1.2 million men is larger than those of Pakistan combined with the Chinese forces in Tibet. The "teeth-to-tail" structure of the land forces is such that India could field considerably more troops than its standing army. Besides, there are some indications that the strength of the army is understated.[24] Indeed, if one includes reserves and paramilitary units that exist beyond the regular army, the country's trained military manpower would be reckoned at a substantially higher level than 1.2 million. As regards the navy, a special ten-year program is under implementation whose outlines are two navies, one each for the western and eastern Indian Ocean, both able to function independently of each other; the development of Vishakapatnam, Bombay, Cochin, and Port Blair in the Andaman Islands into large naval bases; 20 to 25 submarines; fast missile-deploying boats; missile cruisers; possibly Tu-22 squadrons for naval reconnaissance up to an arc of 1,000 miles; and increases in naval fixed-wing aircraft of the fleet air arm.[25]

In spite of the projected growth in its military force posture over the third phase, India's conventional military reach will remain basically limited to the Indian subcontinent. The need, if it arises, to extend the spatial context of Indian military power beyond the subcontinent could be met only through a deliberate decision to acquire a nuclear strike and delivery force. No such decision appears to have been taken. It is obvious, however, that India could not for long conceal a decision to purchase a nuclear strike force. Trigger lists of items and activities that lead toward nuclear force acquisition are maintained by the great powers, and an Indian effort in that respect would be quickly revealed.

It would appear that—even assuming affirmative intent—India is not in a position to go in for an operational nuclear strike force at present. Such a capability will come within its reach by the end of the current phase, and then only the need for a nuclear strike-force "decision" will make it possible. Meanwhile, it is useful to consider the commensurate military application potentials that the country is set to acquire through its civilian nuclear and space programs.

India's civilian nuclear establishment is among the largest in the world, and among noncommunist third world countries it is the oldest and largest. As with other Indian endeavors, it is highly autarkic in function and capability. Beginning with the construction without foreign help of Asia's (outside of the USSR) first nuclear reactor in 1965, India has a half-dozen experimental nuclear research reactors, all but one built without foreign participation; three 500-megawatt nuclear power stations and two more at different stages of construction and design; the ability to design and construct, from equipment manufactured indigenously, one nuclear power station of 500-megawatt capacity every second year—the first country after the United States, the USSR, Canada, Western Europe, and Japan; the ability to provide or fabricate all sensitive nuclear instrumentation, fueling assemblies, special alloys and materials, heavy water, fissile plutonium and thorium from its own separation plants, and, according to speculation, thermonuclear fissile substances; Asia's largest and first nationally constructed variable-energy cyclotron; a major research establishment outside Bombay, which employs approximately 8,000 research and engineering personnel; a second research structure at Kalpakkam (Tamil Nadu) on the lines and scale of the Bombay establishment for specialized research in thorium-fueled breeder-reactor technology; a cadre of trained nuclear research personnel that figures at around 30,000, this being the number included in the nationwide nuclear safety-badge service; and an integrated public-private sector, industrial-units organization to back the nuclear autarky drive in all stages from the mining of ores to the commissioning of nuclear power plants.[26]

In effect, India's nuclear program has been comprehensive and general purpose so that in technical capacities, it could support a weapons project and civilian needs simultaneously. With the completion of the 1980-85 phase of nuclear activities, India will be producing three tons of fissile plutonium annually. Most of this explosive material will be required for the running of civilian nuclear power stations, but the extended military options from possession of explosive elements in such quantities are evident. Indian scientists have also discovered processes for separating fissile U-233 from thorium, are known to be working in laser-applied experiments for uranium enrichment (U-235) technology, and can acquire thermonuclear explosive compounds such as deuterium, lithium, and tritium from existing facilities. In the context of the preceding competencies, India's nuclear explosion of May 18, 1974, amounted to a major political decision but a relatively modest technical event.

The backup organizationally, managerially, and technically in rocket delivery systems is already available in short-range categories and in process of acquisition for long-range purposes. The rocket development program began earnestly in 1967. Between 1970-74, space research establishments in India had developed and tested inertial guidance systems, telemetry equipment, rate gyroscopes, heat shields, nose cones, electronic payload systems, and a wide variety of high specific-impulse solid and liquid propellants.[27] In 1975, a locally fabricated 300-kilogram satellite was launched under an agreement with the Soviet Union using a Molniya rocket, a second one went up in 1978. On June 19, 1981, India launched its first experimental telecommunication satellite. According to a press release from the Indian Space Organization in Bangalore, the satellite was placed in a high geostationary orbit and was more sophisticated than three other Indian satellites launched earlier. In this instance, India combined forces with the European Space Agency and the rocket carrying the satellite was launched from French Guyana. A project for the development of a four-stage rocket with orbital-launch capability and the lofting of further satellites was due to be completed by 1982. Current reports suggest successful test firings of clustered rockets using single boosters, a development with straight military application possibilities. Earlier in 1974, the chairman of the Indian Space Commission had stated that the country then possessed the ability to produce missiles of 1,800 to 2,000 mile range with locally developed solid fuels and guidance systems.

The Indian space program appears to have been sharply upgraded since May 1972—that is, after the Bangladesh events. Set up at that time were a Space Commission and a Department of Space, both charged with time-bound schedules for technical and applied achievements. Because of a late start, India's space decisions indicate a pattern of achievement aims that appear to tumble over each other. Simultaneously, a short-range rocket, a medium-range rocket, a space launch vehicle, and scientific satellite fabrication and lofting capabilities were in various stages of inception. The first phase of the program, to be completed by the mid-1980s, was to enable India to lift 1,200-kilogram payloads into geostationary earth orbits at 40,000 kilometers in space.

The stated objective of Indian space work is to achieve a satellite launch facility for communication and educational purposes.[28] India is already the first country in the world to experiment with a large-scale program of televised instruction by satellite transmission. Approximately 9,000 personnel already support the space effort, and still larger numbers are being trained. As with the nuclear program, Indian policymakers will inherit military launch capabilities along with the civilian purposes of the space-related activities.

If we assume the ability exists, the need to convert nuclear explosives and civilian-use rockets into weapons and missiles will depend primarily on events and their course beyond the subcontinent. The main actors in this regard will be the superpowers, and the activities that might influence an Indian strategic-force purchase decision are among the following: the level and extent of superpower naval deployments in the Indian Ocean; the incentives and instances of external intervention in the affairs of the littoral states; indirect or direct support of Pakistan by way of weapons supply or otherwise*; increased dangers of war in regions adjacent to India due to the scale of arms transfers therein; the joint use of military bases by Pakistan outside of its territory; the possibility that Pakistan may develop nuclear weapons capability; and negative developments in relations with China. It is not clear, however, at what point Soviet aggressiveness in Afghanistan, or possibly in Iran or Pakistan might cause New Delhi to reconsider its position toward Moscow. Whether Soviet maneuvers are likely to cause the Indians to develop nuclear weapons remains a matter of considerable conjecture at the present time. India seems more inclined toward reducing tension with all its near neighbors.

It is as permissible to assume that the geostrategic environment for India will be benign as to suggest that it will be malevolent. The former situation does not destroy the case for continued research in nuclear and rocket work since the civilian purposes remain and amortize the expenses undertaken. However, if nuclear weapons and delivery systems are eventually sought by India, their impact in an Indian Ocean context may involve the following assumptions:

1. Strategic capabilities have a larger meaning than victory in a nuclear war. They connote the ability to achieve general foreign policy goals, and nuclear weapons increase the potential in this respect before a military clash.

2. For modest nuclear powers, "strategic parity" may require no more than the development of a nuclear defense system sufficient to discourage each other and the dominant nuclear powers from forcing a showdown.

3. Dominant nuclear powers cannot, for all their denials, treat modest nuclear powers as nonnuclear powers.

4. The options for a modest nuclear power would be substantially greater where the vital interests of the dominant powers are not threatened.

---

*On July 10, 1981, Indira Gandhi intimated that the sale of F-16 aircraft to Pakistan by the United States had "pushed" the subcontinent into a new arms race. India, it was argued, had nothing to compare with this advanced weapons system.

5. A sea-launched nuclear capacity—as India might seek—is not a simple strategic capability, however small its complement, and however much it is publicly degraded by the dominant powers. As a semblance of a first-strike potential, it remains a dangerous trigger, cannot be detected easily, and creates a range of uncertainties for the great powers.

6. The threshold for achieving a protected, second-strike deterrent system may be much lower than assumed on the basis of superpower dialogues about parity needs. Likewise, "unacceptable damage" is an unobservable criteria, and its base line may be lower for some states than for others.

7. While unbridled nuclear proliferation may be viewed with alarm by the dominant powers, it is not certain that modest, uncommitted, but potential nuclear allies are wholly disadvantageous to their separate interests or roles.

8. The probability of nuclear threats arising in the "penumbra" zone of interstate relations is likely to be reduced for modest nuclear powers.

9. If nuclear umbrellas were viewed skeptically by those to whom they were offered in the past, it is possible that they would become more certainly available with the acquisition of a "nuisance" nuclear capability—though unasked for by the modest nuclear power or publicly withdrawn by the dominant power.

India's security framework continues to remain geopolitically confined to the subcontinent, and there is little reason other than in speculation to suggest that India will embark upon a nuclear force purchase. The country has no gains to make by exacerbating relations with either superpower as long as there is no attempt to overturn its own regime's ideology and function. If future conditions in the Indian Ocean do raise the possibility of their acquisition, nuclear defense systems would be valued by Indian policymakers as stabilizing low-level disagreements with the great powers while simultaneously increasing the costs of attempts to change the status quo to India's disadvantage—it is hoped, beyond their being worthwhile. As a result the disincentives then as now to move India away from "nonalignment," internally and externally, are likely to be greater, and so would efforts to coerce a negative change. According to Indian analysts, an appropriate environment for India's strategic interaction with the great powers is one that simultaneously precludes their country from being ignored or coerced. In some imperceptible measure, India would move up in the international hierarchy of power. In special circumstances the country's bargaining position, especially in the regional and subcontinental environments, would improve.

The value to India of a strategic strike force does not have to be tied to war scenarios in relation to China. In inner policy counsels, it is probable that a nuclear force purchase will be conceived as a minimax solution for general, unforeseen purposes that have largely to do with political relations with the great powers and little with the country's immediate neighbors. The real reasons certainly lie beyond Pakistan and probably beyond China and other regional powers and perhaps relate mainly to the regime's quest for general system autarky.

In other ways, an Indian nuclear force would most likely increase the regime's legitimacy at home and among third world states—for example, in reducing to some extent the "soft state" image. If strategic weapons are produced, then the country's military power acquisition process will have been somewhat slower than China's over the same period, but perhaps only marginally less comprehensive.

CONCLUSIONS

India's ideological affirmation could be described as sympathetic to the Left, irrespective of the rhetoric of any particular leadership in power. The country's nation-building objectives are broadly defined by parameters that enclose choices that result from such ideological affirmation. At a general level, the security effort grew in size and scope to contend with an international system some of whose members have had ideological or territorial demands on India. At a narrower level—not part of this study but definitely affecting the choices made—arise security objectives conditioned by the internal environment of poverty, population, and multiethnicity. India's "permanent" security threat lies in the potential for a mobilized peasantry. Were such a condition achieved, then all current depictions of the country's national security needs would become inappropriate.

Unlike an earlier generation of Indian political leaders who generally believed in a connection with Western states, a newer generation is now assuming positions of power. Many of them below the top echelons are too young to understand the impact of colonialism or, born after independence, hold a more assertive view on behalf of their state. By 1980 the last officers of the Indian Civil Service created during the British Raj had retired. They have been replaced in crucial appointments within the Indian government. Innocent of Sandhurst, Oxford, or Cambridge, this new generation of senior Indian civil servants is more routinely schooled in the "new state" problems of the country, more functionally adept, and more nationalistic in attitude. Among them, along with ranking self-criticisms of many of the conditions of their society, runs a parallel image that projects India as a future major-power contestant.

In the evolving international strategic system, India's position is in the process of a slow and perhaps favorable stabilization. Subcontinentally, there is no significant conventional threat that India could not contend with. Regionally, the possible effects of developments over which India has no control can be neutralized—to the extent that they impinge upon the country—by a continuation of the steady but low-key program of strategic investments initiated since 1965. The basic thrust of Indian military power and policies designed in relation to it is the acquisition of systemwide autarky. Current dependencies will end in the 1980s. Sometime through this decade, India will possess the potential and face the decision for achieving relative strategic independence.

In a wider framework, India's national role conceptions are those of a big state. They seek symbolic, universalist, and pragmatic gains. The search for independent political and military power is an inevitable concomitant of such societal self-images. In real terms, India's force-acquisition processes reflect objectives in consonance with its own evolving interpretation of the general posture of "non-alignment"—the refusal to accept, even while weak and poor, the world view of other large, powerful, or affluent states.

NOTES

1. For a comparative assessment of the local effects and extent of Iranian and Saudi Arabian arms purchases, see Onkar Marwah, "Iran as a Regional Power: Flexibility and Constraints," in *Conflict and Cooperation in the Persian Gulf*, ed. Mohammed Mughisuddin (New York: Praeger, 1977), pp. 29–45.

2. Lorne J. Kavic, *India's Quest for Security* (Berkeley: University of California Press, 1967), p. 61.

3. Ibid., p. 61.

4. *Independence and After: Speeches of Jawaharlal Nehru, 1946-1949* (Delhi: Publications Division, Ministry of Information and Broadcasting, Government of India, 1949), p. 205.

5. Ibid., p. 217.

6. Kavic, *India's Quest for Security*, p. 23.

7. For a detailed study of the 1965 war, see Russell Brines, *The Indo-Pakistani Conflict* (London: Pall Mall Press, 1968).

8. See Robert Jackson, *South Asian Crisis* (New York: Praeger, 1975).

9. From interviews with a senior Indian official.

10. See Ministry of Defense, Government of India, *Annual Report, 1975-76*; K. R. Singh, "U.S. Relations with India in a Strategic and Security Perspective," in *Great Power Relations, World Order and the Third World*, ed. M. S. Rajan (New Delhi: Vikas, 1981).

11. Richard J. Barber Associates, *LDC Nuclear Power Prospects, 1975-1990: Commercial, Economic and Security Implications* (Washington, D.C.: Department of Commerce, National Technical Information Service, ERDA-52, 1975), p. 87.

12. National Committee on Science and Technology, Government of India, *Draft Science and Technology Plan (1974-79)*, 1974.

13. Ministry of Defense, Government of India, *Annual Report*, 1975-76.

14. SIPRI, *Resources Devoted to Military Research and Development* (Stockholm: International Peace Research Institute, 1972).

15. Kavic, *India's Quest for Security*, p. 136.

16. All subsequent information, unless otherwise stated, concerning the defense plans is derived from *Annual Reports* of the Indian Ministry of Defense for the period 1963-64 to 1975-76. See also K. Subrahmanyan, "The Challenge of the Seventies to India's Security," *India Quarterly* 26, no. 2 (April-June 1970): 32–45.

17. SIPRI, *Resources Devoted to Military Research and Development*.

18. *India Weekly* (London), August 15, 1974. Interview with V. C. Shukla, India's former minister for defense production, p. 11.

19. From interviews.

20. *India Weekly*, August 15, 1974, interview with Shukla.

21. Ibid.

22. *Far Eastern Economic Review*, June 3, 1974, p. 30.

23. Ruth Leger Sivard, *World Military and Social Expenditures 1976* (Leesburg, Va.: WMSE Publications, 1976), p. 26.

24. Ravi Rikhye, "India Continues Military Buildup," *Armed Forces Journal*, August 1972, p. 29. According to Rikhye, "Informed sources say that Indian military strength is greater than India admits. These sources say that India has at least 33+ division equivalents, whereas only 27 are on the books. The Air Force and Navy appear similarly underrated."

25. *Far Eastern Economic Review*, June 3, 1974, p. 30.

26. For further details, see Onkar Marwah, "India's Nuclear and Space Programs: Intent and Policy," *International Security* 2, no. 2 (Fall 1977): 96–121.

27. For further details, see ibid.

28. India is a prime mover in promoting the new international information order. Opportunities for training in broadcasting and telecommunications as well as in journalism are being made available to third world nations and are aimed at breaking the monopoly enjoyed by the Western world. *India News*, June 29, 1981, p. 3.

4

PAKISTAN'S NATIONALITIES DILEMMA: DOMESTIC AND INTERNATIONAL IMPLICATIONS

Lawrence Ziring

India's most important immediate neighbor is Pakistan. The two countries have been bitter enemies ever since their joint independence in 1947, but after three costly wars (1947-48, 1965, and 1971), there are some indications that they may be inclined to reduce the antagonism that has caused them so much concern and grief. Pakistan shows no desire to regain its eastern wing in Bengal, and although Kashmir is a persistent irritant, the likelihood of renewed hostilities in or near the cease-fire line is at this writing judged to be remote. Diplomatic relations were resumed in 1976, and both governments appear eager to promote cordial and proper relations, hence the stepping up of the movement of people and goods across their mutual frontier. From the Indian vantage point Pakistan remains a potential problem, but it is confident that its armed forces are an adequate deterrent to possible adventures. The overthrow of Zulfikar Ali Bhutto in July 1977 by the Pakistani military and the emergence of General Zia-ul-Haq as the Muslim nation's chief spokesman was cause for anxiety in New Delhi. Subsequent actions by the martial law authorities in Islamabad have not arrested fears that the new Pakistani government contemplates aggressive moves. Indeed, tensions increased between the two countries when the Indo-Bangladeshi relationship was strained in 1975, eased during Morarji Desai's tenure as Indian prime minister, and grew again with the Reagan administration's decision to modernize the Pakistani army and air force. Nevertheless, Islamabad is preoccupied with the Soviet occupation of Afghanistan and could hardly contemplate let alone carry out an aggressive move against India.[1]

In point of fact Pakistan can ill afford to threaten any of its neighbors, and especially India. Pakistan is passing through still another difficult period of trial that requires giving full attention to national issues. Pakistan remains a house divided against itself. It is therefore a threat more to its own existence than to others. Moreover, the lessons of the 1971 civil war and the Red Army presence on the Northwest Frontier are clear. If Pakistanis are unable to resolve their own domestic troubles, and particularly the fundamental question of national unity, the temptation to outsiders to meddle in the country's turbulent internal affairs may be uncontrollable.[2] This chapter examines Pakistan's continuing struggle to sustain its territorial integrity, the principal centrifugal forces, and the domestic and international implications of its nationalities dilemma.

THE TWO-NATION AND THE MANY-NATION THEORIES

Ever since its inception Pakistan leaders have cautioned the nation against the "poison" of provincialism. Provincialism has come to mean the elevation of province and local region over country, the preference for peculiar ethnic, linguistic, and tribal groups at the expense of the larger nation. Pakistan, which was born as the result of an appeal to the Muslims of South Asia to protect their religion from the larger community of Hindus in their midst, has not been sustained by that same appeal. While the Islamic religion remains a dominant life-force and Pakistanis are considered devout followers of Muhammad, faith has not prevented different Pakistani nationalities from harming one another, and thus undermining their national structure.[3] Those leaders like Muhammad Ali Jinnah, who believed in and pressed the Two-Nation Theory, obscured what others have identified (if not always articulated) as the Many-Nation Theory.

The Two-Nation Theory was a negative reaction to events that were reshaping the destiny of South Asia in the first half of the twentieth century. Muslims residing in areas where the Hindus predominated sensed a helplessness that could only be reckoned with by the creation of a separate self-governing Muslim nation in India. Their demand, however, was for a state to be carved out of those regions where the Muslims were in a majority and where essentially they were not threatened by the larger community. They did not insist on the acquisition of territory where they resided and with which they were more familiar. Instead the call went out to all Muslims to rally behind the cause of their principal party, the Muslim League, and together to save their endangered religion. In the fury of the charge toward freedom and independence, and for what now must be considered a brief historic moment, the promise of a new Muslim state in India temporarily drove out or subdued other loyalties and national claims.[4] When the dust had settled, however, the Pakistan that had been created, or rather superimposed over Muslim regions that were to a greater or lesser extent Muslim political entities in their own regard, showed itself to be something less than the hoped-for promised land. The exodus of millions of frightened and impoverished Muslims from India and their entrance into Pakistan brought the Two-Nation Theory into regions that were not fully prepared to adapt to the new situation. In the metropolitan areas of the Punjab, as in Dacca and Karachi, the main point of contact between the refugee and indigenous populations, greater sophistication and degrees of cosmopolitanism permitted the assimilation of the Two-Nation Theory, but in the vast outer reaches of the country, the Many-Nation Theory resisted all attempts to extinguish it.

THE EAST BENGAL CASE

Although the Muslim League had a comparatively easier time in winning adherents in East Bengal* than in the provinces of the west wing, it was ironically in the former region that the first signs of serious division appeared and the Many-Nation Theory had its first genuine expression. Virtually on the eve of independence, the Bengalis of Pakistan sensed they were not the masters of their own destiny and that the promise of independence was instead a thicket of thorns. The primary issue focused on the Bengali culture and especially their Bengali language, which had been so passionately cultivated by an emerging semienlightened intelligentsia. From the outset, the distant Karachi government insisted that Urdu would become the lingua franca for the entire country.[5] Sensing that this was the beginning of an elaborate program by West Pakistani authorities to confine them to inferior positions, the Bengalis, led by the student community, rioted. The government's reaction was harsh and grossly unconciliatory. The disturbances were attributed to Hindu members of the intelligentsia who it was said were exploiting a volatile issue in order to destroy the Pakistani state.[6] The population of Pakistan was reminded that the government of India had not yet given up the idea of a united Indian state and that Congress leaders had predicted Pakistan would not last one year. The forcible ouster of Hindus from positions of responsibility and their flight from Pakistan, however, did not bring the expected calm to the country. When Bengali Muslims revealed that their views were no different from those expressed by their Hindu counterparts, they were accused of being anti-Pakistan and in league with the country's number-one enemy. Gag orders, bans on public demonstrations, the imprisonment of numerous political figures, and other police actions followed, but the only real effect was the steeling of Bengali resolve and a growing hatred for their brethren in the western wing.[7]

The departure of the Hindus of Bengal to the greater security of India drained East Bengal of some of its most productive citizens. Into this vacuum came Muslim refugees from India who along with entrepreneurs from West Pakistan and in cooperation with the Pakistani government, began to assume the important economic, financial, and commercial roles in the province. While the Bengali Muslims were prepared to make a place for the displaced Indian Muslims, they were totally unprepared for the influx of these powerful non-

---

*The term East Bengal is used throughout this chapter rather than the term East Pakistan as it was the original description for the province and is considered more germane when discussing the nationalities problem.

Bengali interests. They were also distressed by the large number of government administrators who were sent to East Bengal from the Punjab or were members of the Indian Civil Service (ICS) who had opted for Pakistan rather than remain in India. Bengali Muslims were unimpressed with the statistical argument that at the time of partition there were only a handful of experienced Bengali civil servants.[8] Insofar as the bureaucracy was the most significant decision-making body in the country, the Bengalis understood that policies affecting their future would be made and implemented by persons largely unfamiliar and generally unsympathetic with their life-style. And to add insult to injury, the Pakistani army, which took up stations in East Bengal, was comprised predominantly of Punjabis, Pathans, and Baluchis. The British policy that did not include the Bengalis among the martial races of India was perpetuated by Pakistani authorities, and the token Bengali force that was finally recruited in no way satisfied Bengali demands. Bengali discontent with the center was manifested in formal criticism as well as in street demonstrations that often deteriorated into rioting and widespread arson.[9]

The language riots of February 1952 marked the end of a phase that now can be described as symptomatic of an ailment that was still treatable, and introduced a new phase wherein the disease was permitted to spread.[10] The destruction of the Muslim League at the polls in the East Bengal elections of 1954 and the continuing reluctance of vested interests in West Pakistan to accept a constitution granting the Bengalis representation commensurate with their numbers (approximately 55 percent of the Pakistani population was comprised of Bengalis) were telltale signs. The Bengalis were convinced they could not expect justice in a state dominated by non-Bengalis. Moreover, the federal government's decision to disregard the 1954 elections in East Bengal and the declaration of president's rule in the province, along with the ousting of the Bengali prime minister, Khwaja Nazimuddin, and the dissolution of the Constituent Assembly by a Punjabi governor general, constituted all the evidence the Bengalis required to justify their intensive campaign for expanded provincial autonomy.[11]

The collapse of the first parliamentary experiment in 1958, hardly two years after the promulgation of the constitution, ushered in 44 months of martial law under the leadership of Field Marshal Ayub Khan. While Ayub made some headway in Bengalizing the administration in East Bengal, distrust and alienation deepened.[12] The attentive Bengali public argued that Ayub's rule had been imposed on the country in order to prevent the Bengalis from displaying their prowess in general elections, and hence martial law had denied them their right to govern the nation. Frustrations increased until most politically conscious Bengalis were forced to acknowledge that they were prisoners within their own country—or worse still, had been recolonized by Asian imperialists! The Bengalis continued to believe in Pakistan, or so they tried to convince themselves. Those in power, however, were not really concerned with the success of the Pakistan design. To the Bengalis the Pakistan movement had been entrapped and victimized by unscrupulous power-hungry personalities whose only purpose was maximizing their privileges and already lucrative advantages. Pakistan had become a fiction and a myth for a large segment of sensitive Bengalis, and their desire for more autonomy was inevitably transformed into a call for seccession.[13]

The collapse of the Ayub regime after more than a decade of highly centralized rule was not caused by external stimulus. The 1965 war with India, with the exception of the Bengalis, was supported by virtually all elements in Pakistan. Ayub was criticized for agreeing to terminate the hostilities. He was widely condemned when he agreed to cooperate in disengaging his forces and signed the Tashkent agreement with Indian prime minister Lal Bahadur Shastri. But the political opposition made very little headway in their campaign to oust Ayub by exploiting these emotional issues. Ayub suffered most because of his inability to understand popular problems and from his lifelong conviction that the military-bureaucratic apparatus was best equipped and hence most able to run the country. What the Bengalis had known for two decades, the West Pakistani intelligentsia and largely urban population came to learn in 1968: that is, that the promise of a better life in Pakistan was linked to the degree of real participation by the general public acting through their chosen representatives. The population had had its fill of the administrative state and demanded a return to competitive politics with all its shortcomings. The riots that were ignited in small West Pakistani towns in 1968 spread to the major metropolitan centers just as the government was inaugurating celebrations heralding the Decade of Development.[14] Statistically Pakistan had indeed made progress, but the masses enjoyed little if any improvement in their standard of living. The disturbances released a pent-up anger that had not been experienced in Pakistan since the dark days of partition. The West Pakistani demonstrators called upon Ayub to step down, and they possibly would have been satisfied with that objective had it not been for the Bengalis. In East Bengal, the opportunity presented itself to alter the entire political system, or so the Bengalis led themselves to believe. When they began to riot it was clear they wanted more than Ayub's resignation.

Reluctant to quell the disturbances, the civilian-military complex that provided the pillars of Ayub's administration called upon their once proud leader to step aside. After fitful attempts at shoring up his government failed, humiliated by Zulfikar Ali Bhutto and Mujibur Rahman, who refused to negotiate a settlement with him, Ayub announced his resignation. However, instead of transferring power to civilian politicians, Ayub revealed that General Yahya Khan would head up the new Pakistani government. Few in Pakistan were pleased with the announcement, but in East Bengal the cynicism was more intense than anywhere else in the country. Mujibur Rahman insisted that the Bengalis could not submit to another military government and he hammered away at the central theme of a semiindependent East Bengal, embodied in his six-point program.[15]

The Yahya Khan interregnum appeared to promise a return to civilian leadership, the reinstatement of the parliamentary system that had been eclipsed in 1958, and most important, the dissolution of the One Unit, the administrative and political province of West Pakistan that had been created in 1955 by amalgamating the provinces of the Punjab, Sind, Baluchistan, and the Northwest Frontier Province. In 1970 the Pakistanis were allowed to vote in the first general election in the nation's history, and this too was taken as a measure of the sincerity of Yahya and the military junta in returning power to the people of Pakistan. But then everything went wrong for the West Pakistani elite.

Mujibur Rahman's party, the Awami League, won a majority of the seats in the National Assembly, but all were in East Bengal. Under the Legal Framework Order of 1970, Yahya Khan had at least agreed to permit the Bengalis representation in accordance with their numbers. As a result East Bengal was allocated more seats than all the provinces of West Pakistan combined.[16] The runner-up party in the election was Zulfikar Ali Bhutto's Pakistan People's Party (PPP), and although it did very well in both the Punjab and Sind it controlled only half the number of seats won by the Awami League. Given their majority, the Awami League had the right to believe it would form the next government of Pakistan, but Bhutto in league with elements in the military had other ideas. Supported by vested interests in West Pakistan who feared a Bengali-dominated government, Bhutto pressured Yahya to hold on to power until he and Mujib could agree on a *via media*. Yahya's efforts at reconciling the two politicians were stymied, however, as Bhutto conspired to undercut the negotiations. Even a settlement entered into by Awami League and PPP leaders (J. A. Rahim among them) was turned aside by Bhutto. As the negotiations had reached an impasse, the Bengali population, seized now by the most radical elements in the Awami League, lost all patience, and cries of secession were magnified. Mujibur Rahman could do little more than follow the tide that now rolled through the country.[17]

The army attack in Dacca on March 25, 1971, on Awami League politicians and their supporters soon escalated into a civil war that India in December of that year internationalized. India's role was decisive. The Pakistani garrison in East Bengal, cut off from its supply base in West Pakistan, was forced to surrender. The Bengalis, after almost 25 years of anguish, formed their own Bangladesh state. The Two-Nation Theory was dealt a mortal blow, but the Many-Nation Theory had only begun to be heard from.

THE RISE OF BHUTTO

Shorn of its eastern wing Pakistan's fate was uncertain. Yahya Khan was blamed for the humiliating losses and forced to transfer his authority to Zulfikar Ali Bhutto and his PPP. The military establishment had been dealt a serious blow to its physical state as well as to its pride. The entire garrison of some 90,000 troops in East Bengal was in Bangladeshi and Indian prison camps, and all branches of the armed forces had suffered heavy losses at Indian hands in campaigns in and around West Pakistan. The military leaders made it abundantly clear that they could not continue ruling the country and also hope to rebuild their battered legions. Moreover, the Pakistani public had sufficient reason to deplore the military's mismanagement of the Bangladesh affair, and it was natural that a civilian politician should be called upon to "pick up the pieces."[18] Bhutto was the obvious choice given his party's victory at the polls in 1970 and his commanding influence over Pakistan's two largest provinces, the Punjab and Sind. Bhutto was by all odds also the only national figure of some standing that the political scene had generated since the beginning of the Ayub years. The pre-Ayubian politicians who remained were either too old or too discredited to gain the confidence of the people. Furthermore, no other party in West Pakistan enjoyed the political organization assembled by Bhutto and his colleagues. It can be argued that Bhutto was at the time the only logical choice and a varied but largely demoralized Pakistani citizenry sought deliverance by coalescing behind his driving leadership.[19]

Bhutto talked about the resurrection of a new Pakistan and introduced policies aimed at realizing this objective. Under the banner of socialist reconstruction, he nationalized the banks, insurance companies, and most of the country's industry.[20] The armed forces were purged of their upper echelons, the government bureaucracy was overhauled; and the many separate services unified into one central system. The highly privileged Civil Service of Pakistan (CSP) was dissolved into the new arrangement and many of its key officials were retired.[21] Land reform was promised the peasant-cultivators, factory workers were offered higher salaries and improved working conditions, educational institutions were all brought under government supervision, and the student community was told its grievances would be aired and efforts made to redress them. Bhutto declared Pakistan could not be recreated in a day and that the process of transformation would take years before meaningful change could be attained. Thus he was emphatic on the matter of broadening and deepening his movement. This also meant strengthening the PPP to a point where it would have no real rivals.

Bhutto's political rivals were aware that their positions were directly threatened by the many programs launched by the new administration. They also sensed that the consolidation of Bhutto's power, the formation of the PPP's people's guards, and a secret police establishment known as the Federal Security Force (FSF) would mean the imposition of a veritable dictatorship in the country, and they were most unreconciled to that possibility. The new constitution promulgated in 1973 also reinforced Bhutto's authority and appeared to guarantee the dominance of his PPP in the central legislature. The picture was somewhat the same in the Punjab and Sind, but in the Northwest Frontier Province and Baluchistan, where the PPP had made little headway, Bhutto had to contend with opposition coalition governments, of which the dominant party was the National Awami Party (NAP) whose overall leader was Wali Khan, the son of the Khudai Khidmatgar mentor, Abdul Ghaffar Khan. After a brief period of cooperation between Bhutto and these opposition governments in the frontier regions, strains developed, and the center, under the pretext of controlling separatist tendencies, moved against them. Both the Northwest Frontier and Baluchistan provincial governments were overthrown and caretaker regimes favorable to the PPP were installed in their place.[22] The Many-Nation Theory again became Pakistan's primary concern. In May 1974 Zulfikar Ali Bhutto gave special significance to the problem when he said that provincialism would mean disaster for all Pakistanis and that not a single federating unit "would be able to escape the catastrophe."

THE NATIONALITIES ISSUE

The inability to reconcile rival moral and political claims between the Pakistani central government and the different nationalities was not confined to problems involving Baluchistan and the Northwest Frontier. Nor was the issue merely a matter of Bhutto's heavy-handed tactics or his lust for personal power. As was suggested by the East Bengal case, the problem was intertwined with historic, political, economic, and sociopsychological factors, and the inability or lack of willingness by leaders like Bhutto to deal effectively with the multidimensional nature of the nationalities issue complicated it to a point of utter despair. An anatomy of the nationalities issue reveals the following components.

First, it is accepted that there was serious opposition to the creation of a separate, independent state of Pakistan and that among this element were many staunch Muslims. The Northwest Frontier Province harbors perhaps the best examples and certainly Abdul Ghaffar Khan was the most outstanding member of this group. But this is not to say that they wished Pakistan ill. It is more logical and possibly more fair to conclude that their vision was more restricted than Jinnah's—hence their steadfast belief in their ultimate absolution. The following extract from the 1939 memoir of Sir William Barton speaks to this point:

> An analysis of the Pathan mentality must take account of the patriotism which in the last century and a half has developed a consciousness of separate political interest. . . . There can be no doubt that the Pathan of the administered areas is not prepared to throw in his lot with India except on terms that would preserve the identity of his people as a nation apart from the people of India. Here it may be observed that there is among the Moslems of the Panjab a tendency to support a scheme for a separate Moslem State in the north to be styled Pakistan (the land of the pure in heart), which would include most of the Panjab, the Frontier Province and Kashmir, whose population is predominantly Moslem. If such a State were formed it is more than likely that in the end it would be united to Afghanistan.[23]

In his famous essay published in 1945, Abdul Qaiyum Khan reveals his determined opposition to the Muslim League and Jinnah's efforts in behalf of the Pakistan movement. His subsequent conversion and service in numerous Pakistani provincial and central governments cannot conceal the fundamental difference of experience between sophisticated Muslims living in the heart of India and those inhabiting the frontier region. For the former, the principal enemy was the Hindu majority; for the latter, who had been engaged in mortal combat with British forces, the Hindus were judged to be more a potential ally than a threat. Indeed, their view of Jinnah's movement was that it played into British hands. Moreover, it was feared the division of India into Hindu and Muslim states would put the less populated, poorer regions of the country at a disadvantage they could not overcome. Notes Qaiyum:

> We resent the fact that we have been cut up into the N.W.F.P., the Tribal Belt and Baluchistan. Why cannot we be just one unit? We should hate to see Bengal or Assam or Punjab or any other natural unit maimed or mutilated. We do not relish the idea of voting for selfdetermination as part of an arbitrarily cut up bigger land mass in which we would be just submerged. We should like to have, and will not rest until we have, the right to decide our own future. We are not upset by the idea of a common Centre for the whole of India.[24]

Unlike Qaiyum, who eventually left the Pathan Red Shirts (Khudai Khidmatgar) for the Muslim League, Abdul Ghaffar Khan never deviated from his original position. Imprisoned by both the British and Pakistani authorities, compelled to live in exile in Kabul and New Delhi, the Frontier Gandhi, as Ghaffar Khan is sometimes called, long ago accepted his martyrdom. While he apparently resigned himself to the existence of an independent Pakistan, there is also no question about his continuing determination to strengthen the cause of the frontier people:

> I want to knit the divided tribes of the Pakhtuns [Pathans], spread out from Baluchistan to Chitral, into one community, one brotherhood, so that they can share their sorrows and sufferings and can play a vital role in serving humanity.... During all these dark and evil days for centuries, spreading from Mogul reign to British rule and Pakistani regime, these helpless people have been subject to tyranny.[25]

The second point that needs to be stressed concerning the nationalities problem in Pakistan was the failure of those in authority rapidly to complete the drafting of a constitution.[26] In the nine-year period between independence and the promulgation of the country's first constitution, the sociopolitical fabric that had been so arduously drawn together in 1947 was deliberately torn apart.

In those first years after independence, there was considerable popular support from all areas of the country. Those who had tried to prevent the formation of Pakistan were defeated through accepted democratic processes, and most were forced to withdraw from the political scene or join the new order. Those few who chose to resist violently were understandably faced with punitive actions. Unfortunately, Pakistan's political leaders could not make the most of their opportunity, and the predicament of East Bengal was replicated, if not as well publicized, in other regions of the country. Jinnah's death only a year after independence left the country without a truly dominant leader. Although Liaquat Ali Khan is said to have picked up where Jinnah left off, the record indicates that he was a relatively weak and ineffective personality. As a member of the Muslim refugee or Muhajir community, he also had little leverage among the personalities who wielded influence in the Punjab, Sind, and Northwest Frontier Province. Although his assassination in 1951 was widely thought to be the work of conspiratorial elements, that charge was never proved. But it did unleash intra- as well as interprovincial passions and social unrest spread throughout the country.[27] The inability of the politicians to achieve a political compromise also made it impossible for them to control discordant sectarian groups. Ultimately the army entered the picture and the civilian-military bureaucracy took over the management of the nation. Its rule, from the vantage point of those outside the Punjab, was hardly different from that experienced under the British Raj. Thus Pakistani unity was short-lived. The country would be held together, but recognizably, through artificial means.

The third area deserving attention in this analysis was the comparatively better economic picture prevailing in the Punjab. The Punjab had been a productive agricultural province during the British colonial era. Sind, Baluchistan, and the Northwest Frontier Province were all backward hinterlands, inhabited by relatively uneducated and largely tribal populations. Karachi was detached from Sind and did not rejoin the province until the capital was shifted northward in the 1960s. By that time the major industrial and commercial complex developed there was largely in the hands of the Muhajir community and the Sindhis came to view Karachi as an alien appendage.[28] Mention has already been made of the non-Bengali commercial monopolies in East Bengal. The more extensive economic opportunities open to the Punjabis and Muslim refugees were contrasted by the meager chances native Sindhis, Pathans, or Baluchis had of rising out of their poverty. Although these elements provided the country with much-needed labor for menial tasks, it was hardly the kind of opportunity to stimulate integration and national consciousness. On the contrary, the success of some was considered the cause for backwardness in the others. Moreover, economic achievement also translated into educational advances, and hence admission into the select ruling circle in the government bureaucracy. Although quota systems were utilized to make it possible to recruit Sindhis, Pathans, and Baluchis into the privileged services, such devices did little to diminish the sense of frustration among these non-Punjabis. The combined result was a heightened sense of regionalism.[29]

In examining the haves versus the have-nots, there is often the tendency to overlook another struggle, namely that one between the so-called more fortunate elements, the Punjabis and Muhajirs. Given the limited resource base in Pakistan, even these groups did not enjoy unlimited opportunity. From the outset, the Punjabis were suspicious and often jealous of Muhajir aggressiveness. In searching for an explanation for political failure among the early politicians, it is necessary to grasp the antagonism that Punjabis directed at those refugees who had attained high positions in government and dominated the economy. Indeed the first province in Pakistan to agitate for a larger share of the national product was the Punjab and its leaders forced Liaquat Ali Khan into situations that generally compromised his policies. At the same time, it is necessary to try and understand some facts about the Punjab that are often neglected. For example, the Punjabis not only were the largest regional group in West Pakistan, but also, of all the provincial peoples of Pakistan, including those of East Bengal, suffered the most in the transition from colonial rule to national independence.

When the Punjabis finally accepted the Pakistan idea (and it should be recalled that the Muslim League resolution calling for a Pakistan state was passed in Lahore in 1940), the province was deeply divided between Muslims, Hindus, and Sikhs. The latter religious group believed the Muslims threatened their survival, and at the time of partition the atrocities committed by Sikhs and Muslims against one another were more tragic than anything experienced in the other provinces of Pakistan or India. In Bengal, Gandhi and the last chief minister of undivided Bengal, H. S. Suhrawardy, a Muslim, combined forces and managed to limit the civil strife. Later Gandhi and Suhrawardy tried to play the same role in the Punjab but were forced to admit failure.[30] It is said that the British transferred power to indigenous representatives of the Indian and Pakistani nations with considerable ceremony and no warfare. Neither the Indians nor the Pakistanis were required to fight for their independence, and there was no experience with liberation struggles. Although an accurate observation, the carnage perpetrated in the Punjab by Muslims and Sikhs, the slaughter of tens of thousands of innocent noncombatants, would suggest that the Punjab was deeply influenced by the struggle for independence. Undoubtedly it was also the appalling loss of life and property in that part of the Punjab linked with Pakistan that led those Punjabis to insist on a significant voice in the state's affairs. If the Punjabis are accused of imposing their customs, dress, and dietary habits on the country, if they supported the effort to make Urdu the national language, if they seemed more ready to tolerate sudden changes in government, it may be because they had sacrificed so much to achieve Pakistan, and they were determined to preserve it. General Zia-ul-Haq, notably a Punjabi and a Muhajir, opted for Pakistan from the East Punjab, a region that became part of the Indian Union. His emergence as the dominant figure in the Pakistani government and his perception of Pakistan as an Islamic State are intertwined with the peculiar Punjabi experience that identifies the survival of the country with the vitality of the Punjab and vice versa.[31] Muzaffar Qadir has attempted to explain the Punjabis' love for Pakistan and urges discriminating between the activities of the self-interested few and the larger population:

> The intrigues of feudal lords like Daultana in 1952, of self-seekers like Ghulam Mohammad, or the creation of the monstrosity of one-unit as an obstacle in the way of Muslim Bengal and other such instances can hardly be quoted as symbolic of the political stance of the real Punjab. They were acts of individuals and should be condemned as such.[32]

Compared with the other nationalities of Pakistan, the Punjabis are more industrious and politically more stable. The fertility of their lands and the abundant yields give the Punjabis an independence and a sense of accomplishment that only a smaller percentage enjoy in the other provinces. The Punjabis are also tradition bound, and their social structure is very much intertwined with their agrarian circumstances. The Punjab, more so than the other provinces, is heavily influenced by caste, and the division between the Rajputs, Jats, and Arains carries even greater significance than the distinction between Punjabi and Pathan or Punjabi and Sindhi. Perhaps this statement can be better understood when it is noted that the Punjab is multilingual. Urdu is acceptable and widely used in the urban centers of the Punjab, but in the rural areas the three Punjabi dialects are more likely to be heard. In central Punjab the language in common usage is Punjabi, in the Multan and Bahawalpur areas it is Saraiki, and in the region around Rawalpindi the spoken tongue is Pothwari. As Salim Alvi has observed, "Punjabis become Punjabis only when they are outside their province."[33]

The Punjabi Rajputs and Jats have a long history of military involvement and Pakistan's army draws most of its recruits from the Punjab. On the other hand, it is important to note that the Pathans have greater representation in the armed forces than would be indicated by their relatively smaller population. This understanding requires an examination of the fourth aspect of the nationalities problem, the psychological dilemma.

Just as the Muslim League raised the cry "Islam in Danger" and mobilized a movement for the independence of a Muslim state in the subcontinent, Sindhis, Baluchis, and Pathans believe their way of life and particularly their distinctive culture are in jeopardy, especially given their experience with the Pakistan movement and their fear of the more numerous Punjabis. In some ways it is the same fear that Jinnah exploited to get the British to partition India. Only now that fear seeks to dismember what is left of the Pakistan that Jinnah created. The question might be asked if the fear is real or imaginary. As has already been explained, many Pathans felt the Muslim League fear of a Hindu-dominant India was unjustified. Today, the Pakistani government would argue that Pathan fears are more a manifestation of attitude than factual experience. The point in all this lies not so much in the availability of tangible evidence as it does in the minds of those who have a feeling of deprivation. It is, in other words, academic if the fear is real or imaginary; what is important is that it is there and it is a threat to Pakistan's survival as a national entity. It cannot be wished away or forcibly purged. If the fear is to be treated, authority will have to come to grips with the psychology of the Many-Nation Theory and foster a political structure that maximizes provincial expression. Pakistan's real quest for identity is quite possibly related to variety and diversity rather than to some mystical sense of ideological unity.

BHUTTO'S LEGACY

Bhutto and those Pakistani leaders who preceded him were so obsessed with provincialism that they engaged in a self-fulfilling prophecy that was by its very nature self-defeating. The more they sought to eliminate separatist tendencies, the deeper the fissures grew in the Pakistan design. In the Northwest Frontier Province, the call for a Pakhtunistan entity predated the creation of Pakistan.[34] But there is no single interpretation of what Pakhtunistan is supposed to mean. Some have argued for a separate, independent and sovereign state for the Pathans on the Pakistan side of the Afghan border. Others have said it means union of all the Pathans and their inclusion in a larger Afghanistan state. Still others claim that Pakhtunistan incorporates an independent Pakistani Baluchistan as well as an independent Northwest Frontier. Finally there are those who argue that Pakhtunistan merely means changing the name of the Northwest Frontier Province and does not affect or alter the region's relationship with Pakistan. But, even if this is the case, it does not in any way diminish the demand for provincial autonomy. Most of the leaders of the respective provinces have traditionally acknowledged their acceptance of a federal government in Pakistan, but they will not tolerate any maneuver by the central authority to reimpose one unit. Liaquat Ali Khan, Ghulam Muhammad, Iskander Mirza, Ayub Khan, and Bhutto have all been accused of fomenting disorder in the provinces in order to justify the imposition of superior federal power. Most of these actions have been attributed to personal ambition and the gluttonous desire for power rather than real need. And it is this intrigue and manipulation that regional leaders claim is destroying Pakistan. Bhutto is alleged to have engaged in such tactics more than any of his predecessors solely for the purpose of eliminating all opposition to his rule.[35]

After the loss of East Bengal and Pakistan's ignominious defeat at Indian hands, Bhutto moved swiftly to refashion Pakistan's political structure. He neutralized the army by dismissing numerous ranking officers and replaced them with others judged to be less politically motivated. He reorganized the bureaucracy, ended the reign of the privileged services, and called for the resignation of or dismissed approximately 1,400 civil servants, many of whom held high positions. He created his own special police, the FSF, and gave it chief responsibility for the gathering of internal intelligence as well as generally protecting Bhutto and his PPP government. Opposition politicians were intimidated and pressured, cajoled and rewarded, and their parties, with the exception of the National Awami Party, the Tehriq-i-Istiqlal, and the Jamaat-i-Islami, were virtually extinguished. Of the three remaining parties only the NAP has served in a governing capacity. The dissolution of the NPA coalition governments in the Northwest Frontier Province and Baluchistan and the 1975 banning of the NAP suggest that the NAP leaders could not be won over and hence had to be removed by force. But the attack on the NAP only tended to increase provincial tension in the country.

The leader of the NAP, and the principal opposition member of the National Assembly was Wali Khan. After the assassination in February 1975 of Muhammad Sherpao, the chief PPP leader in the Northwest Frontier Province and a member of Bhutto's inner circle, Wali Khan was arrested along with all of his colleagues. His party's offices were closed and its accounts frozen.[36] Wali Khan, it was alleged, had been the brains behind the assassination plot. The NAP leader denied any involvement in Sherpao's murder and intimated that Bhutto had had his associate killed simply to provide the pretext for destroying the NAP. The suggestion was that in a game for high stakes individuals like Sherpao were expendable. Wali Khan's trial was long, high on drama, but ultimately indecisive. It was still going on when Bhutto was overthrown by the army in July 1977, and several months later the martial law government of General Zia-ul-Haq terminated the proceedings and released Wali Khan and 40 others who were standing trial with him. In addition, the martial law government announced that approximately 11,000 political detainees would also be released. These included 5,522 from the Punjab, 4,184 from the NWFP, 1,050 from Sind, and 353 from Baluchistan. History continues to repeat itself in Pakistan. It can be recalled that Mujibur Rahman had been accused of conspiring with India against Pakistan and had been put on trial by Ayub Khan. The Agartala conspiracy trial was also terminated and all charges were dismissed as Ayub was losing control of his government.[37] But the release of Mujibur Rahman did not prevent East Bengal's secession and it can only be speculated if this gesture by Zia-ul-Haq arrested the movement toward separateness in the frontier region.

Zia-ul-Haq has inherited a divisive legacy. Destiny now requires him to work with and where possible accommodate the provincial leaders. This also means granting the provinces more power over their local affairs than they have ever enjoyed before. Moreover, it requires the developing of more harmonious relationships between the different provinces, rather than exploiting their deep-seated fears of one another. Wali Khan has argued with some justification that it was Bhutto who fanned the fires of interprovincial hatred in Sind and elsewhere. In a 1974 interview for the weekly publication *Outlook*, Wali Khan made the following charges:

> Starting off with Sind, we had the Urdu-Sindi trouble, when one Pakistani cut the throat of another Pakistani. He [Bhutto] tried the same trick in Baluchistan. He attempted to pitch Pashtoon [Pathan] against the Baluch in the province. He tried to pitch the Punjabis against the Pakhtoons [Pathans], having this drama played on 23rd March, 1973 in Liaquat Bagh, Rawalpindi, where some people were killed and scores injured. Now all this was engineered so that the Punjabis fought it out with the Pakhtoons. So, it is clear, that he is not making a council or something in [Azad] Kashmir for the betterment of the area. What he wants to do is to rule everywhere, even where he has no locus standi. In Baluchistan, in the Frontier. One lame duck in the NWFP and one lame duck in Baluchistan, and Mr. Bhutto rules everywhere.[38]

In the same interview Wali Khan saw dire consequences in Bhutto's arrest of Baluchi leaders Khair Bakhsh Marri, Mir Ghaus Bakhsh Bizenjo, and Sardar Ataullah Khan Mengal, all members of the ousted Baluchistan government. The closing of parliamentary institutions and the prevention of public meetings, he cautioned, will drive the disaffected members of the population into the arms of the extremists. The latter was not reluctant to use violent methods, and they found conditions throughout the country favoring their brand of political activity. The Baluchi Youth Organization, the Popular Front of Armed Resistance Against National Oppression and Exploitation in Baluchistan, and the Pakhtoon Student Federation in effect took over where the political parties left off. These radical groups found common cause with elements in Afghanistan, especially after a 1973 coup d'etat brought Daud Khan back to power in Kabul. Daud Khan had revitalized the Pakhtunistan issue within days of his assumption of power. Wali Khan opined that if Bhutto did not work with "people who speak of the rule of law and the constitution in this country, well, if you eliminate us, you are only strengthening the extremists—and this is precisely what he is doing."[39]

THE CENTER AND THE PROVINCES

The shah of Iran devoted considerable attention to mediating the dispute between Pakistan and Afghanistan and as a result of his efforts Daud Khan and Bhutto exchanged visits in 1976, while General Zia visited Afghanistan soon after his assumption of power. Daud again visited Pakistan in March 1978 and was warmly received in Islamabad. Daud's death, a few weeks later, at the hands of his disaffected military, and the establishment of a Marxist revolutionary council in Kabul, however, set back the movement toward a rapprochement. It is now evident that there was a Soviet role in the coup. The Soviet Union had been very active in Afghan affairs and the mountain country's dependence on Soviet military assistance was pronounced. Approximately $1 billion in Soviet military equipment was poured into Afghanistan from 1968 to 1977. Afghan officers received their training in the Soviet Union and Marxist-Leninist indoctrination has been made a part of their education. Moreover, the Soviet Union tunneled through the mountains between Soviet Central Asia and Afghanistan, and a superhighway was constructed from the Uzbek frontier clear through the principal cities of Afghanistan to the Pakistani border, a land route that placed Soviet convoys within 18 hours of the Pakistani frontier.[40]

The Soviet presence in Afghanistan following their December 1979 invasion and the flight of hundreds of thousands of Afghans across the Pakistani frontier has made even more imperative Islamabad's resolution of the Pathan nationality question. It has been speculated that Daud was overthrown because the Afghan president appeared to be not only reconciling his relations with Pakistan but, more important, moving toward closer ties with the shah of Iran.

The shah's observations that his country was being surrounded by Marxist regimes cannot be ignored. Moreover, the political system in Pakistan is inchoate at this writing, and although Zia is dismantling Bhutto's quasi-socialist system and replacing it with a more traditional Islamic program, the future character of the Pakistani government is very unpredictable. Nevertheless, Pakistan must still come to grips with Afghan claims to Pakhtunistan. At the very least Afghanistan will have continuing interest in the Pathans on the Pakistani side of the border. A full-scale civil war on the frontier could precipitate the disintegration of the Pakistani army, and Pakistan's survival at that point would be highly questionable. Looked at in this context, a renewed Afghan campaign, given the support of the Soviet Union, for an independent Pakhtunistan must be judged serious.

The Afghan perception of Pakhtunistan is illustrated in a postage stamp issued in 1969 that depicts all of the Northwest Frontier Province and Baluchistan. This idea of Pakhtunistan has been ridiculed by Pakistanis who note that it does not also take into account the Pathans of Afghanistan but does include the Baluchis of Pakistan.[41] These same critics point to the divisions in Afghanistan between the traditional rulers who have been Persian-speakers, as well as the Afghan Tajiks, Turkmen, Uzbeks, and Hazaras, who have little in common with the Pathans on their eastern frontier. The creation of a Pakistani Pakhtunistan, they argue, must have an impact on the Afghan Pathans, who might also insist on the right of self-determination. It is therefore a reasonable guess that the new Marxist Afghan elite, if it intends to press for the creation of a Pakhtunistan state, eventually expects to absorb such a state. The Afghans have long judged the Gandamak treaty of 1878 and the Durand Frontier agreement of 1893 as illegal, and their claim of Afghan irredenta extends well beyond the Hindu Kush to the river Indus. The Afghans have always argued that these treaties with the British were entered into under duress, that their land had been taken from them and their people separated from one another in order to enhance Great Britain's defense of its Indian empire. Therefore no Afghan government has ever resigned itself to Pakistan's control of the Pathan population on the frontier, and they have all periodically publicized their intention to assist in the creation of a Pakhtunistan state.

While beleaguered political movements that are intent on pressing their demand for autonomy or self-determination often come to lean on outside support, there is considerable reluctance on the part of Pakistan's Pathans to become too dependent on Kabul or Moscow. On the one side, these Pathans do not want to escape the grip of Islamabad only to find themselves ensnared in a Soviet-Afghan scheme of expansion. On the other, the Pakistani Pathans are divided between those who see the Soviet Union as an aggressor in Afghanistan and hence a dire threat to the frontier people, and those who are ideologically committed to communist doctrines and actively seek the support of the Kremlin.[42] Abdul Ghaffar Khan and his son Wali Khan have long warned against Soviet encroachment in the region. Abdul Samad Achakzai, the leader of the Wrore Pushtoon movement in the Pashtu-speaking areas of Baluchistan, who was assassinated in 1973, was another who warned against Soviet machinations in the tribal areas. But Ajmal Khattak, a leader of the frontier NAP who spent many of the Bhutto years in exile in Kabul, is unequivocal in his call for an independent Pathan state and, it is alleged, has requested both Afghan and Soviet aid. General Zia's decision to release Wali Khan and the other provincial personalities was taken no doubt with the knowledge that the Pathans and other nationalities need their own leaders, and Pakistan needs those personalities who can provide that leadership and still foster the maintenance of Pakistani unity. As a Punjabi, Zia will have to prove to men like Wali Khan that Pathans, Punjabis, and other nationalities need no longer fear one another and that they all have a stake in preserving Pakistan's integrity. If the Many-Nation Theory gains respectability in Pakistan, it will be simpler to distinguish between the reasonable or moderate leaders and those who are determined to change radically the region's orientation as well as its sociopolitical structure.

The avoidance of situations that are a breeding ground for extremists is also important in Baluchistan and Sind. In Baluchistan the Bhutto government, somewhat encouraged by its relationship with Iran, mounted a major military effort aimed at crushing alleged separatist movements. The Pakistani central government poured several army divisions into the province and mobilized numerous local and paramilitary groups to help scatter the tribal insurgents. The establishment of a Baluchistan Liberation Organization in both Pakistan and Iran and its use of radio facilities in Baghdad added still another international dimension to the problem. The reported uncovering of an Iraqi plot to channel arms to

Baluchi guerrillas through the Iraqi embassy in Islamabad was additional grist for the mill. The Iraqis, it was alleged, were more concerned with making the shah of Iran uncomfortable than with promoting secession in Pakistan. But they were also disturbed by the use of Baluchi recruits in the war against the insurgents in Oman. Nevertheless, the intervention by an Arab state in Baluchistan and the behind-the-scenes role of its mentor, the Soviet Union, gave the Baluchistan unrest particular urgency.[43]

The strategic position (near the Persian Gulf) of both Pakistan and Iranian Baluchistan seemed to make it imperative that dissident movements be controlled. In part this explains the Iran-Iraq agreement of 1975 in which Iran pledged not to support the independence movement of the Iraqi Kurds (see Chapter 6) and Iraq promised it would cease aiding the tribal movements in Iranian Baluchistan. The shah's attempt to calm some of his frontier problems also led him to mediate Afghanistan's dispute with Pakistan. Although these efforts may have borne fruit, the revolutions in Afghanistan and Iran, the demise of Sardar Daud and the shah of Iran in 1978 and 1979 respectively, as well as the Soviet invasion of Afghanistan in December 1979 and the Iraqi invasion of Iran in September 1980, made reconciliation impossible. Although Pakistan's Northwest Frontier Province is an historic area of tension and conflict, it is in Baluchistan where the explosive condition is most evident.[44]

The population of Pakistani Baluchistan is less than 50 percent Baluchi. In the northern area of the province Pathans predominate. In the Sibi and Lasbela districts Sindhi or Saraiki languages are common. In Quetta-Pishin and Loralai the languages most used are Punjabi and Pushtu. The vast Kalat district is Brahui speaking. The dominant Baluchi-speaking tribes are to be found in the border area with Iran. These are the districts of Kharan, Makran, and Chaghai. The ethnic mixture in Pakistani Baluchistan seems to belie a concerted drive for Baluchi independence and this makes the linkage with the Iranian Baluchis more significant. This also helps to explain why many Pathans have urged the integration of Baluchistan with their call for a Pakhtunistan. Clearly, Pathans and Baluchis claim some of the same territory, and this makes them suspicious of one another and often brings them into conflict. The transcending of these narrower nationalisms, however, has been attempted more by local leaders than by the Pakistani government. But the exploitation of tribal differences by the Pakistani center has also defeated these efforts before they had a chance to succeed.[45] Because of the feeling that the government in Islamabad could not be trusted, Marxist extremists, usually students from Karachi, have been able to infiltrate Baluchistan, and it is they who have attempted a workable linkup between hard-pressed Baluchis and disaffected Pathans. They have also joined forces with radical elements in Iranian Baluchistan, where a sporadic insurgency continues to fight Khomeini's revolutionary guards.

Moreover, the Reagan administration's decision to step up arms transfers to Pakistan is interpreted in Pakistani Baluchistan as a frontal attack on the

Baluchi autonomy movement. The 1973–77 conflict that pitted tribesmen against crack Pakistani army divisions is estimated to have cost approximately 10,000 lives on both sides and the use of American weapons by the Pakistan armed forces is not lost on the Baluchis. Bhutto's removal was supposed to herald a change in Islamabad's policy toward the region. And while the Zia government has emphasized greater self-government and has directed that more development funds should be allocated to the province, the Baluchis continue to complain that they are not only being neglected, but that the Punjabis are moving into their region in great numbers, at their expense. The latter migration is seen as deliberate government policy, promoted by Zia to dilute the traditional power of the Baluchi sardars or tribal leaders. In this context, many sardars along with their loyal followers perceive the Soviet invasion of Afghanistan as an opportunity for them to enlist Kremlin support for their independent programs. The sardars are not unmindful of Soviet heavy-handedness but their dissatisfaction with Islamabad's martial law government is so deep and their ties to Pakistan are so weak that they often seem prepared to welcome an external party to relieve them of their immediate problem. Such activity is not unknown in the subcontinent.[46] Indeed, for centuries, warring factional groups have sought the assistance of outsiders to "settle" their quarrels, only to expose themselves to a new maximum ruler. The appearance of the Central Asian moguls in the subcontinent in the sixteenth century is a case in point.

Some Baluchi sardars do not consider themselves Marxists, and prefer the designation "nationalists." Others, however, appear to have been radicalized. Khair Bakhsh Marri, leader of the 120,000 Marri Baluch, is generally judged to be a Communist. So is Akbar Khan Bugti, the leader of another 100,000 tribal people. Both men held high posts in the Bhutto government before running into difficulty over policy toward Baluchistan, and the Baluchi insistence on becoming more independent of Islamabad. Two other personalities who also played roles in the provincial government during the Bhutto period are Ataullah Khan Mengal and Ghaus Bakhsh Bizenjo. They too are considered leftists but less extreme than Marri or Bugti. All, however, have had long and unpleasant experiences with the Pakistani central government and despite their historic rivalries, seem prepared to combine their forces in opposition to the administration of Zia-ul-Haq.

The sardars learned not to trust the Pakistan government during the tenure of Zulfikar Ali Bhutto. Bhutto exploited their factious and divided state to sustain the rule of the federal government. Many of the sardars were arrested and incarcerated for extended periods. One of Bhutto's last acts before his overthrow was to declare the end of the sardari system, which was publicized as turning power over to the people but was actually a guise for imposing greater central control. The Baluchis therefore have little reason to trust Islamabad and they are even more determined to thwart the actions of Zia-ul-Haq. Moreover, the sardars are interested in sustaining their influence and they must compete with the

Baluchi Students' Organization (BSO), which allegedly receives its funds from Soviet actions in Afghanistan and in fact is believed to be in league with Ajmal Khattak, a National Awami Party leader who obtained political asylum in Kabul during the Bhutto years, and who continues to press for the merger of Pathans and Baluchis and the creation of an independent state.

It is important to note that the majority of Baluchis live in Karachi and in western Sind—that is, outside their native province. At the same time they are still a minority in these areas and not likely to pose a genuine challenge to the population there. It is believed, for example, that almost a million Pathans are also living in or around Karachi. Indeed, the Pathans and Baluchis comprise the backbone of the factory and menial labor force in Karachi and are therefore a vital component of Pakistan's industrial economy. It is also this labor force that has been exposed to Marxist ideas and that the leftists among the student community seek to form into a forceful socialist movement.

The Baluchis remaining in Baluchistan are divided into more than a score of major and minor tribes and clans. The Marri and Bugti are supposed to be the largest and are believed of Arab origin. By contrast, it is speculated that the Mengals, another large order, are descendants of early Mongolian invaders. The Brahui, who live among the Baluchis, are often thought of as the original inhabitants of the area. They are Dravidian and as such relate culturally to the dominant ethnic group in southern India. Because of their close and long intimacy with the Baluch, however, the Brahui have developed affinities with their immediate neighbors. What tends to give coherence to this otherwise confused ethnic picture has been the semifeudal, or sardari system. The sardar, or headman, is a symbol of the particular tribe's security vis-à-vis the other rival tribes.[47] Seldom have the sardars shown an inclination to cooperate with one another, and the more centralized regimes of outsiders have exploited this running rivalry to bolster their own preeminence at the expense of the tribes. The constant bickering between sardars has also taxed the resources of the Baluchi people and many observers have concluded that, on the one side, the sardari system is a promise of protection, while on the other it has smothered any hope of raising the Baluchis out of their backward penury.

A new version of the Sandeman system of administration (which the British developed in the region during the nineteenth century) is envisioned by the Zia administration. The Zia government hopes that traditional Baluchi behavior will prevail. The Marxist view represented by Aijaz Ahmad, however, sees the situation quite differently: the Bizenjos, Bugtis, Marris, and other sardars are doomed to struggle with each other due to the "inherent weakness and fragmentation of the feudal class." In other words, the Marxists believe the system is so full of Marxist-Leninist contradictions that it must inevitably collapse. No amount of effort can prop it up, let alone save it.[48] If the Marxist forecast proves correct, Afghanistan with Soviet encouragement might be tempted to support the Pathans as well as the Baluchis in Baluchistan.

Soviet objectives in Afghanistan are speculated upon in the following chapter. Here it is only necessary to point out that the Kremlin envisages specific geopolitical gains as a result of its direct presence in the Central Asian country. Given a successful occupation of Afghanistan, the Soviet Union would be in an ideal position to influence if not dominate both the Strait of Hormuz on the Persian Gulf and the Arabian Sea/Indian Ocean region through the Iranian port of Chah Bahar and the Pakistani harbor of Gwadar. Assuming the fracturing of central authority in both Iran and Pakistan, hardly a farfetched notion, both Iranian and Pakistani Baluchistan might either break away as one or more independent states, or quite possibly form part of a redefined new Afghanistan. Should any of these possibilities materialize, the Soviet Union could claim new client-states and thereby, access to the warm, open water.

Baluchi bitterness with their respective governments in Islamabad and Tehran is tailor-made for Soviet exploitation. Attempts by the government of Zia-ul-Haq to focus Baluchi attention on Soviet aggression in Afghanistan and the brutalizing of a fellow-Muslim people have not reduced the ill-feeling directed at the government. Slogans appearing in Baluchi towns are more likely to display antagonism for the military regime than dissatisfaction with Moscow. In fact, considerable support is shown for the Soviets in Afghanistan among younger Baluchis, suggesting that the problem of dealing with the nationalities in Pakistan is also a generation-gap dilemma. Older members of the Baluchi community have been visibly shaken by the Soviet invasion of their neighbor state and their concerns are more clearly linked with their Islamic way of life. The youth of the region, however, are by contrast less religiously inclined and more concerned with material rewards that they fervently argue the Islamabad government has deprived them of. Moreover, the older generation continues its support of the sardari system, whereas the younger generation is largely critical.

Another aspect of Soviet policy toward the Baluchistan question is the number of Pakistani Baluchis who have been posted in the Persian Gulf sheikhdoms, and especially in Oman. These forces currently defend traditional rulers from subversive elements aided and trained in Marxist South Yemen with help provided by both the Soviet Union and Cuba. Upwards of 5,000 Baluchis are alleged to be included in the Omani armed forces and they have demonstrated considerable skill in neutralizing guerrilla forays in the Dhofar sector of Oman. This contingent has also risen in importance given the Ayatollah Khomeini's decision to withdraw Iranian troops from Oman. In the mid-1970s it was the Iranians dispatched by the shah who thwarted efforts to overthrow the Omani monarchy. The Baluchis have filled the vacuum left by the Iranians and the Kremlin is very interested in curtailing the flow of recruits from the Baluchistan Mekran Coast to the Persian Gulf. Related to this activity is the knowledge that the Pakistanis are "rich" in trained manpower, especially with military experience or capacity. The possible stationing of Pakistani army divisions in Saudi Arabia is but one more instance of how the Pakistani military government could be judged an obstacle to movements seeking revolutionary changes in the area. In this context, the exploitation of nationality grievances by Moscow must always be anticipated.

India is perhaps more interested in what happens in Sind and the Punjab than on the Pakistani frontier, although it cannot ignore any of these nationalities problems. Prior to partition the Congress Party made gestures of friendship toward Afghanistan and, it is alleged, promised that landlocked country a land route to the sea through Baluchistan if Afghanistan could assist those elements on the Northwest Frontier in their effort to keep the Muslim League and Pakistan out. India might again be inclined to strike a deal with Marxist Afghanistan if Pakistan should again begin to disintegrate. Thus, if Pakistan were about to crumble, there is every reason to believe that India would join with Afghanistan and the Soviet Union in rearranging the political geography of the area. And the key to India's role seems to lie in Sind, where since independence a movement started by the late G. M. Syed remains vital.

Sind, perhaps more than the other provinces of Pakistan, has witnessed an extensive influx of people, first from India and then from the other provinces. These people were not assimilated by the Sindhi culture, but rather they clung to their primary traditions, life-style, and languages. Moreover, many of the refugees were far better educated than the native Sindhis, and as Pakistan's economy developed, especially the industrial and commercial complexes between Karachi and Hyderabad, it was these non-Sindhis who monopolized the choice managerial as well as entrepreneurial positions both in the private and governmental sectors. As has already been noted, even the principal labor market was drawn from the frontier regions, leaving the Sindhi a comparatively stagnant pauper in his own house. In the Sind hinterland, the dominant wadera landlord system perpetuated a relationship in which the peasant was completely dominated by his paternal lord.[49] Moreover, the acquisition of Sindhi lands by Punjabis and former members of the military and bureaucracy, especially those lands reclaimed by the extension of irrigation systems, could not be expected to improve the well-being of the Sindhi. Thus after Bangladesh gained its freedom from Pakistan and Bhutto, the first Sindhi to have assumed the maximum political position was installed in power, and young Sindhi intellectuals began to demand redress for their grievances.

The call for a Sindhu Desh, or Sindhi homeland in the 1970s was primarily directed at the refugee Muhajir community that controlled the economy and cultural life of Karachi and its general environs. The Muhajirs had led the movement to make Urdu the national language of Pakistan and now the Sindhis viewed Urdu as an obstacle to their gaining control over their own affairs. Instead of Sindhis learning Urdu, the Muhajirs who had shown virtually no interest in learning Sindhi, were called upon to adopt the latter. Furthermore, provincial government came under the direct influence of Bhutto and his family members.

Their policies reinforced the power of the provincialists, especially as the Bhutto regime was interested in undermining the status of the entrepreneurial class. Having nationalized much of their holdings, Bhutto recognized that they wielded little, if any, political power, but they were still articulate representatives of society, and it was judged best to neutralize their expression. In addition, by manipulating the relationships between this class and the critical Sindhis, Bhutto hoped to make the Muhajirs dependent on him for their continued prosperity. At the same time he amassed popular support by appearing to further Sindhi nationalism. Ultimately, Bhutto sought to use both the Sindhu Desh people and the Muhajirs against his landlord opponents in the rural areas of Sind.

"Sind for the Sindhis" was promoted by the students and intelligentsia in the province. As such it developed similar leftist or Marxist characteristics identified with other nationalities movements pressed by Pakistan's young people. Bhutto's mannerisms and symbols were cut to fit this reality. His dress, his public statements, his party's manifestos and programs, his governmental policies were all keyed to absorbing what he judged to be a socialist tide sweeping the country. It is perhaps for this reason that he was also determined to isolate those organizations and political parties that emphasized Pakistan's Islamic heritage. The election campaign of 1977 and its aftermath suggest that Bhutto had exposed a weakness he could not overcome. When his political opposition accused him of anti-Islamic profanities, even more stalwart supporters had difficulty defending him.[50] Bhutto had heaped ridicule on the country's religious leaders and after years of political atrophy, years in which no politician could hope to achieve national standing, much of what passed for local leadership had been assumed by these religious teachers. Along with a handful of secular politicians, they led the demonstrations that ultimately caused the army to intervene again in Pakistan's political life. Bhutto was swept from power by the military coup, but the nationalities dilemma that he sought to take advantage of continued to fester.

Sindhis are especially critical of the military regime in Islamabad. They not only view Zia-ul-Haq as an usurper and murderer of their beloved leader, they are also convinced that the entire affair was a Punjabi plot aimed at destroying countervailing power in the country. The Punjabis, it is stressed, have long sought domination. It is argued that the Bengalis would have remained within the Pakistan fold had it not been for Punjabi expressions of superiority and their monopolization of power and influence in the country. Although the Sindhu Desh Movement may be somewhat muted, it lies just beneath the surface of Pakistani domestic life and could erupt at any time to further jeopardize the stability and integrity of the larger Pakistan nation. Moreover, Zia-ul-Haq's reluctance to permit political dissent and party organization adds to the frustration and makes it more likely that when the political scene again becomes active, the provincialists and separatists will hold center stage.

CONCLUSIONS

If Pakistan is to be saved from itself, Pakistanis throughout the country will have to adjust their perceptions and behavior. And because this may not be possible among the impoverished, illiterate masses, it will have to be accomplished by enlightened people, and particularly by the country's leaders in political, social, religious, and economic affairs. The Muhajirs will have to learn how to live with the Many-Nation Theory and undoubtedly will have to adapt to the provincial culture around them. The Punjabis will have to give up the idea of dominating the entire country, despite their being more than 60 percent of the population. Pathans and Baluchis, given a larger voice in shaping their destiny, will have to create their own reasons for perpetuating the Pakistani state. Having achieved the autonomy that they have long struggled for, they might find it in their own interest to hold Pakistan together. Pakistan's governmental leaders, at the center and in the provinces, members of the military elite and bureaucracy as well as the major figures in the political parties, are the principals in this major shift in national orientation. Their wisdom and clairvoyance will dictate the success or failure of this incomparable challenge.

None of this operates in a vacuum. There are those within Pakistan who are determined to transform it in such a way as to bring it down. There are those outside the country who are also interested in these transpiring events. None of them can stand by and simply let things happen if Pakistan should crumble. India, Afghanistan, and the Soviet Union all have immediate stakes in the future of this troubled country. And because the world has yet to resolve the fundamental question of "global security," China and the United States are also major actors in the unfolding scenario.

NOTES

1. Pakistan's Foreign Minister has many times refuted Indian charges that his country's attempt to reequip its armed forces is a threat to India's national security. *Pakistan Affairs* 34, no. 9 (May 1, 1981): 1, 3. See also Lawrence Ziring, *Pakistan: The Enigma of Political Development* (Kent, England: Dawson, 1980), pp. 134–66.

2. See Subrata Roy Chowdhurry, *The Genesis of Bangladesh* (London: Asia, 1972); Anthony Mascarenhas, *The Rape of Bangladesh* (Delhi: Vikas, 1971); and Mohammed Ayoob and K. Subrahmanyam, *The Liberation War* (New Delhi: S. Chand, 1972).

3. K. K. Aziz, *Party Politics in Pakistan, 1947-1958* (Islamabad: National Commission on Historical and Cultural Research, 1976), pp. 139–78.

4. See, for example, the informative book by Chaudhry Khaliquzzman, *Pathway to Pakistan* (Lahore: Longmans, 1961).

5. Ishtiaq Husain Qureshi, *Education in Pakistan* (Karachi: Ma'Aref, 1975), pp. 168–90.

6. *The Statesman*, March 16, 1948.

7. Note the attack on H. S. Suhrawardy by Prime Minister Liaquat Ali Khan in the Pakistan Constituent Assembly, *Constituent Assembly Debates*, Official Report (Karachi:

Government of Pakistan Press, May 18, 1948), p. 41. See also Lawrence Ziring, "The Second Partition of Bengal," *Scrutiny* 3, nos. 1-2 (January-June and July-December 1976): 65-79.

8. Ralph Braibanti, *Research on the Bureaucracy of Pakistan* (Durham, N.C.: Duke University Press, 1966), pp. 48-49.

9. Industrial and urban unrest has its roots in the history of Bengal. See for example L. S. S. O'Malley, *A History of Bengal, Bihar and Orissa Under British Rule* (Calcutta: Bengal Secretariat Book Depot, 1925), pp. 538-39.

10. For a glimpse into the relationship between cultural and political nationalism in Bengal see the poem by Chowhury Lutfur Rahman in *Ekusher Kabita* (Dacca: Naya Dunya Prakashani, n.d.), p. 12.

11. For a Marxist view, see Tariq Ali, *Pakistan: Military Rule or People's Power?* (London: Jonathan Cape, 1970), pp. 54-55. See also David Loshak, *Pakistan Crisis* (London: Heinemann, 1971); and L. Rushbrook Williams, *The East Pakistan Tragedy* (London: Tom Stacey, 1972).

12. Lawrence Ziring, *The Ayub Khan Era: Politics in Pakistan, 1958-1969* (Syracuse, N.Y.: Syracuse University Press, 1971), pp. 31-32.

13. Kalim Siddiqui, *Conflict, Crisis and War in Pakistan* (New York: Praeger, 1972), pp. 129-34.

14. Shahid Javed Burki, "Ayub's Fall: A Socio-Economic Explanation," *Asian Survey* 12, no. 3 (March 1972): 201-12.

15. Rounaq Jehan, *Pakistan: Failure in National Integration* (New York: Colombia University Press, 1972), pp. 167-71.

16. Ziring, *Ayub Khan Era*, p. 194.

17. An interesting analysis explaining how Mujib and Bhutto were both heavily influenced by their more radical constituencies will be found in Rounaq Jehan, "Elite in Crisis: An Analysis of Mujib-Yahya-Bhutto Negotiation," a paper delivered at the National Seminar on Pakistan/Bangladesh, Columbia University, February 26, 1972.

18. Robert LaPorte, Jr., "Pakistan in 1972: Picking up the Pieces," *Asian Survey* 13, no. 2 (February 1973): 187-98.

19. Hasan Askari Rizvi, *The Military and Politics in Pakistan* (Lahore: Progressive, 1974), p. 248. See also Khalid B. Sayeed, *Politics in Pakistan: The Nature and Direction of Change* (New York: Praeger, 1980); and Shahid Javed Burki, *Pakistan Under Bhutto, 1971-77* (New York: St. Martins Press, 1980).

20. Moinuddin Baqai, "Economic Progress During the People's Rule," in *Pakistan After 1971*, ed. Zahid Malik (Lahore: Ferozsons, 1974), p. 62.

21. Lawrence Ziring and Robert LaPorte, Jr., "The Pakistan Bureaucracy: Two Views," *Asian Survey* 14, no. 12 (December 1974): 1086-1183.

22. See Government of Pakistan, *White Paper on Baluchistan* (Islamabad: Printing Corporation of Pakistan Press, 1974).

23. Sir William Barton, *India's North-West Frontier* (London: John Murray, 1939), p. 13.

24. Abdul Qaiyum, *Gold and Guns on the Pathan Frontier* (Bombay: Hind Kitabs, 1945), p. 74.

25. Quoted in D. G. Tendulkar, *Abdul Ghaffar Khan: Faith Is a Battle* (Bombay: Popular Prakashan, 1967), pp. 529-30.

26. Useful studies on Pakistan's constitutional problems are Safdar Mahmood, *A Political Study of Pakistan* (Lahore: Sh. Muhammad Ashraf, 1972); and Richard S. Wheeler, *The Politics of Pakistan: A Constitutional Quest* (Ithaca, N.Y.: Cornell University Press, 1970).

27. Of special importance is the report of the *Court of Inquiry Constituted Under the Punjab Act II of 1954 to Enquire into the Punjab Disturbances of 1953* (Lahore: Government of the Punjab Press, 1954) and *An Analysis of the Munir Report: A Critical Study of*

the Punjab Disturbances Inquiry Report, trans. and ed. by Khurshid Ahmad (Karachi: Jamaat-i-Islami, 1956). See also Theodore P. Wright, Jr., "Indian Muslim Refugees in the Politics of Pakistan," *Journal of Commonwealth and Comparative Politics* 12, no. 2 (July 1974): 189–205.

28. Gustav F. Papanek, *Pakistan's Development: Social Goals and Private Incentives* (Cambridge: Harvard University Press, 1967), pp. 40–42.

29. Henry Frank Goodnow, *The Civil Service of Pakistan* (New Haven: Yale University Press, 1964), pp. 160–62.

30. E. W. R. Lumby, *The Transfer of Power in India* (London: George Allen and Unwin, 1954), p. 192.

31. For an examination of the Punjabi, Pathan, and Sindhi phases of Pakistan's history see Lawrence Ziring, "The Phases of Pakistan's Political History," in *Iqbal, Jinnah, and Pakistan: the Vision and the Reality*, ed. C. M. Naim, South Asia Series, no. 5 (Syracuse: Maxwell School, 1979), pp. 145–74.

32. Muzaffar Qadir, "Fear in the Punjab," *Outlook*, October 21, 1972, p. 12.

33. Salim Alvi, "A Nation's Halting Evolution," *Outlook*, May 11, 1974, p. 11.

34. See the autobiography of Ghaffar Khan as narrated to K. B. Narang, *My Life and Struggle* (Delhi: Hind Pocket Books, 1969); and Olaf Caroe, *The Pathans* (London: Macmillan, 1958). Also note the work of Shanti Ranjan Bhattacharya, *The Demand of Pakhtoonistan* (Calcutta: Lala Jan Khan, n.d.). Lala Jan Khan was general secretary of the Pakhtoon Jurga-e-Hind.

35. "Twilight of Justice" is but one example of a flood of articles published by *Outlook* before its banning for the second time. *Outlook*, February 9, 1974, pp. 9–12.

36. Lawrence Ziring, "Pakistan: A Political Perspective," *Asian Survey* 15, no. 7 (July 1975): 629–44.

37. G. W. Choudhry, *The Last Days of United Pakistan* (Bloomington: Indiana University Press, 1974), pp. 22–27.

38. Yusuf Lodi, "An Interview with Wali Khan," *Outlook*, July 6, 1974, p. 7.

39. Ibid., p. 8.

40. Zubeida Mustafa, "Afghanistan and the Asian Power Balance," *Pacific Community*, January 1975, pp. 286–89.

41. See William Branigan "Pakistan's Baluchis Distrust U.S. Aid," Washington *Post*, February 8, 1980, and "Baluchi Harbor A Lure to Soviets," Washington *Post*, February 9, 1980.

42. Ibid., pp. 296–99. See also Yu. V. Gankovsky, *The People of Pakistan* (Lahore: Peoples, n.d.) for a Soviet scholar's influential study of Pakistan's nationalities question.

43. "Iran-Pakistan Tandem," *Outlook*, March 30, 1974, pp. 6–8, and "Inside Baluchistan," *Outlook*, July 13–19, 1974, pp. 4–7.

44. A contrary view is held by Hafeez Malik. See his "Problems of Regionalism in Pakistan," in W. Howard Wriggins, ed., *Pakistan in Transition* (Islamabad: Islamabad University Press, 1975), pp. 60–132.

45. See Selig Harrison, *In Afghanistan's Shadow: Baluch Nationalism and Soviet Temptations* (New York: Carnegie Endowment, 1981).

46. C. I. Eugene Kim and Lawrence Ziring, *An Introduction to Asian Politics* (Englewood Cliffs, N.J.: Prentice-Hall, 1977), p. 124.

47. Stephen and Carroll McC. Pastner, "Adaptations to State-Level Polities by the Southern Baluch," in *Pakistan: The Long View*, ed. Lawrence Ziring, Ralph Braibanti, W. Howard Wriggins (Durham, N.C.: Duke University Press, 1977), pp. 117–39.

48. Aijaz Ahmad, "The National Question in Baluchistan," in *Focus on Baluchistan and Pushtoon Question*, ed. Feroz Ahmed (Lahore: People's, 1975), p. 39.

49. M. Masud, *Hari Report: Note of Dissent* (Karachi: Hari, 1976), pp. 9–11.

50. M. G. Weinbaum, "The March 1977 Elections in Pakistan: Where Everyone Lost," *Asian Survey* 17, no. 7 (July 1977): 599–618.

5

THE FUTURE OF AFGHANISTAN

Lawrence Ziring

Although the Afghans have been classified with the world's more independent people, Afghanistan itself has seldom known genuine freedom. Paradoxically, the hardy, undisciplined population of the mountain state exhibits enormous pride in their local habitat, but have displayed little interest in their extended nation.[1] Afghanistan's classic "backwardness" can be attributed to an absence of community. Despite the passage of centuries, Afghan loyalties have remained narrowly defined by tribe and kinship. What perceptions of statehood and national unity exist have been developed by a relatively small fraction of the nation and this element has been almost exclusively contained within the major urban areas. The overwhelming majority, however, preferred and opted for isolation and a life of self-regulation. The only meaningful government for the latter was found in their own traditions and codes, and among their own folk.

The Kabul government, especially in the days of the monarchy, was tolerated but not necessarily supported. So long as the monarchs refrained from interfering in the lives of the tribal people, the latter were prepared to give it their token support. Any change in this relationship predictably led to instability and conflict. The reforms of Amir Amanullah in the 1920s, like the reforms of Nadir and Zahir Shah in the 1930s and 1950s respectively, were doomed to failure because they violated the cardinal rule that superordinate authority was anathema to the Afghans.[2] But if the Afghan population generally shunned their own government, they were even more opposed to foreign interference. Thus the people of Afghanistan absorbed little in the way of positive experience from those not immediately conversant with their traditions. Their combative nature, an aggressive defense of their privacy, caused the interlopers to pay a high price for their adventures; but the beleaguered Afghan central government could not prevent Persians, Moghuls, Sikhs, Englishmen, or Russians from undermining the country's integrity.

Afghanistan occupies a stretch of territory which, although inhospitable and containing little material resources, makes it extremely susceptible to foreign intrigue. Afghanistan is the land bridge between the Middle East and the Indo-Pakistan subcontinent. It is also the southern extension of Central Asia and provides a meeting ground for the world's most populous states, i.e., the Soviet Union, India, and China. A succession of Kabul governments sought to modify Afghanistan's geography in the hope that the country's geopolitical position could be strengthened. In the nineteenth century the British thwarted Afghan plans in order to bolster their own status in the region, and to ward off a perceived Russian advance into the rim of Asia.[3]

In the twentieth century, Afghanistan saw its greatest opportunity for correcting territorial weaknesses. The withdrawal of Great Britain from South Asia in 1947 caused the Afghans to lay claim to the northwestern region of the subcontinent. The people residing in this sector were related to the people of eastern Afghanistan, and Kabul insisted their coerced separation should be ended. The British, however, did not depart South Asia until they had established the two sovereign and independent states of India and Pakistan. And Pakistan became the heir to British India's northwest frontier, not Afghanistan. Independent India, however, was sympathetic to the Afghan claim, primarily because New Delhi identified Pakistan as its number one enemy and a friendly Afghanistan was deemed to be in its interest.[4]

The Soviet Union also looked favorably on a redefined Afghanistan. Observing the hostility of its neighbors, Pakistan came to depend on the United States, which had an interest in protecting the new state's territorial integrity. Although the United States was hardly in a position to replace the British, the Americans, along with their Pakistani allies, once more frustrated Afghan chances at "correcting" their exposed, landlocked condition.

This chapter examines Afghanistan's quest for unity, modernity, and security. It attempts to place the current Afghanistan drama in meaningful perspective and it aims at ascertaining the long-term implications of the Soviet invasion and occupation.

HISTORICAL SHADOWS

Afghanistan emerged as a political entity as the great Asian migratory movements were drawing to a close. For almost two milennia, the region known as Southwest Asia, stretching from the Mediterranean across modern Turkey and through Iran to Afghanistan, was overrun by warring tribes that filtered through the Caucasus Mountains and the eastern side of the Caspian Sea.[5] A direct result of these movements was the erection of a sophisticated Central Asian culture, cast in an Islamic motif. The scientific and artistic achievements of Central Asia were remarkable. Indeed, the achievement is even more striking given the constancy of the defense requirement. The settled populations were under persistent pressure from marauding armies and although the civilization that was raised in the region prevailed, the nomadic tide could not be stemmed. Central Asia's development, however, influenced the behavior of the tribal people. While hardly capable of taming their rapacious nature, the invaders were often sedentarized and signs of sociability surfaced.

Little is known of Afghanistan's prehistory from a socioethnic point of view.[6] Some of the great armies of antiquity and the middle ages coursed through the region. Alexander, Ghengis Khan, and Tamerlane put their imprint on the region. Nevertheless, information is sparse and speculative on the original inhabitants, and their origins remain an enigma wrapped in a mystery.

When Afghanistan first appeared as a political entity in the mid-eighteenth century, the character of the state reflected the life pattern of the ethnic Pathans, believed to be the most indigenous claimants to the territory. The Pathans (Pashtuns or Pakhtuns) inhabit the eastern half of present-day Afghanistan and the northwestern portion of Pakistan. Residing in barren mountainous terrain, they have steadfastly held to ancient traditions and have opposed all attempts to alter their proud independence.[7] Given epoch-making but indecisive clashes between Turkic and Persian forces, the Sadozai Pathans under the leadership of Ahmed Shah, laid the foundation for contemporary Afghanistan. In 1747, the Durrani dynasty was formed by Ahmed Shah and the Pathans joined with the new monarchy in not only repelling the invaders, but in assaulting the Moguls in their Indian stronghold. In a brief period, not only the Moguls, but the Indian Mahrattas and Sikhs were also defeated, and Afghan rule was extended over a good portion of northern India.

After Ahmed Shah's death, the Durrani dynasty was shattered by internal dissension and the young Afghan empire crumbled. Sikh power expanded as a consequence of the Afghan decline. Dost Mohammad, a Mohammadzai, assumed the Afghan monarchy in the early segment of the nineteenth century. Under his leadership, the Sikh advance into Afghanistan was stymied and eventually they were forced to retreat to India. But by this time the British began to play a vital role in the affairs of the subcontinent. The Europeans were less inclined to support the Afghans given their efforts at wooing the Sikhs, and their determination to consolidate their own control over India. Dost Mohammad thus was the first Afghan leader to address himself to serious relationships with neighboring states. Observing the power arrayed against the Afghan nation, Dost Mohammad entertained assistance from Iran and Imperial Russia. The pattern of international relations thus established was destined to carry into and through the convulsions of the twentieth century.

Tsarist policy called for the expansion of empire and midway through the nineteenth century the Russians slashed their way into Muslim Central Asia and subdued the inhabitants. By the 1870s the imperial army had successfully consolidated its hold over the northern bank of the Amu Darya and Great Britain nervously envisaged a thrust through Afghanistan to Iran and the Persian Gulf on the one side, and through Afghanistan to India on the other. Determined to prevent a direct confrontation with the Russian tsar, the British both signaled their intention to fight to protect their interests, and to negotiate treaties of mutual benefit. In 1907, the British and Russians signed the Treaty of St. Petersburg, in which Iran was divided between them and Great Britain maintained its pre-eminence over the Persian Gulf. Britain earlier persuaded the Russians to establish the Amu Darya as the border between Russia and Afghanistan, thus creating a buffer zone between their rival ambitions.

In the last quarter of the nineteenth century the Afghans came more under the tutelage of the British then the Russians. However, Russian attempts to gain advantages from anti-British sentiment prevailing in Afghanistan were reasonably successful. The collapse of the tsarist empire during World War I and the revolution that brought the Bolsheviks to power, however, nullified Russian interests in Afghanistan. The Red Army was preoccupied with consolidating the revolution, and in Central Asia its task was complicated by British support for the White forces that remained loyal to the notion of monarchy.[8] The Bolsheviks, however, had promised independence to the people of Central Asia. Sensing that the Bolsheviks would assist them in regaining their freedom, some Central Asians enthusiastically supported the Red Army. The Whites suffered a string of defeats and were finally deserted by the British, who left them at the mercy of the victors. With the British no longer a factor, the Bolsheviks destroyed the White resistance. They also retreated from their promise to the inhabitants of Central Asia who were forcibly integrated into the Bolshevik state. The new leadership in Moscow called for the creation of a series of socialist republics in Central Asia and the Red Army was ordered to use force in order to gain compliance. The indigenous population was ill-equipped to defend itself against the Bolsheviks and they eventually succumbed to superior power in 1922–23.[9] Those Central Asians who found Soviet rule intolerable were left with one option, to flee across the Amu Darya.

Thousands of Uzbeks, Tajiks, and Turkomans settled in Afghanistan; others moved into British India while still others sought refuge in Iran and in the Turkish Republic. But given the haven that many Central Asians found in Afghanistan, the Soviets were noticeably disturbed lest they influence their brethren remaining behind in the Central Asian republics. To prevent such a possibility, the Soviets renewed an older policy of the tsars by reopening relations with Kabul. It was not until World War II had run its course, however, that the Soviets found the climate conducive for drawing Afghanistan into their orbit. The withdrawal of British power from the region created a power vacuum that the United States could not entirely fill. Although the Americans could appeal to the regimes in Iran and Pakistan, the Soviets reckoned Afghanistan was beyond their reach and hence could be made subject to Moscow's infuence. Although Afghanistan was perceived a buffer between the Soviet state and the

Indian Ocean countries, Moscow considered Afghanistan a forward area capable of challenging the post-World War II American "containment" program. The Soviets therefore became heavily involved in Afghanistan without directly threatening the country's national integrity—that is, until conditions in the area were dramatically altered by the United States retreat from Iran, and serious rifts developed between Washington and Islamabad. It was at this point that the Soviets sensed the time was ripe for the epoch crossing of the Amu Darya.

SOVIET LONG-TERM INTERESTS

From the outset of their invasion of Afghanistan the Soviets have insisted they were behaving as a responsible and concerned neighbor. Not only were they honoring treaty agreements with the Kabul government, they were also insistent that the mountain state was being subverted by foreign elements that were as much concerned with weakening the Soviet Union as they were in bringing Afghanistan under their influence.[10] Significantly, Afghanistan's destiny has been so intertwined with that of the Soviet Union that the Kremlin is unable to conceive of an Afghan republic independent from itself. The Brezhnev doctrine limiting the sovereignty of the East European satellites has been applied to Afghanistan. The "socialist commonwealth" is paramount and more narrowly defined loyalties are condemned as "chauvinistic" and a threat to the integration of the extended community. Such perceptions explain the oft-repeated charge that "imperialistic" powers foment, assist, and nurture the rebellious groups in Afghanistan. The United States, Pakistan, and China are described as the chief meddlers in Afghanistan's affairs. Egypt and Saudi Arabia are considered lesser culprits. Hence the calls for the withdrawal of Soviet troops from Afghanistan by the United Nations, the Islamic Summit, and the Islamic Conference as well as the principal nations in the Western world have been answered by the Kremlin with a counterdemand that the "real" interventionists are those distant parties who are bent on converting Afghanistan into an anti-Soviet base.

What is also overlooked is that the Soviet Union, ever since the Bolshevik Revolution, has considered itself the protector of Afghanistan's integrity. As such, Moscow has come to believe that its role in Afghanistan is not only more progressive but also more honorable. Moreover, given Marxist-Leninist ideology, the substitution of a modern state apparatus for a perceived antiquated, corrupt, feudal, and repudiated monarchial and tribal order was a Russian responsibility. Efforts by any other state to establish its influence in Afghanistan could only be judged a nefarious move aimed at defeating "progressive" forces in Afghanistan and thwarting the interests of the Soviet state. The notion of a "capitalist encirclement" has undergone significant modification in the aftermath of World War II, but Moscow is ever mindful of its weaknesses.[11] Threats to its position in Central Asia, no matter how remote, are taken very seriously.

Furthermore, the so-called Islamic revival that provoked a new level of excitement with the assumption of political power by the Islamic fundamentalists in Iran, is viewed as both regressive and primitive. Islamic ideology is also at variance with Marxism-Leninism, and its all-embracing character is considered an obstacle to Soviet policy and purpose. More important, the Islamic challenge represented in the call for Muslims to protect their traditions and unite in common cause, is judged a ploy of the Americans and their clients. Even though relations between the United States and Iran are strained by events related to the former's support of the shah, and Americans are widely denounced in the Muslim world for their assistance to Israel, Moscow still believes the United States seeks to gain advantages from the Islamic resurgence. The connection between Islam and "reactionary" behavior, between Islam and capitalism, or between Islam and monarchialism leads the Kremlin to conclude that their adversaries in the West stand to gain from this current display of Muslim "fanaticism." Islam has been publicized in the West as an impediment to communist penetration, but the Soviets argue that internal contradictions are so severe in the Muslim world that the ultimate collapse of Islamic-oriented governments is assured.

In this regard, the Soviets have a historical view of conditions in the Islamic countries. Believing the upheaval in Muslim societies offers opportunities for the rearrangement of power relationships and structures, the Kremlin often finds it useful to join with those Islamic movements that appear willing to accept their help. This is especially true in situations where the same adversary is identifiable. United Front movements are a salient feature of Soviet tactics and marriages of convenience do not rule out Soviet collaboration with groups and personalities otherwise judged to be antithetical. Just as Stalin was capable of joining with Hitler in the division of Poland in 1939, so too Brezhnev and his colleagues are inclined to support the forces represented by the Ayatollah Khomeini in Iran. The fact that both the ayatollah and Moscow have criticized one another does not prevent their association given actions that foreclose other relationships, i.e., Iran-U.S. collaboration.

The savage attack on the Socialist-oriented Muslims identifying with Abolhassan Bani-Sadr did not prevent the Tudeh Party (the communist party in Iran) and the Soviet Union from continuing their support for the Islamic fundamentalists.[12] Moreover, the Mujahiddin,* who have borne the brunt of the mullahs' ire and who have been placed under enormous pressure by the regime's revolutionary guard, were the arch enemies of the Fedeyeen and the Tudeh, the more radical and more secular organizations in Iran. The clash between the

---

*The Mujahiddin of Iran in this chapter are to be distinguished from the mujahiddin of Afghanistan. The former represents an organized Islamic-Marxist movement; the latter speaks of popular resistance to Marxism by Afghan devotees of Islam.

mullahs and the Mujahiddin weaken their capacity to manage the revolutionary experience. In time, given the passage of Khomeini and the decline of the fundamentalists as well as the possible discrediting of the Mujahiddin, the Tudeh and the Fedeyeen, with Soviet assistance, can be expected to assume control of the Iranian government. Moscow's apparent flirtation with the Khomeini government therefore must be viewed as a tactical maneuver.

The Soviets have practiced similar associations in the Arab world. Collaboration with the Palestine Liberation Organization (PLO) and Libya, and quasi alliances with Syria, the People's Democratic Republic of Yemen (South Yemen), and to some extent with Iraq indicate the Kremlin is capable of making successful inroads into the Arab world, despite the broad identification of the people of these countries with Islam.[13] Furthermore, so significant are these ties that even Soviet aggression in Afghanistan has not caused these Muslim countries to alter their relationship with Moscow. United Fronts do work—especially where political conditions are judged more salient than religious or ideological expression.

The Soviet Union understands the divisions in the Muslim world. Demands that it withdraw its troops from Afghanistan are neutralized by a lack of Islamic solidarity. The concern with "Islam in Danger" is not considered genuine. When the Egyptian and Saudi governments declared their support for the Afghan mujahiddin, Moscow's reaction was that they were either acting under pressure from Washington, or were using the incident to bolster their fragile domestic authority. The Kremlin is not moved by popularity contests, nor does the Politburo believe Anwar el-Sadat, his successor Hosni Mubarak, or the Saudi aristocrats speak for the Arab, let alone the Muslim people. The Russians therefore will not bow to public displays of verbal dissatisfaction. Nor will they be dissuaded in their course of action, which in their thinking demands they take advantage of the current chaos in southwest Asia. Moreover, since the late 1960s, Moscow has sought an Asian collective defense arrangement with its neighbors.[14] Although this Russian idea was initially rejected, events over the last decade may convince the targeted governments that it is in their interest to reconsider the proposal.

Afghanistan is of course the nucleus for this Asian collective security system. The status of forces agreement that Babrak Karmal signed permitting the Soviet Union to "legitimize" their occupation of his country, coupled with the 1978 treaty of friendship and cooperation entered into with Noor Mohammad Taraki sealed the fate of Afghanistan. The Soviets are now busily engaged in reconstituting the Afghanistan government. Soviet officials serve in important capacities in all the ministries and decision-making responsibilities are no longer an Afghan affair. More significant, the Soviet Union intends to transform Afghanistan into a willing satellite. The liquidation of the opposition has involved the elimination of a large segment of the sophisticated population. Moscow sees little purpose in emphasizing the role of the older generation. Its attention has been focused on the nation's youth, and it is they who are being courted, trained, and prepared for leadership roles in a future Afghanistan government.[15] But Soviet operations extend beyond finding the persons to fill the administrative posts in government. They are also interested in reconditioning Afghanistan's social fabric.

The Soviet program in Afghanistan can be characterized as "carrot and bludgeon." On the one hand, there is the frantic effort to fabricate popular support for the Babrak Karmal government. On the other, there is the savage attack on the mujahiddin and other dissident elements. Under a protocol entered into in 1980, Afghan students are being "educated" in the Soviet Union. Several thousand have undergone training in Soviet universities and technical institutes. These young people are meant to form a new cadre of leaders with a special dependency on the communist regime in Kabul and its Soviet mentors. The Soviets are also revamping Afghanistan's educational institutions. Textbooks are being prepared and instructors have been indoctrinated with a view toward legitimating the Soviet-backed administration. While this process of transformation proceeds, so too does the unleashing of violent forces on the resisting population. Clashes have intensified between Soviet and Afghan guerrillas. Attempts to recruit fourteen year olds for military service have not been very successful. Nor has a new draft law that was promulgated in January 1981. This law extended the length of military service to two and a half years and was aimed at stabilizing the Afghan army. Defections and desertions, however, have crippled the Afghan army. The Soviet army therefore finds itself not only the central policing agency in the country but also the principal combat arm in the struggle against the insurgents.[16] The more ubiquitous military role played by the Red Army means that they are also taking heavier casualties. And as Soviet losses multiply, the occupation force is driven to acts of cruelty. The destruction of entire villages and the terrorizing of those Afghans who would not or could not flee the country is not destined to gain supporters among the Afghan population.

The Soviet Union is fully aware that it cannot win the affection and support of the Afghans. Moreover, the harshness of Moscow's policies has also made it difficult for even leftist Afghans to work in the Karmal administration. Not only are these individuals targets for the urban guerrillas, they are also becoming more conscious of their national degradation and humiliation. In 1980 Afghanistan's deputy representative to the United Nations defected. The Afghan spokesman at the meeting of the nonaligned states requested asylum and accused the Soviet Union of genocide. Afghanistan's delegate to the United Nations Educational, Scientific, and Cultural Organization also left his post. In March 1981 four diplomats of the Afghan embassy in New Delhi requested asylum in the United States. Even Babrak Karmal's economic advisor, Mohammad Farhang, asked for refuge outside the country, explaining the Soviet Union had betrayed the Afghan nation.[17] Other signs of strain within the Karmal government were revealed in early 1981 when the deputy prime minister, the interior minister, and the army commander disappeared from public view along with other officials.[18]

In December 1980, Babrak Karmal endeavored to stem the tide of dissatisfaction by announcing the formation of a National Patriotic or Fatherland Front. The basic idea behind the front was the unification of disparate ethnic and political forces. The Soviet Union described the organization (and the meeting, originally slated for March 1981 but which was not convened until June and then abruptly terminated after one day) as a coalition of peasants and workers, religious teachers and tribesmen, students and businessmen. Moscow revealed that the purpose of the front was the civic education of the masses. Karmal had been instructed to form the organization during his extended stay in the Soviet Union in the fall of 1980. He was also counseled to heal the rift between the two factions of the People's Democratic Party of Afghanistan (PDPA), the Khalq, and the Parcham.

Relations between the two wings of the Marxist organization had been permanently ruptured by the savage attacks on the one group by the other. During the brief tenure of Taraki and Hafizullah Amin, the Khalqis had the upper hand and they often proved merciless in their treatment of the Parchamis. With the takeover by Babrak Karmal the Parchamis took their revenge and the two groups became implacable foes. Despite these impediments, Babrak Karmal attempted to consolidate his power. Initially, Karmal held the offices of president of the revolutionary council and prime minister. He also made himself responsible for labor and social security, for religious instruction, administrative reform and provincial affairs, and economic development. In all these activities, however, Karmal was dominated by his Soviet advisors who drafted and authorized all policies emanating from government house. Even the calling of a Loy Jirga or tribal assembly was judged to be a Soviet decision. Karmal was instructed to offer the tribal leaders political amnesty. He was also empowered to make financial gifts to those willing to collaborate with his regime. But none of these tactics were successful in tranquilizing Afghanistan. Moscow was compelled to recognize that their handpicked leaders were incapable of achieving Soviet objectives.

Although it was necessary to perpetuate the fiction of an independent Kabul regime, Moscow recognized that it could not avoid more obvious involvement in the country's affairs. With Soviet encouragement, the Ministry of Tribes and Border Affairs was renamed the Ministry of Tribes and Nationalities. As in the USSR, attention was given to the unique qualities of each ethnic group. In point of fact, the program aimed at keeping the various groups from unifying their purpose. The Soviets still believed the individual tribes could be bought off.

Another tactic forced Karmal to relinquish the prime minister's office in 1981. Although he continued as president of the Revolutionary Council and secretary-general of the party, the Kremlin appointed Sultan Ali Keshtmand as the new prime minister. Another Parchami, Keshtmand's assumption of the office revealed Karmal's inability to heal the Khalq-Parcham schism. It also suggested that Moscow might be losing faith in Karmal, and looked to other more capable members of the party to unite the factions and stabilize the regime.[19]

If there was an answer to the Soviet dilemma, it was not likely to be found in the traditionally constituted Afghan state. Rather the situation called for placing Afghanistan in its larger regional context and for rationalizing, according to Soviet logic, the area's geosocial and geoeconomic positions. Only in this way could the Soviet Union's geopolitical interests be realized. Given the continued fighting in the Afghan countryside, the tenacity with which the mujahiddin sought to preserve their way of life, and the uncertainties of the international equation in light of the American decision to supply Pakistan and China with sophisticated weapons, the Kremlin was bound to recognize that its irreversible course in Afghanistan would in time compel it to widen the conflict to include Iran, and especially Pakistan.

THE PAKHTUNISTAN QUESTION

Relations between Afghanistan and Pakistan have been strained ever since the independence of the latter in 1947. The Afghans did not look kindly on the creation of a Muslim state in the northwestern quadrant of the subcontinent. Like the Congress Party of India, they interpreted the partition of the subcontinent as a British tactic aimed at maintaining European influence in the area.[20] Pakistan, it was stated, was a product of Great Britain's *divide and rule* policy and the Europeans were the only party standing to gain from the emergence of still another national entity in the region. Both the Indians and Afghans shared historic enmities toward Great Britain, and both concluded that the creation of Pakistan would disrupt rather than facilitate indigenous development. The Indian National Congress spent considerable energy wooing the Pathans on the Northwest Frontier. A Congress Party was installed there in the preindependence period and although brothers in Islam, the Pathans were slow to show enthusiasm for the Muslim League, which had earlier called for the carving out of a self-governing Muslim state within the subcontinent. Only feverish activity on the part of Muslim League leaders managed to win over the Pathan population to the Pakistan idea. Even then, the Indian National Congress sought to cling to its hold on the area and it only yielded when Muslim sentiment developed into an overwhelming tide. At that point, the Congress began to explore other avenues with Afghanistan, which was only too willing to assist in containing Muslim League influence.

Afghanistan had serious differences with the British. And with the imminent emergence of an independent Pakistan, Kabul realized those differences would remain unresolved, and perhaps even more difficult to address. Uppermost in Afghan thinking was the Durand Line dividing Afghanistan from British

India and which was soon to become the border between Pakistan and Afghanistan. The Durand Line was unacceptable to the Afghans who argued that it had been imposed upon them by superior British power.[21] They also refused to accept the separation of the Pathan population, half of whom remained on the Afghan side of the Durand Line, and the other half in Pakistan. Kabul insisted that the division was a cruel, savage act and that Afghanistan would use every opportunity to reunite the tribal Pathans, even if that meant weakening the new Pakistani state. It is alleged that prior to the transfer of power establishing a sovereign, independent Pakistan, Congress leaders and members of the Afghan government agreed to a plan wherein Afghanistan would be provided an outlet to the sea, identified as the port of Karachi, in return for Indian-Afghan collaboration in either thwarting the creation of Pakistan or, later, in undermining the new state.[22] These allegations have never been proven but subsequent events appeared to reinforce their validity.

The Pathans of the Northwest Frontier had also perceived the British as the primary enemy. With the latter's withdrawal from the region, it was the Pakistan government that inherited the ill will generated by more than a century of deadly combat. Pakistan had every intention of integrating the Pathans along with the country's other nationalities into a coherent, purposive community. But the Islamic theme around which the nationalities were expected to rally was deficient in producing the anticipated objective. The Pathans, like the Sindhis, Baluchis, and Bengalis, were suspicious of Punjabi influence in the new Pakistan government. Moreover, many Muslim refugees from India settling in Pakistan assumed high positions in the country's government and economic sector, often at the expense of less sophisticated indigenous nationalities. These were abrasive issues, and given the Pathan perception that Islam was not in any danger in their part of the country, they had difficulty in grasping the threat to their religion in other areas of the subcontinent. In other words, the Muslim League cry of "Islam in Danger" was at best an abstract idea for the Pathan population. More generally it was viewed as a Pakistan government ploy, publicized to gain adherents and weaken older relationships.

More than a decade before the declaration of the Muslim League's Lahore Resolution (1940), which called for the creation of Muslim states in those areas of British India where the Muslims were in the majority, the Pathans had raised their cry of independence. The formation of the Khudai Khidmatgar by Abdul Ghaffar Khan in the late 1920s dramatized the sophistication of the Pathan demand for an independent "Pakhtunistan."[23] That demand was picked up by other tribal groups all along the Northwest Frontier, while to the south the call mixed with a similar, although more primitive Baluchi demand.[24] Thus by the time Pakistan surfaced as an independent state, other national movements were already well underway. The difference, however, was that Great Britain played the role of midwife at the birth of Pakistan whereas only Afghanistan consistently and openly championed the Pathan/Baluchi cause.

Both Pathans and Afghans have argued that Pakhtunistan is not part of the Indian subcontinent but inextricably tied to Central Asia. By the same reasoning, Pakhtunistan nationalists argue that the people of the frontier were never consulted by either the British or later by Pakistani authorities and they "never acceded to it [Pakistan] by their own free will."[25] The Afghans assumed responsibility for sustaining the Pakhtunistan Movement, knowing that this would permanently embitter relations between Kabul and Islamabad (earlier Karachi). The Afghans apparently gave little thought to the need for cooperation and mutual defense with Pakistan. There is little in the official record that addressed itself to the stabilization of relations between the two Muslim neighbors. Afghanistan preferred to see Pakistan as its primary problem and adversary and Afghan leaders were not inclined toward antagonizing either the Soviet Union or India. The concept of Muslim solidarity remained a verbalization, empty of any genuine significance. But Pakhtunistan, the claim against the Pakistan state, received preeminent attention in Kabul:

> Any claims made by Pakistan on Pakhtunistan, as heir or successor to the British Indian Empire, is . . . void and invalid. Britain did conquer and occupy parts of Pakhtunistan, but she was never in possession of the country as a whole. . . . In consideration of the gravity of the situation, and considering her moral obligations as well as her ties and interests in the affairs of the people of Pakhtunistan, Afghanistan cannot take the position of a disinterested bystander. . . . Any calamity arising out of this restive situation is bound to affect the peace of the region in general and of the neighbouring countries of Afghanistan, Pakhtunistan and Pakistan, in particular.[26]

Afghanistan therefore attempted to block Pakistan's admission to the United Nations. It supported tribal insurrections such as the one led by the Faqir of Ipi in the early years following Pakistan's independence. It gave assistance, encouragement, and asylum to Abdul Ghaffar Khan and other Pakhtunistan Movement leaders. In the 1970s it became the principal conduit for supplies to Baluchi rebels.[27] It also offered sanctuary for Baluchi defectors and generally displayed sympathy for the tribal "liberation" movement. The tension caused by these events brought the periodic severance of diplomatic relations and the closing of the Pakistan/Afghanistan frontier to Afghan commercial goods transiting Pakistan to the port of Karachi. The rupturing of trade relationships had a telling effect. Afghanistan found it necessary to use the Soviet Union for its international trade and an even greater dependency on Moscow was created. In the 1960s, the Soviet Union became Afghanistan's chief trading partner. The Soviets also assumed major responsibility for supplying Afghanistan with staples and other necessities. In return, Kabul permitted the Soviets a free hand in developing the country's road network. The Salang Tunnel was built through the mountains separating Soviet Uzbekistan from Afghanistan.[28] The Russians also improved and constructed Afghan airfields and expanded the telecommunications system. The Afghan military establishment, aided by the United States and Turkey after World War II, also became an almost exclusive concern of the Russians. In sum, if Afghanistan had any opportunity following World War II to develop distance in its relationship with the Soviet Union, it was lost in the passion of the Pakhtunistan affair. When the shah of Iran moved to reverse the prevailing situation in the early 1970s and offered Kabul the use of Iranian port facilities and also pledged financial assistance, it was already too late.

AFGHANISTAN IN TRANSITION

The overthrow of King Zahir Shah by his cousin and brother-in-law Sardar Daud in 1973 was countenanced by the national Marxist organizations; more importantly it had the approval of the Soviet Union. Daud's decision to terminate the Afghan monarchy also appealed to these parties. Daud's call to the Pathans on Pakistan's Northwest Frontier to join with him in the creation of their Pakhtunistan state was also captivating. King Zahir Shah had made the mistake of seriously entertaining better relations with Great Britain and the United States. He also had responded positively to the shah's call to mediate the dispute between Pakistan and Afghanistan. None of these actions were deemed to be in the interest of the local Marxists or the Kremlin leadership and Daud became their willing instrument in destroying the king's authority.[29]

Sardar Daud, however, did not fully understand the extent of his country's commitment to the Soviet Union. He could not be oblivious to the omnipresence of Soviet advisors in his country; nor could he ignore the heavy indebtedness of Afghanistan to the Soviet Union in the economic and developmental sectors. Nevertheless, he was a proud, shrewd, ruthless figure. He had strong ties to the Afghan military establishment as well as the tribal Pathans. He therefore believed the Russians needed him even more than he needed them. Daud, however, soon found himself under extreme pressure from his Soviet advisors to admit more Marxists into his administration. The Soviets were also determined to ideologically indoctrinate the Afghan military units that came under their influence. By 1976 Daud realized he needed new leverage in dealing with Soviet subversion of his authority. Thus, like the king he had overthrown, he turned toward Iran and again the shah entered the picture.

By this time Iran was an accepted power in the region.[30] The Iranian military had demonstrated its prowess in quelling the Omani insurgency. Moreover, the Shah had forced the Iraqis to accept a peace treaty that granted Iran its long coveted "rights" on the Shatt-al-Arab. In return the shah pledged he would cease supporting the Kurdish national movement that was then directed against Baghdad. Iran had become the principal recipient of U.S. armaments, had established its control over the Persian Gulf, and the shah had begun to talk of his country's larger destiny. In addition, the steep rise in petroleum prices in the mid-1970s and Iran's principal role in the Organization of Petroleum Exporting Countries (OPEC) also earned the shah stature heretofore beyond his reach. It was in these circumstances that Daud sensed the necessity of drawing closer to Iran and of reconciling differences with Pakistan. The question remained if he could also avoid raising suspicions in Moscow. In the final analysis, Afghanistan was linked to the Soviet Union, and Daud was expendable.

In April 1978, just a few weeks after his return from a goodwill mission to Pakistan, Daud was overthrown in a bloody coup that all but wiped out his family as well as his top colleagues. Military units loyal to the Marxist People's Democratic Party of Afghanistan (PDPA) carried out the action and immediately turned over control of the government to the leaders of the radical organization. Moscow immediately publicized its support for the new government and promised all necessary assistance. Under the leadership of the Khalq faction of the PDPA, the Afghan government renewed its call for Pakhtunistan and all but nullified the efforts of the previous year. Although the Pakistan government indicated its desire to keep the negotiations alive, there was little encouragement from Kabul.

Given the disarray in Afghanistan, however, the Pakistan authorities were able to bring an insurgency in Baluchistan under control. The Northwest Frontier also passed into a relatively tranquil stage of wait and see. Moreover, Pakistan's government had been seized by its military establishment in July 1977 and the regime of General Zia-ul-Haq was preoccupied with consolidating its power. The basic equilibrium that settled over Pakistan, however, contrasted with continuing turbulence in Afghanistan. The PDPA factions could not control their rivalry despite Soviet efforts. The Khalqis forced the Parchamis from key positions and proceeded to recreate Afghanistan according to their own predispositions.[31] Noor Mohammad Taraki, although the titular leader, was not the real power in the Khalq. His deputy, Hafizullah Amin, was the more effective personality and he insisted that Babrak Karmal, the leader of the Parcham should be eliminated in order to free the Khalq to implement its program for Afghanistan's transformation. Taraki was unable to mediate the dispute between Amin and Karmal but rather than antagonize the Russians (who preferred Karmal), Taraki assigned Karmal to a diplomatic post. Even then Amin sought to liquidate his nemesis, but Karmal had the support of Soviet authorities and he was eventually provided sanctuary in Moscow.

In the meantime, Amin moved to change the Afghan way of life. Reforms were announced that aimed at bringing Afghanistan into the contemporary age, but as was expected, the tribal people were unalterably opposed to government actions. Other Afghan leaders had attempted to break the tribal circle and had failed; but this time there was no hesitation in bringing force to bear on the situation. Moreover, the Afghan army had been developed into a formidable strike force and Amin believed his troops could break the resistance of the fragmented, rebellious tribes. Amin too proved to be in error. The opposition rallied behind the cry of "Islam in Danger" and the warriors of the faith, the mujahiddin, not only repelled government troops, they also began murderous assaults on government officials, foreign advisors, and innocent travelers.[32] The tenacity of the struggle convinced the Kremlin that Amin was too aggressive, too ambitious, and therefore a threat to the consolidation of the revolution. Taraki was called to Moscow and ordered to dismiss Amin and his followers, to clean up the Khalq, and to permit Babrak Karmal and the Parcham to rejoin his government. He was also instructed to reduce the pressure on the tribal population. When Amin learned that he was targeted for elimination, a dispute broke out and in the struggle that ensued Taraki was shot and killed. Amin proclaimed himself the preeminent ruler of Afghanistan.[33] Moscow, however, was unprepared for this development and orders went out to correct the situation before it could threaten Soviet security.

Observed from Moscow, Amin was both an embarrassment and a questionable servant. The Kremlin despatched high-ranking officials, including members of the Politburo to Kabul. These officials were charged with either taming Amin, or preparing his destruction. One such official was the Soviet first deputy minister of internal affairs, Lieutenant General Victor Paputin. Apparently the information sent to the Kremlin recommended Amin's execution. Amin had replaced Taraki in September 1979 and hardly three months later he too was dead, killed by unknown persons, but allegedly by or under Soviet orders. The mysterious death of Paputin during the same period suggests a shoot-out between forces loyal to the Afghan leader and the palace-domiciled Russian forces.[34] The death of Amin would have been a major event in itself had not the Soviet Union decided to open a full-scale military campaign in Afghanistan. The day that Amin died the Soviet army poured across the Oxus River and fanned over the country quickly seizing the principal metropolitan areas, military installations, and airfields. Soviet paratroopers were airlifted into Kabul and Babrak Karmal returned to his capital from Moscow to assume command of the country's new Revolutionary Council.[35]

Moscow stunned the world by its invasion. Nevertheless, the Soviets had calculated there would be minimum opposition to its invasion, and that even then the assault would be verbal not physical. Insofar as the Afghan guerrillas were concerned, the Soviets expected to crush their resistance. In the meantime the Kremlin was not silent. Claiming it had responded to an Afghan government request and that it was merely honoring a treaty commitment, the Soviets argued that Afghanistan had been invaded by foreign provocateurs and they singled out Pakistan as the principal source of the trouble.[36] Aided and encouraged by the United States and China, Pakistan, according to Soviet official statements, was determined to destroy the Marxist revolution in Afghanistan. Soviet troops would be withdrawn from Afghanistan only when Moscow was assured that such foreign intervention had ceased and all attempts at subverting the revolutionary government were terminated.

Pakistan had obvious sympathies with the Afghan mujahiddin, but the Islamabad government hardly influenced their behavior. Indeed, Pakistan had never been able to bring its own tribal population into line with government policy. The Russians knew this. The Soviet charge therefore that Islamabad had instigated, organized, and fueled the insurrection could not be taken seriously. Moreover, the ill will expressed toward Pakistan by Afghanistan in connection with the Pakhtunistan Movement reemphasized Islamabad's essential inability to manage guerrilla warfare against the Afghan regime. There was little doubt that the Afghans were behaving as was their wont; they had always resisted reformers that tampered with their life-style. They refused to yield to the modernizing monarchies and they were no less defiant in resisting the modernizing Marxists. Finally, the use of lethal violence against reluctant tribesmen only added fuel to the fire. The Afghans dedicated themselves to the preservation of their traditional values and Islam became the symbol that linked otherwise disparate groups in common cause.[37]

The inability or reluctance of the Afghan armed forces to crush the resistance, their defection and general demoralization, was a telltale signal to the Soviet officers attached to Afghan units. Sensing that they could not maintain discipline and facing threats to their person, these officers demanded that they be withdrawn or that the Kremlin order in large contingents of Soviet troops. Conditions in Iran and also Pakistan seemed to both aggravate the situation in Afghanistan and to provide the Soviets with an opportunity to assert their authority. In Iran, the Islamic revolutionaries had seized the American embassy in Tehran. The embassy staff had been seized and held hostage. Iranians by the tens of thousands demonstrated in the streets outside the diplomatic compound in a gross display of passionate anti-Americanism. Within a few weeks of the Tehran embassy takeover, the American embassy in Islamabad was also assaulted and destroyed by a mob identified as students and Islamic fundamentalists.[38] The double-barrel assault on American installations and personnel (as well as reverberations elsewhere, i.e., India, Bangladesh, Libya) virtually paralyzed the United States and captured the attention of other nations. Thus when the Soviets moved their troops into Afghanistan, Moscow counted on the world's other preoccupations. Moscow was not only interested in protecting a Marxist revolution from Muslim "fanatics," it was also ready to effect a historic change in the geopolitical structure of Central, South, and Southwest Asia.

The Russian scholars attached to the Soviet Academy of Sciences had studied the Afghans and Pakistanis in great depth.* They knew the tribal people would resist their invasion and that the struggle would be savage and unrelenting. The Soviet military, however, was given no option other than to crush the

---

*Special note should be made of Yu. V. Gankovsky, *The Peoples of Pakistan: An Ethnic History* (Lahore: People's, n.d.).

rebellion. The protracted nature of the fighting, the difficulty of the terrain, and the decision thus far to maintain an effective but not overpowering force in the country caused the conflict to settle into a "hold and pulverize" pattern. The Soviets intended to hold the metropolitan centers and to pulverize the remote villages. The Russians did not expect to bring the tribals to heel. They did, however, anticipate winning the support or the acceptance of the more sophisticated elements in the urban areas. Moreover, as they went about the business of reforming Afghanistan, the Soviets were also in the process of driving the more primitive population into Pakistan. By mid-1981 it was estimated that more than 2 million tribal Afghan refugees had sought refuge in Pakistan's Northwest Frontier Province.

It is possible to speculate with the theory that the Soviet intention was to force Afghanistan's less pliable population upon the Pakistanis. The problems that this influx of people creates for the Islamabad government extends well beyond the question of providing for their welfare. The Soviet Union is making it impossible for these people to return to their homes and it is becoming more evident that they will be taking up residence in Pakistan on a more or less permanent basis. The political implications of this shift in population are intriguing. First, the Soviet Union is determined to consolidate the Marxist revolution in Afghanistan. There is no reason at this point to question their ability to succeed. Second, the Kremlin has reopened the "Pakhtunistan question" in a way that has not previously been conceived. The shift of almost 20 percent of Afghanistan's population to Pakistan, the vast majority Pathans, will enflame, not dampen the Pakhtunistan issue. The Pathans may have reason to despise the Soviet Union, but in their desperation they have even greater need for a homeland. Unable to defeat the Soviet army they are destined to turn their attention toward Islamabad. Moreover, given Islamabad's inability or reluctance to serve their needs, the Pathans are programmed to become a threat to Pakistan's integrity. In time, the Soviets could even assist in rearranging the geography of the area. Just as the Soviet Union has moved to annex the Wakhan corridor, it is likely to partition Afghanistan.

THE WAKHAN CORRIDOR

Evidence of Soviet intentions in Afghanistan are illustrated by Moscow's haste in consolidating its hold over the Wakhan corridor, the thin territorial salient that provided Afghanistan a short border with the People's Republic of China (PRC), and separated the USSR from Pakistan. Reports filtering out from the region insist the Soviet force in the Wakhan is being reinforced and that the territory is to be annexed within the Soviet state.[39] These allegations are supported by information that Soviet Tajik forces comprise the principal garrison (Tajikistan borders on the Wakhan corridor), and that a redefinition of the Soviet frontier is being effectuated. Given the Kremlin's primary concern with security, occupation, and ultimately control of the salient will not only close off China from Afghanistan, it will also place Soviet firepower in closer proximity to the PRC nuclear facility at Lop Nor. It will also give the Soviet Union a shared border with Pakistan. Hence communications between Soviet Tajikistan and Wakhan have improved. A motorized road has been constructed and will be made more permanent. Bridges are being erected across mountain chasms, and tunnels are contemplated to facilitate the movement of troops and supplies. Telecommunications have also been rigged to meet the needs of the occupation army. Nor can this strenuous activity be justified by the current military campaign. There has been little if any resistance to Soviet troops in this area of Afghanistan, and if the purpose of the invasion was merely to quell disturbances and neutralize threats to the Kabul regime, such objectives could have been realized without so extensive a commitment. Even noting the Soviet tactic of overkill, that is overwhelming its adversary with more than the required numbers to do the job, the Moscow action forces the conclusion that the Wakhan corridor is to be absorbed within the Tajikistan republic.

The Wakhan is a rugged mountain region near the Pamir Mountains. In the nineteenth century it gained attention because of British-Russian competition in Central Asia. That contest, known historically as the Great Game, was precipitated by Imperial Russian advances through Central Asia. The British, concerned that their lifeline to India by way of the Middle East, their dominance on the Persian Gulf, and their Indian colony were all jeopardized by the Russian advance moved to stem their drive. A Forward Policy was implemented by Lord Lytton and later expanded by Lord Curzon that brought the British into direct conflict with the Afghan nation. Two Anglo-Afghan wars were fought in the nineteenth century and a final one following World War I.[40] By these engagements Great Britain demonstrated its resolve to keep the Russians from reaching the warm water areas. The wars also caused the Afghans to perceive the British as their primary enemy, and thus the Russians saw an opportunity to ingratiate themselves with the leaders in Kabul and among the tribes.

In 1893 Great Britain settled for a buffer zone solution. The border between Afghanistan and British India was drawn by Sir Mortimer Durand, who eventually won the support of the Afghan king, Adbur Rahman. Earlier the British entered into an agreement with the Russians and the Afghanistan frontier in the north was drawn at the Amu Darya (Oxus River). During that negotiation in 1873, Great Britain and Russia agreed the Wakhan territory from Badakshan to the Pamirs would remain a part of Afghanistan, thus physically separating India from the Russian empire. This understanding was affirmed and legalized in a treaty accepted by London and St. Petersburg in 1887. By this time, Great Britain controlled Afghanistan's foreign relations, and the Amu Darya was consecrated as the border between Afghanistan and Russia. Although the 1887 treaty seemed to relieve tension in the area, that segment of the border involving the Wakhan corridor and focusing on the source of the Amu Darya was never clearly settled. In 1889 the Russians made a number of forays into the Wakhan and in 1891 a Russian exploration expedition attempted to claim it.

The British were again provoked to intervene. With the assistance of Abdur Rahman, the British convinced the Russians that a more complete demarcation of Afghan domain was necessary. As a result of these efforts, a joint boundary commission was assembled that included Russian representatives, and the Wakhan corridor was officially recognized as coming under Afghan sovereignty in 1895-96. The Chinese, who were also affected by the drawing of this border, did not participate in the deliberations of the boundary commission. They insisted the entire endeavor was a European imperialist plot aimed at further subverting their independence. Indeed, the Chinese did not accept Afghanistan's control of the Wakhan corridor until the PRC agreed to sign a separate agreement with Kabul in November 1963.[41]

The USSR confirmed its acceptance of the boundary with Afghanistan following the Bolshevik revolution and it was again proclaimed in the Afghanistan-USSR Treaty of 1946, which applied the Thalweg principle in identifying the Amu Darya boundary.

The Soviets, however, were never convinced that their fiat carried only up to the river frontier. The agreements entered into with the Afghans and earlier with the British were always assumed to be temporary. Given changing conditions, there was no reason to continue a policy that had lost its tactical value. The Russians had paused at the Oxus for a century, waiting for changes to occur in the political environment. But once such changes were judged irreversible, it was incumbent on the leaders in Moscow to press their claims. The annexation of the Wakhan corridor can be observed as a consequence of history. The Soviets would argue scientific inevitability had manifested new circumstances and that their actions were linked to the inexorable forces of history. Others might describe this latest Russian advance as undisguised imperialism. But however judged, the Soviet invasion signaled Moscow's determination to spread its sovereignty into areas long coveted and now deemed ever more vital to the country's security.

AFGHANISTAN AND ITS IMMEDIATE NEIGHBORS

Afghanistan is experiencing permanent metamorphosis. Politically, socially, economically, and geographically it will never return to its previous condition. Monarchy is a thing of the past. The republican interregnum introduced by Daud in 1973 has given way to a Marxist system. But even that system is inchoate and will be made subject to refinement by Soviet authorities. Afghanistan appears destined to follow a pattern of government in intimate relationship with the Soviet Union, with Outer Mongolia the probable model. Outer Mongolia legally maintains a separate, independent, and sovereign identity but politically it is totally dependent on and wedded to Moscow. Like Outer Mongolia, Afghanistan can no longer sustain the fiction that it is a free agent. Moreover, as with Outer Mongolia, Afghanistan's social and economic character will undergo significant modification. Afghanistan already services the Soviet Union's requirement for natural gas, and its economy has long been intertwined with that of its northern neighbor. Policies now being implemented will assure the continuation of this relationship.

The Afghans are already a subject for Soviet planners. For the foreseeable future Afghanistan's material development will reflect the needs of the Soviet state and the socialist commonwealth, not the isolated requirements of a developing nation. In the same context, the Soviet Union intends to break the back of tribalism in Afghanistan. Tribal behavior is an impediment to progressive change. It sustains parochial loyalties that cannot be tolerated in a highly centralized multinational state. Moreover, Afghanistan must learn to pay its own way, and this will be possible only when the available resources are used to the fullest. As in the Central Asian republics of the Soviet Union, it will probably prove necessary to develop an intergrated plan in which Afghanistan is given a specific mission in an all-embracing political design.

While the transformation of Afghanistan from a primitive to a modern, contemporary Marxist state falls heaviest on the indigenous population, changes in the country's geography are slated to impact on its immediate neighbors. The Soviet annexation of the Wakhan corridor is a harbinger of what is to follow. Moscow's concerns focus upon the division of ethnic groups not only between Pakistan and Afghanistan, but also between Iran and Afghanistan, and especially between Afghanistan and its own Central Asian republics.[42] Conversant with the nationality question, it is the Kremlin's intention to redefine political frontiers in order to rationalize and stabilize ethnic groupings. The success of such efforts will be read in the reduction of tension between the parties. Tajiks, Turkomans, Uzbeks as well as Baluchis and Pathans are expected to find new satisfaction in territorial arrangements that better represent their unique heritage. None of these developments, however, signal tranquility for Pakistan and Iran.

Pakistan and Iran are fragile political actors. Their territorial integrity already bears deep scars from earlier violations. Both countries are seriously threatened by centrifugal forces from within and foreign adventurers without. Revolutionary Iran seems headed for a disastrous end. The weakness of the mullah-dominated central government and the eventual collapse of the Islamic state provide new opportunities for separatist movements, ethnically based, to gather momentum and in time to assert their authority. The immediate beneficiaries of the shah's demise may have been the Shiite clergy, but the long-term "winners" are more likely to be Iran's disparate nationalities. As Iran becomes more convulsed by internecine strife, the Kurds will continue to press for an independent Kurdistan, and Turkomans and Baluchis also appear determined to reap dividends from the disorder. Moreover, tribal groups such as the Bakhtiari,

Quashqai, and Azeri are not likely to remain quiescent. They too have territorial demands and although not necessarily realizable, their actions could help accelerate Iran's disintegration.

Pakistan gives the appearance of a "bastion of stability" in the area when contrasted with conditions in Afghanistan and Iran. But appearances are misleading. Beneath the surface, Pakistan faces the greatest challenge to its integrity and independence since its loss of East Pakistan in 1971. The creation of Bangladesh was an event of unprecedented dimensions. It represented the only instance since the end of World War II in which a country established its independence as a result of civil war. Notably, Bangladesh did not emerge as a sovereign entity until the internationalization of the conflict by India and the indirect support provided by the Soviet Union. It is doubtful the Bengalis would have been successful had it not been for the midwifery of these external powers. Nevertheless, it is important to note the alacrity with which the global community accepted the new state and Pakistan's dismemberment. There is then no reason to believe that the world could not adjust to other rearrangements in the political map of South and Southwest Asia. Indeed, it already appears that many governments are prepared to recognize the inevitability of the changes.

The maturing "Pakhtunistan" question and continuing (even if more subdued) unrest in Pakistan Baluchistan address themselves to issues that have been enormously complicated by the Soviet presence in Afghanistan and the flight of more than 2 million Afghans to Pakistan. Assuming the intensification of political conflict between the Zia-ul-Haq administration and his domestic political detractors, and the inability to fashion an acceptable political system based upon a common Islamic ideology, Pakistan's stability could rapidly give way to anarchy. What strengthens Pakistan and gives it the possibility of survival is the resourcefulness and discipline of its armed forces. But even the military cannot be insulated from divisive elements within the country. It remains to be seen to what extent the threat posed to Pakistan by the near proximity of the Red Army can submerge national antagonism. But the Zia government is certainly counting on that perception to reinforce his otherwise shaky authority.

Read in this context, Pakistan's determination to construct an atomic weapon (although persistently denied by Islamabad) is judged necessary to sustain the pride and integrity of the armed forces. It is also viewed as a defense of Pakistan's territorial configuration and independence.* Moreover, the Reagan administration's generous offer of military assistance to Pakistan is not only a total reversal of American policy toward Islamabad, it is also predicated on the assumption that Pakistan is the only bulwark against further Soviet encroachment

---

*A preemptive strike against Pakistan's nuclear facility must be considered more plausible, given Israel's destruction of the Iraqi reactor in July 1981.

in the region. Washington envisages disaster in Iran with subsequent repercussions throughout the Persian Gulf if the line is not held in Pakistan. And while relations between Washington and Islamabad are cool, President Reagan's concern in maintaining the integrity of Pakistan makes it possible for the two governments to interact at levels of mutual self-interest. Thus the Reagan administration has let up on the pressure aimed at preventing Pakistan from acquiring nuclear capability. It has also promised to refurbish the Pakistani armed forces with the most sophisticated weapons systems in the American arsenal. Furthermore, President Reagan, unlike his predecessors, appears indifferent to Indian complaints. Not only does the American administration display impatience with New Delhi, it is also more ready than any of its predecessors to characterize India as playing Moscow's game.

India's reaction has been predictable. On the domestic scene, New Delhi speaks of the necessity to match the American arms transfer to Pakistan. Pakistan has also been warned that India will have to gear up its own nuclear arms program if Islamabad persists in its course. Internationally, India has given lip service to the withdrawal of *all* foreign forces from Afghanistan, but its dependence on the Soviet Union prevents it from citing Moscow as the source of the conflict.[43] New Delhi's need for allies and its rejection of an American connection, coupled with U.S. support for its two arch enemies, Pakistan and China, make the Soviet option a fundamental requirement of Indian foreign policy. Moreover, India is concerned with the possibility of Pakistan's expanded role as policeman in the Persian Gulf. Possessing a nuclear deterrent and the recipient of American arms, Pakistan could be convinced to take up positions in "defense" of the Persian Gulf. Discussions with Saudi Arabia have reviewed the possible movement of Pakistani infantry and armor units as well as air squadrons to the Arabian peninsula.[44] In return for this trained manpower, Saudi Arabia has offered to pay for the weapons that Islamabad intends to obtain from the United States. Initial reports indicated the Saudis were prepared to bankrole Pakistani purchases up to $2.5 billion dollars. More recent accounts cite a lower figure, said to be approximately $500 million—and this sum to be spread over a ten-year period.[45] Definitive decisions are still in the offing. Nevertheless, the direction and the purpose is clear.

The Soviet Union's invasion of Afghanistan is not being treated as an isolated event.[46] Soviet and Southwest Asia are criss-crossed by contradictions that threaten the independence of the states of the region. Concomitantly, older, more established political systems seem less able to sustain their integrity and authority. And as the region moves from crisis to crisis, opportunities arise for outside as well as internal parties to take advantage of the situation. The merging of these opportunistic interests and the means developed to counter their activities will dominate events for the foreseeable future.

NOTES

1. See James W. Spain, *The Pathan Borderland* (The Hague: Mouton, 1963); and Fredrik Barth, "Pathan Identity and Its Maintenance," in *Ethnic Groups and Boundaries*, ed. B. Barth (Boston: Little, Brown, 1969).

2. See Louis Dupree, *Afghanistan*, 2d. ed. (Princeton: Princeton University Press, 1980).

3. W. K. Fraser-Tytler, *Afghanistan: A Study of Political Developments in Central Asia* (London: Oxford University Press, 1950), pp. 90–91.

4. S. M. Burke, *Pakistan's Foreign Policy: An Historical Analysis* (London: Oxford University Press, 1973), p. 75.

5. Lawrence Ziring, *Iran, Turkey and Afghanistan: A Political Chronology* New York: Praeger, 1981), pp. 37–40.

6. Olaf Caroe, *The Pathans, 550 B.C.-A.D. 1957* (London: Macmillan, 1958), p. 26.

7. Khalid B. Sayeed, "Pathan Regionalism," *The South Atlantic Quarterly* 63, no. 4 (Autumn 1964): 478–506.

8. Edgar O'Ballance, *The Red Army* (London: Faber and Faber, 1964), p. 89.

9. See Alexander Park, *Bolshevism in Turkestan, 1917-1927* (New York: Columbia University Press, 1957).

10. Henry Trofimenko, "The Third World and U.S.-Soviet Competition," *Foreign Affairs* 59, no. 5 (Summer 1981): 1039–40. See also Commentary by Drew Middleton on President Ronald Reagan's suggestion that the United States may begin supplying the Afghan guerrillas with arms. New York *Times*, March 28, 1981.

11. Seweryn Bialer, "The Harsh Decade: Soviet Policies in the 1980s," *Foreign Affairs* 59, no. 5 (Summer 1981): 999–1020.

12. New York *Times*, July 16, 1981.

13. *The Manchester Guardian Weekly*, May 17, 1981, p. 1.

14. Phillips Talbot, "The Subcontinent: Menage ā Trois," *Foreign Affairs* 50, no. 4, (July 1972): 707.

15. Eliza Van Hollen, "Afghanistan: A Year of Occupation," *Special Report No. 79* (Washington, D.C.: U.S. Department of State, February 1981), p. 4.

16. Nancy P. Newell and Richard S. Newell, *The Struggle for Afghanistan* (Ithaca: Cornell University Press, 1981), p. 136.

17. Keesing's Contemporary Archives, May 22, 1981, p. 30880. See also S. Enders Wimbush and Alex Alexiev, *Soviet Central Asian Soldiers in Afghanistan* (Santa Monica: Rand, 1981), pp. 1-18.

18. New York *Times*, January 2, 1981.

19. Eliza Van Hollen, "Afghanistan: Eighteen Months of Occupation," *Special Report No. 86* (Washington, D.C.: U.S. Department of State, August 1981), pp. 1-2.

20. See Feroz Ahmed, *Focus on Baluchistan and Pushtoon Question* (Lahore: People's, 1975).

21. Mujtaba Razvi, *The Frontiers of Pakistan: A Study of Frontier Problems in Pakistan's Foreign Policy*, (Karachi: National, 1971), pp. 144–45.

22. Confidential interviews involving the author in October 1965.

23. See Abdul Ghaffar Khan, *My Life and Struggle* (Delhi: Orient Books, 1969).

24. Robert G. Wirsing, *The Baluchis and Pathans*, Report No. 48 (London: Minority Rights Group, 1981), pp. 14-15.

25. Rahman Pazhwak, *Pakhtunistan: A New State in Central Asia* (London: Royal Afghan Embassy, 1960), p. 22.

26. Ibid., pp. 25–28.

27. See Government of Pakistan, *White Paper on Baluchistan* (Islamabad: Printing Corporation of Pakistan Press, 1974).

28. Zubeida Mustafa, "Afghanistan and the Asian Power Balance," *Pacific Community*, January 1975, p. 285.

29. Congressional Research Service, *Afghanistan: Soviet Invasion and U.S. Response*, Issue No. IB80006 (Washington, D.C., July 22, 1980), p. 2.

30. Sepehr Zabih, "Iran's Policy Toward the Persian Gulf," *International Journal of Middle East Studies* 7 (July 1976): 345–58.

31. Newell and Newell, *The Struggle for Afghanistan*, pp. 73–74.

32. A. G. Noorani, "Soviet Ambitions in South Asia," *International Security*, Winter 1979–80, pp. 31–59.

33. Raju G. C. Thomas, "The Afghanistan Crisis and South Asian Security," paper presented at the annual meeting of the International Studies Association, Philadelphia, March, 1981, p. 12.

34. Marshall D. Shulman, "Tales of Afghanistan, Moscow Style," *Current Policy*, No. 143 (Washington, D.C.: U.S. Department of State, February 1980), pp. 1–2.

35. Congressional Research Service, *Afghanistan*, p. 4.

36. *U.S. Statement on Afghanistan*, a statement by Ambassador Donald F. McHenry to the U.N. General Assembly, *Current Policy*, No. 248 (Washington, D.C.: U.S. Department of State, November 20, 1980), p. 2. See also Francis Fukuyama, *The Future of the Soviet Role in Afghanistan* (Santa Monica: Rand, 1980), pp. 1–31.

37. G. H. Jansen, *Militant Islam* (New York: Harper & Row, 1979), p. 193.

38. Lawrence Ziring, *Pakistan: The Enigma of Political Development* (Kent, England: Dawson & Sons, 1980), pp. 242–43.

39. *Dawn Overseas Weekly*, November 8, 1980, p. 2.

40. Mary B. Watkins, *Afghanistan: Land in Transition* (Princeton: D. Van Nostrand, 1963), pp. 52–54, 58, 252.

41. *Dawn Overseas Weekly*, November 8, 1980, p. 2.

42. Allen Hetmanek, *Afghanistan Invasion: The Soviet Muslim Factor* (Washington, D.C.: Congressional Research Service, June 6, 1980).

43. Vijay Sen Budhraj, "India's Response to the Crisis in Afghanistan," *Punjab Journal of Politics* 4, no. 1 (January-June 1980): 1–9.

44. Thomas, "The Afghanistan Crisis and South Asian Security," p. 19.

45. William Beecher, "The Pakistan Nuclear Mystery Deepens," Boston *Globe*, July 31, 1981.

46. See Anthony Arnold, *Afghanistan: The Soviet Invasion in Perspective* (Stanford: Hoover Institution Press, 1981).

6

IRAN AND SAUDI ARABIA: INDIA'S OTHER NEIGHBORS

Lawrence Ziring

India's preoccupation with South Asian affairs is being modified by events over which it has no control. The retreat of British power from that vast region anchored on the eastern extremity at Singapore and in the west at Suez has unleashed forces of considerable complexity. The simplicity inherent in the Pax Britannica that dominated the Indian Ocean for a century has given way to a chorus of strident voices that speak of rivalries and maneuvers heretofore not experienced in the area. At the geographic center of this unfolding scenario is India, and although its traditional and historic relative isolation would seem to suggest a posture of nonentanglement, other more contemporary signs indicate a deepening and expanding commitment to broader and possibly more aggressive international involvement.[1] India would prefer playing the role abandoned by Great Britain—that is, balancing and controlling the competitive regional powers along the southern marginal of the Asian continent. But it clearly lacks the power and organization to effect such a position. Moreover, the United States and the Soviet Union have displayed significant interest in the Indian Ocean, and their presence rules out any hegemonial posturing by a comparatively weaker Indian state.[2] India, however, has expressed its dissatisfaction over superpower rivalry in the Indian Ocean and has encouraged great-power discussions aimed at gaining their withdrawal. At the same time India has shown increasing interest with two countries that are its near neighbors, namely, Iran and Saudi Arabia. In an era of revolutionary change these countries must be judged important variables in any equation describing power relationships in southern Asia as well as along the Indian Ocean littoral. Iran and Saudi Arabia are the subjects of this

Research for this chapter was made possible by a Western Michigan University Faculty Fellowship.

chapter. Their individualized purposes and pursuits, their interaction with the immediate region, their linkages with the Indian subcontinent, and the larger question of regional security will be scrutinized.[3]

THE EMERGENCE OF TWO POWERS

The 1970s produced some very unexpected events, and among them was the rise to prominence of Iran and Saudi Arabia. Both countries owed their conspicuous roles to the large reserves of oil stored in huge subterranean mines beneath their soil and immediately offshore. By 1974, Iran and Saudi Arabia accounted for roughly half the world's energy exports. This unique and indispensable natural resource brought these two states incredible wealth (in 1981 it is estimated Saudi Arabia received approximately $123.5 billion in oil revenues while Iran was believed to have earned around $60 billion prior to the Iraqi invasion in September 1980). These enormous earnings enabled Iran and Saudi Arabia to influence the world economic order, and concomitantly, to affect the political behavior of numerous associated and dependent states. The banking giants that traditionally monopolize economic policymaking found it essential to shape their programs in cooperation with Saudi and other Persian Gulf experts. Governments in many parts of the world found it necessary to reconstruct political positions that might be offensive to the dominant oil producers. Investment of surplus capital in the industrialized nations in addition to the storage of huge cash reserves in European banks gave the key oil-producing states extraordinary leverage in the shaping of those countries' national policies. During the reign of the shah, Iranian interests purchased 25 percent of the Krupp industrial works in West Germany. The London Water Board borrowed $1.2 billion for its expansion program and the French government obtained financial credits of roughly $1 billion from Tehran. Between 1975 and mid-1977 it is estimated Iran invested $7 billion in 34 countries and five international organizations.[4] Since the shah's fall, however, Iranian investments abroad have been virtually at a standstill, moreover, a number of holdings have been liquidated or are in legal limbo pending the solution of complicated financial transactions brought on by the 1979–80 revolution. Oil exports from Iran have been drastically curtailed by the Iran-Iraq war, hence removing the influence that the country has heretofore wielded.

Saudi Arabia, however, has been especially active during the same period (see Table 6.1). Saudi production was increased to make up for the loss of Iranian and Iraqi crude. Saudi earnings also skyrocketed. Its assets abroad totaled approximately $145 billion in 1981, and interest earned on this vast sum was well in excess of $10 billion. The Saudis enjoy a substantial voice in international financial circles, controlling $20 billion in bills, bonds, and notes of varying description from the United States government. They also have made large purchases of West German and Japanese currency, and their deposits in 65

TABLE 6.1

Estimated Oil Production of OPEC Countries, 1980

Country	Estimated Production (million b/d)
Saudi Arabia	10.00
Iran	1.36[a]
Kuwait	1.52
Iraq	0.45[b]
Abu Dhabi	1.71
Qatar	0.45
Oman	0.297
Dubai	0.232
Bahrein	0.068
Libya	1.68
Algeria	1.00
Venezuela	2.33
Nigeria	2.03
Indonesia	1.62
Ecuador	0.21

[a] 1974 production 6.128 b/d.
[b] 1974 production 1.829 b/d.
Source: Central Intelligence Agency, quoted in the New York *Times*, May 27, 1981. 1974 statistics from *Oil and Gas Journal*, December 30, 1974.

of the Western world's leading banks are without peer. On March 27, 1981, the International Monetary Fund (IMF) announced that Saudi Arabia had agreed to lend it $4.9 billion a year for two years. This large infusion of money was earmarked for use by the poorer countries and it moved Riyadh close to Washington with its capacity to influence IMF decisions. But even the Saudis realize that their capital empire is so complex, and so expansive that they may have reached a point where effective management is impossible.[5]

History reveals no parallels for so meteoric a rise of generally classified minor powers. It should also be noted, however, that this newfound power and notoriety is intoxicating. Saudi Arabia, like Iran in the 1970s, will insist on a forward policy, not simply static defense, given the role that history has thrust upon it, and which it cannot ignore.

Before 1970 neither Iran nor Saudi Arabia could be judged potential military powers. Located astride important geopolitical land and sea routes, both countries had to ward off outside pressures and frequently they yielded to superior alien forces. Neither country failed to meet the test of self-preservation, however, and their cultural roots remained deep and intact. Of the two, Iran had the more varied and more complex history. But each suffered from foreign impositions, and as a result both have had their view of the world colored by a form of xenophobia. Each in turn has evolved a distinctive culture that is as much in evidence today as it was when they were weak and submissive. It is their distinctive cultures that also separate them from one another. Although both countries are members of the larger Islamic world, their religious expression is different, as are their psychic and physical characteristics. The Saudi Arabians are the keepers and the primary protectors of the holy places of the orthodox Sunni community of Muslims, not only among the Arabs, but the world over. The Iranians may speak only for themselves, but they do represent the dominant Muslim minority known as Shia, and the establishment of Shiism as the state religion of Iran is traced back several centuries. Iran is in some respects the Saudi counterpart in sustaining and defending a different version of Islam. This understanding coupled with the awareness that Arabs and Persians (Iranians) have seldom promoted amicable relationships adds validity to the view that the emergence of Saudi Arabia and Iran as influential powers in the late twentieth century did not imply they will effortlessly pool their resources in order to ensure their collective well-being. On the contrary, it is more likely that the one perceives the other as a threat to its position and hence will augment its military capability to secure itself against not only those outsiders who covet their riches but also from each other.[6]

The Saudi government has been a severe critic of the revolution in Iran. The Ayatollah Khomeini's attempt to spread the fire of revolution throughout the Islamic world, and particularly in the Persian Gulf area, has caused considerable distress in Riyadh. The attack on the Great Mosque in Mecca housing the Kaaba in November 1979 was directly attributed to the fulminations of the Ayatollah. The Saudis were hard-pressed to crush the dissidents who temporarily seized the holy site, and were embarrassed by the challenge to their authority in so sensitive a place.[7] Moreover, the comparisons made between the shah's administration and that of the Saudi dynasty suggest Saudi Arabia could also fall victim to popular rebellion. The Saudis therefore see the Iranian Islamic state as more threat than promise; and when Iraq invaded Iran in 1980, the Riyadh government was among the first to provide encouragement, and offer material support for Baghdad.

Iran was a primary purchaser of military hardware in the 1970s. The shah spent many of the billions of dollars earned from the sale of oil on the latest military equipment, in the construction of fortifications, harbors, and telecommunications systems. And although the monarch was mercilessly criticized for squandering the country's revenues on paraphernalia for the Iranian armed forces, it was that elaborate arsenal which Iran fell back upon when the Iraqi army poured across the Shatt-al-Arab in the fall of 1980. The Iraqis predicted a brief encounter with what they believed were divided, demoralized Iranian units. But the Iranians put up stiff resistance and when the human as well as material costs were examined, Baghdad ordered its troops to consolidate their gains, dig in and wait for political and socioeconomic forces to destroy the Iranian revolution. In the meantime, the Iranians drew upon the military stores obtained by the ousted monarchy and hoped to gain sufficient time and leverage in the outer world to force the Iraqis to withdraw from their territory.

Relations between Iran and the United States were ruptured when the Ayatollah Khomeini assumed the leadership of the country. The United States was accused of numerous crimes, uppermost being its support of the shah and the atrocities that he is alleged to have ordered against his opposition. But even when the shah fled Iran in 1979, never to return, and the United States after great hesitation agreed to permit him to enter the country for medical treatment, Khomeini's followers could not be appeased. The shah's appearance in the United States was the pretext for the seizure of the American embassy in Tehran and for the retention of its personnel.[8] Despite efforts by the United States government to gain the release of the hostages, it was not until 444 days later and just moments after Ronald Reagan took the oath as president of the United States that the Americans gained their freedom. The long deadlock over the fate of the embassy staff plunged Iranian-American relations to new depths and when Iraq invaded Iran the great majority of Americans seemed to cheer the Iraqis on. Others, however, more conversant with the geopolitics in the region, were concerned that the former "anchor" in the West's security network in the Persian Gulf had been lost and the region was seen drifting toward chaos and ultimately toward Soviet interests.[9]

The swift collapse of the shah's regime and the reluctance of the United States government to attempt a dramatic rescue distressed the Saudis. The survival of the autocratic, monarchial system in the Arabian peninsula was now more in question. So too was the survival of a form of state capitalism that blended well with the Western industrialized world. Although the Saudis concluded that the Americans were less dependable allies, they were also convinced their security was linked to the acceleration of their military expansion and modernization programs, as well as their more deliberate efforts in the diplomatic arena.

The pace of the arms buildup in Saudi Arabia has been met with mixed feelings in the West and with some apprehension in the Soviet Union as well as Israel. For Americans and Europeans there can be no mistaking the economic value of the weapons shipments and the related training and defense infrastructures that the Saudis have contracted for. Recycling petrodollars, especially where it helps offset an extreme deficit in the balance of payments brought on by the high cost of petroleum, is a continuing dilemma for the Western industrialized nations. In this respect the billions of dollars spent for Western manufactured weapons systems are in some circles considered beneficial. On the other hand, the view held by many experts that Saudi Arabia cannot successfully deploy and maintain so much sophisticated hardware and therefore remains dependent on outside assistance over the long term raises questions about Western involvement in local quarrels. The extent to which the Saudis require substantial and advanced military capabilities and the real consequences of an unlimited arms race in the area must be weighed against a desire to defend their territorial integrity, and the tendency that the acquisition of so much military paraphernalia might precipitate a military coup or a preemptive attack by a power, or powers, that feel seriously challenged. This introductory statement raises some important issues that can only be pursued and analyzed by examining the international political and military policies of Iran and Saudi Arabia in the 1980s.

KHOMEINI'S IRAN

Iran is among the world's oldest countries, tracing its history back several millennia. Like China, Egypt, and India, it has had its moments of glory as well as suffered extended periods of decline and humiliation. It is this consciousness that motivates the country's leaders today, and especially the Ayatollah Khomeini, who is recognized as the supreme decision maker. Despite Iran's oil wealth and the modernization programs sponsored by the prerevolutionary government, the great majority of Iranians continue to live in medieval squalor and poverty. Moreover, the overthrow of the shah showed the largely peasant-based society is moved more by religious fatalism than government schemes, and their resistance to change is formidable. Still it is the conservative and generally passive peasant society that helps reinforce Khomeini's administration vis-à-vis the discontented, radical elements in the urban centers. Efforts by this latter group, and especially members of the student and intellectual communities, to organize the peasantry against the revolution have thus far failed. The principal Iranian nationalities and tribes, such as the Azerbaijani, Turkoman, Arab, Kurd, and Armenian on the one side, and the Persian Lurs, Bakhtiari, Quashqai, and Baluchi on the other, are determined to maintain their distinctive languages, customs, and traditions in the face of heavy-handed government policies. The more radical opposition hopes to capitalize on their increasing dissatisfaction.[10] Iran is an old country with a developed culture, but it is less than the integrated corporate entity that its leaders publicize.

Shiite Islam and Persian culture provide Iran with the thin veneer of popular unity that it enjoyed. And Ayatollah Khomeini insisted on a form of politics that aroused the passions of the devout. Secular government leaders like former President Abolhassan Bani-Sadr endeavored to outmaneuver the religious leaders (mullahs) by attempting to merge socialism, nationalism, and Islam, and before his impeachment in June 1981 there were signs of growing support among those groups which found the theocratic emphasis stifling. These elements, however, were brutally suppressed when they dared to show their support for Bani-Sadr.

The mullahs who dominated the revolutionary council did not hesitate to call for the imprisonment or the death of anyone who would incite the masses against their stated program. Moreover, this confrontation took an ugly turn when dissidents exploded a bomb at the headquarters of the Islamic revolutionary party and killed more than 70 government officials, including Ayatollah Baheshti, a leading member of the ruling circle. A similar bombing in late August 1981 took the lives of newly elected President Mohammad Ali Rajai and Prime Minister Javad Bahonar. A few days later, Hojatoleslam Ali Qodussi, the revolutionary government's general prosecutor was also murdered.

Despite these events, Khomeini and the mullahs continued to talk openly about building the perfect Islamic state in Iran, and the country was urged to perform a divine function for Muslims everywhere. Martyrdom had become a general act of faith. Irrespective of continued opposition to the clergy's declarations, the mullahs insisted their interests and those of the larger population were identical. The opposition, they declared, consisted of extraterritorial and ideological elements conspiring with foreign powers. All aimed at subverting Iranian society. Ayatollah Khomeini identified his detractors as agents of "satan," essentially capitalists and Communists, aided and abetted by the United States and the Soviet Union respectively. Iran's capitalists were troublesome due to their close identification with the West. The Iranian radicals, however, were a more long-term threat since they engaged in urban terror, street demonstrations, and assisted ethnic rebellion.[11]

To shore up their domestic and external defenses the mullah-dominated government had organized an elaborate police system that resembled the shah's hated SAVAK, or secret police. The result was a veering away from the much heralded Islamic democracy to an absolute dictatorship. Moreover, the new one-party state proclaimed by the mullahs added credence to the complaint that one tyranny had been substituted for another. The Islamic Republic Party, directly responsible to the leading mullahs, dramatized the government's determination to promote political conformity.[12] Given a largely passive peasantry and a supporting network of revolutionary guards and religious zealots, Khomeini's political system had form and structure. But total political control by Iran's clergy and persistent police surveillance were not conducive to social change and economic development, let alone fighting a successful war against Iraq.

The Islamic revolution, launched in 1979, imposed itself on the entire society, but it was far from a popular success. Economic productivity came to a standstill. Iran's industrial boom was suspended. Agriculture was in shambles as farmers continued to leave their land for the cities. Petroleum revenues fell sharply. Fuel was in short supply throughout the country. Iran required food imports and it lacked the purchasing power to acquire them. At the same time, it was the peasantry that had to take up the labor tasks in the industrial sector, and their lack of training, education, and skill as well as their entrenched social customs and religious scruples impeded successful adaptation. The reluctance of the more educated Iranian classes to involve themselves in tasks requiring manual labor also led observers to conclude that Iran could never industrialize despite the best intentions and strenuous efforts of the government. The Persian temperament, with its stress on humanism and a historic, nonscientific conditioning of the senses, crystallized in an attitude that did not lend itself to aggressive nation building.

There was no question about Khomeini's desire to reestablish Islam's lost glory. But Iran's leftist intelligentsia resented the notion that Khomeini was infallible or that he and the country were one and indivisible. They did not accept his role as a visionary charged with the responsibility of engineering a new Persia. Rather, their perception of him was that of an instrument of change and transition; the radicals believed the real revolution had yet to materialize.[13]

The moderate opposition included many of those who worked for the revolutionary regime. They were inclined to look more at Iranian society for an explanation of the country's predicament. These elements respected Khomeini and saw him as an extension of the Iranian character. The real problems of Iranian life, they suggested, lay deep in the mentality of the people. For them, the passing of the shah had only ushered in an era of expanded chaos out of which new rulers with even stronger authoritarian tastes had emerged.

IRAN'S NATIONAL SECURITY DILEMMAS

It is against this background of domestic strife and uncertainty that Iran's international and military posturing must be analyzed. The key factor promoting national equilibrium remains the armed forces. The shah held strongly to the opinion that Iranian solidarity and political unity were possible only through the organization and development of a large, well-disciplined fighting machine. To this end he felt it essential to provide the military with everything that money could buy, and the boom in oil prices made this possible. The expansion of the Iranian armed forces was in many respects prompted by domestic needs, but it also created a new elite that further aggravated the domestic scene. After all it did evoke the idea of a greater authoritarian order. But the idea was not synonymous with reality. Once the shah's unpopularity waxed into widespread civil disorder, and the armed forces could not or proved reluctant to quell the unrest, army units broke discipline, deserted their stations, and frequently joined with the demonstrators. Even after the shah departed the country, the military establishment failed to close ranks. Differences within and among the branches, and pressures exerted by the United States government, broke the resolve of those officers who believed the armed forces should fill the political vacuum.[14] Finally, it was a rebellion within units of the air force that sparked the collapse of the military establishment. Within a brief period, and almost without a struggle, the military surrendered to their less equipped, relatively poorly trained civilian revolutionaries. All homage was paid to the Ayatollah Khomeini and the Islamic revolution.

The mullahs, however, were not content to leave the armed forces intact. First, the highest ranking officers were arrested by revolutionary guards. These were followed by lower echelon personnel and troops believed loyal to the monarchy. In the first months following Khomeini's return to Iran, scores of military leaders were executed along with former politicians, businessmen, police officials, and administrators.[15] Fearing for their safety, many officers and men deserted their service. Some fled the country. Others attempted to melt into the larger society.

The armed forces not only suffered a sharp loss in experienced personnel, it was also demoralized and uncertain about its future. Moreover, the regular armed forces played a secondary role behind that of the revolutionary guard, which came under the direct control of the mullahs. It was only when Iran's nationalities, i.e., the Kurds, Turkomans, Baluchis, and Arabs began to agitate for greater autonomy and armed struggle erupted in several regions of the country that the formal military establishment again began to play a role. The Iran-Iraq War, however, was the primary catalyst in the revival of the Iranian armed forces. Nevertheless, it remains a questionable entity, and its overall capability a significant conundrum. Iran's forces have been trained to use American weapons and the problem of resupplying, updating, and training Persians to use as well as maintain this equipment are all stymied by the break in Iranian-American relations.

The Iranian army numbered in excess of 300,000 before the revolution, by far the largest force on the Persian Gulf. The air force had another 80,000 and the navy was growing beyond an estimated 20,000. The military's primary mission had been defense, and the Soviet Union's perennial interests in the direction of the Persian Gulf were taken as constant.[16] Iranian authorities did not believe they alone could prevent the Soviet Union from forcing its presence on Iran, and the weakened defense posture seemed to expose Iran to greater threat.[17] The possibility of an armed Soviet thrust across the Iranian frontier until most recently was judged to be remote. But the Red Army's invasion of Afghanistan has altered all calculations. Nevertheless, the pattern of Soviet activity since the end of World War II minimizes direct Soviet operations against Iran. The Soviets are more inclined to work through dissident leftist and nationalist groups within the country or to support neighboring states, like Iraq, whose relations with Iran are embittered. Soviet support for the outlawed Iranian Tudeh Party (the country's chief communist organization) and other clandestine groups as well as its pact with Iraq illustrate this observation.

If the Iranian armed forces have as their primary mission the defense of the country, and if the 1,200-mile border that Iran shares with the Soviet Union can no longer be secured by the United States, Iran's task in safeguarding the Persian Gulf is also questionable. From this body of water passes more than 60 percent of the world's exportable oil supplies—that are in major part destined for the Western industrialized world! It is this strategic passage that Iran would like to continue dominating. Indeed, the Iranian state, as currently constituted, would be in serious jeopardy if the Gulf came under the control of hostile forces. But Iran is hard put to extend its limited power over the Gulf and it is notable that the United States has seen fit to station a sizable fleet near the Strait of Hormuz and in the Indian Ocean. Iranians may complain about this American presence in their waters, but it is also possible that the Iranian military establishment might welcome the U.S. naval force.

Furthermore, Iran occupied the islands of Abu Musa and the Greater and Lesser Tumbs in November 1971 with the full knowledge of the United States and Great Britain. Thus far Iran shows no interest in evacuating these territories. The islands dominate the Strait of Hormuz, and the fear persists that the federation known as the United Arab Emirates (UAE) would be unable to ward off a possible aggressive Iraqi move aimed at commanding the narrow waterway.[18] In the case of Abu Musa, the Iranian occupation took place after an agreement was signed with the ruler of Sharjah (a member of the UAE), who received $3.5 million annually in Iranian aid. Iran was permitted to install fortifications on Abu Musa, but Sharjah retained control over the island's civil affairs. In the case of the Tumbs, claimed by Ras al-Khaymah (also a UAE member), there was no equivalent agreement, and the islands were taken by force. This latter event caused Iraq to sever its relations with Iran, and tension increased along their mutual frontier. Thus when the Iraqi Kurds renewed their military campaign against Baghdad in the 1970s and demanded the establishment of an autonomous Kurdish state, Iran openly supported the insurgents.

Proof that the Iranians were less concerned with self-determination for the Kurds and more interested in improving their defense posture was revealed in March 1975 when a treaty was signed by Iran and Iraq that sealed the fate of the Kurdish people. In a dramatic move Iran forced Iraq to reconcile their long-standing border dispute in return for Iran's decision to close its border to Kurdish insurgents, to remove whatever forces it had in Iraq, and to cease all shipments of arms to the rebellious tribesmen. In return Iraq pledged not to incite Arabic-speaking tribes in the Iranian province of Khuzistan and to curtail assistance to the United Baluchi Front, active on the Iranian-Pakistani frontier.[19] Although the Kurds of Iran were less troublesome at the time than their Iraqi counterparts, any success by Iraqi Kurds could have had repercussions in Iran. Iranian governments have consistently pursued a policy of rigidity where tribal demands are involved. The crushing of Quashqai resistance to the land tenure program demanded by the shah's White Revolution as well as the pressure placed upon the Bakhtiari were cases in point. The Khomeini regime has continued the practice, violently countering all tribal and ethnic political demands at deviance with the Islamic revolutionary government.

On March 6, 1975, the shah and Iraq's Saddam Husein signed an agreement in Algiers in which the latter renounced territorial rights of a century and a quarter's standing. Iraq accepted the Iranian claim that the Shatt al-Arab frontier between the two countries ran along the Talweg, the line of deepest water, and not the Iranian shore of the river. It should be noted that in 1969 the shah had unilaterally repudiated the 1937 treaty with Iraq and since that time had used the Shatt al-Arab as if the river were within the joint sovereignty of Iran and Iraq. While the shah reigned the Baghdad government did little to challenge the fait accompli, and the costly Kurdish conflict apparently convinced Iraq that formal acceptance of the Iranian position would serve its interest. The price of this reconciliation, however, resulted in the collapse of the 14-year struggle of the Iraqi Kurds for national autonomy and the virtual annihilation of their forces.

The Kurds therefore had no reason to view the Iranians as any more friendly than the Iraqis. Insofar as the Kurds were concerned, both countries intended to prevent them from realizing their age-old objective of a free, autonomous if not independent Kurdish state. Thus when the Sunni Kurds in Iran displayed their unhappiness with Ayatollah Khomeini's vision of a Shiite Islamic state and demanded greater self-government, the struggle between the main-line Persians and the tribal people began anew. This time, however, the Iraqis not only wanted to negate the terms of the 1975 treaty, they were also provoked by the Iranian mullahs' call to their Shiite Brethren in Iraq to unite with them against the Sunni leadership of the Baathist socialists in Baghdad. Saddam Husein understood he had a tiger by the tail. More than half of Iraq's population was comprised of Shiite Muslims and they had long been dissatisfied with the Sunni-dominated government. Saddam Husein judged he had to protect his regime from such revolutionary appeals. He was also an ambitious personality, harboring aspirations that extended his influence beyond Iraq to the larger Arab world. Observing Iran's chaotic state, therefore, he unilaterally abrogated the 1975 treaty with Iran and sent his Soviet-equipped war machine across the Shatt al-Arab into Iran's oil-rich province of Khuzistan.[20]

Khuzistan, with its large Arab population, was identified by the Iraqis as Arabistan and Saddam Husein left little doubt he intended to link the province with Iraq. The seizure of Khoramshahr and the siege of Abadan, Ahwaz, and Khuzistan's other principal cities illustrated the determination of the Baghdad government to consolidate its hold over the vital region. Efforts by international agencies and especially the Islamic Conference to mediate the dispute proved fruitless. Moreover, Jordan and Saudi Arabia expressed their support for the Iraqis while Syria and Libya sided with Tehran. Pakistani President Zia-ul-Haq attempted to use his good offices to reconcile the warring parties, but his mission also failed. The Iranians insisted there could be no cease-fire and no resolution to the dispute until the Iraqis withdrew to the original line of control. Saddam Husein, for his part, had committed too much to the fray to withdraw without significant gains.

Apparently able to obtain additional military stores to replenish their forces, rumored to have been aided by both the Soviet Union on the one side and Israel on the other, the Iranians launched a major counteroffensive in the last week of March 1982. By early April thousands of Iraqi troops had been captured, thousands more were said to have been killed, and Baghdad's once-celebrated legions fell back to their own frontier. Although some observers were quick to describe a stunning Iranian victory, others were more cautious and expected the fighting to continue. At first glance, however, it appeared the Khomeini regime had won a great test of its endurance. At the same time the Iranian military establishment had assumed a prominence not enjoyed since the fall of the shah.

THREAT PERCEPTION:
THE SHAH AND THE AYATOLLAH

Iran has long been preoccupied with subversive movements it alleges are supported by the superpowers and by neighboring Arab states. The shah argued that the problem was not of recent vintage. Egypt's Gamal Abdul Nasser embraced the Soviet Union as early as 1955, and in the 1960s he sent his forces into Yemen to assist the antiroyalists. In 1961 the shah declared his primary defense concern was the increased Egyptian activity in the vicinity of the Persian Gulf.[21] The British withdrawal from Aden in 1967 and their replacement by a South Yemenite Marxist government, along with the presence of Egyptian forces in North Yemen, seemed to confirm the perception that radical movements were encircling the region. If additional evidence was needed, it could be found in Iraq's desire to dominate and possibly absorb Kuwait. Iran's response to this multiple threat was two-pronged. On the one side, friendly relations were encouraged between Iran and the conservative Arab states. On the other, the Iranian military establishment was overhauled and programs were developed to obtain the latest weapons, and in numbers that could match anything provided Iran's adversaries by the Soviet Union.

The first significant test of Iranian diplomacy was the shah's decision to give up his claim to the island of Bahrein. The office of the United Nations secretary-general conducted a plebiscite among the population of Bahrein with the shah's concurrence, and they chose independence. The Iranian parliament promptly approved their decision in May 1970. The gesture was obviously directed at Saudi Arabia and Kuwait, the two countries with which the shah most sought to develop amicable relations and the very countries that would have been most disturbed had Iran insisted on seizing the island on the departure of the British. At the same time Iran did not hesitate to make clear its intention to keep Bahrein free of radical influence. In this regard the shah again announced his desire to organize a Gulf defense alliance.

On January 7, 1968, the Iranian government called for joint military collaboration. In the years following that declaration not a single Arab state declared its intention to join such an arrangement. Apart from the historic enmities between Persians and Arabs, Iran's relations with Israel acted as an impediment. But perhaps uppermost in Arab minds was the awareness that Iran was the largest power on the Gulf and any alliance with it would tend to formalize Iranian supremacy as well as legitimize its interventionist role on the Arab side of the Gulf. Nevertheless, Iran was not discouraged from promoting bilateral contacts with the Arab Gulf states, and it demonstrated a willingness to use its forces in behalf of those states if it found the reasons compelling.

Just such a situation erupted at the entrance of the Persian Gulf in the sheikhdom of Oman. An insurgency in the Dhofar district of Oman had commenced in the 1950s, and with the independence of the People's Democratic Republic of Yemen (South Yemen), which sided with the guerrillas, the struggle took on new ferocity in the late 1960s. The reigning sultan of Oman was overthrown by his son in 1970, and in an effort to stabilize the country the young monarch ordered the building of long-delayed public projects. But public confidence was not so easily achieved. The new sultan appealed to Saudi Arabia and other conservative Arab states to assist him in putting down the Dhofar rebellion, which he insisted was communist inspired. When the Arab states indicated a reluctance to fight other Arabs, the same appeal was made to the shah of Iran, who responded with alacrity. The first contingents of Iranian troops arrived in the Dhofar in 1973 and went immediately into combat. By 1975 the insurgency had been reduced, and although sporadic acts of terrorism continued, the threat posed to the Omani regime had at least for the time being been removed.

New concerns were aroused in 1976, however, when it was reported the Popular Front for the Liberation of Oman and the Arab Gulf (PFLOAG) was now receiving assistance from Cuba and that Cuban forces that had been sent to South Yemen might enter the fighting. These revelations led the Iranian government to break diplomatic relations with Havana on April 7, 1976. In a 1975 pledge to the Omani sultan, the shah guaranteed the defense of the sheikhdom's airspace, and when an Iranian reconnaissance plane was shot down over South Yemen in 1976, it was speculated the Cubans were involved. The Cuban role in South Yemen, as with Cuban operations in Africa, was known to be linked with Soviet machinations in the area.

Before the death of Mao Zedong and particularly when Lin Piao wielded power in the People's Republic of China, it was the PRC that provided major assistance to South Yemen.[22] The regime of Hua Kuo-feng, however, apparently reversed a policy of direct intervention in Middle East disputes, and the Cubans quickly filled the power vacuum. Fear of stepped-up Soviet and Cuban operations in the vicinity of the Persian Gulf was shared by Iran and Saudi Arabia.[23] Such concerns also caused the U.S. government to play a more active role in the Persian Gulf as well as along the Omani coast and around the Horn of Africa.

Preparations were made for a U.S. base on the Oman island of Masirah, U.S. military aid was despatched to the Sudan, Saudi Arabian arms sales escalated, and somewhat ambivalently, the United States pondered arms transfers to Somalia as that country took steps to break away from the Soviet orbit.

In September 1977 an alleged secret directive was leaked to the American press that revealed President Jimmy Carter's National Security Council (NSC) had sent the Pentagon a memorandum said to be the culmination of six months of study. It reported "foreign aggression" in the vicinity of the Persian Gulf and that the United States must consider the possibility of direct action to counter a possible Soviet attack. A Central Intelligence Agency (CIA) study made public in May 1977 asserted the Soviet Union would become a net importer of oil and would soon compete with the United States for Middle East petroleum reserves. (In 1981, the CIA revised its estimates and indicated the Soviet Union would produce more than enough oil to meet its needs through the 1980s.) It was thought this document had provoked the NSC study. Nevertheless, the president's directive to the Defense Department not only made the American people aware of the seriousness with which its government viewed developments in the region, it also sought to warn the Soviet Union that any overt move against Iran or other area states would be contested. In a press conference on January 12, 1978, the president again made reference to Soviet and Cuban activities in the region, and this time he was especially critical of the heavy arms shipments and Cuban troop buildup in Ethiopia, which he insisted were being engineered from Moscow. It was the Washington view that the conservative nature of the governments in Iran and on the Arabian peninsula and the more moderate position taken by Egyptian, Sudanese, and Somalian leaders made them more vulnerable to internal aggression if strong external forces provoked a conflict in the area.

The timing of the disclosure emphasizing the volatility of the Persian Gulf sector coincided with an extended debate in the U.S. Congress over arms shipments to both Iran and Saudi Arabia. In both countries arms sales became a major instrument of American foreign policy. Carter's statement on May 19, 1977, that his administration would use the utmost restraint in future arms sales and transfers and that they would be used "only in instances where it can be clearly demonstrated that the transfer contributes to our national security interests"[24] created an expectation that the United States could not satisfy in the Iranian and Saudi Arabian situations. For the Carter administration, but not for a number of influential congressmen and senators, the Iranian weapons purchases were an "exceptional foreign policy implement." Iran had purchased or contracted for more than $15 billion in weapons between 1972 and 1977, making it the largest customer for American military hardware. Superiority in numbers, however, did not translate into superiority in performance, and many questions were raised about Iran's capacity to absorb the amount and high sophistication of the weapons it obtained and still intended to receive from Washington. Iran's heavy dependence on expensive foreign employees and

American servicemen could not be ignored. For example, Iran's F-16 fighter-bombers required at least 1,000 American experts to help with their maintenance. A U.S. Senate staff report made public in August 1976 cited the problem created in purchasing overly sophisticated equipment and the need for substantial numbers of American personnel. It noted Iran's inability to wage a future war "without U.S. support on a day-to-day basis."[25]

The general opinion prevailed in the United States that Iran was very concerned with its defenses but that its weapons purchases, especially where aircraft were concerned, were motivated by what was available, not genuine need. Few Pentagon officials believed the shah's forces could effectively utilize such aircraft. The U.S. Congress was particularly critical about the shah's desire to purchase seven radar-equipped Boeing 707s known as AWACS (Airborne Warning and Control System). The seven planes were slated to cost $1.2 billion and represented the most advanced development in communications and air battle management systems. AWACS was scheduled for deployment by NATO in the 1980s, and it came as some surprise when Carter argued for the sale of the aircraft to Iran. If the Pentagon was concerned with Iran's capacity to utilize the equipment already delivered, how, it was conjectured, would Iranians be able to operate the most sophisticated piece of military weaponry in the conventional arsenal?

The Congress sensed a deepening commitment to Iran by the United States, given the indefinite stationing on Iranian soil of thousands of highly skilled American technicians. The Carter administration, in justifying the sale of AWACS, insisted that Iran's special status in strategic planning made it necessary. President Carter also attempted to blunt criticism about Iranian ability to protect such advanced weapons systems. He noted that the Iranians would be given a simpler, modified version of AWACS and that the shah's forces had a good record in safeguarding their military equipment. What the administration did not say was that the Iranian purchase of AWACS, as with other ultraexpensive weapons systems, reduced the unit cost of the system, and thus made it more readily available to Pentagon purchasers. It was therefore difficult to separate real defense needs from other factors in these military purchases. But it was obvious that the shah intended to proceed with his military building program and that the Carter administration was very helpful in those efforts.

Iran's relationship with the United States was close and intimate through 1978. Parallels could only be found in the American commitment to NATO and Israel. The controversy between the executive branch and the American Congress over future shipments added a degree of strain to Iranian-American relations, but the region had the U.S. government's highest priority and little if any change was forecast. Carter's New Year's Eve visit in Tehran with the shah and the subsequent announcement that the United States intended to construct from six to eight nuclear power stations for Iran confirmed his judgment. So too did President Carter's statement in Iran that the Middle East nation was a bastion of stability in the region.[26]

But the Carter-shah dream was suddenly transformed into a recurring nightmare. Within weeks of Carter's departure from Tehran, demonstrations that had been on the rise spread all over Iran. In the oil refinery city of Abadan a fire in a local theater caused several hundred deaths and the government was accused of deliberately setting the blaze in order to justify action against radical dissidents. Despite the administration's attempt to prove that enemies of the monarchy were responsible for the tragedy, few believed the government's story.[27] This calamity was perhaps the most significant in a long chain of violent events that totally alienated Iran's diverse population. Led by the mullahs, who expressed their support for the leadership of the exiled Ayatollah Khomeini, Iran's devout population received their marching orders in the thousands of mosques across the nation. The call was to revolution, the destruction of the monarchy, the withdrawal of all foreign and especially American forces, and the recreation of Iran as a model Islamic state.

The forces of the revolution included groups and individuals with varied interests, experiences, and philosophies. All, however, were united in their determination to terminate the monarchy. Thus the never-popular shah, despite strenuous efforts at clinging to power, was dramatically called upon to yield. Tension within the armed forces had led to splits in the ranks, and finally to an outright refusal by troops to forcibly quell the demonstrators. Uncertain of their capacity to sustain military discipline, the shah's handpicked officers hesitated to assume direct political control. Moreover, Washington cautioned against a military coup, sensing that it would be better to accept the more moderate revolutionaries and hopefully to win their favor. The exiling of the shah and the collapse of his chosen successor, Shahpour Bakhtiar, however, paved the way for Khomeini's tumultuous return to Iran.[28] The spiritual leader took command of the revolution and immediately called for the changes that had been broadcast earlier. The Ayatollah let it be known that Iran would cease the implementation of all the shah's policies, and that the Americans should not only leave Iran, but also remove their presence from the Middle East. Washington sorrowfully acknowledged that its primary ally in the Persian Gulf had suddenly transformed itself into an arch foe and that other means would have to be found to secure the oil lifeline to the Western world. Not insignificant, the United States also lost the use of bases in Iran, some of these being electronic listening posts on the Iran-Soviet frontier. The United States was forced to find other locations for surveiling the Soviet Union, and American relations with Turkey, which had soured over the Cyprus issue, suddenly improved. In return for Turkish assistance, the United States agreed to resume military aid to that Middle East nation.

While the United States was engaged in negotiations aimed at shoring up defenses in the region of the Persian Gulf, e.g., agreements with Oman and Somalia for base rights, it also ordered a large flotilla of warships into the Indian Ocean and began organizing a Rapid Deployment Force (RDF). The new Iranian authorities perceived these American gambits as proof that the United States government remained Iran's primary enemy. Ayatollah Khomeini repeatedly lashed out against the Americans, calling the United States the "great Satan," and insisting that Washington was intent on destroying the Islamic revolution. Khomeini and his followers were convinced that the Americans would attempt to restore the shah to his throne, just as they had done in the 1953 countercoup perpetrated against the government of Mohammad Mossadegh. The Iranians therefore were equally determined to sever all ties with the United States. Moreover, in the foreign policy field the revolutionaries assumed positions almost the reverse of those developed by the shah. Iran immediately welcomed the Palestine Liberation Organization and housed it in the Israeli embassy, which had been sacked by demonstrators earlier. Signals were sent the Muslim rejectionist states, particularly to Libya, Syria, and Algeria, identifying Iran with the struggle against Israel. By the same token, Tehran disturbed the more traditional Arab states and was scornful of Anwar el-Sadat's role in bridging Egyptian-Israeli differences. Countries like Egypt, Saudi Arabia, Morocco, Kuwait, the United Arab Emirates, and Jordan, according to the Iranians, were client states of the United States and hence anti-Islam as well as antiprogressive. The mullahs called for popular uprisings in all these states, much as they had in Iraq. These fulminations were clearly intended to excite rebellion and the reaction in the targeted states was not unexpected. Sadat characterized Khomeini as anti-Islamic and essentially mad. This view was echoed by other Muslim leaders, even some who wished to show sympathy with the revolution but who were not only fearful of its repercussions but also embarrassed by its excesses. Tehran therefore began to isolate itself from the larger world as well as its more immediate neighbors. The seizure of the American embassy and hostages in November 1979 may have proven good revolutionary theater in Iran, but it also made the country's isolation more complete. Iran ruptured its economic ties with the outside world, which may have reinforced its martyr complex, but it did nothing to lift the country from the chaos of its own making.

Politically unstable, economically dislocated, socioculturally confused, the Iranians were also called upon to contain ethnic conflict in several parts of the country, the most severe fighting occurring in Kurdistan. Domestically as well as internationally Iran was in disarray and its future course uncertain. The Soviet invasion of Afghanistan and the Red Army's appearance on still another Iranian frontier was also cause for alarm. Moreover, it was this fundamental disequilibrium which convinced Saddam Husein that the moment was opportune to solidify Iraq's claim over the Persian Gulf and possibly the oil of Khuzistan too. Indeed, if Iran was headed for disintegration, if the Soviet Union was again intent on establishing soviet republics in Iranian Azerbaijan and Kurdistan (as they had tried to do in the immediate aftermath of World War II), then it certainly seemed appropriate for Iraq to play defender of the Arabs in Khuzistan. Iranian battlefield achievements against Iraq in its spring 1982 campaign, however, seemed likely to destroy Saddam Husein's quest, and possibly his administration too.

Iran's problems are nevertheless legion. Ayatollah Khomeini is an ailing octogenarian and the symbol of the revolution. But neither the Islamic state that the ayatollah envisages, nor Iran's integrity, can be sustained by this frail mortal. The forecast in Iran is for stormy weather once Khomeini passes from the scene. Iran's controversial factions are destined to clash in an epoch-making struggle. And while the initial contest pitted nationalists, socialists, and the Mujahiddin Khalq against the mullahs, the more extremist Cherik Fedyeen el-Khalq as well as the Tudeh Party have yet to play their hand. Most important, only the Tudeh Party had direct ties to, and was capable of using the influence of a superpower. Bridges to the West were virtually nonexistent, especially after Bani-Sadr was given sanctuary in France. The Soviet Union seemed to sense that the United States had had its chance, and now it was the Kremlin's turn to influence Iran's future.

SAUDI ARABIA

Opposite Iran on the other side of the Persian Gulf is Saudi Arabia. Although a comparatively small country by population count (roughly 6 million), Saudi Arabia plays the role of an economic superpower in contemporary international affairs. The country has the largest known reserves of petroleum and is the world's primary exporter of oil. Its prominent position in regard to this most vital of resources has not only brought the country riches undreamed of in the fabled Arabian Nights but has also given its leaders a voice in the political and economic halls of power. Fifty years ago the land that is now Saudi Arabia was nothing more than a vast, barren desert inhabited by quarrelsome nomadic people whose primary concern was day-to-day survival. The Romans and Egyptians had little success in bringing the region under their control, and it remained for the Ottoman Turks to impose something resembling settled rule over parts of the peninsula. The British were perhaps more successful in developing a lasting association as they established trading posts along the coast and tied them to their imperium in India.

The history of the larger portion of Arabia, however, belongs to the Saudi family of Najd. The Saudis are Wahhabi Muslims, judged among the most austere devotees of Sunni Islam. At the turn of the nineteenth century, the Saudis had lost their dominant stature, and their traditional capital at Riyadh was occupied by despised competitors. One hundred years earlier they had seized the holy city of Mecca and laid waste to Kerbala, the center of the Shia sect (in Iraq). But constant warfare took its toll, and eventually the Saudis were defeated by a larger Muslim coalition and forced to take refuge in the least hospitable Arabian terrain. The reemergence of the Saudis came when the founder of the modern state, Abdul Aziz ibn Saud, regained Riyadh and during World War I joined with the British in a common struggle against the occupying Turks. By 1925 Ibn Saud was strong enough to defeat the Hashemites of the Hejaz and regain control of the spiritual cities of Mecca and Medina. (The defeated leader of the western kingdom of the Hejaz was the great-grandfather of King Hussein of modern Jordan.) With this victory the Saudis established themselves as the dominant force in Arabia, and the British, who were the general power in the Middle East, recognized Abdul Aziz ibn Saud as king of the Hejaz and of Najd and its dependencies. In 1932 the kingdom was officially designated Saudi Arabia.

Saudi Arabia, until recently, was never considered a potential military power. The primary mission of its armed forces, like its police and paramilitary groups, was internal control, protection for its leaders, and the safeguarding of its religious shrines and petroleum and communication installations. Occasionally the country had problems with Iraq, South Yemen, and some of the Persian Gulf sheikhdoms over rival territorial claims, but the fighting was low scale and hardly threatened the state's security. The most significant challenge confronting the Saudi government today comes not from another Middle East state but rather from disenchanted social elements with radical ideas who seek to modify Saudi Arabia's traditional structure and behavior. These radicals are usually identified with a relatively young generation of Arab youth who earlier followed Egypt's Nasser and continue to insist that the wealth of Saudi Arabia should be utilized to promote greater Arabdom. They are usually vociferously anti-West and single-minded in their hatred for Israel and its supporters. Since Nasser's death these elements have displayed their fervor by joining with terrorist organizations and so-called armies of liberation. They are usually motivated less by Islam and more by Marxist-Leninist notions of violent change.

The conservative, ritualistic methods of the Saudi government, its affiliation with the capitalist, industrial West, and the concentration of power and wealth in few hands arouse the hostility of these young revolutionaries, and a number have joined the PFLOAG against the Saudi establishment. The growing influence of Moscow in the region is therefore a problem of great moment to Riyadh. The Saudis understand that the bands of revolutionaries seeking to undermine their position often obtain their support from the Soviet Union. Libya has also posed a problem. The ouster of King Idris of Libya, an ally of the Saudis, and the destruction of the monarchy by the Libyan army led by Muammar el-Qaddafi precipitated a move against the Saudi royal system. In 1969, a coup plot was uncovered in the air force, and the director of the air force academy in Dhahran was arrested along with many officers. In addition, a number of government officials were imprisoned, including several from PETROMIN, the government agency in charge of industrial development of petroleum and minerals.[29] More recently, the fall of the shah of Iran, his ignominious exile, and death in Egypt have raised greater concerns. Although overwhelmed by popular dissatisfaction with his rule, the shah was also victimized by outside forces, allegedly sponsored in part by the Libyan government. Elements of the PLO were similarly involved and they were celebrated for their efforts by high members of Iran's revolutionary council soon after the consolidation of the revolution. The Saudis have reason to be concerned with Qaddafi's determination to assist terrorist organizations and so-called liberation movements. Moreover, Libya's Ugandan escapade as well as its occupation of Chadian territory means Riyadh can no longer consider the Libyan strongman a short-term dilemma.

Iraq's shift toward the Soviets after the 1958 murder of its king and the liquidation of his court as well as the establishment of a radical regime in South Yemen are also developments that the Saudis dare not overlook. Nor have they been oblivious to Soviet-related actions against Afghanistan, Pakistan, Egypt, Jordan, the Gulf states, the Sudan, Iran, and on the Horn of Africa. This preoccupation with communist drives in areas closely identified with Saudi security has tended to diminish, at least for the time being, the conundrum posed by Egypt's negotiations with Israel. At first glance, it would appear that Saudi Arabia and Egypt have much in common and that their individual interests are linked in common cause, even if they dispute the methods to be employed in dealing with the Israelis.*

The first oil concession granted to Western companies was made in 1933, and it eventually resulted in the formation of the Arabian-American Oil Company (ARAMCO).[30] Ibn Saud personally pursued the arrangement, believing it would begin a process of modernization in the country. When he died in 1953, Ibn Saud left behind a solid governing structure, but only the faint rumblings of societal change were experienced. His eldest son, Saud, succeeded him, but his lack of administrative skills and excessive extravagance brought the country to the brink of bankruptcy in a few short years. His younger brother, Crown Prince Faisal, was considered the enlightened member of the family, and his presence was especially felt when Saud was implicated in a plot to kill Nasser. Saud disappeared from public life when Faisal first became prime minister. He lost his position completely when his brother ascended the throne in a bloodless coup in 1964.

Faisal's power rested on the loyalty of the religious establishment and the wealthy Hejazi merchants. The religious leaders, who are led by the Al-Shaykh family, are descendants of Muhammad ibn Abdul Wahhab and Faisal's maternal family. The religious ideology is the principal legitimating force in Saudi Arabia, however, the growing importance of the Hejaz merchants and the nouveau riche is eroding the once preeminent power of the religious class and especially the al-Shaykh family. The ability of the Saudi elite to satisfy both groups while at the

---

*Egypt applauded the U.S. decision to sell Saudi Arabia AWACS aircraft as well as other sophisticated weaponry. The assassination of Anwar el-Sadat also appeared to draw the two Arab countries into a more intimate embrace. Moreover, there is evidence the Saudis are now prepared to assume a broader leadership role in the Arab world, with Egypt a supportive player.

same time using the one to check the other is still the key to Saudi rule. This task is complicated by the vast development program underway throughout the country, the modernization of the Saudi armed forces, the presence of thousands of foreign technicians, advisors, and military personnel, and the need to draw labor from the surrounding Arab and other Muslim states.

Faisal's most notable accomplishment was the Arab oil embargo, which he directed in the wake of the Arab-Israeli war of 1973. The embargo precipitated higher prices for world petroleum, gave the Organization of Petroleum Exporting Countries (OPEC) a newfound unity and phenomenal political as well as economic leverage, and in general made it possible for the developing countries to challenge the power of the industrial states. Above all it gave Saudi Arabia a major voice in the councils of the mighty and enormous wealth that could be used for both domestic and international enterprises.

Faisal perceived communism and Zionism as two sides of the same problem. According to the Arabian king, the Communists had implanted Zionism in the Middle East in order to spread their imperial designs. Thus Saudi Arabia's revenues from oil would be used to combat the dual menace. Faisal understood that Saudi Arabia could not overnight develop a powerful military establishment, but plans were drafted and policies executed to begin the process. In the meantime all possible assistance was to be provided Egypt, Jordan, and Syria, the major confrontation states with Israel. Such assistance, it was anticipated, would help wean those states away from their dependence on the superpowers; and it would be especially useful to Egypt and Syria, which were heavily indebted to the Soviet Union for their modern armaments. With Saudi money it would be possible to purchase the necessary weapons from a number of interested sellers, and the political strings usually attached to superpower aid could be avoided. This was particularly important to Faisal, who viewed the Soviet Union's activities in the Middle East with considerable trepidation. The record would suggest that of the two major threats to the Arab world, Faisal saw communism as primary and Zionism as the lesser evil.

The death of Faisal at the hand of an assassin in the Saudi capital on March 25, 1975, apparently had a greater impact on the larger Arab world than it did on Saudi Arabia. After Nasser's death, the Arab world was again in search of a leader.[31] Faisal had begun to assume that role when his life was taken. The assassin was identified as a disgruntled young member of the royal family (of which there are approximately 3,000 members, including the collateral branches), and there was not the slightest suggestion that he had acted as the instrument of a larger conspiracy. Nevertheless, Faisal's death heralded a scramble for the title of chief Arab spokesman, with the principal contenders being Anwar el-Sadat of Egypt, Hafez el-Assad of Syria, Saddam Husein of Iraq, and Qaddafi of Libya. The struggle between these four men intensified over the next six years, with the Lebanese civil war, Sadat's historic visit and peace overture to Israel, the revolution in Iran and the collapse of the shah's political system, and Iraq's invasion of

Iran providing the dramatic backdrop. Moreover, the death of Sadat in October 1981 reduced the field to three aspirants. The Saudis therefore were finally influenced to reassert their claim and to provide the Arab world with another choice.

King Khalid ibn Abdul Aziz al Saud has been described as a retiring, unassuming personality, well-liked by members of the royal family but in poor health and not expected to put himself forward as a driving, ambitious leader. Nevertheless, as his predecessor, he held the offices of prime minister, commander in chief, and supreme imam of the Wahhabis. The crown prince, Fahd ibn Abdul Aziz al Saud, is first deputy prime minister and vice-president of the council of ministers. It was Fahd who was reputed to be the most dynamic figure in the new administration. Fahd had worked closely with Faisal while Khalid was content to remain in his more remote, tribal surrounding during his tenure as crown prince. Fahd was also younger, in better health, and actively involved in promoting the country's development. Fahd's visit to Washington in June 1974 and his meetings with Henry Kissinger concluded on a positive note in Saudi-American relations. Fahd was quoted as saying "an excellent opening in a new and glorious chapter in relations between Saudi Arabia and the United States" had begun.[32] Given his new and powerful role, Fahd was apparently determined to hold to the general course initiated by Faisal. Moreover, the threat posed to the regime by the Soviet Union drew the Saudis into a far more intimate embrace of the United States. Fahd's relations with the United States were redefined in 1981 when the Reagan administration acknowledged Saudi influence and even prompted Riyadh to play a more influential role in Middle East security.

Saudi Arabian policy since the death of Faisal has been resolutely anticommunist. Indeed, the stability demonstrated by the Saudis in the transition from Faisal to Khalid was deemed essential to ward off any meddling by those desirous of exploiting an in-house and destructive quarrel among rival family members. Attempts have been made to distribute power among those with a common stake in the perpetuation of the Saudi system. Thus the promotion of Prince Abdullah ibn Abdul Aziz to the offices of second deputy prime minister, deputy vice-president of the council of ministers, and most important, commander of the national guard was made over the head of Sultan ibn Abdul Aziz, who continued to hold the post of minister of defense and aviation. It is conceivable that the juxtaposition of these appointments preserved a prestigious balance between the claims of the various branches of the royal house. Further evidence on this point was the appointment of Prince Saud ibn Faisal as minister of state for foreign affairs. This post had been held by a commoner during Faisal's reign. The legitimacy of the Saudi system remained the responsibility of the extended family, with its capacity to limit and control fraternal competition. So long as this equilibrium was maintained, it would be very difficult for external forces to challenge the system. Moreover, the unity of the royal family was strengthened by the Saudi constitution—the Sharia, or Sacred Law of Islam. So long as the royal house stands together, an attack upon it will also be judged an attack on Islam. The assault on the central mosque in Mecca in November 1979 was a direct attack on the Saudis and their system. The response from Riyadh therefore was predictable. The decision was made to use all available means to crush the fanatics and to deal with them according to Islamic principle and law. After a protracted battle, the surviving members of the religious sect were seized, quickly tried and executed, the majority suffering beheading. The Saudis were embarrassed by this dramatic display of defiance to their rule and they came under direct criticism from their detractors in the Islamic world. But the point was also made that Saudi sovereignty and Islamic interests were interrelated.

A major test of the Saudi leaders is their wisdom in managing to preserve an old tradition while promoting profound material change.[33] It is this latter dilemma that has caused the Saudi rulers to feel they must insulate themselves against communist philosophies and subversion. It also helps to explain why Saudi Arabia has become so concerned with radical conflicts in their vicinity. The huge foreign work force in the country is both a source of strength and weakness. Saudi development is impossible without them. Their ubiquitous presence, however, is a constant dilemma for Riyadh. Including dependents, the foreign component is estimated to be 2.5 million or approximately one-third of the indigenous population. Moreover, the foreign workers are industrious, but generally nonconversant with Saudi tradition and values, and sometimes influenced by critics of the royal family. One million are Yemenites, 75,000 are Palestinians, and 300,000 more are Egyptians and Arabs from other countries. In addition, there are more than 300,000 Pakistanis, Indians, Bangladeshis, Sri Lankans, and South Koreans in the labor force. The fear persists in Saudi ruling circles that a significant number of the Arab workers could be recruited by dissident organizations and terrorist groups. But they are also troubled by the different life-styles that the foreigners bring to Saudi society. Nevertheless, the Saudi government is dependent on the foreign workers for the successful completion of their five-year plans and their near permanent presence in the country is unavoidable.

Economic development in the Arabian state is without precedent. The Second Five-Year Plan (1975–80)* earmarked $142 billion for a vast array of projects and the Third Five-Year Plan (1981–85) projects expenditures in excess of $250 billion.[34] These figures do not include the military budget, which for 1981–85 is slated to total $105 billion. Saudi Arabia already possesses a modern telecommunications system, a network of fine highways, an efficient electric power grid and numerous contemporary structures. The most sophisticated air-

---

*The First Five-Year Plan (1970–75) was more modest, reported to be approximately $40 billion.

ports have been constructed at Riyadh, Dhahran, and Jidda. New industrial cities are going up at Yanbu on the Red Sea and at Al Jubail on the Persian Gulf. These cities will house the most extensive petrochemical complexes in the world when they are completed and Saudi oil will be transported directly to them via a newly constructed pipeline. With this development the country is expected to dominate the refined as well as the crude oil market. Natural gas recovery is also being made more efficient and the Saudis should become a major factor in the plastics and other petroleum-related industries.

Protecting this unprecedented drive for material progress has been the tandem development of the Saudi armed forces. Before 1978 Saudi Arabia never had a full-blown military establishment. Its main military arm has been the national guard, organized in 1964 by the merger of the royal guard with the army. The national guard is a force of approximately 26,000 desert Bedouins—mostly loyal tribes from the Shammar region—and is led by a member of the royal family. The army is another 45,000-man force, which is being modernized along with the national guard. In the last few years the national guard was re-organized into four brigades, trained and equipped by the United States as mechanized light infantry. Although the Saudis speak of the national guard as an army that is destined to take its place beside other Arab forces in the fight against Israel, its mission is essentially internal security. While contingents of Saudi soldiers were sent to Syria and Jordan during the 1973 war with Israel and remained there for almost three years, and despite frequent declarations about the need for a Jihad, or holy war, against the state of Israel, there is little evidence to suggest the Saudis are poised for attack. It is more likely that the government sees the need for an improved military establishment as a strategic reserve, given the country's more complex evolution.

The Saudi Air Force has received particular attention. There are now esti-mated to be 17,000 men in this elite service. Moreover, the force is acquiring the most advanced aircraft in the American weapons arsenal. The F-15 replaces the F-5E, and the Reagan administration will equip the new aircraft with the addi-tional equipment that Jimmy Carter had decided to withhold. The paraphernalia includes attachable fuel tanks that extend the range of the aircraft, and air-to-air and air-to-ground missiles that make the F-15 a formidable offensive weapon. The Israelis have been highly critical of the U.S. action, arguing that the planes will have the capability to attack their population centers. The United States government, however, insists the Saudis have growing defense needs and that the equipment is meant solely for local protection. The Israelis were also distressed over President Reagan's decision to sell Saudi Arabia several fully equipped AWACS systems. Opponents to the sale in the American Congress as well as the Israelis complained bitterly about the transfer. As with the projected sale of AWACS to the shah of Iran, those opposing it questioned Saudi motives. Many congressmen and senators sustained the view that Saudi Arabia should be con-cerned with more basic defense needs and that the entire military assistance program should be reevaluated. The Reagan administration, however, was committed to the AWACS sale, and despite intense lobbying by the opposition, the American Senate yielded to the president's authority.

Saudi Arabia has accelerated its military building program. The government spent approximately $21 billion on its armed forces in 1981, and the AWACS package added $8.5 billion more to the military budget. New airbases and army installations were constructed in different parts of the country, with a major complex located northeast of Riyadh. Here again the Saudis were very dependent on foreign technicians and advisors. The principal expertise was derived from approximately 1,000 Americans and 2,000 Pakistani servicemen. (There are 45,000 Americans overall in the country and perhaps an equal number of Europeans.) To bolster their defenses the Saudi government also pondered the offer extended by General Zia-ul-Haq to station several Pakistani infantry divisions in the country. In return for such assistance, Saudi Arabia was expected to pay for the modern arms that the Pakistanis wished to acquire from the United States. Pakistan was rich in human resources and it was believed the two countries were eager to promote their growing intimacy. Pakistan therefore began to loom large in the defensive thinking of Riyadh.

Saudi Arabia has always demonstrated a preference for the United States over other world powers. Despite consistent support for Israel by successive American presidents, that orientation remains unaltered. Saudi fascination for American technology and mutually beneficial political and economic ties involving military supply and training components predate the Arab-Israeli conflict. The United States has always emphasized the importance of Saudi oil reserves, and Riyadh has encouraged American cooperation in the protection of the vast petroleum complex in and around Dhahran. Saudi reluctance to request military aid from other Arab states (instead of the United States) is linked to their fear that such cooperation could precipitate an unwanted change in their prevailing political structure. Alliances between Arab states have never been stable and yesterday's confidants are often tomorrow's enemies. Such was certainly the case in 1963–65 when Saudi Arabia and Egypt took opposite sides in the civil war in Yemen, and turned their guns on each other. The bombing of Saudi villages by Egyptian war planes forced Riyadh to realize the deficiencies in their defense structure, and the United States was requested to construct an air defense system as well as help train the national guard and a modern army. The pace of these developments was accelerated in 1974 when the United States prepared a survey of Saudi defense needs for the 1980s.[35]

The United States outfitted the national guard brigades with armored personnel carriers, Dragon antitank missiles, and Vulcan antiaircraft guns similar to those used by American mechanized units. Each brigade was provided with a small tank force, adding to its firepower without diminishing mobility. The United States also sold the Saudis more than 100 F-5 fighter aircraft and equipped them with both Sidewinder air-to-air and Maverick air-to-ground missile capability. The U.S. Congress, however, was still reluctant to provide all the missiles that the Saudis contracted for, and this created some strains in their relationship. Other controversies involved Saudi desires to purchase AWACs air control aircraft and F-15 supersonic fighters. Sensing that such sales would destroy the balance of power between Israel and the Arab states, the Congress tried to prevent the transfer but finally gave its approval in October 1981.[36]

STRATEGIC CONCERNS

The Saudis seek to compensate for their military weakness by associating with those countries that can perform the tasks they cannot do themselves. And of course they are prepared to pay handsome sums of money for the services rendered them. This somewhat explains their connection with the United States and Pakistan, and to some extent the numerous Arab states that they financially aid. At this juncture, however, the Saudis realize they must assert themselves in the Persian Gulf. Iran is no longer the dominant power in the region and keeping the Gulf open may well be Riyadh's responsibility. This may explain why Saudi Arabia was instrumental in forming a security council of Gulf states. In February 1981, Bahrein, Kuwait, Oman, Qatar, and the United Arab Emirates agreed to join the Saudis in a collective arrangement aimed at defending their interests in the volatile area. None of these states want either Iraq or the Soviet Union to increase their influence in the region. Nevertheless, in order to ward off closer alliance with the Soviet Union, Saudi Arabia has supported Iraq in its war with Iran. This posture, however, must be seen as a Saudi diplomatic gambit, not a military decision. Saudi diplomacy also attempted to defuse the Syrian-Israeli missile crisis in Lebanon in May and June 1981. Again, Riyadh was primarily concerned with diluting Russian influence in Damascus.

While the Saudis are disturbed over the situation in the Persian Gulf, they also have more than a passing interest in the Red Sea and the Horn of Africa. At Saudi request the U.S. Corps of Engineers is building a port facility at Jidda for both naval and commercial use. A similar installation is at Al Jubail on the Persian Gulf. In 1972 the United States began a ten-year program to provide the Saudi Arabians with the nucleus of a navy; six corvettes, four minesweepers, two coastal patrol craft, four troop-carrying landing craft, three training ships, and two tugs comprised the initial consignment. In 1977 the Saudis ordered an additional 29 large and medium patrol craft. Most of these vessels were scheduled for duty in the Red Sea and at the southern end of the waterway known as the Bab al-Mandeb. Control of any part of the Red Sea by powers opposed to the Saudi or Egyptian governments is judged a serious security threat. The small 4,000-man Saudi navy cannot defend either the Red Sea or the Persian Gulf and the large U.S. naval presence near the Strait of Hormuz and the American bases in Oman and Somalia are welcome. Approval has also been given for joint U.S.-

Egyptian cooperation and the opening of Egyptian military installations to U.S. forces.

Just as the shah denied mastery of the Persian Gulf to radical regimes, the Saudis, with Egyptian and especially U.S. cooperation, wish to do the same in the Red Sea. The Marxist regime in South Yemen and Soviet penetration of Ethiopia have increased tension in the area. Moreover, Libyan attempts at ousting the Sudan's Jafar Numayri have made countermeasures imperative. The Egyptians have pledged their full support to Numayri, and the joint defense pact initiated by Sadat has been perpetuated by his successor Hosni Mubarak. Egyptian support for the Sudan parallels Pakistani assistance to Oman. Both actions have the approval of the Saudis, who have also agreed to pay for the arms that the Sudan and Oman receive from the United States.

The importance of the Red Sea to Saudi Arabia and Egypt is multidimensional. The reopening of the Suez Canal in June 1975 once more transformed the Red Sea into a major naval and commercial artery. It is the key strategic sea linking the Mediterranean with the Indian Ocean and therefore Europe with the Orient. It is the conduit through which flows much of the oil destined for Western Europe. Arab dominance of the Red Sea also puts the Israelis in an awkward position, given their dependence on maritime shipping passing through the Bab al-Mandeb on its way to the Israeli port of Eilat.[37] Control of the Bab al-Mandeb by the Egyptian navy means Egypt could reach into the northern Indian Ocean in the vicinity of the Persian Gulf and hence could help Saudi Arabia balance radical influences and power on both sides of the Gulf. But the success of this effort also requires neutralizing Aden as a principal Soviet naval and air station.

Revolutionary Iran is aware of Saudi-Egyptian maneuvers in the Red Sea, and although interested in denying it to the Soviet Union and its allies, they are very uneasy over the long-range consequences. The Iranians have criticized those Arab governments that refer to the Persian Gulf as the Arabian Gulf. They have condemned Saudi Arabia, Jordan, and Kuwait for their support of Iraqi aggression in Iranian Khuzistan. The Iranians also believe that Saudi operations on the Red Sea are a beginning for a broader policy of hegemony that will ultimately extend to the Persian Gulf. For the time being, however, the Red Sea gambit provides Saudi Arabia with an opportunity to demonstrate its new military prowess. And their long-term objective is the neutralization of Soviet and Cuban influence in South Yemen and Ethiopia. Saudi overtures of assistance to the government in South Yemen have somewhat moderated the aggressive behavior of the People's Democratic Republic of Yemen (PDRY) but the Russians, Cubans, and East Germans show no indication of withdrawing their "advisors" from the country.[38] Ethiopia, on the other hand, is firmly in the Marxist camp and the Saudis are hardly in a position to persuade the Mengistu regime to modify its foreign policy.[39]

The overthrow of Emperor Haile Selassie in September 1974 and the emergence of a Marxist regime in Addis Ababa gave the Soviet Union a presence in Ethiopia up to that time enjoyed by the United States. The Soviet Union was already entrenched in Somalia, and its efforts to befriend the Ethiopians complicated their relations with the Somalis, who perceived Ethiopia as their number-one enemy. Soviet policy gave attention to the Horn of Africa, and its bases at Berbera in Somalia and on the South Yemen island of Socotra were considered keys to its Indian Ocean activities. When Somalia aspirations could no longer be served in alliance with the Soviet Union, the Berbera base was placed in jeopardy, hence the shift of Soviet forces to Aden. Saudi Arabia was given its opportunity to win Mogadishu's confidence by replacing the aid that the Soviets had curtailed. Fidel Castro visited Somalia and offered to mediate the dispute with Ethiopia but found the situation hopeless. The Somalis would be satisfied with nothing less than Somali irredenta, and they increased their pressure on Ethiopia's Ogaden region. The Ethiopians were already hard pressed by two Eritrean factions that had the support of Iraq, Syria, Egypt, and Saudi Arabia, and the large-scale fighting on several fronts threatened Ethiopia with dismemberment.

The Soviets realized their links with Somalia were expedient, not ideological, and an all-out effort was martialed to save Ethiopia from collapse. By January 1978 the Soviet Union had sent the regime of Mengistu Haile Meriam a half billion dollars in modern weapons, and another half billion was in the pipeline. A thousand Soviet advisers were reported in the country, and Cuban troops were transferred from their bases in Angola to front-line positions in Ethiopia. The U.S. Department of State reported on February 10, 1978, that Cuban forces were already in combat against the Somalis, and the Somalis claimed Ethiopian planes were being flown against them by both Soviet and Cuban pilots. Reports from Somalia insisted that Soviet warships had shelled Somali installations. Information on the fighting was sketchy, however, and the United States sought to verify the claims and counterclaims. Secretary of State Cyrus Vance announced in a press conference in mid-February that the United States had been given assurances by the Soviets that they would not nor would they permit Cuban or Ethiopian troops to invade Somalia. Vance noted that, so long as the Somali frontier was respected, the United States would refrain from direct involvement.

U.S. policy toward Somalia, on the surface, appeared hesitant and indecisive. Somalia had terminated its treaty of friendship and cooperation with the Soviet Union in November 1977. It had also broken diplomatic relations with Cuba. Having lost its Soviet cornucopia, Siad Barre's Somali government requested aid from the United States. After indicating that it would provide such assistance, the United States drew back, asserting that Somalia had invaded Ethiopia and that the United States could not encourage such behavior. At the same time, the Somalis had asked the Soviet Union to vacate its base in Berbera, and the United States was obviously gratified with this turn of events. Thus a program was mounted to safeguard Somalia with help provided by its neighbors.

Saudi Arabia, Egypt, and the Sudan were prepared to increase their support, but they first had to obtain weapons from the United States and other West European nations. The shah of Iran also displayed a growing interest. In December 1977 the Pentagon announced the sale of 12 F-5 fighter aircraft to the Sudan. In January 1978 the Carter administration took the last step before formally revealing its decision to sell Saudi Arabia 60 F-15s. In February, Sadat visited Washington, and although he spent most of his public time talking about his difficulties in arriving at an understanding with the Israelis, he also discoursed at length about the situation on the Horn of Africa. The Egyptian president was blunt in calling for American assistance, particularly F-5 aircraft (approximately 100 were requested), which he declared would not be used against Israel. The only conclusion to be drawn was that Sadat and other conservative Arab leaders were increasingly alarmed by the armed presence of the Soviet Union and Cuba in their immediate vicinity, and they had to find a way not only to help Somalia but also to insulate themselves against the creeping radicalization of the area.

The United States called a meeting in Washington of representatives from Great Britain, France, West Germany, and Italy in January 1978, the subject being Soviet-Cuban operations on the Horn of Africa. Soon thereafter, Ethiopia ordered the West German ambassador to leave the country, accusing his government of aiding the Somalis. The French also agreed to maintain their garrison in Djibouti, and both the United States and France implied they would not be disturbed if the Egyptians and Saudis "Arabized" the Red Sea. These diplomatic maneuvers were matched by the Cubans when Raul Castro turned up in Moscow reportedly to coordinate plans for their campaign in East Africa. And the Israeli government complicated matters by officially announcing that it had been aiding Ethiopia in an effort to ward off Arab dominance at the mouth of the Red Sea.

Siad Barre visited Saudi Arabia, Kuwait, the United Arab Emirates, Pakistan, and Iran in an effort to arouse greater support for his forces. On his return to Mogadishu, he declared there was little likelihood of a negotiated settlement, given the Soviet Union's objectives in the region. "No one will be able to convince the Soviet Union to stop the war," he said. The Soviet bloc "is conducting a war to teach African countries that if they don't obey they will be punished."[40] Somalia, he noted, had no choice but to defend itself, but it did need outside help.

The Russian and Cuban presence in Ethiopia and South Yemen added a new dimension to Soviet machinations. In March 1978, Somali forces retreated from the Ogaden. Despite Soviet assurances to the United States, the Kremlin had its sights on destroying the Siad Barre government. If a regime more favorable to the Soviet Union could be installed in Mogadishu, the Berbera base may again be operational for the Soviet navy and air force. And if the Ethiopians could fight their way into Somalia, they might seize Djibouti as well. With Djibouti in Ethiopian hands and Somalia no longer a threat in the Ogaden, the Soviet Union might convince Mengistu and his Dergue (the military regime in

Ethiopia) to give up Eritrea to the Eritrean People's Liberation Front (EPLF), the Marxist faction that has dominated the fighting there. An alliance between Marxist Ethiopia and the EPLF could easily eliminate the conservative Eritrean Liberation Front and thus complete the radicalization of the Horn of Africa. Moreover, its linkup with South Yemen would give the Soviet Union dominance over the vital sea lanes extending out from the Persian Gulf and the Red Sea. It would also put the Russians in easy striking distance of the Gulf and of course enable them to control the Bab al-Mandeb. Thus, the December 1977 declaration by the government of South Yemen that it was expanding its territorial waters from 3 to 12 miles and would establish an economic zone of 200 miles greatly disturbed the Saudis, Egyptians, and Sudanese. Saudi Arabia reminded the Yemenites that the 1968 Geneva Convention stipulated that no state should extend its sovereignty over more than half the width of a waterway common to more than one country. To protect its interests Riyadh called for the construction of electronic devices to guide navigation in the strait and announced that it too had responsibility for protecting shipping through the waterway. Because of the envisaged costs in strategic position and prestige, none of the contestants in this scenario was expected to quietly steal away.

Skirmishes between Ethiopia and Somalia continued through 1979-80. Ethiopia, however, was reluctant to move its forces into Somalia and the latter was too weak to threaten the Mengistu regime. Moreover, war and drought and refugees had subdued both nations, and their governments were ill-equipped to tend to the desperately impoverished thousands within their midst, let alone to marshal full-scale battle formations.[41] The Soviet Union also wanted more time to consolidate its gains in Ethiopia and they continued to pressure Mengistu to organize a sophisticated Communist Party system. Somalia's Siad Barre, however, was targeted, but survived assassins and dissident elements who conspired to remove him. In the hope of strengthening his regime, Barre agreed to permit the United States to use the port of Berbera. In return, Washington, with Saudi encouragement, promised the Somali government replacement military stores.[42]

The ever-shifting alliances and relationships described in this chapter address themselves to a fluid geopolitical situation in that great arc extending from the coast of East Africa around the Red Sea, the Persian Gulf, and the Arabian Sea to Pakistan and India. This "crescent of crisis" or "arc of crisis" identified by officials in the United States government describes a vast region, rich in human diversity and natural resources, but plagued by controversy and unreconciled conflict. The area is important not only to the people who inhabit it, but to the larger world that is so dependent on its resources and strategic position. It is also in this region where the United States and the Soviet Union are in direct competition. More than Western Europe in the 1980s, the arc of crisis threatens serious confrontation between the superpowers. The collapse of the shah's regime and the Soviet penetration of Afghanistan more than hint at a changing correlation of forces in the vital region. Indeed, what is described as "crisis" in Washington, has become "opportunity" in Moscow. The Kremlin moved quickly to capitalize on the American retreat from advance positions in Southwest Asia. The Soviets sense the tide of history runs in their favor and nowhere has the line been so clearly drawn between the forces of radical change and those wishing to sustain a traditional way of life.

CONCLUSIONS

This chapter has presented a broader perspective from which to view Indian Ocean and South Asian questions. The Indian Ocean has never been, is not now, nor is it ever likely to be dominated by a single littoral power. India's pretensions and declarations that it has a clearer interest in the Indian Ocean than any other state are platitudinous and unrealistic. Its concern with American operations on the island of Diego Garcia can be accepted as genuine, but the withdrawal of the United States from this remote base will not in itself transform the Indian Ocean into the much-heralded zone of peace. The Indians have competition in the Indian Ocean from regional states (that is, not only superpowers) that are reluctant to submit to the hegemony of any of their near or distant neighbors. Given opportunities heretofore unavailable or foreclosed to them, they are now in the process of charting out spheres of influence that they believe are vital to their security. The absence of an integrated world structure or a more limited regional system means that individual states will, wherever possible, attempt to strengthen their strategic postures according to their own lights.

The passing of the European age has unleashed the anarchical forces of nationalism on a global scale, and it is these forces that drive the engines of contemporary international politics.[43] Even the mighty superpowers are swept along and back and forth by the tides of national self-indulgence. No power, irrespective of its enormous military capacity, can control, let alone tame, the volatile situation. The archrivalry between the United States and the Soviet Union, their inability to achieve more than a modicum of understanding, and the deep mistrust of each for the other's motives and intentions, all guarantee the supremacy of these nationalistic drives. India continues to harbor some noble ideas about peace and order, but it too pursues security through military strength, and it certainly cannot be surprised that other states are similarly involved.

In November 1972 the shah of Iran spoke hauntingly of his country's power extending beyond the Persian and Oman gulfs into the Indian Ocean. His thoughts were expressed almost a year before the 1973 Arab-Israeli conflict that produced a chain of events highlighted by the steep ascent in world petroleum prices. He was determined then to assert Iran's claim to a position of significance in the constellation of great powers. The shah commented at the time that events in the world were shaping a destiny for his administration that he could not ignore. The enormous riches gained from the sale of Iran's oil in the years that followed confirmed for him a policy that was already predetermined, and he noted:

> I admit that until three or four years ago I only had the defense of the Persian Gulf in mind. This was because most of our wealth existed in regions to the northwest of Bandar Abbas and the Strait of Hormuz.
>
> We wanted to safeguard that wealth and keep open the way through which they could reach the outside world. But then came events which forced us to think of the Gulf of Oman and Iran's coast there. Then other events in the world taught us that the sea contiguous to the Gulf of Oman, and I mean the Indian Ocean, recognizes no frontiers. Iran was no longer merely thinking of defending Abadan, Khosrowabad, Bushehr or even Hormoz and Bandar Abbas.
>
> We are not even thinking merely of defending Jask and Chah-Bahar. We are thinking of Iran's security perimeter and I am not speaking in terms of few kilometers.
>
> Anyone versed in geopolitical, strategic matters and especially in possibilities of naval and air forces of today would guess how distant that frontier could be from Chah-Bahar.[44]

The shah declared then that it was his primary objective not only to modernize the Iranian armed forces but also to provide them with the most advanced military equipment available anywhere in the world. He explained that the defense of the country was a patriotic duty but that this otherwise natural responsibility was made ever so much more important because of the need to protect Iran's coveted resources. The value of the installations of Kharg Island alone, he recalled, was equal to the total value of all structures in Iran in 1941.

There has been an abundance of commentary about the shah's desire to resurrect the Persian empire and to transform Iran into a major regional power. Nor did the shah keep his intentions secret. He accepted the adage "the best defense was a good offense." Iran had an opportunity to make itself more secure than it had been in centuries. But timidity and hesitancy were not deemed to be the methods likely to produce meaningful results. A forward policy, albeit an aggressive one, while it raised the level of risk, offered the possibility of wider choice and hence of measured accomplishment. To accept a secondary position when the power of decision is made available is a negation of leadership, and the shah had lived with power and threats to his authority too long to miss this opportunity. The shah and his government therefore operated on two separate but linked planes of reality. The first plane involved Iran and its immediate surroundings. Here the emphasis was not only on self-defense and if possible the limitation of superpower rivalries in the region of the Persian Gulf but also the need to isolate and eliminate localized revolutionary and terrorist movements. The second plane projected Iran on to the world stage. This was a multi-dimensional activity involving investments in Western industrial and financial enterprises as well as the organizing of a common defense and economic system for like-minded Asian and oceanic countries. On his tour of India, several Southeast Asian countries, Australia, and New Zealand in 1974, the shah spoke of the need to establish a common market to promote the region's collective well-being. Before this trip India had voiced dissatisfaction with Iran's military building program, but at the end of the shah's visit Prime Minister Gandhi publicly agreed with him that "safeguarding stability and peace in the Gulf was the exclusive right of the littoral states."[45] The shah and prime minister also signed a $1 billion industrial agreement whereby Iran offered Indian soft credit for the purchase of Iranian oil and also sponsored the construction of steel and aluminum works. This assistance placated the Indians and momentarily stilled their fears but scarcely reduced the rivalry between the two nations.

Iran had moved its principal forces in the direction of the Indian Ocean. The military command center at Bandar Abbas, which included the largest naval station in the country, lay astride the Strait of Hormuz. Another naval facility was being erected with American assistance on the Indian Ocean at Chah Bahar in close proximity to the Pakistani frontier. Moreover, in 1972 Iran obtained the right to use the naval base on the island of Mauritius. Nevertheless, it is doubtful that Iran seriously envisaged an extended Indian Ocean policy.[46] The mission of its armed forces, apart from the preservation of the monarchy and the maintenance of national unity, was the building of a defense system that could attract willing allies while not overly antagonizing recalcitrant neighbors.

But even with its mighty arsenal, Iran's forces were largely untested in battle and recognizably short on sophisticated skills. And while the shah outwardly received the loyalty of his military leaders, the occasional defection of a ranking officer, such as Major General Ahmed Moqarrebi, who was executed in December 1977 for what was officially described as spying for a foreign power, left searching doubts. These doubts were justified when mass rioting swept the country in 1978-79, and the shah, despite his vaunted power, was forced to flee his country.

To what extent was the shah's authority weakened by the heavy emphasis on military expansion? The shah had seen many of his counterparts in neighboring Pakistan, Afghanistan, and among the Arab states displaced by their once faithful military supporters. Although in this case the military did not move directly against the monarch, they also did little to preserve his throne.

The passing of the Pahlavi dynasty brought an end to Iran's contemporary quest for big-power status. Momentarily mesmerized by their success, the Iranian revolutionaries did not grasp the consequences of their self-inflicted blows. The Islamic leaders were not content with the liquidation of a despised figure and an antiquated institution. Their sights were focused on the larger society, and no less important, the extended Muslim world. They saw themselves in the vanguard of a great crusade, reviving a faith that really did not need revival. Islam was a durable, vital, and growing force. Its devotees ranged over the globe and totaled in the hundreds of millions. Modernization schemes and technological innovation raised problems that Muslims were required to cope with, but they did not endanger the fundamental Muslim way of life. What the mullahs of Iran failed to understand was that political weakness not spiritual decay was the primary problem. The religious teachers committed the cardinal error; they attempted to rid themselves of politics rather than to understand it. The result was not only political myopia, but a surrealistic world view. Instead of binding up the nation's wounds, redressing grievances, and reconciling competitive demands, the mullahs equated protest with treason. The country was plunged into protracted conflict that sapped its energy and demoralized its folk. The Islamic revolution ceased to be a revolution for human freedom and became a vindictive, punishing force that removed virtually all opportunities for compromise. Thus the revolutionaries turned against one another and Iran's survival was threatened by the very elements that claimed to save it.

What lessons can Saudi Arabia draw from the Iranian experience? Saudi Arabia cannot and should not attempt to fill the power vacuum created by the collapse of the shah's regime. It must also recognize that its foreign policy is an extension of its domestic condition and any attempt to divorce the one from the other will prove ruinous. The shah fabricated a very successful foreign policy. Indeed, the same could be said for the late Zulfikar Ali Bhutto. But both of these strong leaders failed to understand the true nature of the local problems besetting their populations and how these impacted directly on their rule. Expertise in international politics could not save either personality. It will not sustain the Saudis. This does not mean that foreign policy should be neglected. Far from it. But a country's foreign policy must be a reflection, and indeed a measure, of its national experience. Foreign policy should enhance domestic policy, supplement and complement it. The two realms should be mutually reinforcing but primary attention must be given to the immediate surroundings. This is the principal lesson of the Iranian experience.

The Saudi dynasty must recognize its inadequacies and deficiencies. It possesses great power, but its capacity to influence and command respect may well be greater beyond than within the state's frontiers. Absolute monarchies, despite their long history, are anachronistic in the last decades of the twentieth century. Although the world continues to show little genuine interest in democratic systems, and dictatorships and totalitarianisms are on the ascendent, the institution of direct monarchial rule is fading. The ruling monarchs, to be distinguished from the ceremonial ones as in Japan or Great Britain, are destined to disappear before the twenty-first century. The family of Ibn Saud senses this but is disinclined to hasten the process. But if they hesitate in taking the initiative, they will only increase the certainty that others will not remain silent or passive. This is the next important lesson of the Iranian drama.

The dialectics of modernization increases stress in society. The dynamics of growth are never without cost. The pace of material and physical change in Saudi Arabia is unprecedented, but there is very little evidence that even a modicum of political development is contemplated. Even a minor change in the political process would seriously affect the controls sustained by the royal family. Nevertheless, recent history shows that economic progress will not guarantee the longevity or the stability of a particular administration. It could, however, accelerate its decline. Even a country like Saudi Arabia cannot close itself off from the rest of the world. It cannot compartmentalize its private and public life. It cannot prevent the passage of ideas. Too many Saudis have and will continue to live, study, and work abroad and their experiences are more complex than those of their desert forebears. Expectation levels have been raised, not so much in a material as in a psychological context. Today the Saudi mind must come to grips with questions that were never imagined by their predecessors. Moreover, police agencies, no matter how efficient, cannot sustain the status quo. Official violence, intimidation, and general repression will neither promote loyalty nor neutralize criticism, hence the third lesson of Iran.

The Saudis are aware that internationally they have more tormentors than friends, more sycophants than supporters. Their near monopoly of the world's exportable oil, extensive investments, and peculiar life-style create jealousies and bitterness. Moreover, the Arabian peninsula is in too strategic a location to be left unchallenged. Enemies therefore abound both within the Arab domains and in the extended world. Like the ever shifting desert sands, relations with area states are unpredictable and subject to constant change. If Saudi Arabia has had one consistent supporter since its emergence as an independent state it has been the United States government. No Arab or Muslim nation has maintained the close ties that the United States has sustained over the last 50 years. Americans have always attempted to bolster not weaken Saudi authority. The intimacy generated between the governments explains why Riyadh would agree to produce more petroleum when their OPEC partners call for drastic reductions, why the Saudis almost alone insist on holding the line on price increases, and why they tolerate the American position in aiding Israel. Washington is no absolute guarantor of Saudi sovereignty and integrity but Riyadh needs the Americans as much as the latter depend upon Saudi oil reserves. Ties to the Arab and Muslim world are drawn by sentiment; relations with the United States are conditioned by realism and necessity. The former sustains the spirit, the latter holds out the promise of survival.

The United States and Saudi Arabia therefore are likely to move more in tandem now that Iran no longer plays linchpin for the West's defense of the Persian Gulf and adjoining regions. The revolution in Iran also spelled an end to the Nixon Doctrine and the United States can no longer remain a distant observer in Southwest Asian affairs. The United States has less of a foothold in the region but paradoxically it is more physically involved than ever before.

The Soviet Union too presents a more ubiquitous posture along the southern rim of the Asian continent, in Africa, and throughout the Indian Ocean. The Russians are an essentially insecure people and when the opportunity to improve their tenuous position presents itself they have usually responded by pressing their frontiers outward from the periphery. The last of the classic empires, the Soviet successors to tsarist imperium have extended their influence if not their fiat to distant corners of the globe. Nevertheless, it is in southwestern and southern Asia that the Soviets display the greatest interest. The forces of the North Atlantic Treaty Organization block their path on the one side. On the other, China is a formidable adversary. The states that fill the expanse between Turkey and India, however, are not only inchoate, they are consumed by self-doubt, unreconciled rivalry, and primitive fantasy. They are easy prey for outsiders who know what they want and have the will and the capacity to pursue it. Islam and Marxism-Leninism are at complete variance but this has not prevented the Soviet Union from enlisting recruits in its drive for regional hegemony. The domination of Afghanistan like the treaties with Syria, Iraq, and South Yemen, arms and technical assistance to Libya, the PLO, and probably to Iran, as well as the establishment of a proper communist system in Ethiopia are tactical maneuvers aimed at satisfying Russian security needs. Nor is this the end of the process. U.S. attempts at bolstering Egypt, Israel, Saudi Arabia, the Gulf states, Pakistan, and Somalia mean an increase not the diminishing of Soviet pressure in the area. Moreover, this pressure would not be lessened even if the United States decided to withdraw its presence from the region. The contest has proceeded too far for that to occur. An American retreat, given that which preceded it, would be an invitation for the Soviet Union to complete its grand design.

There is no escaping the realities of the 1980s. The United States and the Soviet Union will continue to raise the ante in and near the Indian Ocean. India, like all the other affected states, will have to make whatever adjustment it deems to be in its interest.[47]

NOTES

1. India's historic interest in the Indian Ocean is explored in K. M. Panikkar, *India and the Indian Ocean*, 2d ed. (London: Allen and Unwin, 1962).

2. Geoffrey Jukes, *The Indian Ocean in Soviet Naval Policy*, Adelphi Papers, no. 87 (London: International Institute for Strategic Studies, May 1972), pp. 12–28; and Robert E. Hunter, *The Soviet Dilemma in the Middle East, Part II: Oil and the Persian Gulf*, Adelphi Papers, no. 60 (London: Institute for Strategic Studies, October 1969), pp. 1–12.

3. See Abbas Amirie, *The Persian Gulf and Indian Ocean in International Politics* (Tehran: Institute of International Political and Economic Studies, 1976).

4. New York *Times*, July 12, 1977.

5. New York *Times*, March 24, 1981. See also Muhammad Loutfi, "Prospects for Development and Investment for Oil-Producing Countries," in *The Middle East: Oil, Politics and Development*, ed. John Duke Anthony (Washington, D.C.: American Enterprise Institute, 1975), pp. 67–68; and New York *Times*, January 24, 1978.

6. See Sepehr Zabih and Shahram Chubin, *Iran's Foreign Relations: A Developing State in a Zone of Great Power Conflict* (Berkeley: University of California Press, 1974); and R. K. Ramazani, *The Persian Gulf: Iran's Role* (Charlottesville: University of Virginia Press, 1973).

7. *Middle East Intelligence Survey* 7, no. 16 (November 16–30, 1979): 123.

8. See the statement on Iran to the Security Council by Secretary of State Cyrus Vance, *Current Policy*, no. 121, December 29, 1979.

9. Washington *Post*, December 3, 1979.

10. The ideas expressed by the radical Left in the assault on the authority of the shah are still valid. See Amir Pouyan, *Iran: The Struggle Within* (New York: Support Committee For The Iranian People's Struggle [SCIPS], July 1975); and *Middle East Intelligence Survey* 8, no. 5 (June 1–15, 1980): 39–40.

11. Lawrence Ziring, *Iran, Turkey and Afghanistan: A Political Chronology* (New York: Praeger, 1981), p. 181.

12. New York *Times*, August 12, 1980.

13. William E. Griffith, "The Revival of Islamic Fundamentalism: The Case of Iran," *Hamdard Islamicus* 3, no. 1 (Spring 1981): 51–52.

14. See William H. Sullivan, "Dateline Iran: The Road Not Taken," *Foreign Policy*, no. 40, Fall 1980; and the Washington *Post*, October 30, 1980.

15. New York *Times*, December 19, 1979.

16. *Middle East Intelligence Survey* 8, no. 5 (June 1–15, 1980): 40.

17. See J. C. Hurewitz, *The Persian Gulf after Iran's Revolution*, Foreign Policy Series 244 (New York: Foreign Policy Association, 1979).

18. See John R. Countryman, "Iran in the View of the Persian Gulf Emirates," Study Project Paper, U.S. Army War College, Carlisle Barracks, Pennsylvania, May 1976.

19. John K. Cooley, "Baluchistan Breakaway Pull Felt by Iranian Government," *Christian Science Monitor*, February 2, 1973. See also F. Ahmed, ed., *Focus on Baluchistan & Pustoon Question* (Lahore: People's, 1975); and Robert G. Wirsing, *The Baluchis and Pathans*, Minority Rights Group, report no. 48 (London, March 1981).

20. *Middle East Intelligence Survey* 8, no. 12 (September 16–30, 1980): 89–95.

21. Chester Bowles, *Promises to Keep: My Years in Public Life, 1940-1969* (New York: Harper & Row, 1971), p. 370.

22. Robert G. Irani, "U.S., Iran and Saudi Arabia: The Dynamics of National Security Interests in the Gulf Area," *Third World Review* 3, no. 2 (Fall 1977): 82.

23. For radical accounts of the struggle in Oman see "The Oman War 1957–1959: A Critical History," and "Political Prisoners in the Oil States: Oman, Bahrein, Saudi Arabia, Iran." Both documents were published by the Organization of Arab Students in the United States and Canada, Eugene, Oregon, 1975. See also "Oil and Investment in Oman," Gulf Solidarity Committee, Eugene, Oregon, 1975.

24. New York *Times*, October 11, 1977.

25. New York *Times*, January 5, 1977.

26. James Bill, "Iran and the Crisis of '78" *Foreign Affairs* 52, no. 2 (Winter 1978/79): 338–39.

27. *Daily Telegraph* (London), November 6, 1978.

28. New York *Times*, February 14, 1979.

29. *Saudi Arabia: Bullish on America*, Middle East Research and Information Project (MERIP), report no. 26, March 1974, p. 11.

30. See David Holden, *Farewell to Arabia* (New York: Walker, 1966).

31. Shahram Chubin, "Iran: Between the Arab West and the Asian East," *Survival* 16, no. 4 (July-August 1974): 173.

32. Quoted in the New York *Times*, March 26, 1975.

33. Edward Cody, "Saudi Rulers Face Conflicting Pressures at Home, Abroad," Washington *Post*, December 2, 1979.

34. New York *Times*, March 24, 1981.

35. "Current Policy: Persian Gulf/Arabian Peninsula," Department of State, no. 2, June 1975, p. 4; and "Saudi Arabia and the United States: Areas of Common Interest," a statement by Alfred Atherton, Jr., Department of State, February 23, 1976, p. 2.

36. New York *Times*, July 19, 1977; New York *Times*, October 29, 1981. See also "Dangerous Illusions and Real Choices on AWACS," *Current Policy*, no. 324, Washington, D.C., U.S. Department of State (October 5, 1981); and "Saudi Arabia and U.S. Security Policy," *Current Policy*, no. 320, Washington, D.C., U.S. Department of State (September 25, 1981).

37. Dale R. Tahtinen, *Arms in the Indian Ocean: Interests and Challenges* (Washington, D.C.: American Enterprise Institute, 1977), p. 34.

38. See the statement of Prime Minister Ali Nasser Mohammad of South Yemen after his talks with Indira Gandhi. *India News*, May 25, 1981.

39. Washington *Post*, April 7, 1979.

40. New York *Times*, January 24, 1978. See also Udo Steinbach, "Arab Policy Around the Horn of Africa," *Aussenpolitik* (English ed.) 28, no. 3 (1977): 302–14.

41. "Somali Refugees," *GIST*, U.S. Department of State, March 1981.

42. "Horn of Africa," *Current Policy*, no. 141, Washington, D.C., U.S. Department of State (February 25, 1980), pp. 1–3.

43. Hedley Bull, *The Anarchical Society* (New York: Columbia University Press, 1977), pp. 3–22.

44. *Kayhan*, (international ed.), November 11, 1972.

45. Robert Manning, "Iran's Powerful Empire-Builder," *Far Eastern Economic Review*, January 24, 1975, pp. 20–21.

46. Alexander Mcleod, "Shah of the Indian Ocean?" *Pacific Community*, April 1976, p. 431.

47. See Larry W. Bowman and Ian Clark, *The Indian Ocean in Global Politics* (Boulder, Colo.: Westview Press, 1980).

7

SOVIET SECURITY INTERESTS IN SOUTH ASIA

Robert H. Donaldson

A visit by the leader of the world's most powerful communist state to the world's largest noncommunist state is of inherent significance, but Soviet President Leonid Brezhnev's December 1980 trip to India was of unusual significance. The trip was his second to India in eight years—a record made more notable by the fact that India is the only noncommunist third world country that Brezhnev has visited even once in over 17 years since he assumed the leadership of the Communist Party of the Soviet Union. Clearly, the Soviet leaders value highly their country's friendship with India, as Brezhnev stressed in his first speech in New Delhi: "It may be said without fear of exaggeration that the Soviet people and their leaders are friends India can rely upon. Friends in good times and in hard times, in clear weather and in bad weather."[1] Welcoming Brezhnev upon his arrival was a familiar partner in these periodic demonstrations of state-to-state friendship—Indira Gandhi, prime minister again after a hiatus of almost three years. Indira Gandhi, Brezhnev's hostess on his previous visit, had herself been received on three formal visits in Moscow. Prime Minister Gandhi was widely perceived as a special friend of Moscow, but the expressions of India's trust and confidence in the relationship of these two powers were not the product of a particular individual's preferences. Indeed, the Janata Party government of Morarji Desai that had held power in New Delhi during the closing years of the 1970s had disappointed some observers who had expected that Indira Gandhi's departure would produce a distinct reorientation of India's diplomatic, economic, and military bonds away from the USSR. On numerous occasions, both Soviet and Indian leaders have cited the stability of their friendship as the key to the maintenance of peace in the region.

Moscow's seeming devotion to the preservation of its friendship with India cannot be ascribed to a compatibility of world view or fundamental purpose. Although the American and Indian points of view are dissimilar in many respects, they are to a great extent more mutually compatible than is either country's outlook and ideology with that of the USSR. Rather, Moscow's relationship with New Delhi has been built primarily on a mutual sense of need—a shared perception in each state that the friendship of the other is essential to the preservation of its own security. This chapter will explore in some detail the Soviet Union's security interests in the subcontinent and the surrounding region, starting with the historical record and moving quickly to an examination of Moscow's more recent relations with states of the area. The chapter will conclude with some observations about the Soviet Union's overall security policies in the wake of the invasion of Afghanistan, examining the widespread thesis that Soviet security needs can be met only through the expansion of Soviet military power to the very shores of the Indian Ocean itself.

From the standpoint of the Kremlin, the primary significance of the states of South Asia lies in their role in the competition between the Soviet Union, China, and the United States for global and regional influence. Moscow's chief purpose in South Asia, pursued ardently for most of the last two decades and likely to persist for the foreseeable future, is the enlistment of India's participation as a counterweight to China in the Asian "balance of power" game. Attainment of this objective requires that Chinese influence be excluded from India and Bangladesh, and that Beijing's influence in Pakistan be held to a minimum. Thus Moscow's friendly posture toward New Delhi has needed to be balanced by the maintenance and even strengthening of its ties with Pakistan and Bangladesh. Given the traditional hostility between India and Pakistan, this has required a delicate balancing act, generally guided by the calculation that Soviet security can best be promoted by efforts to stabilize the situation in the subcontinent. From the Soviet viewpoint, India's role in this enterprise of deterring Chinese military action and containing Chinese influence in South Asia is furthered by her visible partnership with the USSR in "collective security" efforts. The more Moscow succeeds in publicly enlisting India in this anti-China campaign, the more confident it can be in the permanence of the hostility between New Delhi and Beijing. While the Soviets currently view China as the greatest threat to their security, Moscow has a second major adversary in Asia, and India's participation is also sought in the limitation of American presence and influence in the region. Thus the Soviets encourage New Delhi to make diplomatic and commercial decisions that assist in reducing American and Western influence.

A third Soviet objective is to encourage the Indian government, as a leader in the third world, to take positions on international issues as close as possible to those taken by the Soviet Union. In both its public pronouncements and its behavior in international bodies, India's support is sought by the USSR. For Moscow, the image of a Soviet-Indian identity of views is valued both for its impact in Washington and Beijing and for its influence on the rest of the third world.

Their Marxist convictions lead the Soviets to believe that India's reliable friendship can best be ensured if her domestic policies and politics reflect an orientation in the direction of a socialist economy and a "progressive" polity. Not since the early years of Khrushchev's leadership have the Soviets viewed the creation of a communist government in India as a practical near-term objective; in recent years, in fact, they have demonstrated their awareness that such a development may create more problems than it would solve. After working rather contentedly with Indira Gandhi's "national bourgeois" government for many years, the Soviet leaders shuddered at her defeat in the 1977 elections. Nevertheless, they soon showed their willingness to cooperate with a Janata Party they had labeled reactionary, so long as it continued a foreign policy acceptable to Moscow. The Soviets resumed close cooperation with Indira Gandhi after her return to power, even though she has moved more openly into conflict with India's two communist parties.

As intermediate goals that help in the pursuit of the aforementioned objectives, the Soviets have sought to build strong and lasting commercial ties with India—both as a way of weakening the fabric of "imperialist" economies and as a useful partner for their own economy—and, through propaganda and cultural exchange, to create attitudes among the Indian elite and mass that are favorable to the USSR. Instrumental in the creation of such attitudes is the fostering of a sense of need among the Indians—a feeling that Soviet support and assistance are vital to the realization of India's own objectives.

In the area of security and regional alignments there appear to be, for the present at least, certain parallels in Indian and Soviet objectives. But there are also certain incompatibilities that raise doubts that the Indo-Soviet relationship will be either permanent or free of tension. The Indians desire more balance in their relations with the "great-power triangle" than the Soviets would like, and the Soviets seek to maintain more balance in their own relations in the subcontinent than the Indians would like. In this arena one occasionally finds that one side's actions arouse suspicions and feelings of betrayal in the other. For example, India has shown its resentment at the Soviet Union's occasional attempt to strengthen its influence in Pakistan, and the Soviets have displayed nervousness over India's efforts to improve relations with Beijing and Washington. In the early 1970s India was suspicious of Soviet-American dealings that appeared to be aimed toward a superpower condominium. Throughout the decade New Delhi assumed a different position on superpower activities in the Indian Ocean than did Moscow. Occasionally, a more generalized tension arose from India's desire to maximize its freedom of action, minimize its dependency, and build up self-sufficiency in the security field. This contrasted with Moscow's attempt to construct a reliable anti-China security system in Asia, and its opposition to the further proliferation of nuclear weapons.

With respect to Soviet and Indian positions on other international issues, there is also a great deal of parallelism, most particularly in the area of opposition to colonial and neocolonial activities in the third world. But the Indians clearly wish to avoid appearances of following the Soviet lead; rather, New Delhi wants to stake out its own positions, which—in the case of North-South issues—may well put an antisuperpower gloss on the issue.

In commercial relations it is not surprising that both sides perceive continuing benefits in their strengthened trade ties. The Indians, however, are pressing for Moscow to purchase more Indian-manufactured goods and to make available more raw materials and nonproject assistance than the Soviets would like. And finally, with respect to India's internal development and political processes, Moscow and New Delhi's objectives are at such variance as to cause strains when Soviet propaganda and other tactics apply pressure on the Indian government to move in a more "progressive" direction.

Although the compatibility of some of their objectives might in itself provide a good basis for Soviet-Indian friendship and cooperation, this is not a sufficient foundation on which to build a friendship that can endure " in clear weather and in bad weather." Far more important in motivating the two states to form a "reliable friendship" is the existence on each side of a sense of dependence upon or need of the other. A country that needs something from another is more vulnerable to its exercise of influence—more likely to change (or sustain) its behavior in a direction that it would not have taken had not the other state deisred it—and thus more predictably cooperative and loyal.[2]

SOVIET POLICY IN THE SUBCONTINENT, 1955-71

From the beginning of its active involvement in the subcontinent, Soviet policy can be viewed in the triangular context. The initial thrust of the Soviet entry into the countries of the Indian Ocean region came in seeming response to the policies both of the United States and of China. Washington's efforts in 1954-55 to enlarge the ring of containment by enlisting allies on the Soviet Union's southern periphery (Iraq, Iran, and in this context, especially, the 1954 U.S.-Pakistani defense agreement) alarmed the Soviets. The hostile reaction to the American policy on the part of the emerging "neutralist" nations such as India encouraged Moscow to counterattack. Moreover, Zhou En-Lai demonstrated anew the possibilities for a Communist-nationalist alliance against the imperialist designs, both with his success in capitalizing on the antiimperialist mood at the Bandung Conference of Asian and African States held in Indonesia in 1955, and by his earlier agreement with Nehru on Tibet that proclaimed Sino-Indian relations would be governed by "the five principles of peaceful coexistence."

Thus by 1955 there was in Moscow a reawakening of the Leninist perception of the third world as the vital "strategic reserve" of imperialism—an arena in which the Soviets could wage the bipolar struggle with solid prospects of success, but at a lower level of risk than would be posed by a direct challenge in the "main arena" of confrontation. The year's significant events foreshadowed the Soviet priorities and techniques in this new arena: Moscow's entry into the Middle East by means of the arms deal with Nasser's Egypt; the visit of India's Prime Minister Nehru to Moscow and the return trip by Khrushchev and Bulganin to India, Burma, and Afghanistan; the dramatic announcement that the Soviets would finance and construct a giant steel mill at Bhilai in India. These early targets of Soviet activity were chosen for their strategic importance in the struggle with the West rather than for any particular features of their internal development, and the early attention given by Moscow to South and Southwest Asia reflected the relative weight these lands carried in Soviet security calculations. Having thus identified their priorities, the Soviets soon set about—with great optimism but little sophisticated knowledge of the domestic affairs of the third world state—to revise the ideological bases of their new policy.

Like Lenin, Khrushchev sensed that so long as the brunt of the independence movement was aimed against the "imperialist" West it would serve the security interests of the Communist East. There was a sufficient community of interest to provide the basis for a temporary alliance against the common enemy—a new "Zone of Peace," he called it. Prime Minister Nehru had already demonstrated his actively neutralist foreign policy in his aversion to the sins of imperialism, and this behavior called forth a warm response from Khrushchev, who pressed India's claim to take a place among the worlds "great powers" and offered support in India's quarrel with Pakistan over Kashmir.

While in India in 1955, the Soviet leader offered his hosts reassurance that strengthened relations need not be hindered by differences in the two states' social systems: "We do not force anything upon anyone; we are not seeking to impose any political obligations."[3] And yet it was Khrushchev's confident expectation that aid from the Socialist bloc could allow the third world countries to break away from the imperialist economic grip and launch their plans for industrialized and truly independent national economies on the model of the Soviet Union's own development. The inevitable result of this process would be the emergence in these countries of a class-conscious proletariat ready to respond to the political program of its communist vanguard and—once the "national bourgeoisie" had revealed the compromising side of its dual nature—to assume political power, even by peaceful means.

But (to paraphrase a remark that Soviet writers would later aim at third world leaders) to proclaim the prospects for socialism is easier than to achieve it. Only a few years after their initial plunge into the Indian Ocean region, the Soviets were discovering that their initial ideological optimism concerning the enlargement of the camp of socialism was misplaced. With only rare exceptions (such as Indonesia), the communist parties in these regions were either still nonexistent, weak, or persecuted by the new nationalist allies of the Soviet Union. Some Afro-Asian communist leaders were bold enough to voice their frustration at this state of affairs. But the primary problem was the unwillingness of the nationalist and revolutionary elites in the new nations to adhere to Marxism-Leninism or "scientific socialism" or to proclaim their willingness to establish "people's democracies" in their countries. The fiercely nationalistic leaders of India and the neighboring countries had their own goals for political and economic progress, and though many of them were influenced by Marxist thought and "socialist" ideals, they were loathe to accept the Soviet approach and model. And needless to say, those leaders who spurned formal communist affiliation were uncomfortable with a Soviet policy that proclaimed their inevitable removable from power. In this early stage, then, the lure of communist ideology was unable to achieve successes for Soviet policy.

The Soviet Union's approach to the Indian Ocean region was developing in truly opportunistic fashion, as exemplified both by Moscow's willingness to modify the Marxist-Leninist doctrine to fit a variety of circumstances, and also by its use of a wide range of instrumentalities for establishing its presence and extending its influence. Moscow's relations with the states of the subcontinent in particular soon extended far beyond the early ideological appeals and spread broadly in the political, economic, cultural, and military spheres. They reached beyond government-to-government dealings and included relationships with both communist and noncommunist parties; contacts and exchanges among trade union, student, scientific, artistic, and other groups (both directly through the Soviet counterpart organization and through various international communist-front organizations); the massive dissemination of both printed material and radio propaganda; the on-the-scene activities of Soviet technicians and advisors, both civilian and military; and so forth. All these instruments were employed extensively in India. Almost 200 Indian delegations of various sorts traveled to the Soviet Union between 1954 and 1957. An ever-increasing volume of books, pamphlets, and magazines made their way from the USSR to India; whereas 17,000 books were sent in 1955, the figure had climbed to 4,000,000 by 1958.[4] Of equal, if not greater, importance in achieving for the Soviet Union a profound impact on Indian consciousness were the offers of economic assistance. The volume of economic contacts rose steadily, and by the 1960s India had become the USSR's most important noncommunist trading partner.

Through the combined effect of this activity, the Soviets sought to wrest India from the economic and cultural orbit of the "imperialist" world. Taken as a whole, the Soviet contacts with India fully exemplified the techniques of what Andrew Scott has termed "informal penetration"—"means by which the agents or instruments of one country gain access to the population (or parts of it) or processes of another country" and in which "the special nature of cold warfare must be sought."[5]

The relatively happy picture of warming Soviet-Indian relations was shattered in the late 1950s by the growing Chinese challenge to both Moscow and New Delhi. According to a Soviet diplomat who defected to the West from the embassy in Rangoon in 1959, a "gentlemen's agreement" in 1955–56 that had recognized Southeast Asia as a "Chinese sphere," and India, Afghanistan, and points west as a "Soviet sphere," was considered by the Soviets to have been breached in 1958 by Chinese "intervention" in India.[6] In the spring of 1959 China charged "Indian expansionists" with having incited and aided a short-lived rebellion in Tibet, and in the summer and fall there were outbreaks of fighting along disputed areas of the Sino-Indian border.

The timing of the Chinese attacks had wider significance since Khrushchev was at this time about to embark on his visit to the United States, where he hoped for results that would show the Chinese that detente and peaceful competition could serve the communist cause better than military force. But if the Chinese sought to sabotage the detente by forcing Khrushchev into a militant stand in support of Chinese claims in India, Khrushchev's reaction was far from obliging. The Soviet leader's stance of studied neutrality emboldened Nehru to adopt a "forward policy" on the Sino-Indian border, thus contributing to the heightening of Sino-Indian tensions. And in August 1962 the Indian Prime Minister announced that he had accepted an offer made by the Soviets in May to supply Mig-21 fighter planes (which had not been supplied to China). The mounting conflict erupted on October 20 in fighting along the northeastern frontier of India, which turned in mid-November into a general Chinese offensive thoroughly defeating India's army and causing Nehru to appeal to Great Britain and the United States for military aid. In this second round of the Sino-Indian border conflict, the Soviet Union at first seemed to side with China. But it must be remembered that the fighting had broken out almost simultaneously with the Cuban missile crisis, and in this delicate period Khrushchev dared not risk provoking disunity in the communist camp. With the resolution of the Cuban crisis, however, the Soviets returned to a position of neutrality on the Sino-Indian conflict, complaining that only the imperialists could benefit from it.

In the wake of the crisis, the Soviets sent a note to the Chinese complaining that "years of hard striving for Indian friendship and Indian neutrality" had gone for nothing as a result of Beijing's actions. Through their initial vacillations, the Soviets had certainly lost standing with Indian popular opinion, while the influence of the United States and Great Britain had risen. The conflict had polarized the Indian political scene, and it had precipitated a conflict within the Communist Party of India (CPI) that resulted in an open split in April 1964. It dramatized for the world the growing breach between Moscow and Beijing and itself became the cause for a further intensification of that conflict.

A consequence of the 1962 border war had been the warming of relations between India's two major adversaries—China and Pakistan. While Moscow was determined to retain the friendship of India, it was reluctant to abandon Pakistan to the exclusive enticements of Beijing and Washington. Thus, as part of the larger campaign to woo the states of the "northern tier," the USSR began to improve its relations with Pakistan. In April 1965 President Ayub Khan visited

Moscow, and the resulting communique seemed to move the USSR toward a position of neutrality on the Kashmir question.

The Pakistanis had been emboldened by the changing situation on the subcontinent to press their claims to Kashmir, and in August 1965 a war erupted over the issue. The conflict was at first ignored in the Soviet press, but then Moscow issued an appeal for an end to the conflict, expressing its desire for Indo-Pakistani relations to be a stabilizing factor in Asia. When China demonstrated its support for Pakistan and made threatening demands on New Delhi regarding the Sino-Indian frontier, the Soviets issued a stern warning to China not to stir up trouble on the subcontinent.

On September 17, Premier Kosygin volunteered to provide the "good offices" of the Soviet Union in helping to settle the conflict. This dramatic gesture, in stark contrast to earlier Soviet behavior in fanning Indo-Pakistani strife, showed how far Moscow had come in its desire to bring stability to South Asia. If a Soviet-sponsored mediation could produce the beginnings of a rapprochement between India and Pakistan, then it would have contributed enormously to Moscow's primary aim in South Asia: the containment of Chinese influence and expansionism.

The Soviets were widely praised for their efforts at mediation, and they managed to derive great propaganda advantage from the image they projected as a peace-loving great power endeavoring, while others fanned the flames of conflict, to bring security to a troubled subcontinent. But the great hopes engendered at the Tashkent Conference were not to come to fruition. Indian and Pakistani leaders were caught in a web of their own making: long years of fanning popular hatred and suspicion were not easily overcome, nor were the large amounts of prestige invested by each state in the emotional issue of Kashmir easily sacrificed by either state. The continuation of the conflict was evidenced in the spiraling arms race that entrapped the great-power patrons of the two combatants. The United States sought to extricate itself, suspending arms shipments during the 1965 war. But India called on the Soviets for more arms, and in May 1968 Moscow responded with a shipment of 100 SU-7 fighter-bombers. In the face of a vigorous protest from Pakistan (and fearing that she might move closer to Beijing) the Soviets agreed in the summer of 1968, following Ayub's cancellation of the lease on the U.S. intelligence base in Peshawar, to sell weapons to Pakistan. The announcement of this deal produced in its turn protests and riots in New Delhi, demonstrating anew the unpopularity that can be reaped by a supplier to both sides in an arms race.

Improving Soviet-Pakistani diplomatic and trade relations were derailed in the spring of 1971 by the outbreak of severe civil conflict in East Pakistan that soon developed into a near genocide. Alarmed at the prospect that the conflict might draw the subcontinent into a protracted struggle in which Pakistan might be supported by China, the Soviets moved decisively to extend their influence and curtail the hostilities.

It is in the context of the larger campaign for "collective security" against China that the Soviet-India treaty, signed on August 9, 1971, must be viewed. Negotiations had actually begun two years before, in the context of sharp Sino-Soviet conflict and splits in Indira Gandhi's Congress Party. The Indians were apparently motivated by the increasing strain of the Pakistani civil war to resume the discussions in the summer of 1971. The other decisive new element in the situation was the trip of Henry Kissinger to Beijing in July 1971—a journey facilitated by Pakistan. Thus, with the cooperation of India's sworn enemy, the United States was making overtures for a new relationship with China, India's second major antagonist in Asia. This dramatic shift raised serious doubts in New Delhi about the American role in a possible Indo-Pakistani conflict.

The Soviets, no less concerned over the prospect of a Sino-American rapprochement, saw the Indian dilemma as an opportunity both to gain influence in New Delhi and to deter another wasteful and destabilizing war on the subcontinent from which they thought only China might gain. The formal linkage of Soviet and Indian interests by means of a treaty might succeed in deterring the Chinese from providing military assistance to Pakistan while placing additional pressure on Yahya Khan, the Pakistani president, to reach a political solution. The formal obligations the Kremlin incurred from the treaty were minimal; its main purpose, from the Soviet point of view, was to formalize and extend Russian influence for the immediate purpose of stabilizing the situation in South Asia.[7]

Although Soviet statements throughout the fall of 1971 grew steadily more critical of Pakistan, Moscow still urged a peaceful solution to the conflict. Nevertheless, the Soviets rushed substantial quantities of arms to India, thus ensuring that their client would be well armed should she find a military solution necessary. In the meantime the Soviets (as well as the Americans) were putting heavy pressure on the Pakistanis to make political concessions to Sheikh Mujibur Rahman's party in East Pakistan.

Nevertheless, India moved her troops into East Pakistan at the end of November. Soviet Ambassador Malik, arguing that Pakistan bore full responsibility for the conflict, used his vetoes in the Security Council to block cease-fire resolutions while the Indians completed their military operations in East Pakistan. The brief war ended in mid-December with the unconditional surrender of Pakistani troops in the east and a cease-fire on the western front.

In the immediate aftermath of the war, the Soviets had every reason to be exultant. Though they had failed to bring about the removal of the refugee burden from India by peaceful means, they had at least played an essential role in India's victory over Pakistan, while their American and Chinese rivals—in the first test of the new "anti-Soviet axis"—had both lined up on the side of the loser. As American influence in India had declined dramatically, so Soviet influence had never been greater.

The Soviets moved rapidly to build their ties with the new state of Bangladesh. Sheikh Mujib visited Moscow in March 1972, concluding agreements on economic assistance that were soon to lead to a substantial Soviet presence in Bangladesh. Two weeks later Pakistan's new leader, President Bhutto, was received in the Soviet capital for a "frank and useful exchange" on the prospects for rebuilding Soviet-Pakistani relations.

In the changed circumstances of the postwar period, however, Pakistan and Bangladesh were overshadowed on the subcontinent by a strengthened and confident India. For the Soviets, the essential point was that whereas prior to 1971 the balance of forces had dictated the well-nigh impossible task of uniting India and Pakistan in a common grouping against Chinese influence, the situation after the December war seemed far more manageable. By Moscow's reckoning, India—grateful for Soviet assistance and dependent on further aid—would be in the new circumstances an even more valuable partner in the effort to outflank China. But Soviet calculations projecting an easy partnership with an increasingly Left-leaning India have been upset by subsequent events—and most notably by India's evident fierce determination to be the client of no other state.

SOVIET POLICIES IN THE SUBCONTINENT
AFTER THE BANGLADESH WAR

A survey of post-1972 Soviet-Indian relations reveals that not only have India's leaders failed to echo the warm references made in Moscow to the Indo-Soviet treaty, strongly reaffirming their continuing nonalignment, but they have in fact made statements strongly critical of "superpower hegemony." Moreover, India has resisted Soviet requests for naval cooperation, and has even refused (despite Brezhnev's personal plea during his visit to New Delhi in November 1973) to give explicit endorsement to the Soviet plan for "collective security in Asia."

The Indians did sign a 15-year agreement designed to put their economic relationship with the Soviets on a stable long-term basis, but they have denied rumors that they plan to seek formal association with the Soviet trading bloc, the Council for Mutual Economic Assistance (COMECON). And there are signs that further growth in Soviet-Indian trade may be limited due both to noncomplementarity in the two economies and Soviet unwillingness to provide certain raw materials needed by India. There are limits also to expansion of Soviet-Indian military cooperation; through the treaty, the Soviets have already extended their pledge of support, and by virtue of her victory in the December war, India now faces a much reduced threat. In a determined fashion India has been seeking self-sufficiency in arms production, and her progress in building a nuclear capability—viewed with a notable lack of enthusiasm in Moscow—suggests that she may be capable of achieving it.

On balance, the Soviet-Indian relationship and the degree of Moscow's influence in New Delhi probably reached a peak in 1971. In the period since then, India's dependence has lessened, and the Soviets may now need India's support more than New Delhi needs Moscow's. If India were to become hostile or indifferent, Moscow would be left with no major asset in South Asia.

In fact, the events of the latter part of the 1970s represented a setback for Soviet interests in the subcontinent. The overthrow of the pro-Soviet government of Sheikh Mujibur Rahman in Bangladesh in the summer of 1975, and its replacement by a more pro-Western (and anti-Indian) regime was viewed with apprehension in Moscow. In the ensuing years, the Soviets displayed considerable reserve in their attitude toward the successor regime of President Ziaur Rahman. As in the political realm, Moscow's economic relations with Dacca were less close in the post-Mujib period. Trade turnover, which had increased rapidly in the years immediately following independence, began to level off in 1975 and fell sharply in 1976. Similarly, the Soviet economic aid program slowed considerably from its initial high level of activity. By the end of the decade, with the West as its major source of economic aid, Bangladesh had improved ties with Beijing and Islamabad while its relations with India were strained. Dacca's denunciation of the Soviet move into Afghanistan, together with its outrage over a Soviet effort to open a consulate in Chittagong without permission, brought relations with the USSR to a new low. The assassination of President Ziaur Rahman in June 1981 brought no evident regret to the Russians, though the Soviet press did try to portray the event as the doing of "pro-Chinese separatists."[8]

The 1977 change in government in Pakistan, like Mujib's fall, was also not much to Moscow's liking. On the occasion of President Bhutto's visit to Moscow in 1974, the Soviet press had noted that, though its path was not "bestrewn with roses," Pakistan was experiencing a "period of renewal" and "progressive forces" were on the offensive.[9] Although they initially welcomed the end to civil strife that followed the military coup of General Zia, the Soviets took pains to praise the "foreign policy moves of the civilian administration which abandoned the disastrous course of confrontation" in the subcontinent and to warn that "the periods of civilian rule were most favorable and fruitful for Pakistan."[10]

These early unhappy premonitions were borne out for the Soviets by subsequent domestic and foreign actions of the Zia regime. In the former sphere apart from their disapproval of the rightward turn in Pakistan's economy and the repeated postponement of elections, the Soviets expressed their sharpest criticism over the April 1979 execution of Zulfikar Ali Bhutto. President Zia had ignored Brezhnev's plea for mercy on Bhutto's behalf, and Moscow showed its anger over the execution by labeling it "an act of cruelty."

But it was in the foreign policy sphere that the Soviets were most critical of Pakistan. In a way, their disquiet was ironic, because it came at a time when Pakistani-American relations were reaching a new low. In the spring of 1979, Pakistan formally withdrew from the Central Treaty Organization (CENTO) Pact and joined the nonaligned powers. And in April Washington announced that it was cutting off all economic assistance (except food aid) to Pakistan in reaction to a evident step-up in Islamabad's drive to obtain a nuclear weapons capability. Although the Soviet press commented with favor on Pakistan's turn toward nonalignment and its distancing from the United States, Moscow's overall stance was critical, for the Soviets saw the sinister hand of Beijing in the background, "fueling" Pakistan's nuclear ambitions and encouraging it to play a destabilizing role in its relations with its eastern and western neighbors.

It was the latter situation—Pakistan's swiftly deteriorating relations with the new Marxist-Leninist government of Afghanistan—that drew the sharpest reaction from Moscow. Throughout the spring of 1979, the Soviet press commented darkly on the alleged machinations of American and Chinese "secret agents" who were stirring up and supporting the counterrevolutionary activities of the thousands of Afghan refugees that were based across the Pakistani border. Pakistan's government was accused of openly ignoring the country's objective national interests and cooperating with imperialist and Chinese schemes to intervene in Afghanistan's internal affairs. In April *Izvestiia* noted that Pakistan's provocations were a "risky undertaking" that could leave it in "an extremely disadvantageous and dangerous position."[11]

Such baleful warnings were accompanied by harsh Soviet press accounts of "seething discontent" among the Pakistani people and characterizations of the Zia regime as a "henchman of the enemies of peace."[12] In an authoritative statement in August 1981, Foreign Minister Gromyko charged that Zia's Pakistan was being manipulated by China and the United States into a "bridgehead that is definitely aimed against the USSR and the countries of Southwest and South Asia."[13] Depicting the United States as the tacit sponsor of the Pakistani drive for nuclear weapons, the Soviet press angrily denounced the Reagan administration's arms deal with Zia as totally unwarranted, provocative, and ultimately destabilizing.[14]

Although Moscow played up the Pakistani threat to India, the chief objective of its concern was the strongly pro-Soviet regime that had come to power in Kabul in a bloody coup staged in April 1978. As a country sharing a long border with the Soviet Union, Afghanistan had been a target of close Soviet attention since the time of Lenin, but relations in the pre-1978 period had been "good neighborly" rather than ardent. Apart from geopolitical necessities, Afghanistan's orientation toward Moscow had been induced by large economic and military assistance programs that dated from the mid-1950s.

Although there is disagreement about the exact degree of Soviet involvement in the coup that brought the Marxist-Leninist regime to power in 1978, there is little doubt that the Soviets had become increasingly disenchanted with the foreign policy of Mohammed Daud. Warmly welcoming the successor government of Noor Mohammed Taraki, Moscow immediately began to dispatch advisors to key positions in both the military and civilian bureaucracies. In

December 1978, with Taraki on an official visit to Moscow, a 20-year Treaty of Friendship, Good Neighborliness Cooperation between the USSR and Afghanistan was signed. It contained the now-familiar phrases promising that "appropriate measures" would be taken to ensure Afghanistan's security and extending cooperation in the military field.

Despite the extremely close relations between the new regime in Kabul and its Soviet patrons that were manifested in a slavishly pro-Soviet tilt in Afghan foreign policy, official Soviet assessments of the Afghan revolution retained a remarkable degree of moderation and reserve. This ideologically cautious assessment of the Taraki regime was in marked contrast to the naive enthusiasm for third world Socialists that had marked the Khrushchev era, but it was also at variance with a seeming Soviet willingness to pour an endless stream of arms and advisors into Afghanistan to save the regime from its internal enemies. These "counterrevolutionary" elements had been provoked in large part by the reckless pace by which the Taraki regime had set about to reorient the Afghan society, economy, and politics. Much of the opposition was aimed at the harsh antireligious (specifically anti-Muslim) measures taken by the People's Democratic Party of Afghanistan (PDPA) government, and the Islamic "counterrevolution" quickly gained the support of both General Zia's Pakistan and Ayatollah Khomeini's Iran. The Soviet press found itself in the strange position of defending the Islamic bona fides of the Taraki regime, while issuing steadily stronger warnings to outside forces that sought to assist the opposition. Soon it began to appear that only Soviet support prevented the total collapse of the PDPA regime. The intragovernment instability that resulted in the murder of Taraki and his replacement by Hafizullah Amin in September 1979, shortly after Taraki had returned from visits to Havana and Moscow, could hardly have comforted Soviet planners as they sought to cope with the burden that the Western press had gleefully begun to label "Moscow's Vietnam." Soviet frustration undoubtedly deepened as Amin proved unwilling to heed Moscow's warnings to slow the revolutionary pace and broaden his political base in an effort to stem the rising tide of rebellion. By autumn's end, the Afghani army was hemorrhaging from desertions as the strength of the antiregime guerrillas was mounting.

The specter of the collapse of the Marxist-Leninist regime in Kabul held grave implications for the USSR. To tolerate the overthrow of a regime in which Moscow had invested so much economic and military assistance as well as the direct aid of thousands of civilian and military advisors, and with which the Soviet Union had concluded a solemn treaty, would have been a tremendous blow to Soviet prestige. From Moscow's standpoint, it would have also posed a security threat of substantial dimensions, since a successor regime would probably have had strong Islamic overtones, blended with anti-Soviet resentment and possible American and Chinese backing. If Afghanistan were to join Iran and Pakistan as militant Islamic outposts on the borders of the USSR, the combined religious and nationalist lure might well have become irresistible for the millions of Soviet Muslims in the region.

Thus the Soviet Union's Christmas 1979 invasion of Afghanistan was the product of Moscow's determination to aim a decisive blow at the anticommunist guerrillas while firmly establishing the authority of a more pliant Marxist-Leninist regime. The timing of the Soviet move was surely influenced by the fact that the United States was distracted by the hostage crisis in Iran. Ignoring the anomalous timing of Amin's removal, Moscow claimed to have been invited in by the new government of Babrak Karmal, and it cited both the Soviet-Afghan treaty and the United Nations Charter as legal justifications for the dispatch of its "limited military contingent"—ultimately to number about 100,000 troops. The Soviets were apparently taken aback by the fury of both American and nonaligned reaction, as manifested on the one hand by the proclamation of a new "Carter Doctrine" for the Persian Gulf–Indian Ocean region and on the other by the one-sided votes that led to condemnation of the Soviet invasion at the United Nations and at the Islamabad conference of Islamic nations.

A heated denial of the Western charges that the Soviet action was directed toward the oil fields of the Persian Gulf region and the "warm waters of the Indian Ocean" came from Leonid Brezhnev in a *Pravda* interview released in mid-January 1980. The Soviet president emphasized the defensive purposes of the action, both to defend Afghanistan's national independence and to safeguard the USSR's own security: "To act otherwise would have been to look on passively while a hotbed of serious danger to the security of the Soviet state was created on our southern border."[15]

But the longer the Soviet "limited military contingent" remained in Afghanistan, the greater became the concern of the other Muslim and South Asian states and the smaller were the prospects that the Karmal regime could ever become anything but a dependent puppet. Bogged down militarily by a fragmented guerrilla force, frustrated in its efforts to hold the Afghan army together or unify the factions in the civilian regime, Moscow intensified its efforts in the winter of 1981–82 to find an acceptable formula for bringing Kabul and its hostile neighbors to the bargaining table. Clearly, the fragile and explosive situation in Afghanistan, as it existed on the second anniversary of the invasion, could not yet be regarded as a "Soviet success" in South Asia.

Not even India escaped the turmoil of the late 1970s. The mounting domestic instability that culminated in Indira Gandhi's proclamation of emergency rule in June 1975 was initially welcomed by the Soviets for its seeming reversal of a mounting "reactionary" tide.[16] But the period of emergency freed Indira Gandhi of any parliamentary dependence on the Communist Party of India (CPI), and the harsh restrictions on political freedom limited the capabilities of Communists as well as other parties. Nevertheless, the election campaign in March 1977, following the lifting of the emergency, saw the Soviet press again supporting Indira Gandhi's regime, though not without a tinge of criticism of her domestic policies and anxiety about the possible consequences. Indira Gandhi's surprising defeat in the elections was attributed by the Soviet press to the "mistakes and excesses" in implementation of the emergency, the halting of progress toward socioeconomic reform, and the Congress' refusal to conclude electoral agreements with the CPI.[17] Hastily shifting its line, the Soviet media dropped labels of "reactionary" and "demagogue" from references to Prime Minister Desai and his colleagues, and the Soviet premier sent a message of congratulations that "expressed confidence that the traditional relations of friendship and all-round cooperation between the Soviet Union and India would continue to grow and develop in the interests of their peoples, peace and international security."[18]

Only a month after the elections, Soviet Foreign Minister Gromyko was in New Delhi to assess the new Indian government at firsthand. Desai's first foreign policy pronouncement—that the Indo-Soviet treaty "must not come in the way of our friendship with any other state; we won't have special relations with any other country"—had undoubtedly occasioned deep apprehensions in Moscow. Nevertheless, six months into the new government's life the Soviet press was showing its relief that "the high hopes of the imperialist forces that Soviet-Indian relations would deteriorate were not justified."[19]

Although Soviet-Indian relations during the almost three-year rule of the Janata Party lacked at times some of the warmth shown by the preceding and subsequent Gandhi governments, the difference was clearly one of degree. On the whole, the Desai's government foreign policy during the closing years of the 1970s did not produce a reorientation of India's diplomatic or economic ties. For most of two decades, political leaders in both India and the Soviet Union have seen it in their interests to foster a perception of reliable friendship, so that regional and global rivals are led to conclude that New Delhi and Moscow can count on each other's support, without fear of abandonment or betrayal.

Nevertheless, Soviet-Indian relations were clearly strained by the Soviet invasion of Afghanistan, which effectively removed the historic buffer between the subcontinent and the Central Asian lands under Moscow's control. Though the Soviet-Indian alliance has been significant for both countries, Indian leaders have always been more comfortable keeping a discreet distance between themselves and the Soviets. Publicly, the Indians sought to view the Afghan events with concern but "understanding," while privately they urged the Soviets to arrange a rapid political settlement and troop withdrawal. The inability of the two countries to agree on a common position was clearly signaled by the absence of any direct reference to Afghanistan in the joint declaration that was issued in December 1980 following the visit to India of Soviet President Brezhnev. There was, however, a paragraph dealing with Southwest Asia that stated: "India and the Soviet Union reiterate their opposition to all forms of outside interference in the internal affairs of the countries of the region." Both sides, it said, "are confident that a negotiated political solution alone can guarantee a durable settlement of the existing problems of the region."[20] This formula was consistent with the public positions of both sides and yet committed neither one to endorsement of the other's views on the specific question of how the crisis was to be resolved. In any case, India's cool and reserved statements on the issue have been publicly appreciated as "sober" and "realistic" by the Soviets, who are undoubtedly pleased to have at least one large noncommunist country abstain from the noisy condemnation of their Afghan adventure.

In light of India's long-standing desire to preserve a measure of balance in her relations with the great powers, it was not surprising in the wake of the Soviet invasion of Afghanistan to see her in conversations with both the United States and China aimed at soothing some of the troubling issues that divided them. An Indian diplomat traveled to Beijing in June 1980 for talks on the sensitive border issue. The Chinese angrily postponed a return visit of Foreign Minister Huang Hua in the wake of India's diplomatic recognition of the Heng Samrin regime in Kampuchea. But in June 1981 Huang's visit finally took place, much to Moscow's consternation. Although Huang publicly agreed to the opening of official talks on the border questions, the Soviet press commentaries sought to dampen any Indian hopes that Sino-Indian relations might actually improve: "In the view of local political commentators, it would be unrealistic and premature to hope and expect that Huang Hua's statements would be followed by concrete deeds on Beijing's part. China's entire current foreign policy gives precious little justification for such hopes. . . . "[21] When the first round of border talks adjourned in Beijing in December 1981 without any visible progress, the Soviets again displayed visible relief.

India's relations with the United States showed a slight improvement in the final months of the Carter administration. But if the Soviets were at all concerned over this seeming improvement in U.S.-Indian relations in 1980, they were surely relieved by the political storm that broke in the spring and summer of 1981, following the Reagan administration's decision to sell a substantial quantity of modern weapons—including the F-16 fighter-bomber—to Pakistan. Although India had herself made major arms purchases from both the Soviets and the British in the previous year, New Delhi viewed the American arms agreement with Pakistan as provocative and destabilizing. For its part, India ostentatiously announced that it had acquired "a few" Mig-25 aircraft, and it began talks with a French delegation interested in selling the latest version of the Mirage.[22]

The Soviets could scarcely contain their glee at this deterioration of Indian-American relations. The American arms deal with Pakistan, together with the Reagan administration's decision to consider arms sales to China, effectively removed the Indian spotlight from the Soviet military presence in Afghanistan and again underscored for New Delhi the value of its alliance with the USSR. On the tenth anniversary of the Soviet-Indian treaty, Foreign Minister Gromyko accused the United States of trying to destabilize Asia by selling arms to Pakistan and China, and he pointedly warned that the Soviet Union would "take all measures" needed to defend itself and its allies.[23]

SOVIET SECURITY INTERESTS
IN THE INDIAN OCEAN

The Soviet Union's friendly ties with India have taken on a wider significance in the years since the 1973 Mideast war and the Arab oil embargo, as global rivalries have focused increasingly in the region of the Indian Ocean. Indeed, from the time in 1968 that two Soviet naval vessels first called at ports in the Indian Ocean, the Soviet naval presence there has slowly but steadily increased in both size and visibility. In recent years, the Soviets have maintained a permanent squadron of 20 or more vessels, with occasional "surges" in times of crisis to well over 30.

There are several hypotheses advanced to account for Soviet behavior in the Indian Ocean. Some see it as an outgrowth of the tsarist "push to the warm water," aimed in the period following British withdrawal from "East of Suez" at the acquisition of a Soviet capability to practice "gunboat diplomacy" and shape events in the region to Moscow's liking. Another explanation sees the Soviet deployment as a defensive reaction to the potential U.S. submarine warfare capability in the area. Yet another focuses on the growing economic-strategic importance of the Persian Gulf oil fields, citing probable Soviet and East European future oil requirements or an ascribed desire to acquire a capability to threaten or actually interdict the vital oil lifeline of the Western countries.

Although the original Soviet deployment probably stemmed from a combination of defensive strategic purposes and the organizational routines of an expanding Soviet navy, the scope and nature of Moscow's behavior over the longer run is best explained in the context of political events and trends in the littoral countries. From this standpoint, the demonstration of Soviet military capabilities, primarily in the form of "showing the flag" in calls at Indian ports, should be understood as the exploitation of yet another instrument for acquiring political influence rather than as the acquisition of a capability for military intervention or interdiction. At times this influence-building activity has focused on particularly strategic countries, and on occasion the Soviets have utilized their capabilities for dramatic demonstrations of resolve to back up their own and their clients' interests in times of crisis (e.g., the Bangladesh war of 1971 and the Arab-Israeli war of 1973).

Seen in this context, then, a certain level of Soviet naval activity seems to be a natural outgrowth of Moscow's acquisition of superpower status and global military capabilities. Though that level may have been heightened by the American response, it is not likely to disappear in any event; indeed, the Indian Ocean provides the most direct route for the routine transferal of Soviet naval units from the Far Eastern to the Black Sea fleets. As for naval activity beyond the level of routine navigational needs, research activity, or "business calls" at the ports of friendly nations, Moscow's own propaganda couches it strictly in terms of a defensive reaction to a growing American and Chinese threat. References in the Soviet press to an American strategic submarine or carrier-launched bomber threat to the USSR itself are usually veiled, clearly subordinated to the alleged challenge posed by U.S. naval activity to the "progressively" oriented regimes in the littoral states.

The logistical needs of the Soviet naval force in the Indian Ocean were at first (unsatisfactorily) met by the use of floating anchorages and by occasional calls at the port facilities of the littoral states. This arrangement necessitated long standstill periods and the presence of a large contingent of support vessels; the perceived need for more extensive and reliable repair and support facilities occasioned Soviet overtures in a number of quarters, including India and Sri Lanka in South Asia, as well as Singapore, Mauritius, Iraq, South Yemen, and Somalia. The most receptive responses (encouraged by large and timely provision of economic and military aid) came from the latter three states. In 1973 the Soviets began to develop for their use the port facilities at Berbera, and by August of the following year President Ford was led to declare that Moscow has acquired "bases" not only there but at Aden and Umm Qasr (Iraq) as well.

But if the concept of "base" is understood in terms of a reliable and secure (not to mention exclusive) facility, the term did not precisely fit these particular situations, as both Moscow and the host states demonstratively pointed out. Moscow's experience with the loss of its Egyptian "bases" is instructive in this context; indeed, the lesson learned there has provoked the Soviets to seek to spread the risk of loss in the Indian Ocean precisely by the development of multiple facilities. But even "spreading the risk" can backfire if, as in the case of Ethiopia and Somalia, it draws Moscow into the embarrassing position of wooing its client's chief rival. The result in this case was, of course, Somalia's expulsion of the Soviets from the Berbera facility in November 1977.

In a region as unstable and volatile as the Indian Ocean littoral, there is little that can be regarded as "reliable and secure." In the larger context of the Soviet effort to maintain and increase its political influence in the countries surrounding the Indian Ocean, we should not overestimate the ease with which Moscow can accomplish this task. The record of Soviet setbacks in the region is instructive; changes of government, Soviet heavy-handedness, creative diplomacy on the part of Moscow's rivals, or simply the sheer force of nationalism and non-alignment—all have helped to cause the Soviet Union to lose positions of influence in Egypt, the Sudan, Bangladesh, Somalia, and Indonesia, and to suffer a serious setback in Iraq.

Despite their long efforts to focus critical attention on American military facilities at Diego Garcia and to protest the innocent intentions of their own activity, the Soviets have found themselves at odds with India and most other Indian Ocean littoral states on the issue of superpower naval activity there. Almost without exception, the littoral states voice support for the idea of limiting superpower naval rivalry and military installations and establishing a "peace zone" in the area. Both Washington and Moscow have objected to any such notion that limits their freedom of navigation on the high seas. In addition, each state has been irritated at the failure of the Indian Ocean countries to distinguish between its own peaceful presence and the "aggressive" activity of its rival. Criticizing the Americans for breaking off their bilateral talks on possible naval limitations in 1978, the Soviets have characterized the proposed U.S. Rapid Deployment Force as an instrument designed to intimidate the littoral states and ultimately to seize the oil fields of the Persian Gulf region. Insisting that it has neither bases nor plans to acquire them, Moscow has also tried (without complete success) to neutralize the Western argument that more recent deployments are a "natural response" to the presence of Soviet troops in Afghanistan.[24]

THE PLACE OF THE SUBCONTINENT
IN SOVIET SECURITY CALCULATIONS

What the record of the Soviet involvement in the subcontinent clearly reveals is Moscow's sense of need to seek influence in the region, stemming from a policy framework that sets a relatively high priority on the region. This Soviet dependence on India has produced a willingness to devote a steady flow of resources and diplomatic energy toward preserving Moscow's rather large investment in the Indo-Soviet friendship. To lose its standing as the "reliable friend" of the strongest regional power in South Asia would cost Moscow heavily. It would entail some risks to its security in a bordering region that has both offensive and defensive value in the Soviet conflict with its primary Asian rival, China. Moscow's substantial stake in the existing order in South Asia thus gives it an interest in helping to stabilize the region by playing the role of "reliable friend" to India.

And yet there was a great deal of discussion in the policymaking community in the early 1980s about a possible shift in Soviet policy in the Indian Ocean region, in a more nakedly expansionist direction. Afghanistan was viewed as a turning point, a forerunner of things to come, even—in the view of the American Army chief of staff—the beginning shot in World War III. But those who assume this stance overlook the special circumstances that existed in December 1979 in Afghanistan and that undoubtedly led the Soviet Union to choose the particular instrument that it did: a client state, challenged by a military uprising, on the periphery of the USSR, vital to Soviet security interests and seemingly not at all related to American interests, a Marxist-Leninist regime linked to the Soviet Union by a solemn security treaty, so that its overthrow would represent a challenge not only to Soviet security interests but also to Soviet credibility. The Soviet Union used military force in Afghanistan to *maintain* an existing regional balance, not to upset it.

The Soviet decision to invade Afghanistan was a calculated and seemingly low-risk response to a set of circumstances that the Kremlin leaders perceived as threatening vital security interests. Contrary to some prevailing interpretations, it evidences neither a blueprint for global expansionism nor an insatiable—indeed paranoiac—sense of insecurity founded on fanatical Bolshevik hostility to the existing international order.

To stress this point is not to lend greater justification or legitimacy to Moscow's aggressive actions in Afghanistan, but instead to argue against the notion that the present-day Soviet leaders' actions in an area such as South Asia are rooted in an unchanging world view, identical to that of their Bolshevik fore-runners. Rather, the shift in what the Soviets term the "correlation of forces" has reduced the relevance of Leninism and the Bolshevik image of the world. The "operational code" of which Nathan Leites wrote was forged in an environ-ment of Bolshevik weakness, in which the enemies of the Soviet state called the tune. As "imperialism" has been tamed, the USSR's sense of threat and aliena-tion from the international system has lessened considerably.

The contrast between the early postrevolutionary period, in which it could truly be said that the Russian working class had "nothing to lose but its chains," and the present position of the USSR in the world is graphically depicted in the statement repeated by Foreign Minister Gromyko at every opportunity that the Soviet Union "is one of the world's leading powers without whose participation no international problems can be settled." This statement reflects an attitude of pride and confidence that is quite different from the earlier aura of hostility and suspicion. As the USSR's stake in the international order has increased, its un-willingness to make a risk-laden challenge to the status quo has been reflected in a marked loss of revolutionary fervor. The Soviets have long claimed that their chief internationalist duty is not the export of revolution abroad, but the build-ing of communism at home.

Events of recent decades have thus helped shape the perceptions held by Soviet leaders in the direction of greater confidence and patriotic pride and a lessened sense of insecurity about frontiers. But to argue this is not to suggest that the men in the Kremlin are, therefore, completely satisfied with the inter-national order or complacent about the USSR's position in it. Nothing said above is meant to deny that the Soviet leadership regards itself as still locked in a highly competitive relationship with the United States, engaged in a struggle for greater influence in far-flung areas of the globe. Indeed, as Robert Legvold has put it, what we have seen in recent years is a "shift in the Soviet preoccupation from the struggle to secure Soviet power against the external world to a quest for a larger place in it."[25] But, to say that the Soviet Union is engaged globally in a competition for influence is not at all to conclude that its vital security interests are everywhere involved, much less to assert that some sense of omni-present threat and possible annihilation is driving the Soviet Union toward world domination. Global involvement has created for the Soviet Union—as for the United States—a far more complex security situation, requiring a more precise assessment of threat and a more careful specification of just which interests are truly vital to its security. And it is on the basis of this assessment that the USSR formulates its estimate of defense requirements.

It is in this context, then, that the Soviet Union has decided that its security interests require a substantial presence in South Asia and the Indian Ocean region. The United States, in contrast, has for most of the past several decades not perceived a need of Indian (or, indeed, Pakistani) support of its more vital objectives, and it has thus had no particular incentive to establish its presence or develop its influence in the subcontinent. Understanding this point should help us avoid being surprised by the substantial Soviet interest and presence in South Asia, and also to avoid being alarmed at the Soviet presence, since we have seen that Moscow's considerable investment has by no means won her inordinate influence or turned India into a puppet state. Rather, much of the Soviet "victory" over the United States in the superpower competition in this region has in effect been accomplished by default.

NOTES

1. "Mission of Peace and Friendship," *New Times*, no. 50, 1980, p. 5.

2. For an extended analysis of this point see Robert H. Donaldson, *The Soviet-Indian Alignment: Quest for Influence*, University of Denver, Monograph Series in World Affairs, vol. 16, books 3 and 4, 1979.

3. "Statements by N. A. Bulganin and N. S. Khrushchev in India, Burma, and Afghanistan," *New Times*, supplement, no. 52, 1955, p. 22.

4. For more details on this activity see Robert H. Donaldson, *Soviet Policy Toward India: Ideology and Strategy* (Cambridge, Mass.: Harvard University Press, 1974), chap. 4.

5. Andrew M. Scott, *The Revolution in Statecraft: Informal Penetration* (New York: Random House, 1965), chap. 1.

6. Alexander Kaznacheev, *Inside a Soviet Embassy: Experiences of a Russian Diplomat in Burma* (Philadelphia: Lippincott, 1962), p. 142.

7. This section draws on Donaldson, *Soviet Policy Toward India*, pp. 225-27.

8. *Pravda*, June 3, 1981, p. 5.

9. *Pravda*, August 13, 1974.

10. P. Mazentsev, "Thirty Years of Independence," *New Times*, no. 32, 1977, p. 13.

11. *Izvestiia*, April 15, 1979.

12. A. Usvatov, "Seething Discontent," *New Times*, no. 36, 1980, p. 12.

13. *Pravda*, August 8, 1981.

14. S. Irodov, "India and the Indian Ocean Problem," *New Times*, no. 26, 1981, pp. 12-13.

15. V. Shurygin, "India: Thirty Years of Independence," *International Affairs*, no. 9, 1977, p. 75.

16. V. Shurygin, "India: A Time of Important Decisions," *International Affairs*, no. 9, 1979, pp. 57-62.

17. *Izvestiia*, March 13, 1977, p. 3.

18. A. Usvatov, "Change of Government," *New Times*, no. 14, 1977, p. 13.

19. Shurygin, "India: Thirty Years of Independence," p. 75.

20. *Pravda*, December 12, 1980, p. 2.

21. *Pravda*, July 3, 1981, p. 5.

22. Michael T. Kaufman, "Diplomacy Swirls Around Pakistan," New York *Times*, August 25, 1981, p. 2.

23. *Pravda*, August 8, 1981.

24. A. Alexeyev and A. Fialkovsky, "For a Peaceful Indian Ocean," *International Affairs*, February 1981, pp. 85-91.

25. Robert Legvold, "The Nature of Soviet Power," *Foreign Affairs*, October 1977, pp. 68-69.

8

U.S. INTERESTS IN SOUTH ASIA AND THE INDIAN OCEAN

W. Howard Wriggins

The Soviet invasion of Afghanistan following the fall of the shah of Iran once again brought South Asia to the forefront of American foreign policy debates. Instead of continuing to isolate Pakistan because it persisted in a clandestine nuclear energy program (suspected of aiming toward a nuclear explosion), in the winter of 1979–80 the Carter administration abruptly changed course. Washington offered modest military and economic assistance to Pakistan that Islamabad promptly rejected; it also committed the United States to defend the Persian Gulf and to urgently seek access to military facilities near the Strait of Hormuz. Following Ronald Reagan's assumption of the Presidency, a more impressive arms transfer to Pakistan became a subject of heated debate in the Congress. Moreover, the nature and size of this military package caused distress in New Delhi and American policy toward India demanded increasing attention.

THE RELEVANT AREA

U.S. interests in South Asia cannot be considered in that area alone, but only as part of a wider context. The states of South Asia, after all, lie immediately to the south of the Soviet Union and China, and a good deal of American policy toward South Asia has been a response to perceptions of the challenge posed to Western interests by the Asian giants to the north.

South Asia is also linked to Southwest Asia, as Pakistan is part of both areas. Suggesting the derivative character of American policy toward South Asia, Western policy toward Pakistan has often been defined largely by Western raw materials and strategic interests in Southwest Asia. These American policies, in turn, have had effects on India's perceptions of American policy toward New Delhi and have had a profound effect on India's approach to the United States and its Asian neighbor. The nexus between developments in South and South-west Asia became particularly salient following the surge in petroleum prices in the early 1970s, the collapse of the shah's regime in 1978, and the Soviet occupation of Afghanistan in 1979–80. Nevertheless, there are distinguishing characteristics about U.S. interests in South Asia that deserve attention.

DIMENSIONS OF AMERICAN INTERESTS

Before examining U.S. interests as they came to be defined in South Asia, it will be useful to consider first dimensions of American interest that might possibly be engaged there (or anywhere else, for that matter). One can identify three dimensions of foreign policy: first, security, concerned with the global and regional structure of power; second, economic relationships; and third, the growing role of international institutions as arenas for competitive or cooperative international politics.[1] These three different categories are not mutually exclusive; phenomena in one spill over into the others. History in the making in practice involves them all, and they often interact in close lockstep. But for analytical purposes, they will be treated as if distinct.

Defense and Security

One aspect of security concerns the global balance between the United States and the Soviet Union at the highest level. This is fundamentally a matter of superpower mutual deterrence; it concerns the awesome matter of nuclear weaponry and the coherence and reliability of the major alliance systems. For our purposes the question asked is: "How do developments in South Asia enhance or erode the structure and functioning of that global balance as the United States perceives it?" In the 1950s, South Asia was thought to be consequential to that balance; in the 1960s and 1970s, it was thought not to matter much. But it appears that the latter view became obsolete with the collapse of the shah and was further undermined by the Soviet occupation of Afghanistan.

Another level of national security interest derives from developments within the area. How do events in South Asia affect the tranquility of and reliable access to areas adjacent to South Asia that are of vital interest to the United States, i.e., Southwest Asia or the Persian Gulf? Conflict between the states of South Asia, internal political eruption, or direct external intervention could all adversely affect U.S. security interests there.

A third level concerns how the South Asian states might be of direct use to the United States—or to its principal opponent? Could they provide facilities of some kind, such as air landing rights, tactical air strips, prestocking locations, naval repair, or rest and recreation possibilities? Where areas are of low security priority, such questions do not arise. But when areas come to be seen as lying near critical fault lines of possible contention, such questions become important.

Economic Relationships

A second dimension of national interest concerns economic relationships. Can an area provide essential resources to the American economy—raw materials or industrial goods at favorable prices, financial resources to be channeled in useful directions, or markets to absorb the products of the United States and earn usable foreign exchange? Has South Asia a role in three-cornered trade relations with other states that then trade with the United States and its associates? The economic dimension for South Asia would not be complete without some notions regarding the role South Asia's future productive systems could contribute to world economic growth or the periodic net burdens South Asian states may impose on the world economy when the monsoons fail, should populations continue to surge, and agricultural productive systems remain insufficient.

"World Order" Considerations

More and more issues of concern to the United States are subject to discussion and joint management through numerous multilateral or international institutions. To that extent the orientation of the states of South Asia toward numerous issues within these institutions will be of some consequence to the United States. When security issues are salient, "world order" considerations seem less important. But they, too, deserve attention.

American assessments of its interests have shown marked changes over time. This is in part a quite realistic response to the changing international environment; it also reflects a learning process that underlined the limits of Washington's capacity to mitigate deeply felt local antagonisms in South Asia. The peculiarly pluralist character of the American political system adds to the changeability. Numerous interests are in play in Washington, each of which tries to present its needs as reflecting the national interest. The president and his entourage often have one perception, different departments press different conceptions on the president and Congress, and the multitude of particular interests in Congress usually bespeaks a variety of ways of defining the national interest. The president and Congress share the constitutional obligation to define a conception of the national interest that will win sufficient popular support to be sustainable. Thus, what becomes policy may also reflect assessments of what the popular traffic will bear. Arnold Wolfers was certainly right when he stressed the ambiguity of the "national interest."[2]

U.S. SECURITY INTERESTS IN SOUTH ASIA

Put most simply, there are two major U.S. interests believed to be at stake in South Asia. First, could the states of the area contribute to constraining Soviet or Chinese expansion southward into Iran, Pakistan, or India? Second, could they affect one way or another access to and the reliability of oil flows from the Persian Gulf?

In the 1950s "containment" of the Sino-Soviet bloc was the first consideration. Following the Korean War and before the Sino-Soviet split became apparent, Washington perceived a unified Asian "heartland" in Sir Halford Mackinder's imagery, stretching from the Baltic to the Pacific. As such, the "global balance" between the United States and its friends and the Sino-Soviet "bloc" seemed threatened. The containment effort called for bolstering individual states on the Sino-Soviet periphery and drawing them together in security collaboration. Both Great Britain and the United States hoped that "joint defense" with India and Pakistan working together would oppose substantial local power to that of the heartland bloc.

In South Asia, however, regional conflict between India and Pakistan remained intense. American assistance to one inevitably alienated the other. India would have been the logical associate if one had had a choice. It was far larger, had inherited the larger army, had well-established democratic institutions, and its leadership was admired in parts of the West. But these same leaders refused to work with the Americans on security matters. They considered Washington's analysis of the Sino-Soviet bloc faulty and its strategy of containment likely to cause more conflict than necessary. They insisted instead on playing a lone hand. The wounds of partition, which the Indians blamed on Muslim Pakistan's intransigence, had by no means healed; both coveted the lovely Kashmir valley; and India saw itself as the rightful heir to the British raj, the properly preeminent power on the subcontinent.[3]

Pakistan had some special assets from Washington's point of view, however. Its position commanded the classic invasion route from Central Asia onto the Indian plains; in addition, it formed part of the hinterland of the oil states of the Persian Gulf.[4] A close working relationship with Pakistan, it was held, could make a contribution to both security objectives. It, too, therefore, was seen as a worthwhile candidate to be a partner in containment, even though it was smaller and divided in two by 1,000 miles of Indian territory. That it was eager to cooperate while the only other South Asian state that mattered was reluctant made the arrangement with Pakistan all the more attractive. The United States sent military equipment to modernize its forces and substantial economic assistance; it also eavesdropped electronically on a nearby Soviet missile test site and U.2 flights took off from Peshawar's airport. There was little intrinsic to South Asia that made it strategically important at the time. It was both the unified threat from the north and interest in the oil flows from the Persian Gulf to the West that led to Washington's containment in association with Pakistan.

By 1965, however, the Sino-Soviet split was unambiguous as Khrushchev and Mao slanged each other and set large numbers of troops on watch along their 3,000 mile frontier. Accordingly, the pressure from the north appeared to ease. So long as the Soviets and Chinese quarreled, the argument ran, they checked each other; the Central Asian balance gave the states to the south greater room for maneuver. As such, South Asia became of lessened security importance for Washington. Moreover, the nagging Indo-Pakistan rivalry that led to a second war in 1965, precipitated by Pakistani efforts to promote rebellion in Kashmir, kept them both weak, and of less use in the containment enterprise than had originally been hoped. Accordingly, events in Central Asia and the mutual quarreling of India and Pakistan led Washington to downgrade the security priority attributed to South Asia.

While American security concern for South Asia diminished following the Sino-Soviet split and the Indo-Pakistan war, the local rivalry between India and Pakistan brought each closer to one of the two rivals in the Central Asian balance. The Chinese threat to India was dramatized by the Sino-Indian war of 1962. This led India to turn increasingly to Moscow. As Indian leaders perceived it, there was more support in security terms to be had from the nearby Asian superpower—the Soviet Union—than from the more distant United States. First, as Indian relations with China worsened, Soviet relations with China were also becoming more bitter. Indians came to believe that the Soviet Union's conflict with China across the center of continental Asia made Moscow the ideal balancer to deter possible future Chinese actions against India, which might turn out as badly for India as the 1962 Sino-Indian war. Thus, Kautiliya's apothegm "my enemy's enemy is my friend" became literal advice to Chandragupta's successors 22 centuries later. The Soviets were also a reliable source of military equipment, and they provided consistent diplomatic support to India in its contention against Pakistan over Kashmir and against China in the Northeast Frontier Agency (NEFA). By contrast, key members of the Indian government saw the United States as a dynamic, imperialist power, actively involved in supporting India's hostile neighbor Pakistan, and thus bent on preventing India from playing its due role as the preeminent power in regional affairs. At the same time, they feared that entering an alliance with the United States would deprive them of their right and their ability to look at each issue "on its merits" and to make up their own minds on important policy issues.

American support for Pakistan from the mid-1950s to the mid-1960s was substantial. It materially improved Pakistan's fighting capacity, but it had the by-product effect of strengthening the military at the expense of fragile civilian political processes. And Americans subsequently learned that Pakistan at that time was more concerned about India and Kashmir than about the hypothetical Soviet drive across the Hindu Kush. American military support for India in the

1962 Sino-Indian conflict demonstrated to Pakistan the obvious and distressing limits to American backing. These limits were confirmed during the 1965 war between India and Pakistan when the United States stopped military supplies and logistical support to both states in an effort to halt the fighting—a far more severe blow to Pakistan's fighting capability than to India's. This was the original source of Pakistan's sense that the United States had been an unreliable ally.

As it perceived more clearly the real outer limits to American support during the first half of the 1960s, Pakistan naturally turned to the most logical nearby source of support—China. Like India, therefore, Pakistan followed Kautiliya's advice. Thus came about the notable cross-linkage that still binds the two most important states of South Asia to opposite contenders in the larger Asian balance.[5]

The Sino-Soviet rivalry may have eased anxieties in the south for those who worried about the Sino-Soviet bloc in the 1950s. But the links India and Pakistan developed with their opposing northern neighbors had liabilities. At least while Mao still lived, the Indians frequently accused the Chinese of clandestinely supporting anti-Delhi movements in strategically sensitive hill areas of Assam and perhaps Bangladesh, since the Chinese believed India had been helping its Soviet opponent. Conversely, the Russians were frequently accused of activating Afghan tribal antagonisms in Baluchistan and Sind aimed at undermining Islamabad's stability since, as Moscow was held to see it, Pakistan had been abetting its opponent China. In one sense, these are "natural" by-products of the Sino-Soviet rivalry and the cross-linked relationships South Asian states have with their larger Asian neighbors. But they marginally complicated the task of South Asia's leaders.

The Central Asian balance retained a certain stability for some 20 years, but South Asia experienced dramatic changes in 1971. The combined follies of Zulfikar Ali Bhutto, Sheikh Mujib, and General Yahya Khan following Pakistan's first free election on universal franchise in 1970 led to huge disorders in East Pakistan and to a third war between India and Pakistan. India emerged from these events even more preeminent than ever, a fact Secretary of State Kissinger officially confirmed in 1974.[6] As India saw it, however, American declaratory policy may have acknowledged Indian preeminence, but Washington made no special effort to consult Indian views nor did it pay any more attention to those they expressed on their own initiative than had been the case before. There was a brief improvement in relations when President Carter replaced Gerald Ford in Washington and Morarji Desai replaced Indira Gandhi in New Delhi in 1977. But as Raju Thomas has pointed out, the underlying politico-strategic conceptions of Washington and New Delhi were so different and in important respects so incompatible that the improvement did not go very deep.[7]

South Asia was thus given relatively low priority in Washington in all three dimensions of security. In regard to the central balance, the Sino-Soviet rivalry was far more inhibiting to both of the Asian giants than anything that might be mounted in South Asia to constrain them; Indo-Pakistan rivalry weakened both these states for possible usefulness in any local contingencies. And after 1965, the United States showed no inclination to use any of the subcontinent's real estate.

A PERIOD OF MINIMUM U.S. INTEREST IN SOUTH ASIA: 1965–79

For nearly 15 years, the U.S. policy of minimum concern for South Asia continued, perhaps encapsulated in the proposition "they can do us little good, but also little harm," with only two brief though important exceptions.

One, already mentioned, occurred in 1971 when President Nixon and Henry Kissinger used General Yahya as an intermediary to begin the opening to China at the very time the general's efforts to return Pakistan to electoral politics exacerbated separatist tendencies. His harsh repression in East Bengal led millions of Hindus to flee East Pakistan and brought the Indian army to East Bengal in a well-planned and well-executed campaign to "liberate" Bangladesh, a success incidentally that restored the reputation of the Indian army. The famous "tilt" toward Pakistan saw the United States outspokenly on Pakistan's side in that miserable episode, and opposed to India.[8]

Nuclear energy raised a second issue. As India moved forward on its nuclear power program, President Carter the engineer became increasingly worried about the risks of nuclear proliferation. With congressional support, he changed the terms previously agreed to for nuclear fuel deliveries to India unless India, like other recipients of nuclear fuels, put their facilities under full international nuclear safeguards. This the Indians refused to do, and they charged the president with having unilaterally gone back on an international agreement. Pakistan's nuclear program, begun under Prime Minister Bhutto in an effort to catch up with India, had led President Carter to stop U.S. economic assistance to Pakistan when General Zia's government refused to desist.

But apart from these two episodes, neither India nor Pakistan figured prominently in U.S. foreign policy considerations.

In the meantime, India's defense establishment became more dependent on the Soviet Union for sophisticated air power while its growing military industrial capacity improved markedly to produce for itself the sinews of conventional warfare, including high quality tanks and even fighter aircraft. A Treaty of Friendship signed with the Soviet Union in the summer of 1971 reassured India as war with Pakistan approached. The Indians may have become restless with their Soviet arms suppliers, but penetration aircraft from France and Great Britain were far more expensive and delivery times protracted, while the Soviets proved to be reasonably reliable in meeting their commitments. China continued to be seen as threatening, and its continued collaboration with Pakistan confirmed in Indian eyes Pakistan's hostility. Though asserting it was still following a non-aligned policy, India rarely deviated publicly from Soviet preferences except briefly at the start of the Janata government in 1977. In Pakistan, Bhutto's efforts to turn Pakistan toward the Persian Gulf reduced his countrymen's obsession with Kashmir and India, and brought new sources of foreign exchange and diplomatic support from the oil sheikhdoms to assist economic development and a rebuilding of Pakistan's shattered military establishment. But he was not prepared to forego his China connection even though he and Indira Gandhi reached agreement on a number of issues at Simla in 1972.

U.S. PRIORITIES

Iran. Sino-Soviet rivalry in Central Asia may have been a source of safety to India and Pakistan, but that did not appear so consequential farther west, where a growing Soviet military establishment faced Iran along a 1,000 mile frontier.[9] Indeed, since the 1950s, Iran played a major role in the American containment effort. Occupying an area that for generations had been contested between tsarist Russia and the British, during World War II Iran had been virtually partitioned for logistical purposes between the Anglo-American allies on the one hand, and the Soviet Union on the other. After the Soviets' reluctant withdrawal in 1946, the United States and Great Britain provided substantial support to the shah's Iran. Moscow promoted the development of the Moscow-leaning Tudeh Party, but the shah with American and British support continued to rule in a way to insulate the Persian Gulf states from Soviet influence and on the whole to assure the continued flow of oil. To be sure, he with Colonel Qaddafi promoted the first oil hike in 1970-71 and again in 1973-74; but he enthusiastically applied a substantial proportion of the additional profits to huge arms purchases, mainly from the United States. For the Nixon/Ford administration, the shah's regime became the protector of the Persian Gulf as the British withdrew from "east of Suez" in the early 1970s, and the Americans, either bogged down or slowly recuperating from Vietnam, proved unable—and unwilling—to take Britain's place, as Washington had done earlier in Greece and Turkey.

The shah's apparent strength had its side effects on U.S. policy toward Pakistan. There appeared little reason to devote substantial resources to Pakistan's problems so long as the shah remained in place and capable. Indeed, the increased incomes of the Persian Gulf states could well have been applied to Pakistan's needs if necessary, and the Carter administration's sensibility to human rights and nonproliferation further encouraged a standoffish American attitude toward Pakistan.

Afghanistan. By contrast to both its neighbors, Afghanistan was assigned a relatively low priority by Washington. No military assistance of any import was undertaken, in part because of its inaccessibility. However, a not inconsequential economic and technical assistance program kept quietly working for many years in the fields of agriculture, irrigation, education, and public administration. A number of governments in Kabul kept up a running quarrel with Pakistan over the alleged mistreatment of the Pushtu-speaking people in Pakistan who have complex familial and tribal connections with the largest single ethnic group in Afghanistan. Soviet officials, including Khrushchev himself, publicly supported Kabul's claim against Islamabad. Most American observers assumed nevertheless the Soviets would continue to respect Afghanistan's integrity as they had for decades. It posed no threat to Soviet security along the Amu Darya; its policy carefully avoided unfriendly actions to Moscow; the Soviets trained their military officers and provided virtually all their equipment. It was a kind of Finland in the south. And the internationally recognized buffer status of Afghanistan had been accepted for nearly a century.

Bangladesh. Devastated by the "war of independence," Bangladesh stirred American interests that were largely humanitarian. To draw Bangladesh back into the realm of functioning governments able to meet at least the minimum basic needs of its people, was to promote stability and good order of the region, and large economic assistance transfers made a substantial difference. Experience had shown that when domestic difficulties and antagonisms mounted beyond a certain point, domestic political upheaval had an immediate and sometimes devastating effect on near neighbors in that overcrowded neighborhood. Acute regional conflicts have resulted that have led to wars which could tempt one or the other major power to the north. American efforts were therefore directed to promoting the rehabilitation of the economy and modest military equipment transfers also took place.

Sri Lanka. On its island south of India Sri Lanka had been a functioning democracy since 1932, with regular unintimidated elections every five years. Its 13 million people had a higher standard of living than the average in either India, Pakistan, or Bangladesh thanks to tea and rubber exports. A number of quasi-socialist governments had sought to insulate the economy from the "vagaries of the world market," and during the 1970–77 period its economy experienced little growth, though it did make some progress toward improved food output. A youth rebellion in 1971 almost unseated the government of Sirimavo Banderanaike only a year after it had come to office. Prompt support came to her from all quarters, including, incredibly enough, China, the Soviet Union, and the United States, and many others. From then on American naval vessels were again welcome to visit Colombo, a particularly attractive port of call for resting crews and for elementary ship repair and resupply. Sri Lanka generally followed a moderate course among the nonaligned, particularly compared to Algeria and Cuba. But neither Bangladesh nor Sri Lanka figured prominently in U.S. security interests in South Asia.

THE INDIAN OCEAN

Accordingly, for most of the 1970s, U.S. security interests in South Asia were thought to be modest. After 1971, only the Carter administration's growing efforts to discourage nuclear proliferation induced Washington to pay attention to the area. At sea, however, there was a difference as both the Soviet Union and the United States showed growing interest, and Iran and India began to expand their navies.[10]

For the United States, the Indian Ocean was farthest from its shores; compared to the North Atlantic or the Pacific, for the most part, U.S. commerce and naval activity were far less prominent. Of vital concern, however, was the northwest quadrant of the Indian Ocean, commanding the entrance to the Persian Gulf, the Strait of Hormuz. Here fanned out the sea lanes carrying oil through Suez to Europe, or by supertanker around the Cape, or across the Indian Ocean through the Malacca Strait to Japan and across to the California coast. As already noted, reliable access to the oil and assured transit to consumers had been taken so for granted that even when Great Britain withdrew from its inconspicuous but stabilizing presence in the Persian Gulf in 1971, Washington made no substantial move to take its place. To be sure, the United States retained a rather obsolescent three-vessel unit on permanent station in Bahrein, and began to upgrade Diego Garcia into a naval communications facility. From 1967–68 there was a notable increase in Soviet naval vessels appearing in the Indian Ocean, however, and proponents of larger naval appropriations warned of our laxity. The United States continued to organize occasional pass throughs of naval task forces from the Pacific fleet heading home through the Red Sea and the Mediterranean. However, the 1973 oil embargo once again turned more urgent attention to the Persian Gulf.

The Soviet Union pushed the development of facilities at Berbera in Somalia, including a missile servicing capability and docking arrangements close to a 14,000-foot runway able to receive anything in the Soviet inventory, and arranged anchorage rights off a number of harbors. Soviet control of the excellent harbor at Aden was virtually complete, thus in effect straddling the entry to the Red Sea. The United States, for its part, gradually upgraded the capability at Diego Garcia from a modest communications facility to a naval task force servicing station. And both navies made periodic visits to a number of Indian Ocean ports. In early 1977, Moscow offered a generous grant to the Maldive Islands for the right to use the former British air and naval station at Gan, but Malle rejected the offer. Gan would indeed be attractive, for it is a well-designed facility in reasonably good condition and lies 400 miles to the north from Diego Garcia and that much closer to the critical Strait of Hormuz some 2,000 miles to the northwest from Diego. Naval competition remained on a fairly low key, however, and in 1977 both Washington and Moscow gingerly approached the problem of defining mutually agreed levels of naval activity to constrain Indian Ocean competition between them.

DOMESTIC POLITICAL DIFFICULTIES

While these interstate affairs influenced Washington's perceptions of American interests, the domestic viability of these states was also observed, but with only moderate concern. To be sure, Pakistan's government remained brittle as ethnic regionalism pulled minorities against Pakistan's centralist regime. Structures for representative rule never were consolidated, and the Bhutto regime was succeeded by another return of the army. In India, the resilient and skilled Congress Party gradually eroded as time carried off the independence leadership to be replaced by men and women of more parochial character; Indira Gandhi used different methods of rule than her father. Troubles in the northeast and disorders in Bihar and Gujerat led to her emergency. Protracted disorders may weaken a state's capacity to rule and tempt outsiders to intrigue. When a state in a strategic position disintegrates from within, regional structures of power may dramatically change, risking conflict between outsiders attempting to preempt their opponents or seeking to establish a distribution of power favorable to themselves. Once the 1971 partition of Pakistan had been accomplished, the domestic political difficulties of all the South Asian regimes, however, were never sufficient to seriously involve outside powers. Until 1978, therefore, Washington showed little interest in what was happening within the polities of South Asia apart from the nuclear issue and occasional expressions of distress over limitation of human rights in Pakistan.

THE STAKES ARE SEEN TO CHANGE: 1978–79

Developments in 1978 and 1979, however, abruptly changed American perceptions of the international stakes involved. The specifics of American interests were sharply redefined as Soviet actions suggested a far more ambitious program for the area—particularly with an eye to approaches to the Persian Gulf—than had been thought plausible by many American proponents of detente. The cumulative effect of a series of steps led to a far more active American approach to the Persian Gulf and thus, inevitably, to its South Asian neighbors.

The surge of Soviet naval activity and a massive airlift that brought 20,000 Cubans and large stocks of sophisticated military equipment to Ethiopia in 1978 suggested a bold bid for a client Ethiopia, which once had been close to the United States. In the winter of 1978 the shah was overthrown, and the government, such as it was, passed into the hands of Islamic zealots.

The government of Iran, which had eagerly taken on the task of being defender of the Persian Gulf, suddenly fell apart; the army disintegrated and the state was at the mercy of the religiously excited mobs. And in late 1979, 80,000 Soviet troops marched into Afghanistan. The Hafizullah Amin government was as promptly overthrown and replaced by Babrak Karmal who had arrived in the train of the Soviet armies. Accordingly, the security situation immediately to the west of South Asia changed dramatically, a development found to affect American perceptions of the security importance of South Asia.

CHANGED PERCEPTIONS OF AMERICAN INTERESTS

The new vulnerability of the Persian Gulf, so vividly dramatized by the collapse of Iran, understandably again gave prominence to Pakistan's location. In the 1950s the Soviet "threat" had been largely hypothetical and American worries about it obviously premature; in the 1980s the presence of Soviet power on the Khyber posed a major and urgent security problem to the government of Pakistan.

It was unfortunate for the people of Pakistan, its officials, and their American friends that the government of Pakistan had not been able to resolve the country's constitutional problem—institutions and conventions supporting representative elections had never been consolidated and the country's ethnic structure and highly centralist administration encouraged separatism. One national election held in 1970 had led to the partition of the country and the second, in 1977, was alleged to have been so drastically corrupted that its results were nullified. The Baluch and Pathan minorities deeply resent rule by the Punjabi majority who dominate the bureaucracy, as well as the army that periodically has taken power. Thus, ironically, the one very exposed major government willing to work with the United States, now at arms length to be sure, is itself lacking in legitimacy and like other South Asian countries, beset by ethnic difficulties.

The government of India played down the security consequences of the Soviet occupation of Afghanistan, reacting rather like it did when the Chinese occupied Tibet in 1953 at a time when India had as good relations with Peking as it now had with Moscow. Some Indian officials urged Indira Gandhi's government to offer strong reassurances to the government of Pakistan, but other counsels prevailed, at least at the outset. Perhaps the government of India saw little cause to worry, since Pakistan lay between it and Soviet forces. Moreover, with Soviet pressures on its western frontier, Pakistan would be more effectively inhibited by the more powerful Soviet presence than it had been by the relatively weak preinvasion Afghanistan. Kautiliya again? To be sure, a weak Pakistan between India and the new Afghanistan might prove to be as effective a buffer for India as Afghanistan had historically been for the subcontinent as a whole. On the other hand, perhaps New Delhi's leaders were rendered cautious by the half-acknowledged awareness that Soviet troops on the Khyber had inevitably changed India's own security situation. George Kennan is said to have once commented that it may take a decade before people come to appreciate the full implications of a major change in their country's security situation.

Whether the government of India would see the possible limiting implications of their changed situation and whether the effects this could have on domestic politics might give the government more room for maneuver in dealing with Pakistan is still not clear.

The government of Pakistan perceived itself under a severe double threat. It could expect Soviet politico-military intimidation at any time if it had to stand alone, and occasional Soviet air intrusions served to remind Pakistan of its exposed position. Its traditional antagonism with India and India's link with the Soviet Union led Islamabad to fear Indo-Soviet collusion designed to bring combined pressure to bear upon it to conform to Soviet or to Indian diplomatic preferences. The China connection was no doubt helpful, but Chinese support was inevitably limited. If Pakistan accepted help from the United States, that might speed the modernization of Pakistan's obsolescent military establishment, but it might also provoke from Moscow the very pressures it feared, without the country being all that much strengthened by the new relationship. In the fall of 1981, after the Reagan administration offered many more resources, Islamabad was eager to purchase advanced military equipment and to receive substantial economic aid. At the same time, trying to avoid the isolation from the numerous nonaligned states that it had experienced when allied with the United States in the 1950s and 1960s, it insisted that it would not become part of a new alliance system. In this way, too, it would be able to protect its growing relationships with the Muslim world in Southwest Asia that might be jeopardized if it were too obviously close to Israel's principal patron.

For the United States, the dilemma was sharp—and familiar. Since the government of India did not share the American perception of the Soviet threat and persisted in arguing that aid to Pakistan inevitably would be turned against New Delhi, as indeed it had been in the past, American assistance to Pakistan risked sharpening antagonism between the two South Asian states and pushing India closer toward the Soviet Union. And, as before, a plausible defense of South Asia could hardly be taken seriously without India at least cooperating. Nevertheless, the location of Pakistan gave it special importance, and the overall U.S. security focus on the Persian Gulf led the administration to support a state that now faced for the first time a direct Soviet presence on its frontier.

To be sure, the United States and the Soviet Union were not the only relevant outside powers. China had had a significant role in pushing India toward the Soviet Union in the aftermath of the Sino-Indian war in 1962. If China could initiate a settlement along the Sino-Indian border acceptable within India's changing domestic politics, and India could find an alternative to its Soviet arms supply, Indian policy might show unforeseen flexibility. At the same time, China was tempted to provide Afghanistan's freedom fighters military supplies to keep up the anti-Soviet resistance, and joined with the United States and nearly all other members of the United Nations in condemning the Soviet occupation. Whether China wanted to make it easier for India to loosen its ties with Moscow and would take steps to encourage that transition remained to be seen.

The evolving American strategy called for a more active American role, which would again involve closer attention to South Asia as well as the Persian Gulf. Washington quickly sought access to facilities in Oman, Kenya, and in Ras Banas, far from population centers on Egypt's Red Sea coast. It replaced Moscow at Berbera in Somalia. At sea, the Carter administration's initial assignment of two carrier task forces to the northwest quadrant of the Indian Ocean was maintained. The Reagan administration sought to work more closely with the states of the Persian Gulf. Its home-based Rapid Deployment Force was urgently beefed up. A by-product of all this activity was the requirement for more ports where American ship's crews, on protracted sea duty far from home ports, could go ashore for rest and recreation. Without that the volunteer navy might have difficulty in recruiting its necessary complements. Would more landing rights, places for prepositioned equipment, and other support facilities be forthcoming?

There were many other uncertainties. Iran had not disintegrated as badly as had been assumed; witness the Iranian spring 1982 offensive against the Iraqis. The Soviets were thoroughly bogged down in a costly, indecisive struggle against fragmented but determined resistance movements in Afghanistan. The extent of U.S. assistance to Pakistan and its effects on Pakistan's capability were not yet clear. No doubt many Americans will have unsolicited advice for Islamabad on how it should deal with its minority and other problems, but only they can judge what steps are feasible to enhance the internal viability of the state, or how best to deal with the Soviet forces on the Khyber. The effects of American policy toward Pakistan on India's policy were also not yet clear. There is little doubt that within Indira Gandhi's government in New Delhi there were growing debates as to what was the best way of coping with the changed security environment of South Asia.

Within the United States there were also differences of view. Under what sorts of circumstances would a Rapid Deployment Force be usefully applied so far from American logistical bases? What were its plausible missions in the face of possible internal disruptions, threatened coups d'etat, regional interstate conflict, or direct Soviet threat? And how could the United States usefully bolster Pakistan against a thrust from the occupying Soviet forces in Afghanistan without the Indians believing such American assistance was mainly directed against them, a view likely to enhance the importance of India's Soviet connection, and make constructive Indian relationships with both Pakistan and the United States the more difficult? Moreover, did not the threat to Pakistan's integrity lie more in the country's overcentralized, bureaucratic administration than in the external military threat?

Security policy is usually a choice among unsatisfactory alternatives where the unknowns are prominent and the predictabilities uncertain. In this respect, policy toward South Asia posed familiar and characteristically intractable difficulties.

THE ECONOMIC DIMENSION

A second dimension of American interests concerns economic considerations, including resources to be obtained, markets to be opened, economic burdens to be shared, and the lot of Asia's millions of poor to be considered.

There is little that the United States obtains from South Asia that is critical to the American economy. No state has yet discovered oil in exportable quantities. Alas for Bangladesh, substitutes are undermining the utility of jute; tea from India and Sri Lanka can also be obtained from East Africa, Indonesia, and China (though none can match Sri Lanka's high-grown teas, as everyone knows). Pakistan's cotton is good and inexpensive, and both India's and Pakistan's quality fabrics, carpets, and ready-made clothing are proving to be attractive to American consumers. India is trying to export some industrial tools, engineering and transportation equipment, and so forth. There are a few useful minerals and other items. To be sure, the United States represents India's largest customer in most years. It is, however, a hard truth that South Asia produces little that the United States really needs.

On the consumer side of the ledger, for those U.S. enterprises that have successfully overcome the difficulties of setting up production in either India or Pakistan, the protected markets have proved highly profitable, though repatriation of investment resources and profits has been difficult. More generally, however, despite the huge numbers, the bulk of the people are so poor they can purchase little but the bare essentials. Official policies seek to protect infant industries from too severe competition from abroad and to insulate their economies from the impact of external economic forces as best they can.

Food, of course, is an essential. Despite notable progress toward food grain self-sufficiency, periodic bad monsoons are likely to require huge food imports, and North America is their external breadbasket. Perhaps only North American farmers producing food grains are significantly affected by whether or not North America has access to South Asian markets.

On the other hand, given the predictions of long-run world food shortages, despite the short-run interest of American farmers in large grain shipments to South Asia, it is to the interest of the overall American economy and the world food balance that South Asian farmers become far more productive. Many parts of the Indus Valley could be as productive as the Imperial Valley of California if the Indus water were properly channeled and farmers organized for optimum output. The Ganges and other valleys in India and the Brahmaputra in Bangladesh, if tamed, could also produce far more. The United States and others in the industrialized world as well as in the third world, therefore, have an interest in doing what they can to encourage more productive use of natural and human resources in all three mainland countries as well as in Sri Lanka.

It is, of course, possible that as India's and Pakistan's economies grow and diversify, their cheap labor and scattered points of technological quality will lead to production of more varied and higher-value goods desired by the outside world. An export-oriented economic drive, if sustained, could not only help reduce South Asia's debt problems by upping foreign exchange earnings but could also materially improve South Asia as a source of middle-level industrial goods that we would not lightly forgo. But such a development seems far down the road and of only marginal economic importance to the United States.

To what extent should the economic well-being of South Asia's millions of poor be an active interest of the United States? To some, the state of South Asia's poor is so shocking and dispiriting as to leave the foreign observer horrified and immobilized. To others, it represents a goad to additional effort and a major source of the drive to change the international economic order, since nearly half the world's truly poor live in South Asia. There is little automatic political linkage between South Asia's poverty and the American people's individual prosperity. However, there is a growing sense that such sharp contrasts in well-being cannot make for a stable or even a viable world order. The world we leave to our children will see far more of the disruptive politics of desperation if we ignore the world's poorest than if we quietly persist in efforts to assist those who seek to improve their well-being and their productivity.

In sum, the first American economic interest in South Asia is to do all that can be done to improve the ability of South Asian states to feed themselves, to diversify their economies and achieve some improvement in the well-being of those worst off. Deriving from the American interest in the sustained ability of South Asian states to maintain national integrity, the second American interest is to ensure insofar as possible that these economies gain resources sufficient to maintain the sinews of effective statehood.

But it must be owned that the experiences of the past 20 years with India, Pakistan, and Sri Lanka underline the limited ability of external resources to make as much difference as, in the more optimistic days of the 1950s and 1960s, the United States often assumed. The Marshall Plan triggered a resurgence of economic forces in Western Europe. However, 15 years of very substantial economic transfers to South Asia have demonstrated their utility but not their automatically beneficent consequences. Bureaucratic, cultural, and political obstacles stood in the way of using external resources to maximum advantage. Until such problems are actively grappled with by local governments, external resources will remain both necessary and useful, but not likely to be the catalysts we and their proponents used to think.

In an economic experiment worth watching, the J. R. Jayewardene government in Sri Lanka took a major turn in 1977.[11] Opting for a freer market approach, more like Singapore's, with substantial help from the International Monetary Fund, Sri Lanka dismantled the elaborate control system based on the Eastern European model previous governments had followed, reduced consumption subsidies, sought foreign investment, and promoted private enterprise. It also accelerated major irrigation and hydroelectric construction. Economic activity surged, creating many new jobs, but a severe inflation gained momentum. Whether the increase in jobs would mitigate the growing and visible contrast between rich and poor remained to be seen. Western government support for the experiment suggests they saw an interest in its success.

WORLD ORDER

A final group of interests centers on the relevance of developments in South Asia to world order. Mention has already been made of the possible consequences of disintegration of either of the South Asian states to the peace and good order of the region. A more obvious aspect derives from the role played by South Asian states in international institutions as they affect the international environment.[12]

There are now numerous fields of activity where collaboration between the states of South Asia and those of Western Europe, Japan, and the United States could make a constructive difference to events. A series of unprecedented problems of world order now call for concerted search for mutually acceptable arrangements. Some of these emerge from grievances of certain third world states, some from concerns of the industrialized states. They are brought forward at the United Nations Conference of Trade and Development (UNCTAD), UN special sessions, UN Food and Agriculture Organization (FAO) conferences, meetings of the Group of 77 and the "nonaligned," in consultations of the Committee of 20 on world financial problems, and so on. These relate to such questions as limiting the fluctuations in raw materials prices, changing international financial arrangements, regularized resource transfers from the "old" and "new" rich to the "poor," the mounting burden of unrepayable developing country debts, population control, accelerating food production, managing environmental and industrial water use, world energy distribution, the Law of the Sea, and so forth. None of these can any longer be worked out satisfactorily by the major powers alone; most require at least the acquiescence, and some require the active collaboration, of many states in the Third World.

It is, of course, possible to argue that the opinion of four states in any one area of the world, in this case India, Pakistan, Bangladesh, and Sri Lanka in South Asia, is not in itself very important to U.S. diplomacy, no matter how skillfully articulated and aggressively organized they may be. However, these are not just any four states. By virtue of their location south of the principal protagonists in the Sino-Soviet contention, their actions are of somewhat greater import to our strategic interest than if they were located, say, in central Africa or at the tip of South America. The very size of the population gives them some claim to be heard. After all, India is more populous than all of Africa and Latin America combined, and even the truncated Pakistan is among the world's large states compared to most members of the United Nations.

Moreover, India and Sri Lanka particularly have played substantial roles in third world forums for many years. They have been far less radical than Cuba, Algeria, Guyana, and a number of others, for instance. Pakistan's and Sri Lanka's skilled diplomats at the United Nations and elsewhere have already given their states' voices a weight their present size and recent political or economic difficulties would normally belie. Since Jawaharlal Nehru's death, India's spokesmen have been somewhat less effective than they were when he was among the first to speak out for what is now known as the third world. But India's weight among the nonaligned nevertheless can make a difference to U.S. activities.

Highly educated specialists from India, Pakistan, and Sri Lanka are disproportionately present in numerous international agencies and third world staff positions. For the most part, they tend to be detached from their lands of origin. Nevertheless, they cannot help but look at certain problems and certain states in some relation to those states' approaches to the problems of their homelands.

All these factors give a number of the states of South Asia a considerable role in political forums in the third world, where the tendency has often been publicly to confront the United States rather than seek collaboration with it.

It has also become increasingly clear during the past decade that U.S. ability to obtain diplomatic support for its initiatives has lessened, that fewer states in the third world particularly are ready to support Washington's positions. Even Western European states have found it more difficult to go along with numerous positions Washington has felt to be important, in part because of the very solidarity often demonstrated in third world forums. This condition was brought home with particular force when the acute vulnerabilities of Western Europe and Japan were dramatized by the Arab oil embargo in 1973. Sharp differences over energy policies emerged between the United States on the one hand and Western Europe and Japan on the other. These differences became more obvious as the decade wore on.

Since the states of South Asia have historically played a significant role in the councils of the third world and are quite as likely to be able to do as much in the future as in the past, the political contribution they can make either to facilitate or to impede U.S. initiatives is a measure of U.S. political interest in having constructive relations with their governments.

To be sure, these world order considerations are not crucial to the immediate political survival of the United States. But if ignored, the weakening of such collaboration and the increase in impediments put in Washington's way could become consequential. The legitimacy of many activities the United States has hitherto taken for granted could be seriously undermined. The states of South Asia, therefore, can help or hinder Washington's enterprises. As such, the United States has an interest in doing what it can to encourage the sympathy, support, and cooperation of the active states in South Asia if a post–Bretton Woods international economic and political order compatible with U.S. long-run interests is to be developed.

In sum, because of the Soviet advance into Afghanistan and the increasing importance of the Persian Gulf following the collapse of the shah, South Asia is again deemed consequential to American security interests. Still, familiar policy dilemmas persist. Bolstering Pakistan still is seen by India as contrary to its interests. Moreover, no solid defense of the subcontinent can be imagined for the long run if India is not prepared to play an important role. Economic issues also are longer term, and derive more from the burden South Asia's masses periodically impose on world food supplies than from any positive contribution South Asia can make to the world's economy. Finally, the role South Asian statesmen are likely to play in the nonaligned movement, the Group of 77, and other worldwide forums will contribute to shaping a world order more rather than less compatible with U.S. long run interests. At a time when security issues have higher priority, Washington will continue to find its task in South Asia a major challenge.

NOTES

1. I am indebted to Donald Neuchterlein for this approach in *United States National Interests in a Changing World* (Lexington: University Press of Kentucky, 1973), chaps. 1 and 2.

2. Arnold Wolfers, "National Interest as an Ambiguous Symbol," *Political Science Quarterly* 67, no. 4 (December 1952): 481-502.

3. For a careful analysis of contrasting strategic conceptions for South Asia held by the United States and India, see Raju Thomas, "Security Relationships in Southern Asia: Differences in the Indian and American Perspectives," *Asian Survey* 21, no. 7 (July 1981): 689-709.

4. Sir Olaf Caroe, *Wells of Power* (London: Macmillan, 1951).

5. H. Wriggins, "The Asian State System in the 1970's," in *Asia in the International System*, ed. W. Wilcox, L. Rose and G. Boyd (New York: Winthrop, 1972). For more detail in relation to Pakistan's policy, see the author's "The Balancing Process in Pakistan's Foreign Policy," in *Pakistan, the Long View*, ed. L. Ziring, R. Braibanti, and H. Wriggins (Durham, N.C.: Duke University Press, 1977); and W. J. Barnds, *India, Pakistan and the Great Powers* (New York: Praeger, 1972).

6. Secretary of State Henry Kissinger, "Toward Global Community: The Common Cause of India and America," *Department of State Bulletin*, November 25, 1974.

7. Thomas, "Security Relations in Southern Asia."

8. For Henry Kissinger's perspective, see his *White House Years* (Boston: Little, Brown, 1979), pp. 842-919. For a critical view by a participant, see Christopher Van Hollen, "The Tilt Policy Revisited: Nixon-Kissinger Geopolitics and South Asia," *Asian Survey* 20, no. 4: (April 1980) 339-61.

9. For an interesting discussion of Anglo-Soviet rivalry in Iran and Central Asia, see the thoughtful article by Giles Bullard, "The Power of Menace: Soviet Relations with South Asia, 1971-1974," *British Journal of International Studies* 2 (1976).

10. For an extensive discussion, see S. J. Cottrell and R. W. Burrell, *The Indian Ocean: Its Politics, Economics and Military Importance* (New York: Praeger, 1972).

11. For a discussion see Howard Wriggins, "Sri Lanka in 1980: The Year of Constraints," *Asian Survey* 21, no. 2 (February 1981): 203-11.

12. For a discussion see Seyom Brown, *New Forces in World Politics* (Washington, D.C.: Brookings Institution, 1974); Miriam Camps, *The Management of Interdependence* (New York: Council on Foreign Relations, 1974); R. O. Keohane and J. S. Nye, *Power and Interdependence* (Boston: Little, Brown, 1977).

9

THE UNITED STATES AND SOUTH ASIA: THE CARTER AND REAGAN ADMINISTRATIONS

Norman D. Palmer

In the context of global objectives, overall foreign policy, and national purpose, South Asia is usually a low-priority area for the United States. It is given special attention only when developments in the subcontinent seem to affect the global concerns of the United States, as in the 1971 crisis that culminated in the India-Pakistan war and the emergence of Bangladesh as an independent nation. More dramatically, the region drew American interest when the Soviets moved into Afghanistan in late December 1979. Moreover, the United States cannot be indifferent to a part of the world that contains more than one-fifth of the world's population, approximately 40 percent of the population of the noncommunist developing countries, and has more people living below the level of decent existence than in any other region of the globe. U.S. relations with the countries and peoples of South Asia have been made at once more difficult by the low standards of living and the difficulties that these countries have had in achieving internal cohesion, political and economic stability, and development. The often unhappy state of their intraregional relations (especially the continuing tensions between India and Pakistan) is aggravated by the competition, occasional limited cooperation, and conflicting interests of the United States, the Soviet Union, and China in the area.

A good summary of U.S. interests in South Asia was made in September 1976 by Adolph Dubs, deputy assistant secretary of state for near eastern and south asian affairs, in a statement before the Subcommittee on International Organizations of the Committee on International Relations of the U.S. House of Representatives:

> In the South Asian region, our primary concerns have been the promotion of regional stability and the normalization of relations between the nations of the subcontinent and the avoidance of inter-

ference by outside powers. We hope that the governments of the region can focus their main attention on their massive human and social development problems. In keeping with American concerns for the developing world, we hold a long-standing interest in the economic progress of the countries of South Asia.[1]

Most of the official U.S. policies and relations in South Asia can be related to these "primary concerns." They are legitimate concerns, but whether U.S. policies in trying to further them have been sound and effective can be, and indeed has been, a subject of divergent interpretations in the United States and in all the countries of South Asia. Fortunately, there are other aspects of U.S.-South Asian relations, even on the official plane, such as cultural exchanges and multilateral as well as bilateral relationships. Moreover, perhaps the most meaningful aspects of the U.S.-South Asian encounter are nonofficial in nature, and these are far more extensive than is generally recognized.

TILTS AND POLITICAL CHANGES

U.S. relations with India reached a low point in 1971 as a result of the so-called tilt toward Pakistan, a much more complicated and less-biased approach than the term suggests. They improved somewhat in 1972-75, but deteriorated again during the emergency in India in 1975-77. While the United States refrained officially from criticizing the eclipse of democracy in India, there was considerable criticism of the actions of Indira Gandhi and her government in the American press and among influential groups in the private sector. Indians in the United States were sharply divided in their views of the emergency. But some Indian groups were very vocal in their opposition to the new direction in India, and many opponents of Indira Gandhi and her government came to the United States to present their case against the emergency rule. Indira Gandhi frequently lashed out against the alleged Central Intelligence Agency (CIA) or other American "machinations" in Chile and elsewhere, presumably including India, and she was quite indignant over criticism of her policies emanating in the United States. It was, at best, a holding period in official U.S.-Indian relations.

In the 1950s President Eisenhower's decision to enter into mutual defense agreements with and to extend military assistance to Pakistan, and the latter's entry into two multilateral security arrangements—the South East Asian Treaty Organization (SEATO) and the Baghdad Pact, later called the Central Treaty Organization (CENTO)—had adverse effects on U.S.-Indian relations. Pakistan became "America's most allied ally in Asia." This special relationship, however, did not last long. It began to come apart in the early 1960s, as illustrated by Pakistan's resentment at the emergency military aid provided by the United States to India during the Sino-Indian border conflict in late 1962 and by the bitter comments of Pakistan's leader, Ayub Khan.[2]

Relations with Pakistan improved somewhat in the late 1960s after the Republicans regained power in Washington. There has long been a widespread feeling in both India and Pakistan that the Republicans tend to favor Pakistan, whereas the Democrats lean toward India. Pakistan appreciated the U.S. position during the early part of the crisis in South Asia in 1971, but was disappointed with the limited support it received from the United States during the Indo-Pakistan war in December of that year. On its side the United States tried to make the best of a difficult situation and welcomed the restoration of civilian government in Islamabad after Pakistan's loss of East Pakistan. It had continuing doubts about Pakistan's new leader, Zulfikar Ali Bhutto, who had often been identified with an anti-American and pro-Chinese position. Nevertheless, the United States was encouraged by Bhutto's apparent success in keeping what was left of Pakistan together and in restoring national confidence and élan.

The year 1977 witnessed significant political changes in all the South Asian countries as well as in the United States. New governments, markedly different in orientation, style, and character from the governments they succeeded, came into power in India, Pakistan, and Sri Lanka, and some important administrative changes were made in Nepal and Bhutan. Moreover, in April 1977 Major General Ziaur Rahman, who had been the real power in Bangladesh since November 1975, was sworn in as president of Bangladesh. All the leaders of the new governments professed complete faith in democracy and pledged to restore democratic rights and freedoms as soon as possible. The Janata government in India and the United National Party in Sri Lanka took steps to fulfill this pledge immediately after their electoral victories. The heads of the essentially military regimes in Pakistan and Bangladesh gave lip service to their pledges of greater democratization; but they continued to rule by authoritarian methods and postponed promised national elections "to save the country from a dangerous crisis," as General Zia-ul-Haq stated when he canceled elections that had been scheduled in mid-October 1977.

In India, Bangladesh, and Sri Lanka, but not in Pakistan, the change to a Democratic administration in Washington was generally welcomed. In the United States the political changes in India and Sri Lanka were also welcomed, but reactions to the changes in Pakistan and Bangladesh were muted and reserved. There were recurring doubts in Washington about the capacity of all the new regimes to survive and govern effectively. But there can be no doubt that in the United States and in at least India and Sri Lanka a new political climate had been created that augured well for improved relations between the Carter administration and these countries. While basic problems remained, the overall climate of U.S.-South Asian relations noticeably improved.

THE NEW CHAPTER IN INDO-AMERICAN RELATIONS

Carter's desire for improved relations and his special interest in India (based, to be sure, more on his general sympathies for third world countries and on his mother's experience in India as a Peace Corps volunteer than on any profound knowledge or understanding of the complex Indian society) were well known and often expressed; and this interest and desire were reciprocated increasingly in official and unofficial Indian circles. The moves toward an improved climate were evident even before the change of government and the ending of the emergency in India.[3] Even Indira Gandhi, who had often been an acerbic critic of U.S. policies and practices, began to modify her criticisms and to express more frequently her interest in improved Indo-American relations.

The improvement in relations became more apparent and contacts became more frequent after the March 1977 elections in India. Indira Gandhi's stunning defeat at the polls was followed by the ending of the emergency that had existed since June 1975 and the installation of the new Janata Party government, headed by the veteran leader Morarji Desai. The termination of the prolonged emergency and the restoration of democratic freedoms in India came as a relief to most Americans who were at all concerned with such matters. While Americans were rather baffled by Morarji Desai's enigmatic personality and personal life-style, including most abstemious habits, they respected him for his experience, ability, and integrity. Furthermore, his views on economic and foreign policies seemed to be much more congenial than those of his predecessor. In particular, Desai favored economic policies that gave more of a role to the private sector and more opportunities for foreign investment and operations than the policies followed by the more socialist Gandhi regime. His emphasis on a more genuinely nonaligned foreign policy was widely interpreted in the United States as more favorable to American interests and less pro-Russian than Indira Gandhi's foreign policies had been.

According to an Associated Press report from New Delhi on July 4, 1977, Prime Minister Desai and President Carter had entered into an extensive private correspondence, in which they exchanged views on a variety of matters of special concern to their two countries, including "such sweeping subjects as the gap between the rich and the poor countries, nuclear safeguards and peace through disarmament."[4] With the change of government in India, official visits were exchanged between the United States and India with unprecedented frequency. The U.S.-India Joint Commission and its subcommissions, which had been quite inactive during the emergency in India, were given a new impetus. During a visit to New Delhi in July 1977 Warren M. Christopher, under secretary of state, said that the United States had decided "to look to India as the leader of South Asia," a statement that pleased the Indians and drew an official protest from the government of Pakistan.

Even the U.S. Congress began to have a more active and sympathetic interest in India. In late March 1977, in a gesture of approval of the political change in India, the Foreign Assistance Subcommittee of the Senate Foreign Relations Committee recommended repeal of a measure adopted by the Congress in July 1974. (India's nuclear explosion in May 1974 had required U.S. representatives to the World Bank and its affiliated agencies to vote against low interest loans to India by the Bank's International Development Association.[5]) In November seven members of the Asian and Pacific Affairs Subcommittee of the House Committee on Foreign Relations led by Chairman Lester L. Wolff visited India "as part of a new Congressional effort to get acquainted with India."[6]

In 1977 two prominent Indian leaders came to the United States for medical treatment—Jayaprakash Narayan in May and President N. Sanjiva Reddy in September. Carter conveyed his good wishes to both of these Indian leaders. Their treatment in the United States seemed to improve their health and also contributed to better feelings between Indians and Americans—although some Indians protested that adequate medical facilities existed in India.

The highlights of the exchange of visits on the official level were President Carter's visit to India in January 1978 as one stop on a whirlwind tour that took him to seven countries in nine years, and Prime Minister Desai's visit to the United States in the following June.

Carter received a warm welcome in India. On his arrival he stressed the theme that pervaded all his public remarks, namely that the United States and India were linked by common moral and democratic values. Desai echoed these statements. The crowd that assembled to listen to President Carter at a public meeting was the largest he addressed during his first year in office. His speech to the Indian Parliament was also repeatedly interrupted by what was described as "desk-thumping, foot-stomping" applause.

In private conversations with Desai, however, a number of differences remained unresolved. Most of these centered around different positions on nuclear matters. In his speech to the Indian Parliament, Carter announced that the United States would resume shipments of enriched uranium for the Indian atomic power plant at Tarapur, near Bombay; but he seemed to be dissatisfied with Desai's reaction to the decision and with his efforts to get assurances regarding nuclear safeguards. An embarrassing situation was caused by a private exchange between Carter and Secretary of State Cyrus Vance that, unbeknownst to the speakers, was picked up and recorded by a radio technician. Carter said to Vance: "I told him [Prime Minister Desai] I would authorize transfer of fuel now . . . it didn't seem to make an impression on him." He then added: "When I get back I think we ought to write him another letter, just cold and very blunt." As one correspondent noted, "Spokesmen of both the President and the Prime Minister spent much of the rest of the day trying to explain these remarks."[7] It could be concluded that warmth of Carter's public reception reflected an improved climate in Indo-American relations, whereas the private discussions reflected continuing differences between the two governments.

Desai's visit to Washington was also characterized by warm public hospitality and behind the scene disagreements. Nevertheless, both governments sought to improve their overall relations. The Indian prime minister addressed large audiences in New York, California, Nebraska, and Washington. Desai appeared on a major network TV-interview program. He also addressed the prestigious National Press Club in the nation's capital. He met with several key members of the U.S. Congress and had long talks with President Carter and other high-ranking American officials. He and Carter continued to differ, however, on a number of important issues, including the role and activities of the super-powers, especially in the Indian Ocean, the nuclear nonproliferation treaty (to which Desai, like Indira Gandhi, was adamantly opposed), and the question of the resumption of U.S. shipments of enriched uranium for the Tarapur nuclear plant.

The exchange of visits by the top leaders of the two countries dramatized what many official spokesmen of both countries described as a "new chapter" in Indo-American relations. This interpretation was widely accepted in unofficial circles as well, but it was questioned, or at least modified, by some seasoned political observers. Girilal Jain, one of India's best-known journalists, for example, wrote of Carter's visit:

> . . . cooperation between two major countries like the United States and India . . . calls for a community of outlook and interests which is plainly missing in this case. *Pax Americana* and Indian nationalism are once again at odds with each other and this time in a strikingly different context. America is no longer the great aid-giver it was and India's need for assistance is no longer as desperate as it was in the sixties. Mr. Carter and Mr. Desai need a great deal of ingenuity to bridge this gulf.[8]

AFGHANISTAN AND NEW TILTS

The improvement in U.S. relations with India and the virtual freeze in U.S.-Pakistan relations that began in 1977 were abruptly reversed as a result of the Soviet invasion of Afghanistan in late December 1979 and by Indira Gandhi's return to power in India's seventh general elections. Moreover, the fall of the shah and the victory of a fundamentalist Islamic regime in Iran heralded a changed geopolitical and religious situation in the critical Persian Gulf region. South Asia thus became an area of greater concern to the United States. The Soviet invasion of Afghanistan seemed to pose a serious threat to South and Southwest Asia. Again the greater American attention to South Asia was due primarily to extraregional and global considerations.

Pakistan, which shared U.S. perceptions of the seriousness of the Soviet occupation of Afghanistan, became a "front-line" state. The Carter administration immediately revised its policy toward that country, moving from a freeze on economic and military aid that had been imposed nine months earlier (because of U.S. apprehensions about Pakistan's nuclear program) to an offer of economic and military aid that in its original form of $400 million was rejected by President Zia-ul-Haq. Subsequent negotiations were long and frustrating to both countries. No mutually acceptable agreement was reached until September 1981, several months after the advent of the Reagan administration, when agreement on a six-year, $3.2 billion economic and military aid package was announced.[9]

The United States recognized that the influx of hundreds of thousands of Afghan refugees into Pakistan, which by midsummer 1981 had reached some 2.5 million people, imposed additional burdens and problems upon Pakistan. Washington participated in bilateral and multilateral programs of aid for the refugees; but Pakistan still had to bear the main burden, in more than a financial sense. It has been speculated the United States is providing some military assistance to the Afghan "freedom fighters"—or "counterrevolutionaries," as the Russians called them—through a variety of direct and indirect clandestine channels. It is also believed Pakistan is involved in moving arms and supplies to the Afghans, despite constant denials that it was engaging in such action. For their part the Afghans have repeatedly complained about the limited assistance and support they were getting from Pakistan and the international community.

India's reaction to the Soviet presence in Afghanistan was of a very different nature. The first comments of Indira Gandhi after her electoral victory seemed to be supportive of the Russian action; but the main burden of her comments was that she was opposed to all forms of foreign intervention, including that of the United States and China. She was reported to have indicated her concern about the Soviet occupation of Afghanistan to Russian leaders at personal meetings and through diplomatic channels, and to have urged the prompt withdrawal of Soviet forces from Afghanistan. But she seemed to be even more concerned about the Pakistan military buildup, and the plans to provide major U.S. military assistance to Pakistan, including F-16 fighter-bombers and other sophisticated weapons and military equipment. Indira Gandhi spoke out more strongly and more frequently about these developments, and about the increasing naval presence of the great powers in the Indian Ocean—with specific reference to the U.S. naval buildup and the development of the Diego Garcia base. She was less outspoken concerning the presence of Soviet forces in Afghanistan and elsewhere in the region.

THE REAGAN ADMINISTRATION AND INDIA
AND PAKISTAN: NUCLEAR AND SECURITY ISSUES

The Republican victory in the American presidential election in November 1980 was welcomed in Pakistan and viewed with misgivings in India. At a press conference in Calcutta on January 3, 1981, even before Reagan assumed office, Indira Gandhi expressed the hope that under the new administration the United States would reverse what she called the "tilt against India" and seek to improve

Indo-American bilateral ties. Shortly thereafter, in a meeting with a 14-member delegation of the Armed Services Committee of the U.S. House of Representatives, she repeated this hope, but she also said that recent U.S. actions and policies had threatened the peace and stability of South Asia and the whole Asian region.

In late November 1980, in presenting his credentials to President Carter as the new Indian ambassador to the United States—some 15 months after his predecessor, Nani Palkhivala, had left—K. R. Narayanan said that "our relations are today warm and cordial and there are brighter prospects for further improving them on the basis of mutual understanding, mutual respect, and friendly reciprocity." He also referred to "widening areas of cooperation" between India and the United States.[10] Six weeks later, however, in an address to the Asia Society in Washington, D.C., the Indian ambassador struck a more somber note: "There is need to clear this layer upon layer of misperception that we have about each other. The United States, being a superpower, had certain strategic considerations and global perceptions of its interest which often tended to weaken the bilateral relationship between the two countries."[11]

The question of the continued supply of enriched uranium for the nuclear power plant at Tarapur remained a bone of contention. According to the U.S. Nuclear Nonproliferation Act of 1978 the president was obligated, after a certain time had elapsed, to cut off any form of nuclear assistance to any country which refused to accept the terms of the international Nuclear Nonproliferation Treaty of 1968 and which would not accept "full safeguards," including international inspection, for all of its nuclear facilities. India had refused to adhere to the treaty, and while it did permit inspection of its Tarapur plant it would not permit the same arrangement for its other nuclear facilities. Hence India and the United States were at an impasse on this issue, with neither side showing any willingness to abandon or even modify its rather intractable position. Under these circumstances the Reagan administration decided to seek India's consent to abrogate the 1963 treaty in which the United States had agreed to supply enriched uranium for the Tarapur plant for a period of 30 years. Apparently Washington was prepared to renounce the 1963 treaty unilaterally if India would not agree to its abrogation. An added irritation between the two countries was the adoption by the U.S. Senate, on October 21, 1981, of an amendment to the Foreign Assistance Act of 1972 requiring a cutoff of foreign aid to India or Pakistan if either country detonated a nuclear device. Other major differences concerned the position of the two countries regarding Soviet activities in Afghanistan, Pakistan (with India strongly objecting to the U.S. decision to provide substantial military aid to Pakistan), Kampuchea (with India recognizing the Heng Samrin regime and the United States the Pol Pot regime), the naval buildup of the United States in the Indian Ocean area, and a variety of Middle East issues.

Prime Minister Gandhi and President Reagan participated in the North-South summit conference in Cancun, Mexico, in late October 1981. They reportedly had amicable and fruitful discussions, but on the main issues of the New International Economic Order and the transfer of resources and assistance from the industrialized to the developing countries the two leaders were obviously far apart. Contacts between India and the United States, however, continued on many levels, official and unofficial.

While U.S. relations with India remained officially good, but were in fact rather cool and distant, relations with Pakistan, which had again become involved rather significantly with larger U.S. interests and concerns, continued to improve. In September 1981 Pakistan agreed to a six-year $3.2 billion military and economic aid package. In a separate agreement the United States promised to speed up delivery of some of the promised F-16 aircraft. These developments were welcomed in Pakistan but strongly objected to in India. Nevertheless Pakistan, like India, objected to the action of the U.S. Senate on October 21, 1981, to require suspension of aid to either India or Pakistan if either country exploded a nuclear device. This action, to which the Reagan administration was opposed, was clearly aimed more at Pakistan than at India. Indeed, suspicion that Pakistan was clandestinely developing nuclear weapons was a major obstacle to the improvement of U.S.-Pakistan relations.

The new U.S. rapprochement with Pakistan was only one reason for the growth of anti-American feeling in India. In an Op Ed piece in the New York *Times* on the very day of the Senate's action on aid and nuclear proliferation a former assistant editor of the *Times of India* wrote: "Not since the era of Dwight D. Eisenhower, when the United States looked upon India's neutralist leader Jawaharlal Nehru as a stooge of Moscow have relations between Washington and New Delhi reached as low a point as they have today. . . . A series of recent events have generated an outbreak of violent anti-American feeling, even among the more responsible quarters of India public opinion. . . . Girilal Jain, editor in chief of *The Times of India*, accused President Reagan of waging a war not so much on the Soviet Union as on third world countries which refuse to fall in line with its policies."[12] This interpretation seemed to corroborate an assessment made three months previously by the seasoned American scholar-journalist Selig S. Harrison, who wrote that Indo-American relations were in "the most dangerous crisis . . . since India won its independence in 1947. . . . Each new Washington pronouncement helps harden the anti-American sentiment that has festered beneath the surface in India as a result of the 1954–1965 American military-aid fiasco in Pakistan and the pro-Islamabad tilt of the Kissinger years."[13]

ECONOMIC RELATIONS

Economic issues have been most extensively discussed between representatives of the United States and India, on both official and unofficial levels—in bilateral official negotiations, in the Economic and Commercial Subcommission of the U.S.-India Joint Commission, in various U.N. forums, including the General Assembly, the World Bank, the International Monetary Fund, the United Nations Development Program, and the United Nations Conference on Trade and Development, in tariff negotiations under the aegis of the General Agreement on Tariffs and Trade, in many international conferences, in the Aid India Consortium, and in private bodies such as the India-U.S. Business Council. In the "wide range of multilateral and bilateral economic, trade and investment issues" that have been discussed are such issues as trade, development assistance, investments, the role and treatment of American-based multinationals in India, and a variety of major international economic issues, with a special focus on the "North-South dialogue" and the demand for a New International Economic Order.[14]

On many of these issues India and the United States are obviously far apart. The United States is the leading nation of the North, and India is perhaps the leading nation of the South. India strongly supports the New International Economic Order, and the United States has reservations about it. The leaders of the two countries hold divergent economic as well as political views. Yet the network of economic relations between the United States and India is quite extensive. They bulk much larger in terms of India's efforts at economic development than they do in the totality of U.S. international economic relations. India is not a major area of American trade or investment; yet American investments are the second largest of all foreign investments in India, and the United States was for some time India's leading trading partner (it is now second to the Soviet Union). Bilateral U.S. aid to India, which totaled over $9 billion, was suspended in 1971 as a result of the decision of Indira Gandhi's government that India could and should get along without it, but it has now been resumed on a modest scale (the Reagan administration requested congressional approval of $258,528,000 for bilateral aid to India in fiscal year 1982). Total U.S. aid to India, through both bilateral and multilateral channels, is quite substantial. The United States is a major contributor to the World Bank and its soft-loan affiliate, the International Development Association, and to the International Monetary Fund (IMF). On November 9, 1981, the IMF approved a loan of $5.8 billion to India to help that country deal with its growing balance of payments difficulties (mainly due to the high prices for its imported oil). This loan, the largest ever granted by the fund, was under negotiation for several months. It was a source of bad feeling between India and the United States because the Reagan administration instructed the U.S. executive director of the fund to oppose the loan. According to a correspondent of the New York *Times*, the "Reagan administration had strong misgivings about the loan to India on the ground that the money would be lent on too easy terms and would be more for development purposes than for meeting specific balance-of-payments needs."[15]

U.S. trade with and investments in Pakistan are very small. As a result of the new relationship that has developed since the Soviet invasion of Afghanistan, efforts are being made to increase both trade and investments. A leading role in these efforts is being taken by the U.S.–Pakistan Economic Council, which was formally inaugurated by President Zia-ul-Haq in October 1980 when he visited the United States. American economic aid to Pakistan was quite limited in the 1970s. It was suspended except for certain emergency relief in 1971 as a result of the crisis in South Asia, and was again curtailed in the spring of 1979 due to the mandate imposed by the U.S. Congress in the Nuclear Nonproliferation Act of 1978. It states that after a certain period aid must be cut off to any non-nuclear country that is developing a nuclear program with weapons-producing capabilities. After the Soviet invasion of Afghanistan this requirement was reluctantly waived by the Congress in the case of Pakistan.

U.S. economic relations with the other nations of South Asia are even more limited, and even more dominated by the aid nexus. The major exception is economic assistance to Bangladesh, a nation that depends almost exclusively on outside aid for its entire development program. For the fiscal year 1982 the Reagan administration recommended a grant of $193,324,000 to Bangladesh. Additional U.S. assistance to that very underdeveloped country (with a population of more than 90 million in an area about the size of the state of Wisconsin) is provided through multilateral channels. Bangladesh receives more than $1 billion of economic assistance annually from all sources. Recommended appropriations for aid to Sri Lanka and Nepal in fiscal 1982 were $78,253,000 and $18,226,000 respectively.[16]

DIPLOMATIC REPRESENTATION:
THE PERSONAL DIMENSION

The Carter administration's interest in improved relations with the countries of South Asia was shown by the quality of the new ambassadors chosen to represent the United States in South Asia. The United States had no ambassador in India for some months after William Saxbe left in late 1976. In April 1977 Robert Goheen, a distinguished private citizen, was named to this post. Goheen was a popular choice in India. He had been born in India of missionary parentage and had his early schooling in Madras. A former president of Princeton University, he was cochairman of the Subcommission on Education and Culture of the U.S.–India Joint Commission at the time of his appointment. In April 1977 Carter nominated a senior career diplomat, George Vest, as ambassador to Pakistan, but later that month he changed his mind, and named Vest to the post of assistant secretary of state for European affairs. On May 23 he nominated another career foreign service officer, Arthur W. Hummel, Jr., as the next U.S. ambassador to Pakistan. A few weeks later W. Howard Wriggins, director of the Southern Asian Institute at Columbia University and author of a well-known book on the politics of Ceylon, was named U.S. ambassador to Sri Lanka. In late 1977 David Schneider, an experienced career officer, became U.S. ambassador to Bangladesh.

For some time after the change of government in India, Kewal Singh, a former foreign secretary, remained as India's ambassador to the United States. In September 1977 he was succeeded by Nani A. Palkhivala, a distinguished lawyer and business executive who had been one of the most outspoken opponents of the abrogation of constitutional safeguards and human freedoms during the emergency in India in 1975–77. Before he left India to take up his new post, Palkhivala said that he would try to promote and deepen cultural as well as political and economic relations between India and the United States.[17] The appointment of such a well-known champion of human rights and democratic freedoms was widely welcomed in the United States. Shortly after he assumed his new post, Palkhivala said that he could not remember a time when U.S.-Indian relations had been better. He left his post in the fall of 1979, and was not replaced until some 15 months later, when K. R. Narayanan, a veteran diplomat, presented his credentials as the new Indian ambassador.

Although Ambassador Goheen left India well before President Reagan assumed office, no successor was appointed for several months. In the fall of 1981 a senior career foreign service officer, Harry Barnes, arrived in India as the new American ambassador. The long delay in replacing Ambassador Goheen and the appointment of a career foreign service officer instead of a distinguished private citizen were regarded by many Indians as further evidence that Reagan and his associates attached little importance to U.S. relations with India.

In 1981 Ambassador Hummel, who was highly regarded in Pakistan, was transferred to Beijing as U.S. ambassador to the People's Republic of China, and was replaced in Pakistan by Ronald I. Spiers, another senior career diplomat. A veteran Pakistani diplomat, Sultan Muhammed Khan, was replaced, after some delay, as Pakistan's ambassador to the United States by a senior Pakistani general, Lieutenant-General Ejaz Azim, who presented his credentials to President Reagan on September 21, 1981. An interesting diplomatic choice was the appointment of a husband and wife, both senior foreign service officers, as American ambassadors to Bangladesh and Nepal—Carlton Coon to Nepal and Jane Coon to Bangladesh.

CONCLUSIONS

It is easy to be very bullish or very bearish about U.S.-South Asian relations. Undoubtedly these relations will continue to be characterized by frequent ups and downs. Recurring expressions of goodwill and mutual interests cannot conceal the relative superficiality and lack of real warmth and understanding in official relations, and the limited contacts and vast misunderstandings and differences in outlook and ways of life on unofficial and personal levels. No real "encounter between civilizations," to use a Toynbeean phrase, has occurred, is occurring, or is likely to occur between Americans and South Asians. Official relations will doubtless remain formally good and correct, with some fluctuations in style and substance, but they will not be as close or as cooperative as many Americans and South Asians think they should be. The view of the world from Washington and from South Asian capitals is a very different one in many respects. So too are the life-styles, outlook, and values of American and South Asians.

The United States sees South Asia as an important part of the world because of the problems of human and national development in the world's second most populous region, because the subcontinent is crucial in the developing world, in the nonaligned movement, and in North-South relations. For South Asians, however, the United States is an important country because it is a superpower and its influence affects them in innumerable direct and indirect ways. The United States is an ever-present reality—a continuing factor, or actor—in the South Asian scene, whereas South Asia does not play a similar role in the American political and social environment.

Except within the larger context of global considerations, such as North-South relations and the rivalries of the major powers, South Asia will continue to be a relatively low-priority area for the United States. For the South Asian countries, the United States will inevitably have a higher priority, in both positive and negative ways. Most Americans will continue to think about South Asia in terms of problems and of human misery, and most South Asians will continue to think about the United States and Americans in terms of both attraction and repulsion. On both sides the images will be mainly stereotypes, often with little relation to reality. There are, and will continue to be, many difficulties, both tangible and psychological, in U.S.–South Asian relations. These cannot be removed by political cosmetics. Much depends on the course of events in the United States and the countries of South Asia, and in the international system generally.

A continuing problem for the United States will be to maintain satisfactory relations with both India and Pakistan—a problem that is complicated by the generally uneasy relations between the two major states of South Asia, and by U.S. "tilts" toward one or the other of these states at different periods. During the Carter period the tilt was toward India, as it had been in the early 1950s. During the Reagan era it had been toward Pakistan, as it was in the mid-1950s and in 1971.

In his article in the New York *Times* on July 15, 1981, suggestively entitled "India, and Reagan's Tilt Toward Pakistan," Selig S. Harrison warned that "the combined impact of the Administration's overtures to Islamabad and Peking has produced the most dangerous crisis in relations between New Delhi and Washington since India won its independence in 1947." "The Administration," he asserted, "seems largely oblivious to New Delhi's emergence as a regional power center, but in the eyes of 650 million Indians this indifference is viewed as hostility because it is linked with pro-Peking and pro-Islamabad policies." This piece prompted a rejoinder by James L. Buckley, the under secretary of state, who took issue with Harrison's interpretation. "The underlying premise of our current initiative [in South Asia]," Buckley argued, "is that a secure, stable and independent Pakistan is essential to the stability of the entire region. The same obviously can be said for India, with which we seek a strong and constructive relationship."[18]

In reality, U.S. relations with the two major South Asian states—and with all other states in the region—during both the Carter and Reagan administrations, before and after the Soviet occupation of Afghanistan, were a "mixed bag" of extra efforts to promote better understanding, increased contacts, limited cooperation, continuing difficulties, and new complications.

NOTES

1. Statement of Adolph Dubs, U.S., Congress, House, Subcommittee on International Organizations, Committee on International Relations, *Human Rights in India*, 94th Cong., 2d sess., September 23, 1976, p. 148.

2. Mohammad Ayub Khan, *Friends Not Masters: A Political Autobiography* (London: Oxford University Press, 1967).

3. An evidence of Carter's special personal interest in India that was widely appreciated and widely publicized in India was his selection of his mother to head the official delegation to the funeral of Fakhruddin Ali Ahmed, president of India, who died in mid-February 1977. "Miss Lillian" took advantage of her first return visit to India since her service as a Peace Corps volunteer to pay a sentimental "homecoming" visit to Vikhroli, a suburb of Bombay, where she had worked for two years (1966–68) as a nurse and medical counselor. See "Homecoming for Lillian Carter," *Times of India*, February 16, 1977.

4. M. V. Kamath, "Indo-U.S. Accord," *Times of India*, July 6, 1977.

5. M. V. Kamath, "U.S. Reverses Stand on Aid to India," *Times of India*, April 1, 1977.

6. "U.S. House Team to Tour India," *Times of India*, August 3, 1977.

7. Dennis Farney, "Carter's Series of Trade, Aid Agreements Seen Most Striking Pattern of Trip So Far," *Wall Street Journal*, January 3, 1978.

8. Girilal Jain, "President Carter's Visit: *Pax Americana* vs. Indian Nationalism," *Times of India*, September 28, 1977.

9. Bernard Gwertzman, "Pakistan Agrees to U.S. Aid Plan and F-16 Delivery," New York *Times*, October 21, 1981.

10. For the text of Ambassador Narayanan's remarks see *India News*, December 1, 1980.

11. Quoted in *India News*, January 19, 1981.

12. Rahul Singh, "Indian Anger at the U.S.," New York *Times*, October 21, 1981.

13. Selig S. Harrison, "India, and Reagan's Tilt Toward Pakistan," New York *Times*, July 15, 1981.

14. See reports of a meeting of the Economic and Commercial Subcommission of the U.S.-India Joint Commission, held in Washington in late October 1977 (in *India News*, November 7, 1977) and of the joint executive committee of the Indo-U.S. Business Council,

also held in Washington, a month preceding (described in M. V. Kamath, "India's Curbs on U.S. Investments to Stay," *Times of India*, September 30, 1977). An unusually frank and wide-ranging exchange of views featured the Conference on the New Perspective on India–U.S. Economic Cooperation, held in New Delhi, August 19–25, 1979. The conference was sponsored by the Association of Indians in America, and was endorsed by both the Indian and U.S. governments and the Indo–U.S. Business Council. Some 200 Indian and American officials, business leaders, and scholars (including the author of this chapter) participated in this conference.

15. Clyde H. Farnsworth, "India Wins an International Loan of $5.8 Billion over U.S. Protests," New York *Times*, November 10, 1981.

16. See tables in U.S., Congress, House, *Foreign Assistance Legislation for Fiscal Year 1982* (pt. 5), Hearings and Markup Before the Subcommission on Asian and Pacific Affairs of the Committee on Foreign Affairs, 97th Cong., 1st sess., March 23, 24, 25, 26, 30, 31, and April 6, 1981, pp. XXIV, XXV, and XXVI.

17. "Palkhivala Will Try to Be Cultural Envoy Too," *Times of India*, September 12, 1977.

18. James L. Buckley, letter to the New York *Times*, August 5, 1981.

INDEX

ABOUT THE EDITORS
AND CONTRIBUTORS

LAWRENCE ZIRING is Director of the Institute of Government and Politics and Professor of Political Science at Western Michigan University. He received his B.S. (1955), M.I.A. (International Affairs; 1957), and Ph.D. (1962) from Columbia University. He has taught at Dacca University (Bangladesh, then East Pakistan) (1959-60), Columbia University (1960-61), Lafayette College (1961-64), Syracuse University (1964-67). He also served as Advisor, Pakistan Administrative Staff College (1964-66). He was a fellow of the American Council of Learned Societies (1974-75). He is the author of *Iran, Turkey and Afghanistan: A Political Chronology* (1981), *Pakistan: The Enigma of Political Development* (1980), *The Ayub Khan Era: Politics in Pakistan, 1958-1969* (1971), *An Introduction to Asian Politics* (with C. I. Eugene Kim) (1977), and *The Middle East Political Dictionary* (forthcoming). He edited *Pakistan: The Long View* (with Ralph Braibanti and W. Howard Wriggins) (1977).

ROBERT H. DONALDSON is Provost and Dean of the Faculties and Professor of Political Science at Herbert H. Lehman College of The City University of New York. He formerly taught at Vanderbilt University and was Visiting Research Professor, Strategic Studies Institute, U.S. Army War College. He is the author of *Soviet Policy Toward India: Ideology and Strategy* (Harvard, 1974), and *The Soviet-Indian Alignment: Quest for Influence* (Monograph Series in World Affairs, 1979); coauthor (with Joseph Nogee) of *Soviet Foreign Policy Since World War II* (Pergamon, 1981); editor of *The Soviet Union in the Third World: Successes and Failures* (Westview, 1981).

ONKAR MARWAH is Deputy Director, Program for Strategic and International Security Studies, Institut Universitaire De Hautes Etudes Internationales, Geneva. He taught international relations at Clark University and was a Research Fellow with Harvard University's Program for Science and International Affairs. He was employed in the Indian Administrative Service and has served with the state government of Bihar and the Union Government of India in development planning. His academic work was undertaken at the University of Calcutta, the London School of Economics, Yale University, and the University of California, Berkeley, from which he holds a Ph.D. Among his publications are: *Asian Alien Pariahs* (1974) and *Change and Modernization in India and China* (1974). He also co-edited *Nuclear Proliferation and the Near Nuclear Countries* (1974).

NORMAN PALMER is Professor of Political Science at the University of Pennsylvania. He received his Ph.D. from Yale University. In 1973-74, he was Visiting Distinguished Professor of Political Science at Duke University. He has been a senior associate of the Foreign Policy Research Institute and is a former president of the International Studies Association. He is author of *International Relations: The World Community in Transition* (with Howard C. Perkins; 1953, 1957, and 1969), *The Indian Political System* (1971), *South Asia and United States Policy* (1966), *Sun Yat-sen and Communism* (with Shao Chuan-leng; 1961), and *Elections and Political Development: The South Asian Experience* (1975).

LEO E. ROSE is editor of *Asian Survey* and Lecturer, University of California, Berkeley. He received his B.A. (1949) and Ph.D. (1959) from the University of California, Berkeley. He served as Director of the Himalayan Countries Project at Berkeley (1960-70). He has been the recipient of Ford Foundation and American Institute of Indian Studies Fellowships for study in India. He is the author of *Himalayan Battleground: Sino-Indian Rivalry in Ladakh* (1963), *Sikkim as a Factor in Himalayan Area Politics* (1969), *Nepal: Strategy for Survival* (1971), *Asia and the International System* (with Wayne A. Wilcox and Gavin Boyd; 1972), and *The Politics of Bhutan* (1977); *Nepal: Profile of a Himalayan Kingdom* (1981).

W. HOWARD WRIGGINS is Professor of South Asian Studies, Columbia University. He was U.S. ambassador to Sri Lanka (1976-80). He served as Professor of Political Science and Director of the Southern Asia Institute, Columbia University (1967-76). He was Chief of the Foreign Affairs Division of the Legislative Reference Service of the Library of Congress and has served on the Policy Planning Council of the Department of State and the National Security Council Staff of the White House. He was a Rhodes Fellow at St. Anthony's College Oxford (1973-74). He is the author of *Ceylon: Dilemmas of a New Nation* (1960) and *The Ruler's Imperative* (1969). He is the editor of *Population, Politics and the Future of Southern Asia* (with J. F. Guyot; 1973) and *Pakistan in Transition* (1975).